Praise for

FATHERLESS AMERICA

"No one writes about the crisis in American family life with more candor, intelligence, and sympathetic understanding than David Blankenhorn."

—Mary Ann Glendon, Learned Hand Professor of Law, Harvard Law School

"*Fatherless America* is the strongest possible refutation to a thesis widely held in our society—that fathers are really not important. David Blankenhorn exposes the multiple ways our culture has convinced itself of this falsehood and shows how to reconstitute fatherhood for the future."

—Don Browning, Professor of Ethics and Social Sciences, Divinity School, University of Chicago

"As much as anyone in American life today, Blankenhorn has opened an important public conversation about growing fatherlessness and its ill effects on our children. *Fatherless America* is a civic wake-up call."

—Jean Bethke Elshtain, author of *Women and War*

"David Blankenhorn has written one of the most important and provocative books of this decade. The book will force those who disagree to deal with Blankenhorn's carefully assembled evidence and tightly reasoned arguments."

—Norval D. Glenn, Ashbel Smith Professor of Sociology and Stiles Professor in American Studies, University of Texas at Austin

"Ten years from now, *Fatherless America* will be remembered as the book that triggered a national response."

—Don E. Eberly, President, National Fatherhood Initiative

"An enormously intelligent and courageous book which will have a profound impact on the national debate. Reattaching men to their children might well be the most urgent task facing those concerned with improving the life circumstances of American children."

—Sylvia Ann Hewlett, economist and author of *When the Bough Breaks: The Cost of Neglecting Our Children*

"Perhaps the most important book written this decade on our greatest social crisis is *Fatherless America*, by New York intellectual David Blankenhorn."

—Elizabeth Schoenfeld, *Policy Review:
The Journal of American Citizenship*

"The publication of *Fatherless America* is a landmark moment for our nation."

—Ken Canfield, President, National Center for Fathering

"If we truly hope to rid ourselves of the epidemic of youth violence, we had better pay attention to the message of this book—ultimately, the way to remove violence from our society is to return fathers to their families."

—Dan Lungren, Attorney General of California

"The bible of the fatherhood movement is *Fatherless America,* by David Blankenhorn."

—*Idaho Statesman*

"With his book, his think tank and his powerful arsenal of facts about fatherhood, Blankenhorn has taken the helm as the de facto navigator [of the fatherhood movement]. Far from promising a trouble-free voyage, he has begun by making giant waves. "Fatherless America" has instantly become a catch phrase."

—*Los Angeles Times*

"It took me a long time to read this book, because I savored every word, footnotes and all. The book closes the debate about the importance of the father, presenting the bountiful evidence that fatherlessness in America may be the most (not the only) important cause of the many social dysfunctions wracking our nation today."

—Dennis Byrne, *Chicago Sun-Times*

"Blankenhorn is a master of dissecting some of the shibboleths about parenthood that we take for granted—as, for example, in his discussion of the "Deadbeat Dad" or the "Visiting Father." Even the footnotes of this book are a rich store of information, and the book provides cultural criticism of a very high order."

—Gilbert Meilander, *Commonweal*

"A crusade promoting the importance of males.... Here is a man preaching that fathers should get married, stay married, and remain a role model for their children—that anything less puts children at risk. It says something about America in the '90s that that message is so hard to take."

—Wyatt Andrews, "Eye on America" profile of
David Blankenhorn, *CBS Evening News*

FATHERLESS AMERICA

CONFRONTING OUR MOST URGENT SOCIAL PROBLEM

David Blankenhorn

HarperPerennial

A Division of HarperCollins*Publishers*

Dedicated to a good father,
DAVID G. BLANKENHORN, JR.

First HarperPerennial edition published 1996.

Designed by Ellen Levine

The Library of Congress has catalogued the hardcover edition as follows:

Blankenhorn, David.
    Fatherless America : confronting our most urgent social problem / David Blankenhorn.
      p. cm.
    Includes bibliographical references and index.
    ISBN 0-465-01483-6
      1. Fathers—United States. 2. Fatherless family—United States. 3. Paternal deprivation—United States. I. Title.
HQ756.B57   1995
306.874′2—dc20   94-40151

ISBN 0-06-092683-X (pbk.)

02 03 04   ❖/RRD 10 9

Contents

Acknowledgments   vii
Introduction   1

PART I
FATHERLESSNESS

1. The Diminishment of American Fatherhood   9
2. Fatherless Society   25
3. The Lost Idea   49

PART II
THE CULTURAL SCRIPT

4. The Unnecessary Father   65
5. The Old Father   84
6. The New Father   96
7. The Deadbeat Dad   124
8. The Visiting Father   148
9. The Sperm Father   171
10. The Stepfather and the Nearby Guy   185

PART III
FATHERHOOD

11. The Good Family Man   201
12. A Father for Every Child   222

Notes   235
Index   317

Acknowledgments

My most important author's debts are to my colleagues Barbara Dafoe Whitehead and David Popenoe, who started this project with me and made enormous contributions in the early stages of the book. Barbara Dafoe Whitehead contributed heavily to the first three chapters, especially her research and insights into the fatherhood debate during World War II. David Popenoe contributed importantly to the research material, especially in the social science and historical fields, used in the book. To these two good friends go my deepest thanks. They do not agree with all the views expressed in this book, but the book is much stronger as a result of our collaboration.

I am also especially grateful to Jean Bethke Elshtain, Mary Ann Glendon, and Sylvia Ann Hewlett for their numerous valuable suggestions, for their advice and friendship, and for their inspiring commitment to improving child well-being in our society.

Grace De George and Paul Hirschfield contributed many hours of research and editorial assistance to this book. I deeply appreciate their help. At Basic Books, Kermit Hummel and Linda Carbone guided me through this journey with great patience and much skill. Other authors should be so lucky. For talking to me about the ideas in this book, and for teaching me a great deal, I am particularly grateful to Charles Ballard, Don Browning, Don Eberly, Lew Finfer, Maggie Gallagher, Norval Glenn, David Gutmann, Heather Higgins, Wade Horn, Leon and Amy Kass, Martin Kessler, Elizabeth Lurie, and Dana Mack.

This book would never have been possible without the support and encouragement of the Institute for American Values. I am especially grateful to the Institute's Board of Directors and financial supporters for making it possible for me to undertake this project.

My wife, Raina Sacks Blankenhorn, read every draft of every chapter with the toughness of an editor, the insight and spirit of a writer, and the generosity of a spouse. I cannot imagine this book, or much else, apart from her. I am honored that a painting of her father, Raymond Sacks, who died when his daughter was ten years old, is on the cover of this book.

Most of what I believe about family life I first learned not from conferences or libraries but from my parents. For this reason, when I describe in this book the importance of committed parents, I am also describing their importance to me.

Introduction

The United States is becoming an increasingly fatherless society. A generation ago, an American child could reasonably expect to grow up with his or her father. Today, an American child can reasonably expect not to. Fatherlessness is now approaching a rough parity with fatherhood as a defining feature of American childhood.

This astonishing fact is reflected in many statistics, but here are the two most important. Tonight, about 40 percent of American children will go to sleep in homes in which their fathers do not live. Before they reach the age of eighteen, more than half of our nation's children are likely to spend at least a significant portion of their childhoods living apart from their fathers.[1] Never before in this country have so many children been voluntarily abandoned by their fathers. Never before have so many children grown up without knowing what it means to have a father.

Fatherlessness is the most harmful demographic trend of this generation. It is the leading cause of declining child well-being in our society. It is also the engine driving our most urgent social problems, from crime to adolescent pregnancy to child sexual abuse to domestic violence against women. Yet, despite its scale and social consequences, fatherlessness is a problem that is frequently ignored or denied. Especially within our elite discourse, it remains largely a problem with no name.

If this trend continues, fatherlessness is likely to change the shape of our society. Consider this prediction. After the year 2000, as people born after 1970 emerge as a large proportion of our working-age adult population, the United States will be a nation divided into two groups, separate and unequal. The two groups will work in the same economy, speak a common language, and remember the same national history. But they will live fundamentally divergent lives. One group will receive basic benefits—psychological, social, economic, educational, and moral—that are denied to the other group.

The primary fault line dividing the two groups will not be race, religion, class, education, or gender. It will be patrimony. One group will consist of those adults who grew up with the daily presence and provision of fathers. The other group will consist of those who did not. By the early years of the next century, these two groups will be roughly the same size.

Surely a crisis of this scale merits a response. At a minimum, it requires a serious debate. Why is fatherhood declining? What can be done about it? Can our society find ways to invigorate effective fatherhood as a norm of male behavior? Yet, to date, the public discussion on this topic has been remarkably weak and defeatist. There is a prevailing belief that not much can—or even should—be done to reverse the trend.

When the crime rate jumps, politicians promise to do something about it. When the unemployment rate rises, task forces assemble to address the problem. As random shootings increase, public health officials worry about the preponderance of guns. But when it comes to the mass defection of men from family life, not much happens.

There is debate, even alarm, about specific social problems. Divorce. Out-of-wedlock childbearing. Children growing up in poverty. Youth violence. Unsafe neighborhoods. Domestic violence. The weakening of parental authority. But in these discussions, we seldom acknowledge the underlying phenomenon that binds together these otherwise disparate issues: the flight of males from their children's lives. In fact, we seem to go out of our way to avoid the connection between our most pressing social problems and the trend of fatherlessness.

We avoid this connection because, as a society, we are changing our minds about the role of men in family life. As a cultural idea, our inherited understanding of fatherhood is under siege. Men in general, and fathers in particular, are increasingly viewed as superfluous to family life: either expendable or as part of the problem. Masculinity itself, understood as anything other than a rejection of what it has traditionally meant to be male, is typically treated with suspicion and even hostility in our cultural discourse. Consequently, our society is now manifestly unable to sustain, or even find reason to believe in, fatherhood as a distinctive domain of male activity.

The core question is simple: Does every child need a father? Increasingly, our society's answer is "no," or at least "not necessarily." Few idea shifts in this century are as consequential as this one. At stake is nothing less than what it means to be a man, who our children will be, and what kind of society we will become.

This book is a criticism not simply of fatherlessness but of a culture of fatherlessness. For, in addition to losing fathers, we are losing something larger: our idea of fatherhood. Unlike earlier periods of father absence in our history, we now face more than a physical loss affecting some homes.

We face a cultural loss affecting every home. For this reason, the most important absence our society must confront is not the absence of fathers but the absence of our belief in fathers.

In a larger sense, this book is a *cultural* criticism because fatherhood, much more than motherhood, is a cultural invention. Its meaning for the individual man is shaped less by biology than by a cultural script or story—a societal code that guides, and at times pressures, him into certain ways of acting and of understanding himself as a man.[2]

Like motherhood, fatherhood is made up of both a biological and a social dimension. Yet in societies across the world, mothers are far more successful than fathers at fusing these two dimensions into a coherent parental identity. Is the nursing mother playing a biological or a social role? Is she feeding or bonding? We can hardly separate the two, so seamlessly are they woven together.

But fatherhood is a different matter. A father makes his sole biological contribution at the moment of conception—nine months before the infant enters the world. Because social paternity is only indirectly linked to biological paternity, the connection between the two cannot be assumed. The phrase "to father a child" usually refers only to the act of insemination, not to the responsibility for raising a child. What fathers contribute to their offspring after conception is largely a matter of cultural devising.

Moreover, despite their other virtues, men are not ideally suited to responsible fatherhood. Although they certainly have the capacity for fathering, men are inclined to sexual promiscuity and paternal wayward-ness. Anthropologically, human fatherhood constitutes what might be termed a necessary problem. It is necessary because, in all societies, child well-being and societal success hinge largely upon a high level of paternal investment: the willingness of adult males to devote energy and resources to the care of their offspring. It is a problem because adult males are fre-quently—indeed, increasingly—unwilling or unable to make that vital investment.

Because fatherhood is universally problematic in human societies, cul-tures must mobilize to devise and enforce the father role for men, coaxing and guiding them into fatherhood through a set of legal and extralegal pressures that require them to maintain a close alliance with their chil-dren's mother and to invest in their children. Because men do not volun-teer for fatherhood as much as they are conscripted into it by the sur-rounding culture, only an authoritative cultural story of fatherhood can fuse biological and social paternity into a coherent male identity.

For exactly this reason, Margaret Mead and others have observed that the supreme test of any civilization is whether it can socialize men by teaching them to be fathers—creating a culture in which men acknowledge their paternity and willingly nurture their offspring.[3] Indeed, if we can equate the essence of the antisocial male with violence, we can equate the essence of the socialized male with being a good father. Thus, at the center of our most important cultural imperative, we find the fatherhood script: the story that describes what it ought to mean for a man to have a child.

Just as the fatherhood script advances the social goal of harnessing male behavior to collective needs, it also reflects an individual purpose. That purpose, in a word, is happiness. Anthropologists have long understood that the genius of an effective culture is its capacity to reconcile individual happiness with collective well-being.[4] By situating individual lives within a social narrative, culture endows private behavior with larger meaning. By linking the self to moral purposes larger than the self, an effective culture tells us a story in which individual fulfillment transcends selfishness, and personal satisfaction transcends narcissism.

In this respect, our cultural script is not simply a set of imported moralisms, exterior to the individual and designed only to compel self-sacrifice. It is also a pathway—indeed, our only pathway—to what the founders of the American experiment called the pursuit of happiness.

The stakes on this issue could hardly be higher. Our society's conspicuous failure to sustain or create compelling norms of fatherhood amounts to a social and personal disaster. Today's story of fatherhood features one-dimensional characters, an unbelievable plot, and an unhappy ending. It reveals in our society both a failure of collective memory and a collapse of moral imagination. It undermines families, neglects children, causes or aggravates our worst social problems, and makes individual adult happiness—both male and female—harder to achieve.

Ultimately, this failure reflects nothing less than a culture gone awry: a culture increasingly unable to establish the boundaries, erect the signposts, and fashion the stories that can harmonize individual happiness with collective well-being. In short, it reflects a culture that increasingly fails to "enculture" individual men and women, mothers and fathers.

In personal terms, the end result of this process, the final residue from what David Gutmann calls the "deculturation" of paternity, is narcissism: a me-first egotism that is hostile not only to any societal goal or larger moral purpose but also to any save the most puerile understanding of personal happiness.[5] In social terms, the primary results of decultured paternity are a decline in children's well-being and a rise in male violence, especially against women. In a larger sense, the most significant result is our society's steady fragmentation into atomized individuals, isolated from one another and estranged from the aspirations and realities of common membership in a family, a community, a nation, bound by mutual commitment and shared memory.

The main character in this book is not a real person. As befits a book about shared narratives, he is a cultural model, or what Max Weber calls an ideal social type—an anthropomorphized composite of cultural ideas about the meaning of paternity. I call him the Good Family Man. As described by one of the fathers interviewed for this book, a good family man "puts his family first."

If this book could be distilled into one sentence, it would be this: A good society celebrates the ideal of the man who puts his family first. Because our society is now lurching in the opposite direction, I see the Good Family Man as the principal casualty of today's weakening fatherhood script. And because I cannot imagine a good society without him, I offer him as the protagonist in the stronger script that I believe is both necessary and possible.

PART I

FATHERLESSNESS

CHAPTER 1

The Diminishment of American Fatherhood

A Michigan high school senior, Kara Hewes, enters a crowded conference room to face cameras and reporters. She is about to make a public appeal to her seventy-three-year-old father. She asks him to admit his paternity. "I'd just like him to be a father," she says. "I want very much to develop a relationship with him."[1] Her biological father, identified through a reliable blood test, is Bruce Sundlun, World War II Air Force captain, Harvard Law School graduate, and second-term governor of Rhode Island.

Kara Hewes gets her wish. Shortly after the press conference in June 1993, Sundlun acknowledges his paternity and agrees to pay Kara's college tuition. She withdraws her paternity suit. Father and daughter dine together in the governor's mansion, and he invites her to visit him and his other children at his Newport estate.[2]

The governor's supporters are confident that the publicity will not damage his political career. After all, this is a complicated case. The thrice-divorced governor was single at the time he fathered Kara. He had already paid $30,000 to Kara's mother to settle an earlier suit, and Kara had been adopted by her stepfather, who later vanished. Another important point in Sundlun's favor, say his supporters, is that the governor has always been forthcoming about his personal life. "His frankness and candidness with the people of this state deserve a great deal of respect," says Julius Michaelson, a friend and former Rhode Island state attorney general.[3]

As for the governor, he is reluctant to dwell on the past: "I think the important thing is not to look back," he later tells reporters in a joint press conference with his daughter. "We're here to look forward and try to create a relationship. You can't wave a magic wand and have a storybook life."[4]

Governor Sundlun's unstorybook story, though a bit more public than most, has become increasingly common. It is a story unfolding in countless courtrooms, lawyers' suites, and welfare offices across the nation. Like the governor, more and more men are fathering children outside of marriage. More and more men are failing to support or even acknowledge their children. More and more men are simply vanishing from their children's lives.

Kara Hewes's story is also familiar. A growing number of American children have no relationship with their fathers. Court and school officials report that many children do not even know what to put in the "Father's Name" blank on printed forms. An even larger proportion of children have only the slightest acquaintance with their fathers. In its 1991 survey of children in the United States, the National Commission on Children described the spreading phenomenon of father-child relationships that "are frequently tenuous and all too often nonexistent."[5]

Fathers are vanishing legally as well as physically. About one-third of all childbirths in the nation now occur outside of marriage. In most of these cases, the place for the father's name on the birth certificate is simply left blank. In at least two of every three cases of unwed parenthood, the father is never legally identified.[6] Not surprisingly, paternity suits are on the rise.

When Governor Sundlun says that we "can't wave a magic wand and have a storybook life," he implies that the storybooks may be unrealistic. The governor need not worry: Even storybooks for children now reflect his kind of fatherhood. "There are different kinds of daddies," one book for preschoolers states, and "sometimes a Daddy goes away like yours did. He may not see his children at all."[7] Another children's book is equally candid: "Some kids know both their mom and dad, and some kids don't." One child in this book says: "I never met my dad, but I know that he lives in a big city." Another says: "I'll bet my dad is really big and strong."[8]

So Kara Hewes and Governor Sundlun are, after all, something of a storybook story. It is one we all know. It is becoming our society's story. We see it everywhere around us. We tell it to our children. It is the story of an increasingly fatherless society. The moral of this new narrative is that fathers, at bottom, are unnecessary. The action of the story centers on what can be best understood as the fragmentation of fatherhood.

Imagine something big, made out of glass, called fatherhood. First imagine it slowly shrinking. Then imagine it suddenly shattering into pieces. Now look around. Try to identify the shards. Over here is marriage. Over there is procreation. Over here, manhood. Over there, parenthood. Here, rights. There, responsibilities. In this direction, what's best for me. In that direction, what's best for my child.

Off to one side, looking nervous, is an emaciated fellow we must now call a biological father, filling out forms and agreeing to mail in child-support payments. Off to the other side is some guy the experts now call a social father, wondering what to do next and whether he wants to do it. In the middle, poking through the rubble and deciding when to leave, are mothers and children. There is much anger and much talk of "rights."

People are phoning their lawyers. People are making excuses. People are exclaiming at how complicated things have become.

Indeed, as fatherhood fragments, things do become complicated. Culturally, the story of fatherhood becomes harder to figure out. For, as we witness the collapse of fatherhood as a social role for men, we become confused and divided about the very nature and meaning of fatherhood.

Parenting experts question whether there is anything truly gendered about fatherhood. Scholars win research grants to investigate whether father absence harms children. Social workers debate whether it helps children, especially poor children, to press for fathers' names on birth certificates. Judges try to sort out tangled custody conflicts, often pitting unmarried biological fathers against "father figures" such as the mother's boyfriend or even former boyfriend. Journalists write stories alternately condemning "deadbeat dads" and sympathizing with the plight of teenage fathers.

As an analogue to the story of Kara Hewes and Bruce Sundlun, consider the story of Ronnell Williams, a student at Taft High School in Cincinnati. Williams is a talented basketball player, averaging twenty-nine points per game for his high school team. He is also an honors student, expected to graduate in the top 10 percent of his class. His achievements are all the more remarkable because he began with so many strikes against him.

His father was killed by his mother's boyfriend when Ronnell was three years old. His mother was addicted to drugs. He repeatedly ran away from home, got caught stealing, and spent time in reform school. But with the support of a coach, his truant officer, and a concerned businessman-mentor, Williams is able to turn his life around. By the time he reaches his senior year, he is a model student, a school leader, and a basketball star. College coaches come calling.

The story should end here. But it doesn't. Just before graduation, Williams is arrested for selling crack cocaine. As he explains to the judge, he was peddling the drug in a desperate effort to raise money for abortions for his two pregnant girlfriends: "I felt I was too young for the responsibility of being a father."

In the *New York Times,* the sportswriter Ira Berkow gives this story a happy ending. The young athlete gets a suspended sentence. He also gets a $25,000 basketball scholarship from American University. He's outta the hood. Berkow's piece ends in a slow fade, with Williams walking away down a sunny street, "dribbling the ball sweetly between his long legs."[9]

As might be expected, some *New York Times* readers object. In a letter to the editor, the Reverend Wayland Brown urges us to consider "plenty of fine young men who are not convicted felons and who have not impregnated several women. Give one of them the scholarship." Another reader asks: "What happened to the two young women who were made pregnant by him? My guess is that they do not have such supporters as loyal coaches, truant officers ... and mentors who recognize and encourage potential talent and ability in them."[10]

In most respects, Ronnell Williams and Bruce Sundlun have very little in common. They come from different sides of the tracks. One is an old, rich, white guy with a lot of power. The other is a young, poor, black guy without (at least yet) much power. But as fathers, these men surely have much more in common than either of them, or most of us, would prefer to admit. As cultural models of paternity, these men are twin brothers. They both embody the collapse of fatherhood as a social role for men. They both embody the trend toward a fatherless society.

Their two stories raise fundamental questions for which we as a society have no coherent answers. What does it mean to be a father in the United States today? What does our society require of fathers? Are some fathers excused from these requirements? For example, are unemployed men excused? What about minority males from disadvantaged backgrounds? What about prominent elected officials who are candid about their personal lives?

Do we stigmatize unwed fatherhood or do we not? Do we jail deadbeat dads or enroll them in jobs programs? How long is a father financially responsible for his child? As long as a child needs his help? Until court-ordered child support expires? Until the child holds a press conference?

Our society is deeply ambivalent and divided about each of these questions. For as fatherhood disintegrates around us, we grow more confused about just what fatherhood is. The end result is hardly surprising: What Governor Sundlun, somewhat mistakenly, calls storybook fathers are in increasingly short supply.

The Shrinking American Father

Prior to fragmenting—breaking into pieces, like Humpty Dumpty—fatherhood in our society spent a long time shrinking. Historically, the contraction of fatherhood both preceded and precipitated its disintegration. In this sense, today's fragmentation of fatherhood represents the end point of a long historical process: the steady diminishment of fatherhood as a social role for men.

Over the past two hundred years, fathers have gradually moved from the center to the periphery of family life. As the social role for fathers has diminished, so our cultural story of fatherhood has by now almost completely ceased to portray fathers as essential guarantors of child and societal well-being. Not to be overly gloomy, but in some respects it has been all downhill for fathers since the Industrial Revolution.

In colonial America, fathers were seen as primary and irreplaceable caregivers. According to both law and custom, fathers bore the ultimate responsibility for the care and well-being of their children, especially older children. Throughout the eighteenth century, for example, child-rearing manuals were generally addressed to fathers, not mothers. Until the early nineteenth century, in almost all cases of divorce, it was established practice to award the custody of children to fathers. Throughout this period, fathers, not mothers, were the chief correspondents with children who lived away from home.

More centrally, fathers largely guided the marital choices of their children and directly supervised the entry of children, especially sons, into the world outside the home. Most important, fathers assumed primary responsibility for what was seen as the most essential parental task: the religious and moral education of the young. As a result, societal praise or blame for a child's outcome was customarily bestowed not (as it is today) on the mother but on the father.[11]

Of course, all of this eventually changed: not marginally, but fundamentally. First, industrialization and the modern economy led to the physical separation of home and work. No longer could fathers be in both places at once. No longer, according to Alexander Mitscherlich, could children typically acquire skills "by watching one's father, working with him, seeing the way he handled things, observing the degree of knowledge and skill he had attained as well as his limitations." The nineteenth century's "progressive fragmentation of labor, combined with mass production and complicated administration, the separation of home from the place of work, [and] the transition from independent producer to paid employee who uses consumer goods" led to "a progressive loss of substance of the father's authority and a diminution of his power in the family and over the family."[12]

The major change in family life in the nineteenth century was the steady feminization of the domestic sphere. Accompanying this radical change were a host of new ideas about gender identity and family life—some focusing on childhood as a special and separate "tender years" stage of life, others on what were believed to be the special capacities of women to care for children and to create, in contrast to the outside world dominated by men, a secure moral ethos for family life.

One important consequence of these new ideas was the relative decline of patriarchy and the shift toward more companionate models of marriage and parenthood. The historian Carl Degler, describing the increasingly "attenuated character" of nineteenth-century patriarchy, concludes that "the companionate marriage placed limits on the power of the husband"

and led to the "relatively democratic role of the father in the nineteenth-century family."[13] As early as the 1830s, Alexis de Tocqueville could praise the "influence of democracy" on fatherhood in America, even as it led to the fact that "paternal authority, if not destroyed, is at least impaired."[14]

From a modern perspective, this philosophical shift, this emerging ethos of the companionate family, is praiseworthy. Certainly our society could not, and does not wish to, recreate for our time the model of the agrarian patriarchal father. Regarding the cultural meaning of paternity, however, the historical evidence is clear: Both the new economy and the new philosophy of the nineteenth century contributed to the sharp contraction of fatherhood as a social role.

Stephen M. Frank summarizes the impact of these basic shifts: "As some fathers began to spend more time at work and less at home, and as family structure shifted away from patriarchal dominance and toward more companionate relationships, paternal requirements shrank."[15] As Susan Juster and Maris Vinovskis put it:

> The transition from the father to the mother as the primary socializer and educator of young children was completed by the nineteenth century. The mother was now regarded as the "natural" caretaker of the child, and the father's role was limited in practice to that of a supervisor or the ultimate dispenser of discipline in the home.[16]

During the nineteenth century, fathers began a long march from the center to the periphery of domestic life. As Joseph H. Pleck observes: "A gradual and steady shift toward a greater role for the mother, and a decreased and indirect role for the father, is clear and unmistakable."[17] As early as the 1830s, child-rearing manuals, now more often addressed to mothers, began to deplore the father's absence from the home.[18] In cases of family dissolution, custody of children shifted decisively from fathers to mothers during this period.

This shift should not be exaggerated. Describing "the continued vitality of fatherhood" in the nineteenth century, Frank's examination of the letters of Civil War soldiers reminds us that many fathers "continued to be enormous presences in their children's lives," fulfilling commitments as both providers and nurturers. "I think of you . . . and wish I could be there to send Ed to bed on time," wrote one soldier to his wife in 1863; "should I ever reach home again I feel thankful to think I am spared on Edwin's account as I know he will grow up a bad boy unless some father guides him."[19] Despite its steady contraction, nineteenth-century fatherhood was almost certainly stronger than its twentieth-century successor.

Yet the overall trend of the nineteenth century is clearly toward the shrinking of fatherhood. "Paternal neglect," warned a New England pastor in 1842, was causing "the ruin of many families."[20] By 1900, another worried observer could describe "the suburban husband and father" as "almost entirely a Sunday institution."[21]

Within the home, the father retained his formal status as chief executive, or head of the family, but had largely ceded to his wife the role of chief child raiser, manager, and decision maker. As Pleck puts it: "The father continued to set the official standard of morality and to be the final arbiter of family discipline, but he did so at more of a remove than before: He stepped in only when the mother's delegated authority failed."[22]

Increasingly, men looked outside the home for the meaning of their maleness. Masculinity became less domesticated, defined less by effective paternity and more by individual ambition and achievement.[23] Fatherhood became a thinner social role. Paternal authority declined as the fatherhood script came to be anchored in, and restricted to, two paternal tasks: head of the family and breadwinner.

In our own century, of course, these two roles as well have undergone profound change. No longer conventional wisdom, each is now a fundamentally contested idea. Both go to the heart of today's great disagreements, anxieties, and conflicts over gender identity and the family. The remarkable generational changes regarding these issues, illustrated in table 1.1, clearly reflect the erosion throughout this century of the last two remaining anchors of the traditional fatherhood script.

Daniel Yankelovich also confirms this steady change in American attitudes:

until the late 1960s, being a real man meant being a good provider for the family. No other conception of what it means to be a real man came even close. Concepts of sexual potency, or physical strength, or strength of character (manliness), or even being handy around the house were relegated to the bottom of the list of traits associated with masculinity. By the late 1970s, however, the definition of a real man as a good provider

TABLE 1.1

Adult Americans who agree that "It is much better for everyone involved if the man is the achiever outside the home and the woman takes care of the home and family."

Age group:	Percent who agree:
18–29	27
30–44	28
45–59	47
60–69	63
70–79	75
80 and up	82

Source: National Opinion Research Center, combined data for 1986–91.

had slipped from its number one spot (86 percent in 1968) to the number three position, at 67 percent. It has continued to erode.[24]

In sum, over the past two hundred years, fatherhood has lost, in full or in part, each of its four traditional roles: irreplaceable caregiver, moral educator, head of family, and family breadwinner. As the historian Peter N. Stearns put it: "An eighteenth-century father would not recognize the distance contemporary men face between work and home . . . or the parental leadership granted to mothers or indeed the number of bad fathers."[25]

The result is that fatherhood as a social role has been radically diminished in three ways. First, it has become, in the most literal sense, smaller: There are simply fewer things that remain socially defined as a father's distinctive work. The script has been shortened to only a few pages.

Second, fatherhood has been devalued. Within the home, fathers have been losing authority; within the wider society, fatherhood has been losing esteem. Many influential people in today's public debate argue that, when all is said and done, fathers are simply not very important.

Third, and most important, fatherhood has been diminished as paternity has become *decultured*—denuded of any authoritative social content or definition. A decultured paternity is a minimalist paternity. It is biology without society. As an extreme example, consider the phenomenon of the sperm bank: fatherhood as anonymous insemination. No definition of fatherhood could be tinier.

A decultured paternity necessarily fractures any coherent social understanding of fatherhood. As fewer children live with their biological fathers, and more live with or near stepfathers, mothers' boyfriends, or other male "role models," biological fatherhood is being separated from social fatherhood. In turn, social fatherhood, once detached from any one man, becomes more diffuse as an idea and elastic as a role—less a person than a style of relating to children.

It is a wise child, the proverb goes, that knows its own father. To the degree that this teaching is true, a decultured paternity brings forth fewer wise children. Though most children certainly disfavor this trend—preferring to understand "my father" as one person rather than a series of disparate relationships—the steady disembodiment and dispersal of social fatherhood are defining characteristics of deculturing paternity, succinctly captured by the title of a 1993 article in the *New York Times:* "'Who Is My Daddy?' Can Be Answered in Different Ways."[26]

A decultured paternity transforms the callings of fatherhood from what might be termed simple but mandatory to complex but optional. To use a military metaphor, our cultural story no longer conscripts men into a uniform fatherhood service. Instead, fathers increasingly comprise an all-volunteer force, small and flexible. No longer unambiguously responsible for a fixed number of mandatory tasks, today's decultured fathers must largely select for themselves, from a complex menu of lifestyle options, the meaning of their paternity. Ultimately, a decultured paternity is incompatible with fatherhood as a defined role for men.

Finally, a decultured paternity signals the growing detachment of fatherhood from wider norms of masculinity. Consider several aspects of this phenomenon. In our elite discourse, masculinity is widely viewed as a problem to be overcome, frequently by insisting upon "new" fathers willing to disavow any inherited understandings of masculinity. In popular culture, the traditional male fantasy of sex without responsibility—the anti-father world view of the adolescent male, as emblematized in the philosophy of *Playboy* magazine, James Bond movies, and Travis McGee novels—is an increasingly accepted cultural model in our society, less an accusation than an assumption about male behavior. In addition, in what the sociologist Elijah Anderson calls the "street culture" of our inner cities, men's glorification of casual and even predatory sex, completely divorced from responsible fatherhood, now constitutes the core of what Anderson calls the "sex code" of young minority males.[27]

All three of these otherwise distinct trends are linked by an underlying idea: the disintegrating connection between masculinity and responsible paternity. Being male is one thing. Being a good father is another. The latter is no longer the pathway to proving the former. "Man" and "father" become separate and even dissimilar cultural categories.

Consequently, as paternity is decultured, the larger meaning of masculinity in our society becomes unclear and divisive. A decultured fatherhood thus produces a doubtful manhood. For without norms of effective paternity to anchor masculinity, the male project itself is increasingly called into question and even disrepute.

Many analysts of gender issues in our century have pondered Freud's famous question: What do women want? Fewer have sought to name the most important question, the core issue, for men. Let me take a stab.

Men, more than women, are culture-made. Fatherhood, in particular, is what the novelist Herbert Gold calls "a metaphysical idea"[28]—an imperfect cultural improvisation designed not to express maleness but to socialize it. It derives less from sexual embodiment than from a social imperative: the need to obligate men to their offspring. Consequently, ideas about masculinity and fatherhood are inextricably rooted in social functions.

For this reason, the core question for men today is almost certainly less about desire than about function. Or perhaps it is that men, more so than women, cannot name their desires without affirming their functions—recognizing and enjoying the special work that society needs them to do.

So the question is not, *What do men want?* but rather, *What do men do?*

Central to that question is the fatherhood script—thus the core question is really, *What do fathers do?* Yet here is our tragedy. Our society is unable to answer this question.

The Collapsing Bases of Good-Enough Fatherhood

Structurally, the preconditions for effective fatherhood are twofold: co-residency with children and a parental alliance with the mother. These two foundations do not guarantee effective fatherhood, but they do sustain the possibility of good-enough fatherhood. Conversely, when one or both of these enabling conditions are absent, good-enough fatherhood is not possible for most men.

Both of these bases of good-enough fatherhood are collapsing in our society. The data in tables 1.2 and 1.3 are sobering. With each passing year, fewer and fewer men are living with their children. Fewer and fewer fathers are willing or able to sustain cooperative partnerships with the mothers of their children.

In 1990, more than 36 percent of all children in the nation were living apart from their fathers—more than double the rate in 1960. The trend shows no sign of slowing down. Indeed, it seems quite probable that, as of 1994, fully 40 percent of all children in the nation did not live with their fathers. Scholars estimate that, before they reach age eighteen, more than half of all children in the nation will live apart from their fathers for at least a significant portion of their childhoods.[29]

TABLE 1.2
Percentage of U.S. Children in Various Family Arrangements

Living with	1960	1970	1980	1990
Father and mother	80.6	75.1	62.3	57.7
Mother only	7.7	11.8	18.0	21.6
Never married	3.9	9.3	15.5	31.5
Divorced	24.7	29.7	41.6	36.9
Separated	46.8	39.8	31.6	24.6
Widowed	24.7	21.2	11.3	7.0
Father only	1.0	1.8	1.7	3.1
Father and stepmother	0.8	0.9	1.1	0.9
Mother and stepfather	5.9	6.5	8.4	10.4
Neither parent	3.9	4.1	5.8	4.3

For most of these children, the possibility of being fathered has largely evaporated. When a man does not live with his children and does not get along with the mother of his children, his fatherhood becomes essentially untenable, regardless of how he feels, how hard he tries, or whether he is a good guy. Almost by definition, he has become de-fathered.

Yet these two father-disabling phenomena have become the distinguishing traits of the fatherhood trend of our time. In historical terms, the spread of these new conditions of paternity marks the essential difference between a fatherhood that is shrinking and a fatherhood that is fragmenting.

When fatherhood is *shrinking*, a father is doing less, and perhaps doing it less well, but he is still a father. His role may be diminishing, but it is still coherent. He is still on the premises. His children see him every day. He is still a husband and a partner to their mother. He is responsible for protecting and nurturing his children. He may not win any Father's Day prizes—he may not be a very good father at all—but he is still recognizably a father.

But when fatherhood is *fragmenting*, the identity and social definition of the father change not in degree but in kind. The new conditions, driven by divorce and out-of-wedlock childbearing, split the nucleus of the nuclear family. Now the father is physically absent. When he comes "home," his children are not there. He is not a husband. Because the parental alliance has either ended or never begun, the mother has little reason or opportunity to defend or even care about his fatherhood. In the most important areas, he is not responsible for his children.

This transmogrification means that there is no longer any coherent structure to his fatherhood. His paternity has become disabled, cut off

TABLE 1.3

Percentage of U.S. Children Living with Their Biological Fathers

	1960	1970	1980	1990
Living with father	82.4	77.8	65.1	61.7
Living apart from fathers	17.5	22.4	32.2	36.3

Tables 1.2 and 1.3 Sources: Donald J. Hernandez, "America's Children: Resources from Family, Government, and the Economy" (New York: Russell Sage Foundation, 1993), p. 65; "Marriage, Divorce, and Remarriage in the 1990's," U.S. Bureau of the Census, Current Population Reports, series P-23, no. 180 (Washington, D.C.: Government Printing Office, 1992), tables M and N, pps. 11–12; "Marital Status and Living Arrangements: March 1980," U.S. Bureau of the Census, Current Population Reports, series P-20, no. 365 (Washington, D.C.: Government Printing Office, 1981), table 5, p. 31; and "Marital Status and Living Arrangements: March 1990," U.S. Bureau of the Census, Current Population Reports, series P-20, no. 450 (Washington, D.C.: Government Printing Office, 1991), table 6, p. 45.

Note: Figures for 1980 and 1990 do not add up to 100 percent due to discrepancies of approximately 2 percent between tables M and N (see *Sources*) regarding the number of children living with two parents in 1980 and 1990.

from its essential supports. In sociological terms, his fatherhood has become deinstitutionalized, or detached from socially cognizable expectations and goals. Consequently, the very meaning of his fatherhood becomes fractured and disorganized. To his children and to the larger society, he becomes largely unrecognizable as a father.

Indeed, it is precisely this quality of unrecognizability, often associated with social confusion and even bizarreness, that emerges as the telltale sign of a fatherhood that is not simply shrinking but breaking into pieces. To illustrate this disintegration, consider several news stories from 1993.

In Texas, Judy has a baby. The father is Larry, her boyfriend. After the birth, Judy and her husband, Randy, decide to dismiss their pending divorce action, keep the child, and cut off all contact with Larry. Unhappy with this turn of events, Larry initiates legal action to establish his paternity and win visitation rights. In deciding in favor of Larry, the Texas Supreme Court strikes down a state law declaring that a married man is presumed to be the father of his wife's child, and that an unmarried man lacks paternal rights regarding the child of an intact marriage.[30]

In Seattle, Megan Lucas, an unmarried mother, leaves her newborn son with her seventeen-year-old sister. After Megan legally relinquishes her parental rights two years later, the child, by then in foster care, is scheduled to be adopted by two gay men who are licensed foster parents. The mother changes her mind about the adoption and files to regain custody. The child's father, the *New York Times* notes, "has not come forward."[31]

In the media, the Texas story is interpreted largely as an expansion of the prerogatives of fatherhood. A father should be able to visit his child, regardless of marital status. Similarly, the Seattle story is portrayed chiefly as an example of lingering bigotry against gay parents. Both stories are essentially about individual rights. Unwed fathers have rights. So do gay adoptive parents. Family law should be updated to recognize these rights.

This interpretation should not surprise us. Increasingly in our national discourse, what Mary Ann Glendon terms "rights talk" trumps most other considerations. Yet surely the fundamental truth, the core social dynamic, of both of these stories is the fragmentation and dispersal of fatherhood. In one case, fatherhood is severed from, then directly opposed to, husband-hood and marriage. In the other, the father never even makes an appearance. This is the trend that produces these and many other similar stories about fathers' "rights."[32]

Moreover, as fatherhood fragments, so do other institutions that depend on fatherhood. Marriage is an obvious example, but consider a less obvious one: adoption. What explains the current explosion of tangled legal quarrels and sensational media stories surrounding the issue of adoption? One frequently offered answer is that we are becoming a more litigious and complex society. Yes, we are. But the more precise answer is that the fracturing of adoption in our society—its loss of institutional coherence—stems directly from the fracturing of fatherhood.

Consider the case of Baby Pete. In Vermont, Angela Harriman puts her newborn baby, Pete, up for adoption. She tells everyone that the father is Marcus Stoddard, her boyfriend. Angela's estranged husband, Daniel, who is living in Louisiana, apparently knows nothing of the pregnancy or the adoption. But when he learns what has happened, he takes legal action to gain custody of a child he has never seen. Blood tests eventually show that he, not Stoddard, is the probable father. Harriman tells a journalist: "I'm not doing this to get back at her. I just want my son."[33]

In the media, the Baby Pete story is widely celebrated as having a happy ending. The adoptive parents will maintain physical custody of Pete, while Daniel Harriman will share legal custody with the adoptive mother and will have visitation rights. The adoptive father, described by the *New York Times* as now becoming "in effect, the stepfather," declared: "Nobody lost, and the baby won."[34] The editors of the *Times* agreed. As they saw it:

> Lawyers are already pointing to this agreement as a possible model for future squabbles over biological parents', adoptive parents' and children's rights. And so it could be. . . . The adults in the case put their own interests and emotions aside to do the right thing for a child. Bless them.[35]

Bless them? Let's see. A one-day-old infant is given up for adoption by a mother who says that her boyfriend, not her estranged husband, is the father. This turns out to be untrue. Lawyers are called in. As a result, the mother drops out of the picture, the baby goes to adoptive parents, and the father, winning a big victory, gets visitation rights. A model for the future?

No, this is a model of the decomposition of marriage and fatherhood as social institutions. More specifically, it is a consequence of the splitting apart of social from biological fatherhood. What results is men who impregnate women, and who at times assert paternal rights, but who find themselves hopelessly tangled up by a rather basic question: Who is this child's rightful father? No one can figure it out. The Baby Pete case is a model of our tortuous struggle to redefine parenthood as we become an increasingly fatherless society.

In this sense, the Baby Pete story has a happy ending in precisely the same way that child-support payments and cooperative divorces constitute happy endings. It is happy only insofar as we define happiness as our capacity to improve our procedures for managing the decline of fatherhood. As is often the case, the *New York Times*'s gushy endorsement of this entire philosophy—"For Once, the Baby Won"—hovers precariously on the boundary between conventional trendiness and self-parody.

In sum, a new fatherhood has emerged in our society. But what is new is not the hands-on, nurturing "new" fatherhood so widely proclaimed and urged in the media and by parenting experts. Instead, measured according to demographic reach and social impact, what is truly new in our generation is a fatherhood that is increasingly estranged from mothers and removed from where children live. Unlike previous fatherhood shifts in our nation's history, these newly dominating conditions of paternity do not simply change or even shrink fatherhood. They end it.

The Rise of Volitional Fatherlessness

Historically, the principal cause of fatherlessness was paternal death. By the time they turned fifteen, about 15 percent of all American children born in 1870 had experienced the death of their fathers. Only slightly more than half reached age fifteen with both parents still alive.[36] At the turn of the century, middle-aged widowed men outnumbered middle-aged divorced men by more than 20 to 1.[37]

But one of the great medical and social achievements of this century has been the steady decline of early parental death. Only about 3 percent of all children born in 1950 lost their fathers through death before reaching age fifteen. More than 90 percent reached that age with both parents still alive.[38]

Today, the principal cause of fatherlessness is paternal choice. Over the course of this century, the declining rate of paternal death has been matched, and rapidly surpassed, by the rising rate of paternal abandonment. The shift began quite early. Even for parents of children born as early as 1910 through 1930, according to the demographer Peter Uhlenberg, "the increase in voluntarily broken marriages greatly exceeded the decline in marriages broken by death."[39]

By 1960, about 9 percent of all U.S. children lived in single-parent homes—not much different from the 8.5 percent who lived in single-parent homes in 1900. Yet in 1900, three of every four single parents were widowed—nearly one of every three a widowed man. Only about 5 percent of all children in one-parent homes in 1900 lived with a parent who was divorced or never married.[40] In 1960, by contrast, the great majority of single-parent homes, almost all headed by women, stemmed not from the death of a parent but from divorce and out-of-wedlock childbearing.

Since 1960, even as paternal death continued to decline, rates of paternal abandonment skyrocketed. In the 1970s, the number of middle-aged divorced men surpassed the number of middle-aged widowed men.[41] By 1992, only about 5 percent of all female-headed households with children had experienced the death of the father; about 37 percent had experienced parental divorce; and in 36 percent of these homes, the parents had never married.[42] For the first time in our nation's history, millions of men today are voluntarily abdicating their fatherhood.

Though paternal death and paternal abandonment are frequently treated as sociological equivalents, these two phenomena could hardly be more different in their impact upon children and upon the larger society. To put it simply, death puts an end to fathers. Abandonment puts an end to fatherhood.

Yet among social scientists who study fatherhood, the equivalency argument is quite popular. Alvin L. Schorr and Phyllis Moen, for example, seek to disprove the notion that contemporary father absence is "unique and deviant": "There have, for hundreds of years, been single-parent families. . . . Early death of the father combined with an extended span of childbearing has made the single-parent family fairly common in the twentieth century."[43] As the historian Tamara K. Hareven put it in her testimony before a congressional committee concerned with family policy: "In fact, divorce now has a similar effect on family disruption that death once had."[44]

In *The Way We Never Were,* the historian Stephanie Coontz emphasizes the same point. To Coontz, people who worry about fatherlessness today are historically illiterate, afflicted by a mental disability called "nostalgia," defined by Coontz as the tendency to believe in a past that never existed. Coontz explains: "Even though marriages today are more likely to be interrupted by divorce than in former times, they are much less likely to be interrupted by death, so that about the same number of children spend their youth in single-parent households today as at the turn of the century, and far fewer live with neither parent."[45]

Leave aside the facts showing that fewer than 10 percent of all children lived in one-parent homes in 1900, compared with 27 percent in 1992.[46] Instead, focus on Coontz's larger thesis: Parental death and parental abandonment are social equivalents. Before, we had one. Now we have the other. Same net result.

This thesis, commonly asserted by scholars and widely repeated by journalists and other commentators, is a sophism. Like all sophisms, it depends upon a superficial correctness of form to disguise an invalid assertion. The equivalence is only formal. Where it counts, death and abandonment are much closer to opposites.

When a father dies, a child grieves. (I have lost someone I love.) When a father leaves, a child feels anxiety and self-blame. (What did I do wrong? Why doesn't my father love me?) Death is final. (He won't come back.) Abandonment is indeterminate. (What would make him come back?)

When a father dies, his fatherhood lives on, inside the head and heart of his child. In this sense, the child is still fathered. When a father leaves, his fatherhood leaves with him to wither away. The child is unfathered. When a father dies, the mother typically sustains his fatherhood by keeping his memory alive. When a father leaves, the mother typically diminishes his fatherhood by either forgetting him or keeping her resentments alive.[47]

Yesterday, when a father died, our society affirmed the importance of fatherhood by comforting and aiding his family. Today, when a father leaves, our society disconfirms the importance of fatherhood by accepting his departure with reasoned impartiality. Historically, we have viewed the death of a father as one of the greatest tragedies possible in the life of a child. Today, we increasingly view the departure of a father as one of those things that we must simply get used to.

Death kills men but sustains fatherhood. Abandonment sustains men but kills fatherhood. Death is more personally final, but departure is more culturally lethal. From a societal perspective, the former is an individual tragedy. The latter is a cultural tragedy.

The rise of volitional fatherlessness constitutes the final diminishment of fatherhood in our time. The fact that we discuss death and abandonment as social equivalents speaks volumes about what is happening to our idea of fatherhood. The fact that paternal death caused such pain and social concern, while paternal departure is now accepted with relative equanimity, tells us with great precision what is truly new about contemporary fatherhood.

CHAPTER 2

Fatherless Society

Fatherhood is a social role that obligates men to their biological off-spring. For two reasons, it is society's most important role for men. First, fatherhood, more than any other male activity, helps men to become good men: more likely to obey the law, to be good citizens, and to think about the needs of others. Put more abstractly, fatherhood bends maleness—in particular, male aggression—toward prosocial purposes.[1] Second, fatherhood privileges children. In this respect, fatherhood is a social invention designed to supplement maternal investment in children with paternal investment in children.

Paternal investment enriches children in four ways. First, it provides them with a father's physical protection. Second, it provides them with a father's money and other material resources. Third, and probably most important, it provides them with what might be termed paternal cultural transmission: a father's distinctive capacity to contribute to the identity, character, and competence of his children. Fourth, and most obviously, paternal investment provides children with the day-to-day nurturing—feeding them, playing with them, telling them a story—that they want and need from both of their parents. In virtually all human societies, children's well-being depends decisively upon a relatively high level of paternal investment.

Indeed, many anthropologists view the rise of fatherhood as the key to the emergence of the human family and, ultimately, of human civilization. As Jane and Chet Lancaster put it:

> In the course of evolution, the keystone in the foundation of the human family was the capturing of male energy into the nurturance of the young. . . . The human family is a complex organizational structure for the garnering of energy to be transformed into the production of the next generation, and its most essential feature is the collaboration of the male and female parent in the division of labor.[2]

In short, the key for men is to be fathers. The key for children is to have fathers. The key for society is to create fathers. For society, the primary results of fatherhood are right-doing males and better outcomes for children. Conversely, the primary consequences of fatherlessness are rising male violence and declining child well-being. In the United States at the close of the twentieth century, paternal disinvestment has become the major cause of declining child well-being[3] and the underlying source of our most important social problems, especially those rooted in violence.

Youth Violence

In November 1993, Joseph Chaney, Jr., made the front page of the *Wall Street Journal*. Arrested in Miami and charged with the crime of armed robbery, Joseph, age thirteen, was ordered by the grand jury to be tried as an adult. Like many American cities, Miami in the 1990s has become increasingly punitive toward children who commit violent crimes. The spread of such crime, according to the local judge, is making Miami "an absolutely deplorable place to live." Across the nation, judges and legislatures are finally running out of patience with children like Joseph—a child who has been arrested more than sixteen times since the age of six.[4]

Joseph's mother, Yvonne Jackson, is thirty-six years old, has never been married, and has three sons, each by a different man. None of the boys ever really had a father or knew his own father. Mario's father is currently in prison. Jovon's father recently died of AIDS. Joseph's father is married to another woman. All three boys have been in constant trouble with the police.

Yvonne's older brother, Willie, is a veteran Miami police officer and the unmarried father of several children. He says he constantly worries about his nephews, and frequently asks his mother and his girlfriend to help Yvonne. (Willie does not ask for help from his and Yvonne's father, who does not live with their mother.)

In addition to receiving occasional help from Willie, Yvonne and her children have participated in a number of programs aimed at helping them. Yvonne completed a drug rehabilitation program, took a parenting course, and has regularly requested and received help from the children's school counselors. Joseph attended a special counseling program for troubled youth.

When Joseph Chaney, Sr., went to visit his thirteen-year-old son, awaiting trial in a Miami detention center, he says he hardly recognized the little boy: "Something told me to go up to him and hug him, but I couldn't. Something's telling me to back off."[5]

In 1994, the Carnegie Corporation devoted an entire issue of the *Carnegie Quarterly* to the topic of "Saving Youth from Violence." In summarizing recent research on the sources of, and solutions for, youth violence, the Carnegie Corporation came up with this list of factors that contribute to youth violence: frustration, lack of social skills, being labeled as "dumb," poverty, drug and alcohol abuse, physical abuse and neglect, violence on television and in video games, school days that are too short, the availability of guns, the failure to use antiviolence and conflict-resolution curricula in school classrooms and child-care centers, inadequate health care programs, the shortage of community-based life skills training programs, and the absence of effective mentoring programs for at-risk young people.[6]

As something approaching panic about the problem of youth violence erupted across the nation during 1993 and 1994—"Teen Violence: Wild in the Streets," announced the cover of *Newsweek* in August 1993—numerous prestigious institutions and scholars emphasized the same basic themes presented by the Carnegie Corporation. For example, the American Psychological Association's Commission on Violence and Youth issued a 1993 report on *Youth and Violence.* The report attributes the rise of youth violence to the following factors: access to guns, involvement in gangs and mobs, exposure to violence in the mass media, lack of parental supervision, physical punishment, substance abuse, social and economic inequality, prejudice and discrimination, and the lack of antiviolence programs and psychological services in schools and communities.[7] Along with just about everyone else, the commission calls for a comprehensive, multiapproach solution to the problem.

But what is wrong with these lists? Surely, all these "factors" can and do, at least indirectly, contribute to youth violence. Yet the single most obvious factor—the one, moreover, most likely to produce the other factors—is conspicuously absent from these reports and recommendations and from countless others like them.

What was most absent in Joseph Chaney, Jr.'s, life? Why is this child going to jail for an adult crime? Admittedly, Joseph faced many problems. A mother who, by all accounts, was inattentive and ineffective. Poverty. A lousy neighborhood, full of guns and gangs. On the other hand, he had an uncle, a police officer, who tried to "mentor" him. He and his family actually received a great deal of help, or at least attention, from various social workers, court officers, school counselors, and community-based life skills training programs.

At the risk of oversimplifying a complex problem, perhaps what Joseph

Chaney, Jr., needed most—and suffered most from not receiving—was paternal guidance from Joseph Chaney, Sr. Indeed, in the story of Joseph's childhood, there is not a single instance of responsible fatherhood. No grandfather. An unavailable biological father. No legal or even informal stepfather. Even Joseph's one male "role model," his uncle, is himself an unmarried father.

Today the city of Miami, like the nation as a whole, is fed up with Joseph and the growing number of children like him. We will put this little boy in jail, hoping that a prison will do what no father in his life was willing or able to do: keep him off the streets and teach him what it means to be a man.

In 1988, a congressional committee investigating the national surge in youth violence heard testimony from members of youth gangs. Here is part of an exchange between Congressman Dan Coats of Indiana and Shawn Grant, an eighteen-year-old from Philadelphia:

MR. COATS: See, the question I'm getting at, Shawn, is I'm wondering where are the fathers.

MR. GRANT: Say it again?

MR. COATS: I'm wondering where the dads are. I'm wondering why the fathers don't rise up and say, "I'm not going to let this happen to my family. I don't want my kid to get killed. . . ."

MR. GRANT: Well, a lot of parents, you know, kids coming up nowadays, they get a certain age, they're bigger than their parents. They intimidate their parents.

MR. COATS: So, just overwhelmed by them.

MR. GRANT: Especially if they're on drugs or they come in the house drunk. Maybe a lady have a child who's about six feet. . . .

MR. COATS: Well, what are you going to do when your son is bigger than you? He's fifteen and comes in and says—

MR. GRANT: See, that's when I'm going to try to take him to the court system or something. Then he'll be put away. I think if he do a little time like I did and sit in somewhere for like—if he did a first offense, maybe just sitting there for like twenty-one days or something like in a detention juvenile center for awhile and think about what you did, I think he'll come around a little bit.[8]

In this remarkable conversation, two themes stand out. Congressman Coats begins by speaking specifically about "fathers," but the discussion quickly shifts to "parents." Boys get bigger than their "parents." Teenage boys can intimidate their "parents." This abstract, genderless vocabulary has become a widely accepted convention in our academic and expert discourse on this subject, now observed even by teenagers from Philadelphia.

But it intentionally obscures the main point. Yes, many teenage boys are bigger than their mothers. But very few are bigger than grown men, and very few can physically intimidate grown men—especially grown men on the premises who act like committed fathers.[9]

Second, Shawn Grant does not seem to have a clue about what fathers do. (He told the committee that he used to "wonder about my father" and resent him for "not being around me.")[10] If a son misbehaves, Shawn Grant's idea is to "take him to the court system or something." Yet Grant did not invent this idea. Indeed, on this very point, he is simply restating the philosophy of the Miami judicial system—lock up Joseph Chaney, Jr.— as well as the larger philosophy in our society, which is adamant about demanding more prisons but not very adamant at all about demanding more fathers.

In *There Are No Children Here,* Alex Kotlowitz meticulously describes the world of Lafeyette and Pharoah Rivers, two boys living in a Chicago public housing project in the late 1980s.[11] It is a world of relentless, pitiless violence. It is a world in which children witness far more murders than they do weddings—and in which welfare mothers commonly purchase funeral insurance for their small children. It is also a world largely without responsible adult males, a world in which Kotlowitz observes a twelve-year-old boy trying to be a man without knowing how, worrying about the safety of his younger siblings "like a father worrying about his children."[12] So closely are these two themes intertwined—growing violence rooted in growing fatherlessness—that Kotlowitz might just as appropriately have named his study *There Are No Fathers Here.*

Yet our society remains curiously reluctant to name this problem. Much of our national discussion of youth crime simply ignores the elephant in the room called fatherlessness. Moreover, many analysts come quite close to viewing all traditional norms of fatherhood not as a remedy for the problem of youth violence but rather as a leading cause of it.

In *Boys Will Be Boys,* Myriam Miedzian seeks to identify the primary source of "criminal and domestic violence" in the United States in what she terms the "male mystique"—the values of toughness, dominance, repression of empathy, and competitiveness that comprise the inherited manhood script in our society. These historically defined male norms, she argues, are the primary seedbeds of violent crime. In other words, modern violence is the result of traditional masculinity. Only by fundamentally revising the latter can we reduce the former.

She describes the father who embodies this destructive masculine mystique:

He does not express much emotion. He doesn't cry. He is very concerned with dominance, power, being tough. His taste in movies runs to

John Wayne and Sylvester Stallone. On TV he watches violent shows like "Miami Vice" and "Hawaii Five-O." Whatever his actual behavior may be, he is likely to indulge in callous sexual talk about women. He may feel that a high level of involvement in child care is unmanly.[13]

Such fathers, she concludes, "reinforce in their sons just those qualities that serve to desensitize them and make them more prone to commit violent acts or condone them."[14]

Miedzian's thesis is widely accepted among the experts in this field, pervading many of the current reports and recommendations concerning youth violence. Yet I would like to offer a good word for this type of father. Doubtless he is far from perfect. But there is one sin of which he is almost certainly innocent. He is not the reason why young boys commit crimes.

In fact, exactly the opposite is more likely to be true. This type of father—playing rough with his children, teaching his sons to be tough and competitive, coming home every night to watch football or crime shows on TV while seeking to repress some of his anxieties or doubts—may not deserve the Dad of the Year Award, but as for the probability that he or his sons will commit criminally violent acts, he is much more likely to deserve a letter of commendation from the local police department than to deserve the charge that Miedzian levels against him.

There are exceptions, of course, but here is the rule: Boys raised by traditionally masculine fathers generally do not commit crimes. Fatherless boys commit crimes.

Both clinical studies and anthropological investigations confirm the process through which boys seek to separate from their mothers in search of the meaning of their maleness. In this process, the father is irreplaceable. He enables the son to separate from the mother. He is the gatekeeper, guiding his son into the community of men, teaching him to name the meaning of his embodiment, showing him on good authority than he can be "man enough."[15]

In this process, the boy becomes more than the son of his mother, or even the son of his parents. He becomes the son of his father. Later, when the boy becomes a man, he will reunite with the world of women, the world of his mother, through his spouse and children. In this sense, only by becoming his father's as well as his mother's son can he become a good father and husband.[16]

When this process of male identity does not succeed—when the boy cannot separate from the mother, cannot become the son of his father—one main result, in clinical terms, is rage. Rage against the mother, against women, against society. It is a deeply misogynistic rage, vividly expressed, for example, in contemporary rap music with titles such as "Beat That Bitch with a Bat."[17]

Another common result of this failure is hypermasculinity, or what is frequently termed protest masculinity: the unrestricted (unmanhandled) aggression and swagger of boys who must prove their manhood all by themselves, without the help of fathers. For these reasons, if we want to learn the identity of the rapist, the hater of women, the occupant of jail cells, we do not look first to boys with traditionally masculine fathers. We look first to boys with no fathers.

Certainly, despite the difficulty of proving causation in the social sciences, the weight of evidence increasingly supports the conclusion that fatherlessness is a primary generator of violence among young men. As Michael R. Gottfredson and Travis Hirschi summarize current findings: "Such family measures as the percentage of the population divorced, the percentage of households headed by women, and the percentage of unattached individuals in the community are among the most powerful predictors of crime rates."[18] Surveys of child well-being repeatedly show that children living apart from their fathers are far more likely than other children to be expelled or suspended from school, to display emotional and behavioral problems, to have difficulty getting along with their peers, and to get in trouble with the police.[19]

According to a 1990 study commissioned by the Progressive Policy Institute, the "relationship between crime and one-parent families" is "so strong that controlling for family configuration erases the relationship between race and crime and between low income and crime. This conclusion shows up time and again in the literature."[20]

Moreover, fatherlessness undermines more than the life prospects of individual fatherless children. Especially as it becomes widespread, it also weakens the larger ethos of protection in a community. As James Q. Wilson reminds us:

Neighborhood standards may be set by mothers but they are enforced by fathers, or at least by adult males. Neighborhoods without fathers are neighborhoods without men able and willing to confront errant youth, chase threatening gangs, and reproach delinquent fathers. . . . the absence of fathers . . . deprives the community of those little platoons that informally but often effectively control boys on the street.[21]

So there is a link between masculinity and violence, but not the link that Miedzian describes. The rapid growth of crime in our society over the past three decades does not derive from traditional male norms but from the decline of certain traditional male norms, particularly the norm of paternal obligation and the duty to provide for children.

Put simply, we have too many boys with guns primarily because we have too few fathers. If we want fewer of the former, we must have more of the latter. There is little evidence to suggest that any other strategy will work.

Social workers, psychologists, mentors, and life skills instructors can frequently help children like Joseph Chaney, Jr., but they cannot even begin to do the work of a father. And despite our current policy of spending ever-larger sums of money on prison construction, our capacity to build new prisons is being far outstripped by our capacity to produce violent young men. We are generating male violence much faster than we can incarcerate it.

Prisons cannot replace fathers. At best, new prisons constitute an expensive endgame strategy for quarantining some of the consequences of fatherlessness. In this sense, locking up Joseph Chaney, Jr., might make us feel better and it might make us safer. But putting this child in jail is not an act of justice. It is an admission of failure, a symbol of our retreat.

Domestic Violence Against Women

Domestic violence emerged as an urgent and distinctive societal concern during the 1970s.[22] During these years, scholars and opinion leaders, especially those within the feminist movement, came to view domestic violence not simply as one subcategory of violent behavior but as conceptually separate from other types of violence—a special crime with its own distinctive logic and institutional sources.

The logic of the crime, in this view, is the logic of patriarchy. Privileged by gender status, men in families oppress women and children, frequently through violence. The main institutional source of the problem is marriage, which sanctions the values of patriarchal fatherhood. This perspective suggests that our current understanding of domestic violence, also frequently termed spouse abuse or wife beating, is defined largely by our understanding of marriage and fatherhood.

"Male violence against women is at least as old as the institution of marriage," Gus Kaufman, Jr., a psychologist, told *Time* magazine in a 1993 cover story on domestic violence entitled "'Til Death Do Us Part." The article explains: "So long as a woman was considered her husband's legal property, police and the courts were unable to prevent—and unwilling to punish—domestic assaults."[23]

In *The Battered Woman*, Lenore E. Walker argues that "the very fact of being a woman, specifically a married woman, automatically creates a situation of powerlessness" that invites husbands to become violent.[24] As Susan Schechter puts it: "Although men no longer legally own women, many act as if they do. In her marriage vows today, the woman still promises to love, honor, and obey.... Battering is one tool that enforces husbands' authority over wives or simply reminds women that this authority exists."[25]

Similarly, Naomi Wolf, angered by the rise of a "rape culture" in the United States, confesses that "when I think of pledging my heart and body to a man—even the best and kindest man—within the existing institution of marriage, I feel faint."[26] From this perspective, marriage culture emerges as a synonym for rape culture, and a marriage license becomes a license for a man to beat his wife.[27]

This idea largely governs television programming on domestic violence, including a great many made-for-television movies such as *The Burning Bed,* a popular 1984 movie starring Farrah Fawcett. In almost every case, domestic violence on television is portrayed as a crime committed by a married man, typically a middle-class, seemingly "normal" married father, usually from the suburbs.

Policy makers also commonly equate marriage with male violence. In West Virginia, legislators recently considered a bill, endorsed by the state medical association, that would require all marriage licenses in West Virginia to carry "warning labels" against domestic violence.[28] The symbolism and logic of this idea are unmistakable: Like alcohol and cigarettes, marriage poses potential health hazards for women.

Even in cases of domestic violence that clearly have nothing to do with marriage, this marriage-based conceptualization of the problem endures. In 1993, the *Wall Street Journal* published an essay by Shawn Sullivan called "Wife-Beating N the Hood." But, despite the title and much of the author's language, the essay itself is not about wife beating at all. It is about girlfriend beating. Thus, Sullivan writes about interviewing men he describes as "alleged wife-beaters" in a Brooklyn court, one of whom "admitted hitting his girlfriend but he added: 'She simply drove me to frustration. Where I come from, you don't take that s—— from your girl.'"[29]

More generally, our public discussion of domestic violence almost never acknowledges, much less analyzes, differences in marital status among men who assault women. Indeed, to avoid making these distinctions, certain rules of language are widely observed. Almost without exception, journalists, legislators, academics, and advocates for battered women adhere to the convention of calling perpetrators of domestic violence "husbands" or "partners," or sometimes, even more elliptically, "husbands and boyfriends." As a result, the public repeatedly hears that men who batter women are either husbands or, well, we would prefer not to be precise.

Thus our currently prevailing paradigm for understanding the problem: Male violence in families is rooted in, and sustained by, male marital privilege. Because of the causal link between marriage and violence, and because husbands are the principal victimizers of women, "wife beating" properly emerges as a generic term for male violence against a female sexual partner.[30]

But if marriage is the problem—if marriage serves to institutionalize and even valorize male violence—we might logically expect the decline of marriage in our society to be accompanied by a decline in domestic violence. More women freed from the restraints of marriage, less male violence.

But apparently, the opposite has happened. As women are living ever more separately, they are also living ever more dangerously. Demographers confirm that the single most significant change in men's lives during the past three decades has been that "men on average spend more time outside of fatherhood"—much less time living with their children and much more time living outside of marriage.[31]

At the same time, while reliable trend-line data are virtually nonexistent, the leading scholars on this issue generally confirm that domestic violence is a growing problem in our society.[32] So the weakening of marriage has not made the home a safer place for women. As more women are living apart from husbands and fathers, more women are being battered by men.[33]

This trend is tragic, and certainly does not speak well for men, but it should not be surprising. In *Fighting for Life,* Walter J. Ong nicely describes the foundation of prosocial behavior among males in human societies. The adult male "counters his tendency to violent domination by placing any violence in him directly at the service of others." Which "others"? In all societies, the male's biological offspring and the mother of his offspring emerge as the primary others on whose behalf he deploys, and in doing so socializes, his tendency toward aggression and adversative relationships.[34]

In their cross-cultural study of homicide, Martin Daly and Margo Wilson conclude that the male propensity toward violence—there is "no known human society in which the level of lethal violence among women even begins to approach that among men"—is rooted primarily in "male sexual jealousy and proprietariness." What social arrangements serve to minimize male violence? Like Ong, Daly and Wilson report that male violence is restrained principally by "paternal investment" in children, achieved through a "reproductive alliance" with the mother. In short, married fatherhood:

> The practice of paternal investment, by reapportioning male reproductive effort away from mating competition, tends to reduce both the fitness prize for high rank and the risk of total reproductive failure. Biparental care for the young thus softens male-male conflict and selects for less dangerous competitive tactics.[35]

From these perspectives, married fatherhood emerges as the primary inhibitor of male domestic violence. By reducing the likelihood of sexual jealousy and paternal uncertainty, and by directing the male's aggression toward the support of his child and the mother of his child, married fatherhood dramatically restricts the tendency among men toward violent behavior.

Do crime statistics in the United States support this theory? In 1994, the Centers for Disease Control and Prevention, an agency of the U.S. Department of Health and Human Services, released a study containing a startling piece of information: Each year, about 6 percent of all pregnant women are battered by their "husbands or partners."[36] In an interview with the *New York Times,* Dr. Julie Gazmararian, the study's principal author, was dismayed to find so many women "at risk, especially during pregnancy, a time when women are bonding more with their mates."[37]

Yet in the tables of the study itself, we learn a revealing and little-reported fact: For every married pregnant woman who reported being abused by her husband, almost four unmarried pregnant women reported being abused by their boyfriends. Moreover, marital status is the strongest predictor of abuse in this study—stronger than race, age, educational attainment, housing conditions, or access to prenatal health care.[38]

In short, in exactly the same way that the language of "husbands or partners" (and of "mates") fuzzes over the key distinction, the reported figure of 6 percent obscures at least as much as it reveals. The Centers for Disease Control might just as accurately, and much more diagnostically, have reported that, compared to married women, unmarried women are three to four times more likely to be physically abused while pregnant.

A recent study of domestic violence in New Jersey confirms this phenomenon. Even though co-resident wives greatly outnumber co-resident girlfriends—nationally, there are only about six unmarried co-resident couples for every hundred married couples—reports of domestic violence against girlfriends in New Jersey actually outnumber reports of domestic violence against wives.[39]

The National Crime Victimization Survey, conducted by the U.S. Department of Justice, provides the most comprehensive source of national data on violent crimes against women. This survey's findings confirm the thesis that violent behavior among men is strongly linked to marital status. For example, from 1979 through 1987, about 57,000 women per year were violently assaulted by their husbands. But 200,000 women per year were assaulted by boyfriends and 216,000 by ex-husbands. Of all violent crimes against women committed by intimates during this period, about 65 percent were committed by either boyfriends or ex-husbands, compared with 9 percent by husbands.[40] Clearly, male violence against female intimates is concentrated not within the marital institution but outside the perimeters of it—either from sort-of spouses (boyfriends) or from former husbands.

More broadly, married women are four times less likely than unmarried or divorced women to become the victim of any violent crime. Marital status is one of the strongest predictors for female crime victimization. From 1973 through 1992, the female violent crime victimization rate—violent crimes against females per 1,000 females age twelve or older—was 43 for unmarried women and 45 for divorced and separated women. For married women, the rate was 11. In short, for women, being married means being safer from violent crime.[41]

Yet simply comparing married to unmarried perpetrators, as revealing as that comparison is, may not take us to the heart of the matter. Recall the core idea: The institutional inhibitor of male violence is married fatherhood. The goal for men, and for society, is paternal investment through an alliance with the mother. But what happens to men when this process fragments? Specifically, what happens when there is fatherhood—or at least some semblance of fatherhood—but little or no alliance with the mother?

During the summer of 1993, several colleagues and I conducted an unscientific experiment. We read two Boston newspapers each day, looking for stories describing local incidents of domestic violence. We had our hands full. As it turned out, that summer Boston experienced a horrifying surge of domestic violence. In reviewing these grim stories, two types of violent men clearly stand out.

The first is the boyfriend-father. He is the biological father of his girlfriend's child, but his relationship with the mother is sporadic, ambivalent, and unstable. On the one hand, he is proud of his child and cares about his child. As a father, he has the right to make claims and to be involved. On the other hand, his commitment to the mother is weak and variable. Moreover, because the mother understands this fact, she may well decide that she no longer wants him around.

For these reasons, he may well treat her with resentment and even rage, in part because he dislikes being obligated to her, and in part because she alone largely controls something that is important to him. In addition, his anger may be stoked by humiliation as he comes to suspect—and to be told by the mother, perhaps as she shows him the door—that he is letting her and their child down and thus failing a test of manhood.

This increasingly common situation is highly combustible—an unstable mixture of sexual proprietariness, concern for offspring, resentment, and relative powerlessness, all operating without the benefit of any institutional coherence or structure. It is a seedbed for male violence. As a result, the boyfriend-father frequently becomes a violent guy, using his fists or a weapon to grab for something—ultimately, perhaps, a sense of control and self-respect—that his situation renders almost inherently unattainable. Here are three examples of this phenomenon from that terrible Boston summer:

After allegedly putting a gun to his ex-girlfriend's head and pulling the trigger, 22-year-old Hernando Cruz went to a friend's house and watched TV news reports to make sure she was dead.... Cruz, of Revere, was charged yesterday with murdering Francisca Guthrie, 18, outside a crowded mall as she pushed their infant daughter in a stroller.... Police and prosecutors said Cruz, a car-rental agency worker, was angry that his girlfriend had left him.... Guthrie, who moved in with her family in Chelsea two days ago, refused to let Cruz see their 2¹/₂-month-old baby, Cassandra.[42]

In March, Patricia Aquino was granted a year-long restraining order to keep her boyfriend away from her.... Yesterday morning, Aquino's 13-year-old daughter, hearing her 2-year-old brother moving about in her mother's bedroom, pushed open the door and found Aquino sprawled at the foot of the bed.... Aquino was pronounced dead at the scene.... Police said they were seeking for questioning Robert (Skipper) Murphy, 34, the father of Aquino's two youngest children.[43]

Ann-Marie Yukevich did almost all the right things—took out restraining orders against her abusive boyfriend, and even got him locked up for six months last year.... [But yesterday] the mother of two—who was three months pregnant with boyfriend Michael Browler's child—died when he allegedly stormed her Watertown home despite a restraining order and suffocated her with a pillow.[44]

The second newly prevalent type of perpetrator is distinctly visible from the National Crime Victimization Survey. He is the ex-spouse: the former husband-father who goes crazy. He was once a married father. Then his world falls apart. He loses his children. He loses his home, his purpose, his direction. Frequently, he loses his grip. Frequently, he becomes a violent guy.

Sometimes, of course, he was a bad husband and father—perhaps even a violent one—before the divorce. In such cases, marriage has clearly failed to inhibit male violence. Yet even after taking this disconfirming evidence into account, the larger trend seems clear: For many men, suddenly losing their identity as married fathers, especially when the loss is involuntary, shatters their world and triggers violence.

Consider three cases involving former husband-fathers, all occurring in Boston within a period of less than two weeks:

The estranged husband of a Roxbury woman broke into her apartment early yesterday and went on a bloody rampage, fatally stabbing his wife's brother and slashing the throats of his wife and 14-year-old daughter.... Neighbors of his wife said he had been distraught about their separation.... [The victim] had obtained a restraining order July 1 against her husband and the pair separated about a month ago.[45]

An Arlington man beat his estranged wife to death and buried her in an East Boston marsh because he was angry about having to pay her $200 a week in child support, a prosecutor alleged yesterday.[46]

A New Hampshire man, angered over the outcome of a bitter divorce case, allegedly shot and killed a Massachusetts man who had once been married to his wife.... Nathaniel Tuttle ... is charged with murder in the death of Joseph Siedentopp ... who had testified against Tuttle in the divorce case.... The victim was the third husband of Tuttle's wife, Matalina, 46. Tuttle is her fourth husband.... The two met in 1978 while Matalina was married to Siedentopp, court papers said. She worked as a bookkeeper for Tuttle's Auto Parts and, in 1979, had a daughter by Tuttle. In 1989, she filed a "palimony" suit against Tuttle, but dropped it after Tuttle agreed to marriage.... Tuttle, who was barred from contact with her as a result of a restraining order, had also been ordered to undergo counseling ... the prosecutor said the divorce decree apparently sparked the shooting.[47]

That summer, the Boston newspapers ran several hand-wringing stories detailing the failure of current public policy to halt the surge of domestic violence in the city. "The major weapon we have against domestic violence, the civil restraining order, is not working," a Quincy District Court probation officer told the *Boston Herald*. "We need to re-look at this in a major way."[48] The *Herald* also observed: "A year ago, Gov. William F. Weld declared 'an epidemic of domestic violence' in the state. Bills were passed and millions of dollars were spent to quell the murders. But today ... advocates wonder just how effective the laws, funds and press conferences have been."[49]

What preoccupied Boston in the summer of 1993 preoccupied everyone in the summer of 1994, when much of the nation became transfixed by the grisly crime of domestic violence allegedly committed by O. J. Simpson, the former football star. If proven guilty, Simpson is yet another example of this growing phenomenon, the killer ex-husband. Moreover, like many males who turn to violence, he grew up without a father.[50]

What is the underlying reality of these dreadful stories? That some people, for whatever reason, simply go bad? That males are prone to violence? That we need stricter laws and tougher enforcement? That we need to teach men, starting when they are boys, to control their aggression? That we are living in an increasingly violent world?

Yes, all of these things are true. But the deeper chord of this narrative is the growing fragmentation of fatherhood in our society. For the plot line running through all of these crime stories is the growing incoherence of paternity and the steady weakening of marriage as an institution that brings order and meaning to men's lives. As marriage weakens, more and more men become isolated and estranged from their children and from the mothers of their children. One result, in turn, is the spread of male violence.

Across societies, married fatherhood is the single most reliable, and relied upon, prescription for socializing males. Thus, a society's procreative norms for men, though seldom recognized as a determinant of violence, do more to determine the level of domestic violence than either legislative action or police procedures.

For if the cultural antidote for male violence is monogamous marriage and responsible fatherhood, the breeding grounds for it are casual sex, family fragmentation, and nonmarital childbearing. As we deinstitutionalize marriage and fracture fatherhood in our society, we must not be surprised by the rapid spread of male violence, especially violence against women.

Child Sexual Abuse

With each passing year, the horrifying crime of child sexual abuse is reported more often and, apparently, is happening more often in our society.[51] It is also, more than any other category of violent male behavior, rooted in what Douglas J. Besharov, a leading scholar in the field, calls "the growing presence of unrelated males in households with children."[52] In short, the spreading risk of childhood sexual abuse is directly linked to the decline of married fatherhood.

This is the trend on the ground. Meanwhile, in the movies and on television, as well as in much of the print media, the portrayal of the sexual abuse of children follows a strict formula. It is never the butler. Always, the father did it.

From television movies such as *Something About Amelia* and *Not in My Family,* to magazine stories such as *Newsweek*'s "The Sins of the Fathers," the essential plot line rarely varies.[53] He gets married. He becomes a father. He seems normal. He molests his child. A 1993 storybook for children, *The Storm's Crossing,* perfectly captures the genre: "On the surface Maggie is a happy-go-lucky, everyday-kind of kid—from a model family living a model life in a good neighborhood. But she is also the unhappy-be-unlucky victim of her father's sexual interests."[54]

As in the case of domestic violence against women, the crime of child sexual abuse is frequently described by scholars and children's advocates as a sickening but predictable consequence of having fathers in the home. From this perspective, child sexual abuse can be viewed as fatherhood run amok. As Judith Lewis Herman puts it, the sexual molestation of daughters is "an exaggeration of patriarchal family norms, but not a departure from them."[55] The presence of fathers, then—especially, it seems, everyday kind of fathers from model families—endangers children by exposing them to the risk of sexual abuse.

Yes, some—too many—married fathers molest their children. But the weight of evidence is clear. What magnifies the risk of sexual abuse for children is not the presence of a married father but his absence. More specifically, the escalating risk of childhood sexual abuse in our society stems primarily from the growing absence of married fathers and the growing presence of stepfathers, boyfriends, and other unrelated or transient males.

Consider stepfathers. A stepfather enters a family as the mother's sexual partner, but not as the daughter's father and longtime protector. As many analysts have pointed out, the incest taboo is significantly weaker in step-father-stepdaughter relationships. Nor is this relationship characterized by what some scholars term "kin altruism"—the profound tendency to sacrifice most for those with whom we share the closest biological ties.[56] For fathers (and for mothers as well), kin altruism exerts its most powerful influence in the case of biological offspring.

Moreover, for the married father, the daily habits of fathering, originating from the child's birth—watching her being born, teaching her to brush her teeth—serve as a strong reinforcement of paternal protectiveness and a strong barrier against the expression of sexual desire for a child. As Judith Wallerstein observes: "the father's role is to protect his daughter, an impulse that is normally more powerful than any excitement he experiences."[57]

In the case of stepfathers, none of these inhibitors of sexual expression is present. Of course, most stepfathers do not molest their stepchildren. But, as numerous studies confirm, stepfathers are far more likely than fathers to do so.[58]

Consider boyfriends. Until quite recently, mothers with live-in boyfriends were considered unfit mothers, largely because boyfriends were considered a threat to the sexual innocence of children. Judges could and did deny such women custody of their children. But today, with the general acceptance of cohabitation, not only has such antiboyfriend fearfulness largely vanished but we seem to have forgotten why we ever had it. In general, mothers with dependent children are free to share their households with boyfriends.

The language we use is revealing. These are not men but "boys." They are not husbands or fathers but "friends." When we think of adult family roles, there are no activities called the "boyfriend role." The language is rooted in fact. Boyfriends tend to be younger and far more transient than either fathers or stepfathers. Regardless of their age, they possess a kind of adolescent freedom. They are unrestricted, not bound by either the father role or the husband role. Most important, they are not bound by probably the most powerful taboo in human society: the incest taboo.[59]

Consequently, the growing prevalence of boyfriends and "play husbands" in households with children poses a direct threat to children's physical and sexual safety.[60] One study conducted by the research firm Westat finds that, of all cases of child abuse in which the perpetrator is known, fully one-quarter are cohabiting "parent substitutes," usually boyfriends—a rate dramatically higher than the rates found among fathers, day-care providers, babysitters, or other caregivers.[61]

According to another recent study from the University of Iowa, of all reported cases of nonparental child abuse, about half are committed by boyfriends, even though boyfriends provide only about 2 percent of all nonparental child care. About 84 percent of all cases of nonparental child abuse occur in single-parent homes. Among the cases occurring in single-parent homes, 64 percent of the perpetrators are boyfriends. The study's conclusion: "a young child left alone with mother's boyfriend experiences substantially elevated risk of abuse."[62]

Regarding sexual abuse, the risk posed by boyfriends is especially high. In the Westat study, cases of sexual abuse by "parent substitutes" actually outnumber cases by natural parents.[63] Michael Gordon and Susan J. Creighton summarize the research findings: "A number of studies have shown that girls living with non-natal fathers [boyfriends and stepfathers] are at higher risk for sexual abuse than girls living with natal fathers."[64]

To make a dangerous situation even worse, many single mothers, especially women who never married and already face obstacles such as poverty and bad neighborhoods, simply do not prevent their boyfriends from showing sexual interest in their daughters. Because she wants a boyfriend who will fuss over her and her children, a single mother "may encourage the current man in her life to 'play daddy,' hoping he will like the role," reports Judith S. Musick in *Young, Poor and Pregnant*. But these mothers often fail to realize that "allowing someone to play daddy under these conditions in effect gives him carte blanche—the child is his to do with as he sees fit. All too many males will see fit to threaten, force, coerce or seduce the woman's daughters into sexual activity."[65]

Finally, consider the rising risk of sexual abuse from male strangers and acquaintances. In the Westat study, approximately half of the confirmed acts of child sexual abuse were committed by "others"—people outside the household.[66] More significantly, there is a clear relationship between the absence of a married father on the premises and the opportunity for "others" to coerce and molest children. Accordingly, many girls in father-absent homes are poorly protected from sexually opportunistic males in the surrounding community. Elijah Anderson observes:

> The local boys may be attracted to the home as a challenge. . . . In such a setting no man, the figure the boys are prepared to respect, is there to

keep them in line. Girls in this vulnerable situation may become pregnant earlier than those living in homes more closely resembling nuclear
families.[67]

According to a recent study from the Alan Guttmacher Institute, among
girls who experience sexual intercourse by the age of fourteen, nearly three-
quarters report that they have at times been physically coerced into it.[68]

According to some observers, men who sexually abuse children seem to
develop special antennae that pick up the signals of vulnerability.[69] Certainly, in several celebrated cases, single mothers have let such sexually
opportunistic men befriend their fatherless children. In Sonora, California,
for example, Daniel Mark Driver "gained the trust of single mothers" by
"moving in religious circles and offering himself as a substitute father." He
then sexually molested the children he was "fathering."[70]

Child sexual abuse is a terrible crime, regardless of the identity or family
status of the perpetrator. Too many married fathers commit this crime.
These are facts. But it is also a fact, despite our widespread unwillingness
to face it, that a child is sexually safer with her father than she is with any
other man, from a stepfather to her mother's boyfriend to guys in the
neighborhood. She is also safer with a father than without one. A child in a
fatherless home faces a significantly higher risk of sexual abuse.

Child Poverty and Economic Insecurity

If the most immediately frightening societal consequence of fatherlessness
is the rise of male violence, the most easily measurable is the rise of child
poverty. Across history and cultures, the foundational tasks of fatherhood
have been twofold: protection and provision. The first is about violence.
The second is about money.[71] For the child, fatherlessness means more of
the former and less of the latter.

A blizzard of statistics and studies confirms the relationship between
fatherlessness and child poverty, but here, at least arguably, are the three
most revealing comparisons. In married-couple homes in the United States
in 1992, about 13 percent of all children under the age of six lived in
poverty; in single-mother families, about 66 percent of young children lived
in poverty—a ratio of 5 to 1.[72] In married-couple homes with preschool
children, median family income in 1992 was approximately $41,000; in
single-mother homes with young children, median income was about
$9,000—a ratio of more than 4 to 1.[73] Of all married-couple families in the
nation in 1992, about 6 percent lived in poverty; of all female-headed families, about 35 percent lived in poverty—a ratio of almost 6 to 1.[74]

One more comparison, regarding the economic well-being of African-American children. Of all black married couples with children under age eighteen in 1992, about 15 percent lived in poverty; of all black mother-headed homes with children, about 57 percent lived in poverty—a ratio of almost 4 to 1.[75]

In *Single Mothers and Their Children,* Irwin Garfinkel and Sara S. McLanahan succinctly summarize the evidence: "Families headed by single women with children are the poorest of all major demographic groups regardless of how poverty is measured."[76] In *Poor Support,* David T. Ellwood similarly concludes that "the vast majority of children who are raised entirely in a two-parent home will never be poor during childhood. By contrast, the vast majority of children who spend time in a single-parent home will experience poverty."[77]

Most scholars now agree that this link between family structure and child poverty is not simply a statistical correlation. It is a causal relationship. Fatherlessness causes child poverty. Indeed, according to numerous scholars, fatherlessness has become the single most powerful determinant of child poverty—more important than race, region, or the educational attainment of the mother. As William Julius Wilson and Kathryn M. Neckerman put it, "sex and marital status of the head are the most important determinants of poverty status for families."[78]

Similarly, Leif Jensen, David J. Eggebeen, and Daniel T. Lichter, analyzing a national child poverty rate that jumped from 14 percent in 1969 to 20.6 percent in 1990, despite much more social spending on children, attribute most of this surge to "the demographic shift of children living in married-couple families to 'high-risk' single-parent families." Echoing other scholars, they suggest that "changing family structure is the greatest long term threat to U.S. children."[79]

In his careful review of the evidence, William A. Galston, currently the deputy assistant to the president for domestic public policy, concludes that current research findings "suggest that the best anti-poverty program for children is a stable, intact family."[80] He might just as easily have said: a married father on the premises.

In 1986, our society crossed an important threshold. That year, for the first time in our nation's history, a majority of all poor families were father-absent.[81] Historically, for most poor children, poverty stemmed primarily from fathers being unemployed or receiving low wages. For most poor children today, poverty stems primarily from not having a father in the home.

In strict economic terms, this trend can be understood as paternal disinvestment: the growing refusal of fathers to spend their resources on their offspring. This trend helps to explain an apparent paradox. Public spending on children in the United States has never been higher. At the same time, child poverty is spreading and child well-being is declining.[82] The explanation is that our rising public investment in children has been far outweighed by our private disinvestment, primarily paternal disinvestment.

Certainly, the clearest economic consequence of paternal disinvestment is rising child poverty, a condition that, in 1992, afflicted 22 percent of all children under age eighteen and 25 percent of all children under age six.[83] But paternal disinvestment also produces an economic ripple effect that extends well beyond the official definition of poverty. For even when fatherlessness does not consign children to poverty, it commonly consigns them to a childhood—and frequently an early adulthood as well—marked by persistent economic insecurity.

For example, divorce typically means lower living standards for women and children. One study estimates that, in the year following divorce, average income for women drops by approximately 30 percent.[84] Even the best postdivorce economic arrangements, in which fathers regularly pay child support, almost always mean less money and more insecurity for children—including fewer traditional childhood activities such as athletics, summer camp, vacations, school trips, and swimming lessons. A 1991 study concludes: "other than paying child support and buying gifts, the majority of [divorced] fathers have never provided assistance to their children."[85]

Moreover, millions of children in our society—from those who have never seen their fathers to those whose absent fathers visit regularly and pay child support—fail to receive any financial support from their fathers precisely when they need it the most: when they are crossing the threshold of adulthood. As they enter their late teens and early twenties, these young people will want to buy a car. They will want to go to college, or make a down payment on a house, or buy furniture for an apartment, or find a co-signer for a bank loan. But, unlike previous generations, these young people will get no help from their fathers. Even among divorced fathers who pay child support, the end of the support order, usually when the child reaches age eighteen, usually signals the end of support. In her study of paternal support following divorce, Wallerstein was dismayed to find that many fathers

> who had maintained contact with their children over the decade, who had supported them with regularity, and who were well able to continue supporting them financially, failed to do so at the time when their youngsters' economic and educational preparation for adulthood was at stake.[86]

For many young people, this paternal disinvestment in young adulthood contributes to downward social mobility. Although many children manage to do well without a father's help, those who grow up without fathers are far more likely to move down, not up, the socioeconomic ladder. Sons are especially affected, since they are the traditional beneficiaries of a father's occupational guidance and role modeling.[87]

In a larger sense, the cessation of the intergenerational transfer of paternal wealth—from father to child and from paternal grandparents to grandchild—is likely to emerge by the early years of the next century not only as a growing determinant of individual economic well-being but also as a new source of social inequality. For as fatherlessness spreads, the economic difference between America's haves and have-nots will increasingly revolve around a basic question: Which of us had fathers?

Adolescent Childbearing

After protection and provision, the central task of fatherhood is cultural transmission. In many respects, the single most consequential development in the story of human fatherhood, powerfully portrayed in classic texts such as the Bible's Book of Genesis, is the movement of males toward understanding their paternity not simply as biological insemination, nor even primarily as providing resources and warding off danger, but also— and perhaps most important—as "manhandling" their offspring: making sure not only that the child survives, but also that the child grows up to be a certain kind of person.

Here we see the essential difference between biological paternity and fatherhood. The former helps to produce a child. The latter helps to produce an adult. In the broadest sense, cultural transmission can be understood as fathers and mothers, in overlapping but distinctive ways, teaching their children a way of life. The result of effective cultural transmission is the development of competence and character in children.

Fatherlessness—the absence of paternal transmission—contributes to a decline of character and competence in children. Today, a growing characterological deficit among children is widely evident in our society, affecting countless aspects of children's behavior and mental health, from school misconduct to eating disorders to the decline of politeness and manners.[88] For this reason, characterological disinvestment by fathers is harder to quantify than economic disinvestment, but it is far more important. For children, doing without a father's money is the easy part. Money influences what you have and what you can do. Fathers shape who you are.

For boys, the most socially acute manifestation of paternal disinvestment is juvenile violence. For girls, it is juvenile and out-of-wedlock childbearing. One primary result of growing fatherlessness is more boys with guns. Another is more girls with babies.

In 1991, the rate of adolescent childbearing, measured as births to teen mothers per 1,000 girls, reached 62.1, the highest level since 1971 (prior to the legalization of abortion). In more than two-thirds of all cases of teenage childbearing today, the mother is unmarried.[89] (In 1960, only 15 percent of teen mothers were unmarried.)[90] Each year, unmarried teen mothers account for a larger share of the nation's total number of child-births. In 1985, for example, they accounted for 7.5 percent of all births. In 1991, they accounted for 9 percent.[91] Adolescent childbearing is inextricably linked to the decline of fatherhood—not only because more and more adolescent boys are willing to impregnate girls without the slightest intention of becoming an effective father but also because more and more adolescent girls are growing up without a father in the home.

A father plays a distinctive role in shaping a daughter's sexual style and her understanding of the male-female bond. A father's love and involvement builds a daughter's confidence in her own femininity and contributes to her sense that she is worth loving. This sense of love-worthiness gives young women a greater sense of autonomy and independence in later relationships with men. Consequently, women who have had good relationships with their fathers are less likely to engage in an anxious quest for male approval or to seek male affection through promiscuous sexual behavior.

Many studies confirm that girls who grow up without fathers are at much greater risk for early sexual activity, adolescent childbearing, divorce, and lack of sexual confidence and orgasmic satisfaction.[92] These problems do not stem primarily from economic status. Scholars have studied this issue carefully, documenting the effects on girls of fatherless homes while controlling for income—that is, eliminating income as a dependent variable in the studies. They have concluded that father absence, not money absence, is the core issue.

For example, Garfinkel and McLanahan, in their careful summary of the research on the many "intergenerational consequences" of fatherless homes, place special emphasis on the "family formation behavior" of girls who grow up without fathers. Among white families, one study finds that "daughters of single parents are 53 percent more likely to marry as teenagers, 111 percent more likely to have children as teenagers, 164 percent more likely to have a premarital birth, and 92 percent more likely to dissolve their own marriages."[93]

These authors favor new public policies that would provide greater economic support for single-parent homes. But they also insist that we confront the research findings that "increasing the incomes of single mothers would alleviate at least some of the educational disadvantages now associated with being a member of a female-headed family, but would not have much of an impact on out-of-wedlock births or on the perpetuation of mother-only families."[94]

For girls, the effects of fatherlessness often emerge most visibly during adolescence, frequently in the form of precocious sexuality. For example, daughters who seemed to have "gotten over" their parents' divorce may suddenly exhibit problems in forming intimate relationships of their own. Of the young women in the California Children of Divorce Study, Judith Wallerstein writes:

> Many of the young women who had done well during their early adolescent years experienced a "sleeper" effect as they moved into late adolescence and became very frightened of failure. Almost all confronted issues of love, commitment and marriage with anxiety, sometimes with very great concern about betrayal, abandonment, and not being loved. In response to this, many of the young women, and some of the young men, appeared counterphobically to have thrown themselves into short-lived sexual relationships.[95]

E. Mavis Hetherington's study of teenage daughters in father-absent families identifies differences between girls who lose their fathers through divorce and girls who lose their fathers through death. Compared to daughters who live with both parents, girls from both widowed and divorced families are less able to interact successfully with men. But while daughters of widows tend toward shyness and inhibition with men, daughters of divorce tend to be overly responsive.[96]

Deprived of a stable relationship with a nonexploitative adult male who loves them, these girls can remain developmentally "stuck," struggling with issues of security and trust that well-fathered girls have already successfully resolved. Judith Musick observes: "The self's voice in these young women may remain fixed on one basic set of questions. . . . What do I need to do, and who do I need to be, to find a man who won't abandon me, as the men in my life and my mother's life have done?"[97]

These unresolved issues pose serious obstacles to meeting what Erik Erikson describes as the central challenge of adolescence: establishing a sense of industry.[98] As Musick puts it:

> Girls for whom basic acceptance and love are the primary motivating forces have little interest or emotional energy to invest in school or work-related activities unless they are exceptionally bright and talented. Even then, the pull of unmet affiliative or dependency needs may be more powerful than anything the worlds of school or work have to offer.[99]

Precisely because these issues are so intimate and important, this form of paternal disinvestment in daughters cannot really be remedied. When a girl cannot trust and love the first man in her life, her father, what she is missing cannot be replaced by money, friends, teachers, social workers, or well-designed public policies aimed at helping her. She simply loses. Moreover, as more and more girls grow up without fathers, society loses.

From a societal perspective, this particular consequence of fatherlessness is very much like most others. It is not remediable. Paternal disinvestment cannot be offset by either maternal investment or public investment. As a society, we will not solve our crisis of fatherlessness with prison cells, mentoring programs, antiviolence curricula, boyfriends, antistalking laws, children's advocates, income transfers, self-esteem initiatives, or even mothers. We will solve it only with fathers.

CHAPTER 3

The Lost Idea

The fatherless family of the United States in the late twentieth century is a social invention of the most daring and untested design. It represents a radical departure from virtually all of human history and experience.

In his classic statement, the anthropologist Bronislaw Malinowski enunciated the fatherhood idea that has guided human societies up to this point in history:

> The most important moral and legal rule concerning the physiological site of kinship is that no child should be brought into the world without a man—and one man at that—assuming the role of sociological father, that is, of guardian and protector, the male link between the child and the rest of the community. I think that this generalization amounts to a universal sociological law and as such I have called it in some of my previous writings the principle of legitimacy.

Malinowski describes significant cultural variations in the expression of the legitimacy principle, but insists upon the universality of the core idea:

> Yet through all the variations there runs the rule that the father is indispensable for the full sociological status of the child as well as of its mother, that the group consisting of a woman and her offspring is sociologically incomplete and illegitimate. The father, in other words, is necessary for the full legal status of the family.[1]

Admittedly, for many Americans, a universal principle is hard to respect. After all, we are a nation with an exceptionalist heritage. Our tradition, as Harold Rosenberg puts it, is "the tradition of the new."[2] Rebellious individualism runs deep in our national character, including rebellion against the family, especially fathers.

Yet even in the United States, the fatherhood idea, as summarized by Malinowski, has endured until quite recently. Indeed, to consider the particulars of the American experience is to grasp just how recent and radical is the idea that children do not necessarily need fathers.

"Bring Daddy Home"

Concern about fatherlessness is a recurring theme in American history. As an immigrant, frontier, and slave-owning society, the United States in the eighteenth and nineteenth centuries presented harsh challenges to family life. Many children lost parents during the journey to America. Compared to life in Europe, childhood in the United States, especially near the frontier, could be chaotic and dangerous. Many African-American children experienced an unspeakably cruel form of father loss, forcibly separated from their fathers at the auction block.[3]

War, in particular, separated fathers from their children. Recruiting soldiers meant breaking up families. During the Civil War, for example, an orphanage official worried that "withdrawing men of the laboring classes from civil life into the army . . . has increased the number of women of those classes who are compelled to seek our sheltering wards, or leave with us their helpless children."[4] And, of course, war brought the terrible threat of untimely death. During the Civil War, the nation's bloodiest conflict, over 618,000 soldiers died. Although not all of these men were fathers—most Civil War soldiers were quite young, between the ages of fourteen and twenty-four—one study estimates that between one-third and two-fifths of all Union soldiers were married men.[5]

In his study of letters written by Union soldiers, Stephen M. Frank shows how these absent fathers struggled to remain involved in their children's lives, questioning and advising their wives on everything from diet to discipline. These men worried about their children's safety—one soldier told his wife to sell his pistol, fearing that his small son would try to play with it—and that their children might forget them.[6]

"I often ask myself whether our little Callie speaks of her 'pa,'" a Southern soldier wrote to his wife. "Does she remember me?"[7] These soldier-fathers especially yearned to see the babies born while they were away. "I want to see the children very bad," wrote another Confederate father; "their is sevril men in the same fix that I am in that hav young babs at home that they never saw."[8] This paternal solicitude is more than touching. It reveals a primary truth of wartime fatherhood: The absence of fathers during war, while obviously painful for individual families, does not constitute an assault on fatherhood as a social role and cultural norm.[9]

In the twentieth century, however, our nation has faced not one father-hood crisis, but two. The second is the one we face today: the rise of voli-tional fatherlessness. The first, very different, fatherhood crisis in this cen-tury occurred during and immediately after World War II. During that war, for the first time in American history, the government conscripted fathers into military service on a societywide scale. This mass conscription of fathers caused widespread debate and protest, including a vigorous dis-cussion among experts and opinion leaders, much of it focusing on the role of fathers in society.

The fatherhood debate of World War II constitutes a little-remembered but important historical moment. For during those years, even as millions of men put on uniforms and left their families, American society was in lit-tle doubt about what fathers do or about the consequences of father absence. Across lines of region, educational attainment, class, race, and gender, the consensus at the onset of World War II was unambiguous: To separate millions of fathers from their children, even temporarily, would present a clear and present danger to child and societal well-being.

Such agreement can derive only from a society's embrace of the father-hood idea: the "moral and legal rule" of a father for every child. Because the United States in the 1990s increasingly ignores this foundational idea, it is revealing to recall a time, not so long ago, when we did not. Because we currently disavow the fatherhood idea that our parents and grand-parents espoused, much of what those people did about fatherhood in the 1940s must surely strike our contemporary sensibility as quaint or anom-alous, perhaps even stunning.

When the United States entered the war, for example, military leaders did not favor drafting fathers. During the early war years, a special defer-ment category was created for men whose children were conceived or born prior to the 1941 attack on Pearl Harbor.

By 1943, however, it had became clear that draft quotas could not be filled solely from the ranks of single men and married men without chil-dren. The Selective Service was forced to turn to the "father class" of roughly 6 million men.[10] As one general bluntly complained in his testi-mony before the Senate Committee on Military Affairs: "If the men are single or if the men are fathers is really immaterial. It is the men, it is the bodies that we need."[11]

The proposal to draft fathers produced widespread alarm and protest. Senator Burton Wheeler of Montana introduced legislation to postpone it, warning the Congress that widespread father absence would be severely detrimental to families. The government's modest dependency allowance for these fatherless homes, Wheeler insisted, was inadequate. Mothers would be unable to make ends meet. Economic vulnerability would spread, harming both domestic and military morale. Mothers would be forced to go to work in factories and shops. With children left at home unsupervised, rates of crime and juvenile delinquency would rise.

In October 1943, military necessity prevailed and the ban on drafting fathers was lifted. Even then, however, the military moved cautiously and reluctantly. As the ban was lifted, General Lewis B. Hershey, the director of the Selective Service, promised to order local draft boards to "first exhaust the pool of available unmarried men, and next the pool of married men without children, before fathers would be called."[12]

Popular opinion remained decisively opposed to drafting fathers. A Gallup poll during the fall of 1943 found that 68 percent of Americans believed that, compared to drafting fathers, it was preferable to draft single men employed in industries essential to the war effort. Public opinion also favored drafting single women for noncombat military service in order to avoid drafting fathers. As George Gallup put it, the public objected to the father draft because "it would lead to the breaking up of too many families where there are children."[13] Among the last-ditch efforts of some congressional leaders to postpone the father draft was a proposal to draft seventeen-year-old boys instead of adult fathers.[14]

As the end of the war approached, there was much public pressure to bring the fathers home first. Late in the war, the military polled soldiers to help determine priorities for early discharge. In the view of most servicemen, the first criterion for early discharge should be combat service. The second should be fatherhood. These opinions served as the basis for a weighted point system devised by the military. For each child under age eighteen, a soldier got twelve points, with up to thirty-six early-discharge points allowed for being a father.[15]

Yet even this pro-father point system did not satisfy the families waiting at home. Members of Congress felt considerable public pressure to abandon the point system altogether and simply bring the fathers home first. Across the country, mothers formed "Bring Back Daddy" clubs to organize lobbying campaigns, presenting members of Congress with baby shoes with tags reading "Bring Daddy Home."[16] Many members of Congress urged a change in the existing policy. As one congressman from New Jersey put it: "a generation of fatherless children would make our country a second-rate power and everything should be done to prevent such a tragedy."[17]

In part, of course, the wartime debate about fathers—whether to draft them and when to discharge them—was rooted in the practical needs of the immediately affected families. It is not hard to understand why mothers would want their husbands to come home soon. But the debate also reflects much more than self-interested lobbying by a particular constituency. It reflects a coherent societal understanding of what fathers do.

This consensus is clearly revealed in the discussion among social scientists of the effects of war on family life.

During the mid-1940s, numerous prestigious academic organizations, including the Social Science Research Council, the U.S. Children's Bureau, the National Conference on Family Relations, the American Orthopsychiatric Association, and the American Academy of Political and Social Science, published special reports on how the exigencies of war influence family life. These reports differ in emphasis and detail, but they agree on the central point: War and its aftermath had unleashed powerful destabilizing influences—including greater mobility, anonymity, and prosperity—that seriously threatened child and family well-being.

In some respects, these scholars pointed out, World War II had simply accelerated family changes that were already evident in a rapidly modernizing society. But not in the most important respect. For the war had created a family phenomenon with no precedent: the prolonged, mass separation of fathers from their families.

"All of the effects of the war upon the family were neither so new nor so radical as this mass separation," argued the sociologist Francis Merrill in a 1948 study entitled *Social Problems on the Home Front*. He continued: "In the temporary separation of millions of families and the permanent disruption of thousands of others, the war exerted a new and unforeseen influence upon this central institution."[18] In brief, fatherlessness was not one social problem caused by war. To Merrill and others, it was the primary social problem caused by war.

Social scientists agreed that war-induced fatherlessness—one scholar called it "mass deprivation"—jeopardized the well-being of millions of children. According to one estimate, about 1.7 million children were relying on dependency checks from the U.S. Army as of June 1944. Yet this figure excludes the children of men in other branches of the service, so the total number of wartime fatherless children is much higher, affecting, according to one estimate, as many as 3 million to 4 million U.S. families.[19]

Many of these soldier-fathers were killed in combat:

> As the casualty lists grow, more and more children are doomed to a family life that includes only one parent. The death of one soldier may mean several fatherless children; another, if he married just before leaving for the front, may be killed in action before his child is born. [These] children grow up with a deep sense of loss, and even though they cannot remember their father, they are sometimes envious of their friends who have fathers who mean so much to them.[20]

Even more soldier-fathers escaped death but remained absent from their families for months or years. Such an absence, scholars observed, cuts in half the strength of the family. Moreover, the issue is not simply two parents. The issue is a father. As one of the reports put it: "The family with the absent father was an incomplete relationship, since there was no one to play the male role in the lives of the growing children."[21]

Particularly worrisome to these scholars was the impact of fatherlessness on boys. Boys growing up without fathers might develop a "mother fixation," or fail to achieve a healthy separation from their mothers, leading to either overdependence on mothers or, alternatively, rebellious anger against mothers. Single mothers might be unable to discipline unruly boys. More generally, child rearing during wartime might become too permissive and too feminized—the exclusive responsibility of overtaxed mothers, grandmothers, and other female relatives.

Because the wartime disruption of children's lives was greater in Europe than in America, many U.S. social scientists looked to Europe, especially Great Britain, for additional evidence on how war affects children. One of the most influential studies on this topic was Anna Freud's analysis of English children who were evacuated from London during the bombings and sent to residential nurseries in the countryside. Freud's work, based on her experience as the director of three of these wartime nurseries, contributed important insights into the effects of maternal and paternal absence on children.

All the London children over the age of two had acquired a practical understanding of the sights and sounds of wartime air raids:

> They realize that the house will fall down when bombed and that people are often killed or get hurt in falling houses. They know that fires can be started by incendiaries and that roads are often blocked as a result of bombing. They fully understand the significance of shelters. Some children who have lived in deep shelters will even judge the safety of a shelter according to its depth under the earth.[22]

Yet what most traumatized these children was not the bombings or the physical danger but the separation from their parents. As Freud put it:

> The war acquires comparatively little significance for children so long as it only threatens their lives, disturbs their material comfort, or cuts their food rations. . . . It becomes enormously significant the moment it breaks up family life and uproots the first emotional attachments of the child in the family group.[23]

The residential relocation of these children cast both mothers and fathers into the role of visitor. Freud found that mothers and fathers handled this role in very different ways. Visiting mothers "behave naturally enough in the nursery, deal with their children in a variety of ways, examine their bodies, cut or curl their hair, rearrange their clothes, bathe, and put them to bed occasionally and, according to their nature, either overwhelm them with sweets or use the short time together for criticism and nagging." Visiting fathers, on the other hand, were more typically "inactive, shy, and awkward."[24]

In some respects, the children appeared not to miss their absent fathers. Upon leaving their homes, they seemed easily to accept separation from fathers, even when the fathers were departing for overseas military service. When distressed or frightened, the nursery child "always calls out for his absent mother. We have never under these circumstances heard a child demand the presence of his father, though in air raids they will sometimes cry out for their fathers."[25]

Yet Freud warns against concluding from these observations that "the presence of a father is of minor importance in the infant's life." Freud points out that the father's role in the family could not be replicated in an institutional setting. There was no single person in the nursery to remind the child, even remotely, of the father. The caregivers in the nursery

are neither the providers of material goods nor the last court of appeal in all matters which concern the child. Impersonal and invisible powers take on the father's role—the organization, the committee, the governors, a board provide the material means for the child's upbringing and, by their decisions, determine the child's fate.[26]

This fact may help explain why the visiting fathers behaved awkwardly. (Indeed, most fathers everywhere tend to do poorly in the role of visitor.) For perfectly understandable reasons, "impersonal and invisible powers" had taken over what these fathers viewed as their main job: protecting and providing for their children. Unlike the mothers, these fathers could not temporarily resume that job during the visits.

Nor could nursery life reproduce, or even recapture during occasional visits, the essential rhythm of the father-child relationship—especially the daily cycle of presence and absence that, in cultures across the world, largely defines the infant's developing relationship with the father, the first "other" in the infant's life. For, in contrast to the more continuous and symbiotic mother-child bond, this daily mixture of closeness and distance, expressiveness and instrumentality, constitutes a typically distinctive feature of the father-child bond, both contributing to the child's development and informing the infant's attachment to the father's bigness and otherness.

However, although the London children could tolerate paternal absence, they could not accept the fact of paternal loss. Freud writes:

All our orphaned children talk about their dead fathers as if they were alive, or, when they have grasped the fact of death, try to deny it in the form of fantasies about rebirth or return from heaven. . . . Visits from dead fathers are, if anything, mentioned more often than visits of ordinary living fathers, and the insistence on their coming is all the greater.

Said one four-year-old boy whose father had died:

My daddy is killed, yes, my sister said so. He cannot come. I want him to come. My daddy is big, he can do everything. . . . My daddy is taking me to the zoo today. He told me last night; he comes every night and sits on my bed and talks to me.[27]

Children born out of wedlock also created fantasies about the fathers they had never known. Freud cited the case of Bob, a little boy who first mentioned his father at age two, when he cried out for him in moments of despair. He asserted over and over that his daddy was real. He would stop in the middle of a game and shout, "Yes, I do have a daddy!" although no one had disputed it. Once his mother brought a man to the nursery. Later, Bob recalled this incident repeatedly, viewing it as an important piece of evidence to support his claim that his father was real.[28]

American social scientists also examined the increase in juvenile delinquency in Britain during the war years, leading them to predict a similar increase in the United States.[29] They had already noted increasing arrest rates in the United States for crimes such as assault and breaking and entering. Equally troubling was the rise in the number of young girls who hung around army bases and "contributed to the war effort by giving . . . [sex] to the man in uniform."[30]

Scholars generally agreed that there were multiple causes for this increase in juvenile delinquency, including wartime residential mobility, the decline of parental supervision, and the relaxation of sexual norms. But of all the contributing causes, one stood out as primary: fatherlessness. To Katherine Lenroot of the Children's Bureau, the central explanation for the spread of juvenile delinquency during the war years was that "fathers are separated from their families because they are serving in the armed forces or working in distant war industries."[31]

In the view of many scholars, moreover, wartime father absence did more than erode the father-child bond. It also weakened the mother-child bond. For when the father leaves home, the mother's relationship with her child changes significantly. In this sense, less fathering during the war also meant less mothering. "It is an observable fact, substantiated by collected data, that a large number of mothers in war work have not provided adequate care and supervision for their children," concluded one sociologist.[32] Concern for latchkey children and "eight-hour orphans" prompted the

American Orthopsychiatric Association to recommend that mothers of children under age three be barred from wartime factory work.[33]

Father absence during the war could also threaten the marital relationship. Some experts feared that a mother on her own might overidentify with her child, thus undermining the spousal bond. Or that a single mother might become so reattached to her own parents or other close relatives that the returning husband would be treated as an intruder.[34] Moreover, the mother's independence as a solo parent and worker might lead to an increase in "sex antagonism" following the war.

Social scientists in the 1940s also explored the war's impact on paternal competence. A Stanford University study of returning fathers found that they had a hard time establishing good relationships with firstborn children. Compared to fathers who did not go to war, these fathers tended to be more critical of the oldest child, to discipline him or her too harshly, and to be more easily annoyed by disruptive behavior. They tended to view their sons' behavior as too babyish or girlish. Overall, these fathers were much more comfortable and relaxed with children born after they had returned home.

In many ways, military service had diminished these men in their roles as fathers and family men. The Stanford study concludes:

> Fathers had to adopt unfamiliar roles of breadwinner, husband, and father all at once rather than in a more orderly, sequential pattern. They were husbands, but unsure of their relations with their wives and novices in the role. They were fathers, but of unknown children whom they had seen only in pictures; they lacked any warm interpersonal relations with these children and were vague and uncertain in the role of father. Finally, they were heads of families, without jobs, without training, and with only the faintest conceptions of what they wanted to do or how to go about making decisions.[35]

A recent study by William M. Tuttle examined the statements of hundreds of middle-aged adults who had been children during World War II. Their recollections describe the varying, and often unenthusiastic, responses of children to the returning father. Teenage children often feared that their fathers, who had known them when they were smaller, would not recognize them or would disapprove of their changed physical appearance. Younger children worried that they might not be able to recognize their fathers. Tuttle tells of one child who thought her father was an impostor and expressed amazement that this fellow could so deceive the mother.[36]

Some children found that they did not like this man very much, later describing him as "solemn," "intolerant," "frustrated," "abusive," or "very nervous."[37] Some children plainly viewed their fathers as intruders. In some cases, fathers literally kicked children out of the marital bed; in other cases, they simply asserted their claim to the mother's time and affection, fostering resentment from the children. Not infrequently, there were more serious problems, such as alcoholism.

There were two areas of domestic life in which the returning fathers seemed particularly anxious to reassert control and influence. One was discipline. As Tuttle puts it: "for fathers coming home after prolonged absence in a military environment in which they either gave orders or promptly obeyed them, there seemed little doubt that their sons and daughters should respond to them as buck privates had to first sergeants."[38]

A militaristic approach to family life provoked resentment and sometimes rebellion among children, in turn leading some fathers to "crack down" even harder. One woman remembers a fighter-pilot father, a man she never really knew, disturbing the secure nest she and her mother had made with her paternal grandparents: "Suddenly, I was no longer a princessly 'half orphan' but a spoiled brat! He scolded, I cried, Mom and Grandma stood up for me. . . . Many years later, Mom told me what a rocky time it was for all concerned."[39]

War-absent fathers also frequently sought to exert special influence over the gender-related behavior of their children. Many fathers worried about their sons' manliness, fearing in particular that their boys would be unable to hold their own in fights or would become "sissyish." One father's story typifies this concern:

> I had a heart-rending experience yesterday. Ray came in complaining about the boy next door. I said, "Don't tell me about it, go out and handle it yourself." Ray said, "What shall I do?" I said, "If he hits you, hit him back." Well, Ray went out and took a terrible licking from that boy. I didn't know what to do. I felt horrible. Instinctively he won't lash out. I don't know why.[40]

Of course, these two issues—rules of discipline and standards of masculinity—are common preoccupations among fathers everywhere. It is not surprising that these returning soldier-fathers would try especially hard to assert themselves in these areas. At the same time, in the view of the Stanford researchers, many of these men went overboard, with results that were frequently stressful to them and harmful to their children. Why?

To the researchers, the behavior of many of these men suggested their fear of paternal inadequacy. Unlike fathers who had lived with their children during the war, these men had missed out on any gradual initiation into fatherhood. They had been denied the opportunity to begin at the beginning. As a result, many lacked the knowledge and the skills they needed to nurture their children effectively. Many felt unequal to the task.

One common male response to the feeling of inadequacy is to strive mightily, if at times wrongheadedly, to assert control.

Indeed, undergirding the entire scholarly discussion of postwar paternal competence is the conviction that, for fathers, family attachments are not only vital to family and child well-being but also relatively weak and vulnerable to disruption, especially when men live apart from their children for long periods of time. For many men, World War II loosened and disrupted family attachments. For some, including many who came home and did their best, this process diminished paternal capacity and effectiveness. For others, family problems stemming from wartime absence became more serious.

During and immediately following the war, there was an upsurge in men deserting their families. Many men simply vanished into the growing anonymity of a nation at war. Social scientists were particularly concerned about a wartime social climate that permitted much greater male disengagement from family responsibility. As one put it: "The exigencies of war not only brought about the forced separation of many families, but made such separation socially respectable."[41]

Paternal uncertainty also increased during the war years. Sometimes fathers could not square children's birthdates with the dates of spousal reunions. Occasionally, a child's looks—a blonde, blue-eyed daughter in a family with brown eyes and dark hair—raised questions about paternity. One man who worked with World War II veterans reported that many fathers were tormented with doubts about whether the children presented to them by their war brides were, in fact, their own.[42]

Unwed childbearing also increased during the war years. Officially, the number of births to unmarried women climbed from 103,000 in 1940 to 128,000 in 1945, but the actual increase was probably higher.[43] Wartime conditions made it harder for men to marry their pregnant girlfriends.[44] Moreover, military service offered an escape hatch for many men who might "have worked out a satisfactory solution with the girl had they not been separated" by the military. Military service also gave more fathers the chance to deny paternity—a trend that, among other things, made adoption more difficult. According to one child-welfare official, the "most thoughtful adoptive parents, who usually make the best homes for children, are eager for such information and are prone to overlook those babies with casual histories."[45]

In some ways, of course, the dangers of war encouraged family solidarity. In many cases, moreover, the war simply served to forestall the dissolution of troubled marriages, since couples could live apart but still remain legally married. But overall, the war clearly undermined male habits of family commitment.

Many wartime marriages, after all, were impulsive matings with near strangers, thus much more likely to prove disappointing. More important, sending young husbands off to war undermined the very foundation of companionate marriage, which depends upon sustained affection and time together. In addition, army life, and the accompanying decline of sexual restraint, constituted a poor preparation for monogamous marriage. One observer asked: "Will army life, which in past wars has initiated many young men to the pattern of sex pleasures without the responsibility of marriage, forge an attitude of cynicism toward marriage and a determination to keep free of its bonds?"[46]

During and immediately after the war, the divorce rate in the United States increased dramatically. In 1942, about 321,000 couples got divorced. By 1945, the total had reached 485,000, and in 1946, it was up to 610,000.[47] (Soldiers were immune from default judgments and therefore did not have to respond to divorce complaints during wartime or for six months after war. Divorce decrees had to await the end of the war.)[48]

Many wartime marriages fell apart quickly. Often, suspicions and jealousies over wartime love affairs eroded trust between spouses. According to some social scientists, women's wartime entry into the workforce may have loosened their commitment to marriage. As one scholar concluded: "It is also obvious from case material that many marriages are breaking up at this time because it is possible for the wife to support herself independently of her husband."[49]

A Culture of Fatherlessness

Only five decades—less than two generations—separate this century's first crisis of fatherlessness from the crisis we face today. In some ways, the two crises are similar. Both are defined by the mass separation of fathers from children. During the war years, approximately 3 million to 4 million families with children experienced fatherlessness, including about 183,000 home-front children whose fathers died in battle.[50] It seems fair to estimate that, during any one of the war years, about 20 to 25 percent of the nation's families with children experienced fatherlessness. In 1992, by comparison, about 21.5 percent of the nation's families with children were headed by mothers only.[51] As of 1990, about 36.3 percent of all children in the nation lived apart from their biological fathers (see table 1.3).

In crude demographic terms, measured as annual rates of fatherlessness, the two crises might be described as roughly the same size. One important difference, of course, is that most of the wartime-absent fathers returned home. Today, almost no absent fathers return home. Moreover, the trend of wartime fatherlessness came to a fairly abrupt halt soon after the war ended. Today's trend toward fatherlessness continues to escalate, is cumulative, and shows no sign of slowing down.

Yet the real difference between the two crises is not demographic. It is cultural. Demographically, the two crises share several common features. Culturally, they are polar opposites. For the wartime father absence of the 1940s occurred within, and was constrained by, what might be termed a culture of fatherhood. Father absence in the 1990s is occurring in, and fueled by, a culture of fatherlessness.

Wartime fatherlessness was largely involuntary. It was a matter of necessity, not choice. Today's fatherlessness is almost wholly volitional—the consequence not of one collective decision, rooted in social necessity, but of many individual decisions, rooted in personal adult preferences. The father absence of the 1940s can be viewed as a version of male sacrifice: a result of service to family and society. Today's father absence is the antithesis of male service and sacrifice. At bottom, contemporary fatherlessness is about personal freedom, a lifestyle choice.

Fatherlessness during the war years stemmed primarily from the actions of government. Today's fatherlessness has almost nothing to do with the actions of government. The earlier fatherlessness resulted from a centralized mobilization of men for a public purpose. Today's fatherlessness is an unorganized dispersal of men for private purposes. The earlier father absence was viewed as an emergency measure, a necessary but temporary evil, to be reversed as soon as the emergency passed. Today, fatherlessness is viewed as normal—regrettable perhaps, but acceptable.

When the soldier-father went off to war—and even when he died in combat overseas—much of his fatherhood remained behind, sustained by memory, in the lives of his children. Today's fatherlessness leaves very little behind. The 1940s child could say: My father had to leave for a while to do something important. The 1990s child must say: My father left me permanently because he wanted to.

American society in the 1940s, even as it waged war, spoke and acted on the basis of an idea: the fatherhood idea. Recall Malinowski's legitimacy principle: a father for every child. In the 1940s, Americans believed in this idea. From all the evidence, including the testimony of the experts, they took it quite seriously. Because they believed in the idea, they viewed the loss of fathers during the war as a grave social problem, worthy of concentrated attention and action, and justifiable only temporarily and on the basis of a national emergency.

In the 1940s, the fatherhood idea catalyzed public action and influenced military decisions. It also informed scholarship. Indeed, family scholars during the war clearly treated the fatherhood idea not as one hypothesis—one possible point of view—but as a core assumption. The fatherhood idea caused scholars to ask questions, including many subtle questions about paternal competence and the male role in family life. But the idea itself was not a question. It was a shared social conviction about the sources of child and societal well-being.

As a result, while many American families lost fathers during the war, American society did not lose the idea of fatherhood. Thus, to study the United States during World War II is to study a society quite different from our own—a society in which citizens and leaders, whatever their other flaws, repeatedly took action based on the principle that every child needs a father.

Today, American society is fundamentally divided and ambivalent about the fatherhood idea. Some people do not even remember it. Others are offended by it. Others, including more than a few family scholars, neglect it or disdain it. Many others are not especially opposed to it, nor are they especially committed to it. Many people wish we could act on it, but believe that our society simply no longer can or will.

Because the fatherhood assumption has largely vanished from contemporary scholarly discourse, family experts today pursue a different set of questions. Are fathers truly important? (Some say yes: some say no; others are not sure.) Is being a good father different from being a good parent? (Here the most common answer is: no.) Do never-married fathers have rights? Can we improve the divorce process? Can stepfathers replace fathers? What is the minimum social requirement of fathers? That they sign paternity papers? That they pay child support? Or is there no minimum requirement at all?

When a society loses the fatherhood idea, these are the emergent questions for the experts. Eventually, of course, these questions dwindle into inconsequence, just as swelling numbers of fathers themselves, without the fatherhood idea, dwindle into inconsequence.

When the author Richard Bach left his family in the 1970s, his wife told their five-year-old son: "His Daddy-part died."[52] In a society that loses the fatherhood idea, the Daddy-part of the society shrinks and eventually dies.

PART II

THE CULTURAL SCRIPT

CHAPTER 4

The Unnecessary Father

For some social tasks, individual volunteers will suffice. But effective fatherhood requires cultural conscription. As a social role, the deepest purpose of fatherhood is to socialize men by obligating them to their children. In turn, the success of fatherhood depends fundamentally upon the success of its cultural story.

For obligating fathers to their children is less a matter of biology than of culture. Compared to mothers, fathers are less born than made. As a social role, fatherhood is less the inelastic result of sexual embodiment than the fragile creation of cultural norms.

It is almost impossible to find a culture in which large numbers of mothers voluntarily abandon their children. Yet to find a culture in which large numbers of fathers voluntarily abandon their children, all we need to do is look around. For this reason alone, a society's fatherhood story—the shared understanding of what it means for a man to have a child—is almost certainly that society's primary indicator of how many children will grow up with fathers, and also, therefore, probably that society's most important determinant of overall child well-being.

In a larger sense, the fatherhood story is the irreplaceable basis of a culture's most urgent imperative: the socialization of males. More than any other cultural invention, fatherhood guides men away from violence by fastening their behavior to a fundamental social purpose. By enjoining men to care for their children and for the mothers of their children, the fatherhood story is society's most important contrivance for shaping male identity.

In the United States today, much of our cultural story of fatherhood is told and shaped by experts—those credentialed authorities on whom modern societies increasingly rely to name the problems, interpret the facts, define the options, and set the agenda for public action. They are among our society's most important opinion leaders. They are the specialists who study the topic and who earn money by conveying their conclusions to the wider society and to other experts.

Many of them have earned graduate degrees, teach in the universities, and write for the professional journals. Others are journalists, editors, columnists, and television commentators. They shape newspaper stories and magazine articles; they influence the themes of novels and movies. They write and review the books, appear on the television news programs, serve on the blue-ribbon commissions, and testify before the legislative committees. They are the panjandrums of our cultural discourse.

Their expertise matters precisely because it claims to—and increasingly does—tell individuals and groups in the society how they are expected to act. In brief, their expertise helps to craft our cultural narratives. The cultural narratives shaped by experts are quite prosaic. In social terms, they are as real as bricks, press releases, or bank accounts. They are also probably more important. As George Gerbner insists: "Those who tell stories hold the power in society."[1]

Functionally, as Carl E. Schneider suggests, cultural narratives serve three purposes. First, they link the individual to the larger society. Cultural stories teach us what other people do and why, and what they are likely to expect from us. They are one means by which we learn to live with others. In this sense, they constitute a potent common language.

Cultural narratives also adumbrate social goals. The morals of these stories, along with the protagonists and the plot lines, are anything but arbitrary. They embody and advocate socially approved norms. Because they ultimately derive more from society than from the individual, their inherent bias is to guide the individual toward what society believes to be prosocial purposes. Accordingly, our prevailing cultural story of fatherhood helps to define the kind of father that society desires and expects.

Finally, and perhaps most important in the case of fatherhood, cultural norms reduce the burden of individual choice by providing authoritative models of human relationships.[2] Peter L. Berger finds that "one of the most archaic functions of society is to take away from individuals the burden of choice."[3] As Alfred North Whitehead memorably put it:

> It is a profoundly erroneous truism, repeated by all copybooks and by eminent people when they are making speeches, that we should cultivate the habit of thinking of what we are doing. The precise opposite is the case. Civilization advances by extending the number of important operations which we can perform without thinking about them.[4]

Effective cultural cues help ensure that fatherhood is not something that every man must reinvent for himself. For fathers, this fact is central. Because the social meaning of paternity is problematic in human societies, fatherhood itself is largely a cultural contrivance. In the case of mother-

hood, cultural stories may be more additive than determinative. But for
fatherhood, they are determinative. Consequently, a special challenge of
any society is to enculture paternity by means of compelling narratives—to
ensure that a man's understanding of fatherhood is firmly influenced by
traditions, ideas, models, and habits acquired from the culture that sur-
rounds him.

For these reasons, today's prevailing elite story of fatherhood carries
profound social consequences. But what is the content of that story? What
is its moral? What are its main ideas about the meaning and purpose of
fatherhood? Consider this thought experiment. What if contemporary
expertise constituted our only source of information about fatherhood? If
you were an alien from another planet, curious about human fathers but
confined to the Current Periodical section of a leading university library,
what would you conclude about fatherhood in late-twentieth-century
America?

The basic answer is clear. Today's expert story of fatherhood largely
assumes that fatherhood is superfluous. More precisely, our elite culture
has now fully incorporated into its prevailing family narrative the idea that
fatherhood, as a distinctive social role for men, is either unnecessary or
undesirable.

An essential claim of the script is that there are not—and ought not to
be—any key parental tasks that belong essentially and primarily to fathers. In
this view, society no longer requires, or can afford to recognize, any meaningful difference between norms of fatherhood and norms of parenthood.

This conception of fatherhood, now widespread, constitutes a unifying
philosophical premise of almost all currently fashionable arguments about
men, masculinity, and fatherhood. Its ideologically diverse proponents justify it on grounds that are both societal and personal, pragmatic and
utopian.

Intellectually, the idea of superfluous fatherhood rests on three propositions. The first is that fatherhood as a gender-based social role is literally
what the dictionary defines as superfluous: exceeding what is necessary.
The second proposition is that men in general, and fathers in particular,
are part of the problem. The third is that social progress depends largely
upon a transformation of fatherhood based on the ideal of gender role
convergence. Accordingly, this final proposition urges that fathers, for
their own good and for the sake of women and society as a whole, transcend gender-specific male roles in favor of essentially gender-neutral
human values. These three propositions order the plot and prompt the
characters of our contemporary fatherhood story.

To reveal the expert story of fatherhood in our time, I propose that we
use the concept of characters in a story or script. The following list gives
the specific sources of the script: the documents and cultural products

that, taken together, constitute a fair and authoritative representation of contemporary elite discourse on fatherhood in the United States. I propose to examine these documents as a movie actor would examine a screenplay: to learn the overview of the story and to locate the cues for what the actors should do.

SOURCES OF THE EXPERTS' FATHERHOOD SCRIPT

1. Scholarly books and college textbooks
2. Popular nonfiction books
3. Children's books
4. Professional journals
5. National professional conferences
6. Congressional hearings
7. National family and children's commissions
8. Popular magazines and parents' advice books
9. National newspaper commentary
10. Interviews with professionals.

There are eight characters in this script. Three are leading characters: the Unnecessary Father, the Old Father, and the New Father. The Unnecessary Father plays the role of the chorus. He is the character who speaks the prologue and epilogue and comments on the action. In this sense, he is omnipresent in the story.

The Old Father and the New Father are also stars of the current script. Both are biological fathers. Both live with their children and father them on a routine basis. Each, therefore, embodies both biological and social fatherhood. Moreover, the New Father represents a growing proportion of actual fathers in the society. The Old Father, on the other hand, as an anti-hero, represents a declining proportion of actual fathers.

The script also features five minor roles, or parts for what might be termed fatherhood understudies. These five almost-fathers are the Deadbeat Dad, the Visiting Father, the Sperm Father, the Stepfather, and the Nearby Guy. The first three are biological fathers, but do not live with their children. The latter two are not biological fathers, but can play fatherly social roles, albeit murky ones. They embody the contemporary dispersal of fatherhood: the growing detachment of social from biological paternity.

Although minor characters, they are quite significant. There are five of them, after all, compared to only three leading roles. They receive considerable attention from the experts, in part because they represent newer, more ambiguous paternal figures. Most important, they are significant because each one represents a growing proportion of men. Indeed, among today's families, it is the latter two of these fatherhood understudies—the Stepfather and the Nearby Guy—who increasingly live with the children.

Each of the eight characters in this script embodies the primary idea that fatherhood is superfluous. Each conveys the notion that fatherhood, as a gendered social role for men, is either unneeded or a problem to be overcome. Each plays its part in the larger expert story of fatherhood, a story that stands as a cultural rationale for the actual trend of fatherlessness in our society. Listen to this story.

Fathers as "Not That Important"

September 21, 1992, constituted an important cultural moment in the United States. That evening, the season premier of the prime-time CBS sitcom *Murphy Brown* assumed what the *New York Times* called "the status of a national event."[5] Earlier in the year, the show's heroine, Murphy Brown, had decided to bear a child outside of marriage, thus becoming, as they say, a single mother by choice. When Vice President Dan Quayle criticized the show for "mocking the importance of fathers," a protracted national controversy erupted, in which Quayle was roundly and repeatedly denounced. On the September 21 episode, watched by a remarkable 41 percent of that night's television audience, Murphy took her revenge, rebuking Quayle on the air for his "painfully unfair" remark about the necessity of fathers and reminding viewers that "families come in all shapes and sizes."[6]

Also in this episode, another of the show's characters, Corky, a straitlaced, rather idiotic staff member at the television station where Murphy works, comments: "I was raised to believe that if you had a child out of wedlock you were bad. Of course, I was also raised to believe a woman's place was in the home, segregation was good, and presidents never lie." (Translation: If you believe out-of-wedlock childbearing is wrong, you are racist and sexist.) In the public relations struggle between Murphy Brown and Dan Quayle, the vice president emerged as the clear loser. "The most obvious result of all the Vice President's efforts," concluded the *New York Times,* "seemed more politically damaging than helpful to him."[7]

On the other hand, the Murphy Brown affair proved quite profitable for CBS, for Candice Bergen, the show's star, and for Diane English, the show's creator-producer. During the controversy, and apparently largely because of it, *Murphy Brown* received an Emmy Award for best comedy series. Accepting the award, Diane English was moved to "thank in particular all the single parents out there who, either by choice or necessity, are raising their kids alone." Candice Bergen not only received an Emmy for best leading actress in a comedy series but was also awarded an honorary degree from the University of Pennsylvania. English, suddenly a star herself, appeared in television ads for Hanes stockings.

Prior to the controversy, a thirty-second commercial during *Murphy Brown* sold for $145,000. But after the eruption of publicity set off by Quayle's remark, the price soared to $310,000—making it the most expensive ad of any television show. By all conventional measures, Murphy Brown's unwed motherhood was an unqualified box office success.[8]

Back now to September 21, 1992. On this same day of the *Murphy Brown* season premier, a front-page article in the *Washington Post* sweepingly announced that the "Conventional Family's Value Is Being Reevaluated." In what seemed intended as journalistic cheerleading for the message of that evening's *Murphy Brown* episode, the article declared that "a searching reevaluation by social scientists" had now demonstrated that "the consequences of absent fathers" on children "have been overstated," and that, as a result, the "conventional two-parent household may be far less critical to the healthy development of children than previously believed."[9]

This article's core theme—the relative unimportance of fathers—derives largely from the scholarly work of Frank L. Mott, a senior research scientist at Ohio State University. The article also cites one other study and quotes five other scholars. But Mott's study, described as "one of the largest and most comprehensive studies" based on "new child databases," is the article's intellectual centerpiece.[10]

The press release summarizing Mott's study captures his basic idea. Fathers, the press release title tells us, are "Important, But Not That Important." Mott's core finding is stated with equal bluntness: "A father's absence from the home is not a major factor in behavior problems or low achievement test scores in young children."[11]

What analysis supports this remarkable conclusion? Mott's 1992 study, "The Impact of Fathers' Absence from the Home on Subsequent Cognitive Development of Younger Children," looks at a national sample of 1,714 children born to very young mothers—between ages fourteen and twenty-one at the time of childbirth. All of these mothers, then, were literally or virtually "teen mothers." The children in the sample were between five and eight years old in 1988.

Mott tabulated these children's reading and math test scores. He also asked their mothers, through a written questionnaire, to evaluate them regarding six possible behavioral problems: hyperactivity, depression, antisocial behavior, peer conflict, headstrongness, and dependency. He then used statistical calculations called regression coefficients in an attempt to measure the relationship, if any, between father absence and child well-being. His major findings are fourfold.

First, "white boys show systematic evidence of socio-emotional disadvantage due to a father's absence from the home." Similarly, the test scores of white boys in fatherless homes are significantly lower than those of white boys living with their fathers. In sum, in comparison to white girls and to black children of either sex, "it does appear that father's absence is most harmful emotionally and cognitively to young white boys."

Second, for white girls, the emotional and cognitive effects of father absence are "similar, although much more modest." Third, Mott finds little or no evidence that black children suffer harm as a result of living apart from their fathers. Indeed, quite the opposite: He finds that fatherlessness actually benefits many black children. In some important areas, black children, especially girls, who live apart from their fathers do better than black children who live with their fathers.

Finally, Mott concludes that the causal link between fatherlessness and poor child outcomes is weakened—though not eliminated—by taking other factors into account, especially the mother's income, her educational level, the presence of a grandparent in the home, and the presence of other men, such as boyfriends. Accordingly, Mott concludes that childhood problems stem at least as much from these other factors as they do from "father's absence *per se*."[12]

With these four findings in mind, return now to Mott's stunning press announcement: "A father's absence from the home is not a major factor in behavioral problems or low achievement test scores in young children." Return to the *Washington Post* story, which informs readers, based on Mott's research, that a child's cognitive development "had nothing to do with whether the child's father was present in the household."

Clearly, a credibility gap separates Mott's research findings from the public description of those findings. Mott's single strongest finding was that fatherlessness harms white children, especially boys. Yet his press release, which formed the basis of the *Washington Post*'s article, emphasizes exactly the opposite point, stressing that fathers are "not that important."[13] The central public message from Mott's research—the notion that fathers are "not a major factor" and "not that important"—is directly and repeatedly contradicted by Mott's own research findings.[14]

This is a big problem. But it's not the only problem. For Mott's study is, at bottom, intellectually unserious. Moreover, his conceptual sloppiness consistently serves his belief that fathers are "not that important."

Mott's work suffers from five flaws. First, he examines an extremely limited range of problems—low test scores and mothers' reports of six specific behavioral problems—in a sample of very young children. Yet ample research demonstrates that fatherlessness is linked to a much wider range of more serious childhood and adolescent characterological problems, such as lower ability to defer gratification, lower achievement motivation, and problems with self-control and secure sexual identity.[15] Mott's study, however, does not directly address any of these problems, in part because they tend to emerge later, as children get older than Mott's sample of five- to eight-year-olds. One scientific strategy for concluding that fathers are "not that important," then, is to base sweeping public statements on ane- mic data that do not even pretend to measure what matters most.

Second, what about Mott's conclusion that, for black children, father- lessness is not very harmful and may even be helpful? Mott finds, for example, "no evidence that the absence of a father is harmful to black girls." Similarly, he discovers "a *lesser* level of anxiousness-depression for black girls when a father is *not present*" and finds that "black girls in homes where a new man is present are less anxious-depressed than their counterparts living with their biological father."

As a matter of social science, Mott in this instance is obviously ignor- ing—or, worse, misunderstanding—what social scientists would call redundant negative influences. The fatherless children in his sample, after all, are essentially children born to unwed teen mothers. Sadly, many of these children, especially the black children, face many detrimental influ- ences, from poverty to unsafe neighborhoods to mothers who are hardly more than children themselves. Adding one more detrimental influence, father absence, does not make a difference large enough for Mott's regres- sion coefficients to isolate, especially among young children and within the small range of variables he sought to measure.[16] The presence of redun- dant negative influences is significant, of course, and sad, but it hardly jus- tifies Mott's bizarrely counterintuitive suggestion that black fathers are somehow less important than white fathers, or that, for black children, having no father can sometimes be better than having a father.

Third, what about Mott's claim that girls need fathers less than boys do? Just as he stresses the comparative insignificance of black fathers, he also stresses the comparative insignificance of the father-daughter relationship, repeatedly suggesting that girls either suffer no harm from fatherlessness, or that they suffer much less than boys.[17] Yet numerous, more careful studies disconfirm this thesis. If the evidence suggests that fatherless boys tend toward disorderly and violent behavior, it just as clearly suggests that fatherless girls tend toward personally and socially destructive relationships with men, including precocious sexual activity and unmarried motherhood.[18] By what possible standard, other than personal bias, does Mott judge one set of these consequences to be "less important" than the other?[19]

The fourth component of Mott's conceptual confusion is his virtual inability to define the word *father*—a definite liability in a study of father- hood. For one of Mott's core hypotheses is that "new father figures"— boyfriends, stepfathers, and other nonrelated males—can and do become "fathers." Or at least, sort-of fathers: guys who can do all or most of what fathers do. This notion adds further theoretical bulk to Mott's master idea that biological fathers are "not a major factor" and "not that important."

Mott's clearest exposition of this theme is found in the journal *Demography*, in which he poses the question: "When Is a Father Really Gone?" His basic conclusion: almost never. The reason, according to Mott, is that about 60 percent of the children in his study who do not live with their biological fathers nevertheless enjoy "access to a male figure either in or out of the home who may potentially be considered a father or father substitute." From this finding, Mott concludes that "defining virtually all of these children as essentially fatherless is in error." Instead, though they do not live with biological fathers, and though most live in what have traditionally been called single-parent homes, they do, when other males are taken into account, experience "significant 'gross' flows of fathers in and out of the household." Mott warns us, therefore, that "traditional analyses," which focus on biological fathers, "could well be misspecified."[20]

Apart from the fact that Mott's thesis—that other men can effectively replace fathers—is decisively contradicted by the weight of scientific evidence, surely the most extraordinary aspect of this analysis is Mott's intentional transmogrification of the word *father*. As he uses the term, it bears no necessary relationship to biological paternity, marriage, co-residence with mother or child, or, indeed, any specified set of rights and responsibilities. For Mott in this case, a "father" may be roughly but accurately defined as: a nearby guy.

The fifth and final flaw in Mott's research is the most complex, but also the most revealing. For, in his effort to show that fathers are "not a major factor" and "not that important," Mott depends almost solely on what Travis Hirschi and Hannan Selvin have classically called "false criteria of causality." Such criteria permit—indeed, require—social scientists to conclude, in their words, that "nothing causes anything."[21]

When Mott concludes that fathers are "not a major factor," he is making claims about causality. He is claiming either that fatherlessness does not cause problems for children or, at a minimum, that fatherlessness is comparatively less important than other possible causes of childhood problems, such as poverty, bad neighborhoods, or poorly educated mothers. To make either claim, Mott must establish credible criteria of causality. He does not. Instead, he brandishes false criteria.

Mott's general approach to the issue of causality can be illustrated by an analogy. Consider this statement of causation: smoking can cause lung cancer. Consider how a Mott-style press release might announce a new study debunking this proposition:

SMOKING: IMPORTANT,
BUT NOT THAT IMPORTANT

Research shows that not every smoker gets lung cancer. Conversely, not everyone who gets lung cancer is a smoker. Thus, many factors other than smoking may contribute to lung cancer. Indeed, new regression coefficient data reveal these key findings: persistent coughing may damage lungs and is positively associated with the presence of lung cancer; healthy lifestyles, positive attitudes, and general physical fitness are positively associated with the absence of lung cancer; and some lungs are genetically more susceptible to disease, including cancer, than others. Therefore, smoking *per se* is probably misspecified as a major cause of lung cancer. Indeed, new data reveal that smoking is not a major factor in lung-related health problems of young children.

The goal is to downplay smoking as a cause of lung cancer. The main strategy is to disassemble smoking: to disaggregate its various aspects into stand-alone components. Then the analyst can cite the causal effect of one component—such as coughing, general physical fitness, or the relative rarity of lung cancer among children who smoke—to suggest that "smoking *per se*" does not cause lung cancer.

Mott's "not that important" argument depends decisively on this strategy. He seeks to disassemble fatherhood just as the analogy disassembles smoking. To take only one obvious example, Mott treats low income and father absence as two necessarily unrelated phenomena. Methodologically, he disaggregates the two. As a result, according to Mott's criteria of causality, any evidence that low income harms children is, by definition, also evidence that fatherlessness does not harm children, or at least does not harm them as much as low income does. Meanwhile, back on planet Earth, a primary role of fathers in all human societies is economic provision for children. It is simply false, therefore, for a scholar to deploy data on child poverty—the absence of economic provision for children—as evidence for an argument that fathers are "not a major factor" and "not that important."

Moreover, even regarding variables that, at least arguably, are unrelated to fatherhood, Mott's thesis still rests on a classic error: the false belief that since variable A appears to matter, then variable B must matter little or not at all.[22] Indeed, absent reliance upon this false criterion, Mott literally has nothing to say about the importance of fathers for children.

In sum, the *Post* story on the unimportance of fatherhood is based on flawed reporting of flimsy evidence.[23] It ignores numerous recent studies that contradict its thesis. Ironically, this article does not simply misdescribe the current social science "reevaluation." It inverts the truth.

For there is nothing new or trendy about scholars who downplay the importance of fathers. The axiom that fathers are essentially superfluous has constituted a major belief among social scientists for at least two decades. To the degree that any "searching reevaluation" of conventional wisdom is occurring, it is occurring precisely because, quite recently, a number of prominent scholars, from Sara McLanahan to Sar Levitan to Norval Glenn, have broken ranks with scholarly fashion in order to emphasize the importance, rather than the irrelevance, of fathers in shaping outcomes for children.

For example, James Q. Wilson of the University of California reports that, in the early 1980s, when he was writing *Crime and Human Nature,* he expected current scholarship to confirm the link between father absence and male juvenile delinquency. Yet he admits that "I did not find what I had expected to find." Yet by the early 1990s, the weight of evidence had shifted. "Since I wrote that chapter," Wilson now reports, "the evidence that single-parent families are bad for children has mounted." It is precisely this emerging shift that constitutes the real social science "reevaluation" of fatherhood worthy of analysis by the *Washington Post*.[24]

Return again to September 21, 1992: Murphy Brown, in prime time, taking comic aim at a hapless politician for his comments on "the importance of fathers," and the *Washington Post,* on the front page, taking scholarly aim at the idea that fatherlessness harms children. The former was based primarily on the views of Hollywood scriptwriters and the entertainment requirements of a national television network. The latter was based primarily on the views of Frank Mott and the journalistic requirements of a national newspaper.

Mott played a small but interesting part in the drama of that day. Indeed, one might describe his role as "important, but not that important." His scholarship blended in nicely with the theme of the day.[25] It supported both the message of Murphy Brown and, apparently, the biases of the *Washington Post.* I examine Mott's scholarship in some detail, then, not because it represents something special but because it represents something quite typical: the widespread belief that fatherhood, at bottom, is unnecessary.

The Chorus of the Unnecessary Father

Does every child need a father? Our society's prevailing answer is Frank Mott's answer: not necessarily. Quite simply, we have changed our minds on this question. In 1991, for example, unmarried mothers accounted for approximately 30 percent of all childbirths in the nation, an increase of 82 percent since 1980, including a doubling of the rate of unwed childbearing among whites.[26] The public opinion analyst Daniel Yankelovich finds that a majority of Americans, in "an astonishing turnabout in mores," now view the prospect of a woman choosing to have a child on her own, without the entanglement of a father, as morally unobjectionable.[27]

Other studies confirm Yankelovich's finding. For example, one forthcoming study finds that a majority of Americans now agree with the proposition that single mothers can raise children just as well as married couples, and disagree with the proposition that children generally do best in intact, two-parent homes.[28] Another recent survey finds that fully 70 percent of younger Americans, age eighteen to thirty-four, now endorse the proposition that it is morally acceptable to have children outside of marriage.[29]

The *New York Times* reports that unmarried pregnant teenagers are now "beginning to be viewed by some of their peers as role models." In 1992, for example, April Schuldt, a high school senior from Eau Claire, Wisconsin, was elected homecoming queen by her classmates when she was five months' pregnant. She told the *Times* that she hoped others would see her as "a pregnant girl, continuing school, planning to raise and care for her baby and being supported by other students."[30]

As Katha Pollitt puts it: "Why not have a child on one's own? Children are a joy; many men are not."[31] Or as Michelle Pfeiffer, the movie star, puts it, explaining her decision to raise a child on her own: "Men are like pinch hitters. So what's the deal?" Should she conceive or adopt? She reviewed her options:

> I thought about all my options, and certainly one of those options was to just have a baby with somebody, which I guess is the obvious option. But when it came right down to it, I just couldn't do it. I thought, I don't want some guy in my life forever who's going to be driving me nuts.[32]

The Unnecessary Father, then, plays a starring role as the chorus in our contemporary fatherhood script. He may be useful in some ways. He may be a nice guy, perhaps even a force for good. But he is nonessential, peripheral, "not that important." His presence may be appreciated, but it is not required. We can and increasingly do get along without him. His good points are frequently outweighed by other considerations. No one holds him up as either the core problem or the core solution. Listen to his voices in today's cultural story.

Listen to Billy, a young father in the popular 1985 movie *St. Elmo's Fire*. Having decided to leave his wife and infant daughter, Melody, to pursue a music career in New York, he explains to his girlfriend: "I thought about hanging around and being one of those 'I'll see you on the weekend' Dads. But that's not what Melody needs. Besides, it would just confuse everybody."

Listen to the 1989 miniseries *The Women of Brewster Place* on the subject of black men. Young, shy woman: "I don't have a husband." Older, wiser woman: "Well, I've had five, and you ain't missing much."

Listen to a police officer question a young mother on the 1993 television series *Homicide: Life on the Street.* Police officer: "Does that baby have a father?" Young mother: "Every baby has a father. I just hope my baby doesn't end up looking like him."

In a 1993 episode of *Roseanne,* the popular sitcom, Roseanne's sister, Jackie, learns that she is pregnant. The father is a not-too-steady boyfriend. She wants the baby, but cannot decide whether or not to tell the boyfriend. Finally, she tells him. He is calm. Trying to be supportive, he promises to stay in touch, in case she needs anything. As they part, she tries to be kind: "Thanks for the child."

More generally, listen to Caryn James, a *New York Times* cultural critic, on the increasing number of unmarried pregnant women now featured on prime-time television dramas and sitcoms. These new shows have kept television "in touch with the shifting realities of women's options," the most important of which is that "women who want children do not need or necessarily want a spouse underfoot."[33]

Indeed, most contemporary network television—with popular but rare exceptions, such as *The Cosby Show*—clearly reflects a Father Knows Worst philosophy, in which fathers are, at best, amiable bumblers. As Stanley R. Graham puts it: "The television shows of the past 20 years often portray father as fool."[34]

Listen to the new storybooks we read to young children: "Carly doesn't remember when her dad lived with them. He moved away when she was a baby. Sometimes Carly wonders what it would be like to have a father. 'Can you miss someone you never knew?' she asks herself."[35]

Listen to Anne Lamott, in her best-selling book about her experiences as an unmarried mother, discuss her infant son, Sam:

> I don't have any idea what I will tell Sam when he is old enough to ask about his father. I'll say that everybody doesn't have *some*thing and that he doesn't have this one thing, but that we have each other and that is a lot. And that for a while his father was my friend.[36]

But she worries about it. She asks a male friend to become Sam's "Big Brother" and an older couple to become his "paternal grandparents." She concludes:

> I'm just going to have to tell him that not everybody has a father. Look at me, I will tell him: I don't have a father, and I don't have a swimming pool, either. But Sam will have a tribe. You can't help but believe that these other men will help Sam not have such a huge sense of loss. They'll be his psychic Secret Service.[37]

By the summer of 1993, when Sam was three years old, Lamott had emerged as an important new public voice on the subject of raising children without fathers. She had became a regular commentator on parenthood for National Public Radio, an essayist for leading publications, and a frequent guest on national television talk shows. By age three, she told the *San Francisco Chronicle,* Sam had become

> very interested in everyone else's fathers, of course. One day when I went up to day care, the day-care worker took me aside and said, "Sam has been telling all the other kids' daddies that he doesn't have a daddy, and he says it very sadly when they come to pick up their children."

The day-care worker suggested therapy for Sam, but Lamott thought her suggestion "was such a lousy trip to lay on a single mother."[38]

Responding to Sam's concerns about his father, however, Lamott began devoting much of her public commentary to a new "Could Be Worse" view of fatherlessness. Sam has no father, but what if he had a lousy father? That would be worse. For example, she wrote in the *New York Times:* "I would give anything for Sam to have a great father, because he wants one so badly, but I will not risk giving him a bad one. It's better to have no father than to have one of those mean, lazy men who couldn't even bring up a houseplant."[39]

This "Could Be Worse" school of thought regarding fathers is increasingly influential in today's family debate, serving as a primary apologia for the Unnecessary Father. Here is how the historian Stephanie Coontz expresses it:

> Of course children benefit from the involvement of a caring father, but they're obviously better off for the absence of an abusive one, and let's not forget that paternal absence has been the norm in many "traditional" two-parent families. Some therapists argue that emotional absence, more ambiguous than physical loss, may be harder to grieve, causing difficulties that show up much later in life than the disruptions caused by divorce.[40]

Let's see, now. "Caring" fathers are, well, okay. But many fathers are abusive. Moreover, because so many fathers who live with their children are "emotionally absent," fatherlessness is frequently better—easier to grieve—than having a father. In short, when deciding on the desirability of maintaining a father on the premises, here is the new rule: better safe than sorry.

This emerging thesis is a paradigmatic example of what Daniel Patrick Moynihan calls "defining deviancy down," or consciously lowering expectations of what is normative. In this case, the intention is to normalize fatherlessness—to remove from it any stigma of deviancy or even undesirability—by insisting that the baseline cause for social alarm is no longer the absence of a good father, but rather the hypothetical presence of a bad father. At bottom, however, to insist upon this new formulation of the problem is to validate the idea of the Unnecessary Father.[41]

Listen to a popular advice book for mothers address the subject of divorce and absent fathers:

> Given time and space, most women discover that the pleasures of being alone are real—and they're not eager to give them up. A single mother can pick her own friends—no more seeing people because of "couple ties." Your children, too, can sometimes pick friends that Dad didn't approve of. And without another adult questioning your values, your child-rearing methods, or your wants, you can come to treasure the sense of being in control that you've worked so hard to achieve.[42]

Are you worried that a father, once gone, cannot be replaced? Don't be. "The best strategy a single mother can adopt is to *establish a support system* to replace the traditional two-parent family." Are you worried about the lack of a male role model for your son? Don't be. Look to that support system. Besides: "The pervading influence of movies, books, and the culture in general driving home male behavior to your son ensures that your own role will be well balanced."[43]

Listen to the family scholars Alvin L. Schorr and Phyllis Moen: "The presence or absence of both parents *per se* makes little difference in the adequacy of child-rearing or the socialization of children."[44] Listen to the family counselor Genevieve Clapp, in *Divorce and New Beginnings,* emphasize the "positive side of parenting solo." She asks: "Are single-parent homes really so different?" And answers: not really. For children, the core requirement is a loving home, she reasons, not the presence of a father.[45] Or listen to the psychologist Charlotte Patterson of the University of Virginia: "Children don't need a father to develop normally."[46]

Similarly, consider social work and the related helping professions. In the United States, argues Martin Wolins, both "social welfare policy and social work practice" are rooted in "an assumption of paternal irrelevance." He warns us that "several millennia of human social existence should have been sufficient as evidence that fathers are worthwhile. Only in the twentieth century have we begun to wonder whether it is possible to do without them and 'get away' with it."[47]

This is the heart of the proposition: that we can do without fathers and get away with it. For example, a number of influential analysts argue that, if poor mothers must choose between welfare payments and fathers, the course of wisdom is to choose the welfare payments, since they are generally more reliable and less bothersome than men.[48] Applying the same logic to the broader society, Anna Coote of the Institute for Public Policy Research in London insists that "[t]he father is no longer essential to the economic survival of the unit. Men haven't kept up with the changes in society, they don't know how to be parents. . . . At the same time, women don't have many expectations of what men might provide."[49]

This view is strongly endorsed in contemporary scholarly discourse on fatherhood. John N. Edwards, for example, urges his fellow social scientists—as if much urging were needed—to rid their studies of "nuclear family bias," since "family structure in and of itself has little or no effect on development" of children.[50] Similarly, Joseph Pleck argues that "data do not really support the case that fathers *per se* (as opposed to, say, a second female adult besides the mother) make a distinctive psychological contribution" to child development.[51] Notice that each of these scholars, exactly like Frank Mott, uses giveaway terminology, thus revealing the analytic intent to disassemble fatherhood: "fathers *per se*" do not make distinctive contributions, and family structure "in and of itself" has little or no effect.

Susan E. Krantz also disagrees with those who feel that "two parents are necessary for the well-being of a child." In that mistaken perspective, Krantz argues, "the role of the father" is "overemphasized" while "the role of other adults" is often "underemphasized."[52] Lula Beatty and Lawrence E. Gary, in testimony before Congress, also report that "family strength is not contingent on family structure."[53] The historians Steven Mintz and Susan Kellogg, in their book *Domestic Revolutions,* in a breathtaking but not unusual case of social science amnesia, find "no clear-cut empirical evidence to suggest that children from 'broken' homes suffer more health or mental problems, personality disorders, or lower school grades than children from 'intact' homes."[54]

Writing in the *Journal of Marriage and the Family,* Alan J. Hawkins and David J. Eggebeen ask the question, "Are Fathers Fungible?" Their answer is yes: "In short, paternity is peripheral to young children's developmental ecologies, and one should not anticipate significant influences of fathers on children's well-being." "Men may be important to children's healthy development," they concede, "but biological fathers can readily be replaced by other adult men."[55] This view, too, is very common.

Similarly, Barbara G. Cashion, in her study of father-absent families, finds not only that fathers are unnecessary for healthy child development but also, echoing Mott's thesis regarding black childen, that fatherlessness produces direct advantages for children. Fatherless girls, for example, are more "independent" and "open" than other girls and, as a result, frequently enjoy higher self-esteem. Father absence is also positively associated with children of high IQ. When fathers are absent, moreover, Cashion finds that family relationships are warmer and closer. She explains:

> The two-parent family is hierarchical with mother and father playing powerful roles and children playing subordinate roles. In the female-headed family there is no such division. Women and children forgo much of the hierarchy and share more in their relationships. . . . Single mothers report that they enjoy their ability to set norms and make decisions about time schedules and routines that suit their own and their children's needs. There is a general lack of conflict, and decisions are made more easily and quickly, provided resources are adequate.[56]

Her one proviso—fatherlessness is better, "provided resources are adequate"—is an inspired touch, a subtle variation of the analytic technique of disassembling fatherhood.

A very few years ago, even among elites, Cashion's position would have been considered extreme. Progressive perhaps, or a harbinger of things to come, but not fully acceptable, not mainstream. Today it is mainstream. I heard it frequently in interviews with divorced mothers. A divorced mother in Chicago had this to say about raising a child alone:

> The mechanics may be difficult, but in a way it's easier, because there's you and there's him and there's not some third party. So in a way it's easier. The communication is there and you don't have someone else who may disagree. The husband may disagree with me, and then the child gets confused. I feel like I have more control. The mechanics are clumsy, because if you work evenings you have to find a sitter, the husband's not home.

Another woman in the same meeting agreed: "I like better having the control of how the kids are being raised myself than with having somebody else."[57]

For perhaps the clearest grassroots description of the Unnecessary Father, listen to the voices of single mothers by choice. They are our society's real-life Murphy Browns: a rapidly growing minority of middle-class mothers—by my estimate, accounting for up to 9 percent of all childbirths today[58]—who have made the deliberate decision to bear and raise a child without a father. Naomi Miller sensitively, and largely sympathetically, chronicles their stories in her book *Single Parents by Choice*.[59] Cynthia, the mother of a five-year-old son, remembers:

> When I was thirty-two I decided that I wanted to be pregnant, but that I didn't want to wait for Mr. OK or the biological clock. So I told an old friend of mine that I wanted to get pregnant. He agreed but did not

want any responsibility, which was fine with me as I didn't want the relationship, but I wanted a child. I named him after my father.

Joyce is a sociology professor:

My relationship with [her boyfriend] George was something I considered apart from having a child. If we got together, it did not hinge on having the child. Even though it didn't work out, he does play an active role as a father. He lives in another state, but I would like it pretty well if he took a job closer. . . . Before, I had thought that if I had a child and I was the one raising him and I was a good parent, it would make absolutely no difference there not being a father in the house, that the child wouldn't miss it. That was before I had Keith, and I am surprised to say that that has changed. I am very glad that his father has a good relationship with him, because my son seems to be really close to his father. Even when Keith was very young and we would go see George, when we left it would really tear me up because I could see that Keith missed having his father around. . . . But I haven't changed in one thing. I do believe that one good parent who makes a good childhood for the child is as good as 90 percent of the two-parent homes I have come across. They have their own problems and their own agendas.

Andrea, a real estate agent, talks about her daughter:

She has asked why she doesn't have a daddy. I told her that when I became pregnant I really wanted to become a mommy, but her daddy didn't want to be a daddy. She asked why, and I told her that some people want to be daddies and some don't, that it's a big decision.

Emily, a freelance writer, talks about her son:

When Ethan was about eight, he did go through a period of feeling rejected and being curious about his biological father. Apparently he wrote something in a class at school that he really would like to meet his father, because his father would like him. At that point, we talked some about that, and how his father's not being around had nothing to do with him. . . . When he was six or seven he became very physically expressive with men. I felt he really needed that contact. If he was with a man, he would wrestle with him or just be physically close. Now that he's older and with his peers, that need has disappeared. I can't see in his particular case that this has been a problem for him. . . . Every one of his friends is from some different family combination, and I just don't think that's an issue for him.

Rachel, who teaches biology in a private high school, discusses her daughter, Jessica:

> She started asking questions when she was two, and I told her that there was a person who was her father and that he had helped put her in my tummy, but that he wasn't part of our lives. . . . She says to me now, "I wish I had a dad," but I think this will come up more fully as she gets older. Jessica came home upset from school one day recently. Her teacher had asked the children to draw a picture of their families. Jessica had drawn a picture of herself with me and Jeff, a man who I have been seeing lately. She is pretty attached to him and told her teacher that he was my friend. The teacher said that a mom and a kid and a friend weren't really a family. I think it would be really helpful if teachers acknowledged more the fact that not all children are growing up today in families that have a mommy and a daddy, and they should be more aware of and accepting of that.[60]

As fatherlessness spreads in our society, so do our acceptance and even endorsement of the trend. For as our society abandons the fatherhood idea, we do not simply become "more aware" of children growing up without fathers. We also become "accepting of that." In a culture of fatherlessness, fatherhood becomes irrelevant.

CHAPTER 5

The Old Father

If the Unnecessary Father is not needed, the Old Father is not wanted. If the former is never seen as the solution, the latter is always seen as the problem. The Unnecessary Father is someone we can get along without. He inspires condescension. The Old Father is someone we cannot get along with. He inspires anger. We can, and frequently do, simply ignore the Unnecessary Father. We can never ignore the Old Father. He is a threat.

In the mind's eye, the Unnecessary Father is small. He is modern. He is youngish to middle-aged. By contrast, the Old Father looms large. He is not modern. He is, well, old. We do not care much, or even think much, about the Unnecessary Father. We are tormented by the Old Father. The Unnecessary Father is someone to forget and to dismiss. He is "not that important." The Old Father is someone to remember and to fear. He is important. We tolerate the Unnecessary Father. We strive to disown the Old Father.

In essence, the Old Father is the paternal embodiment of what the family therapist Frank Pittman calls "mascupathology" or what several analysts term "the masculine mystique." For Pittman, the tragedy of such fathers is their embrace of "the suicidal absurdity of our masculine models." Pittman reminds us that

> qualities that were useful in protecting primitive societies from saber-toothed tigers have few practical functions these days. Cities full of men stomping around flexing their muscles and growling manly noises at one another have become our modern jungles. Men fight for turf and wrestle for control over people and things, whether through war, armed robbery, or corporate takeovers. . . . Heavy doses of masculinity are unquestionably toxic, and no longer socially acceptable.[1]

Of course, denouncing "masculine models" is virtually obligatory in today's public discourse on fatherhood. In 1993, *The Chronicle of Higher*

Education published a review of no fewer than twenty-eight current and forthcoming books on fatherhood and manhood in America. What unites all of these otherwise diverse books, concludes the *Chronicle* reviewer, is their "sharp critique of patriarchy" and their animosity toward "stereotypes of masculinity," especially "Marlboro Man" images of maleness.[2]

Similarly, a 1992 survey of thirteen books on manhood in *Contemporary Sociology* concluded that "most men" are "trapped in stifling old roles and unable to implement the changes in their lives that they want."[3] As that ubiquitous cultural weathervane, Phil Donahue, sums it up, "technology has made strength and aggression not only less necessary but perhaps even maladaptive." Accordingly, our inherited manhood norms, which "associate potency with violence," only teach boys and men to "dehumanize others—especially women."[4]

The Old Father, through his paternity, injects this toxic mascupathology into family life. He is the carrier and the essential progenitor of the masculine mystique. He is, in the phrase of Kyle D. Pruett, author of *The Nurturing Father,* "the barbed wire of the old masculine stereotypes."[5] This is why no one likes him.

Certainly, no one likes him as he existed in the 1950s. To most contemporary cultural critics, the 1950s represent a particularly noxious decade in American history. (Because many of the strongest critics are baby boomers who themselves grew up during that decade, much of our contemporary discourse on the 1950s consists of a generational elite vilifying its own parents.) Moreover, much of what is deemed wrong with that decade hinges on a view of the Old Father of the 1950s. He was not a great guy.

For Father's Day 1992, the *Boston Herald* profiled Steve Crafts, who "leaves work early every other Wednesday to spend quality time with Nathan, his son from a previous marriage." Crafts's own father was a "typical dad of the '50s." Crafts recalls: "His job was to go out and earn the money and punish the kids when he got home. He had trouble showing affection or admitting he had made a mistake. I resolved not to be like him."[6]

Similarly, the author Ralph Keyes remembers: "My father did not play a big role in our family life. He worked hard, traveled at times and didn't say much when home. Occasionally, Dad would pull out a flat old baseball glove and play catch with his four kids. Sometimes he'd take us to the drive-in."[7]

Keyes's father comes off better than many. Andrew Ferguson, a reporter who attended the First International Men's Conference in Texas in 1991, describes "Dad-hating" as the animating core of the contemporary men's movement, the emotional hot spot for both leaders and participants. At a conference workshop, for example, John, the leader, "suggested the men break up in little groups, according to what kind of Dad they had":

One fellow had to sit all by himself, because he said his Dad was okay. This brought John up short. Momentarily. "We'll talk about this Dad later. Because let me tell you," John said, full of pity, "this Dad—the one who did a pretty good job—this Dad is the toughest of all. We've got some work to do."[8]

In *The Fifties,* David Halberstam detects important cultural meaning in the story of Ozzie Nelson. In the 1950s television series *The Adventures of Ozzie and Harriet,* Nelson was a wonderful father. But in real life, it seems, he was a terrible father: a dictatorial, domineering workaholic who exploited his children, especially his son Ricky, for commercial purposes. Halberstam clearly believes that this fact tells us something about the fathers of that era. Thus his peroration: "Ricky Nelson, the charming, handsome All-American boy, was, to all intents and purposes, the unhappy product of a dysfunctional family."[9]

Similarly, for the historian Stephanie Coontz, an apt metaphor for much of 1950s fatherhood is that "radiant Marilyn Van Derbur, crowned Miss America in 1958, had been sexually violated by her wealthy, respectable father." To Coontz, this fact symbolizes a harsh reality: "Beneath the polished facades of many 'ideal' families, suburban as well as urban, was violence, terror, or simply grinding misery that only occasionally came to light."[10]

When not preoccupied with incest and terror, the Old Father of the 1950s was busy remaining physically and emotionally distant from his family. To Barbara J. Berg, family life in the 1950s was characterized by "the virtual absence of the father."[11] The historian William H. Chafe recalls that the "commuter father left home almost before daybreak, returning home just in time for a romp with the kids, perhaps a quick swing, then a kiss goodnight."[12] Steven Mintz and Susan Kellogg agree: "Fatherhood, according to a popular conception of the 1950s, was increasingly characterized by psychological distance and part-time involvement." Meanwhile, a "wife's primary role was to serve as her husband's ego massager, sounding board—and housekeeper."[13] Similarly, for Wini Breines, the typical 1950s dad was a "dubious father,"

> often emotionally unavailable to his wife and children, coping instead with his own needs and new work demands. Although postwar values encouraged their active participation in family life, there is evidence that middle-class fathers were not only emotionally unavailable, but physically absent a good deal of the time . . . the father was both an unavailable and unpromising role model for boys. Expected to be more involved in the family, he was unable and ill-equipped to do so.[14]

Moreover, fatherhood in the 1950s occurred within broader cultural norms—described by Breines as a "moralistic national family ideology"[15]—that most contemporary analysts find deplorable. Coontz complains that men were "pressured into acceptable family roles."[16] Chafe complains that sex roles in the 1950s "achieved a new level of polarization in the suburban family," since the "effort to reinforce traditional norms seemed almost frantic."[17] Elaine Tyler May attributes this "frantic" effort to, well, the communists. She detects in the cultural familism of the 1950s a "domestic version of containment" that "undermined the potential for political activism and reinforced the chilling effects of anticommunism and the cold war consensus."[18]

Fathers with Fangs

This critique of the 1950s father constitutes but one dimension of a larger, and generally more hostile, contemporary broadside against the Old Father. At bottom, much of this assault centers on the problem of paternal authority: the use of power by fathers in family life and in the larger society. The Old Father stands guilty of abuse of power.

As James Garbarino puts it: "Traditionally, men's 'work' in the family has focused on the assertion of authority and power—the wellsprings for family violence and suppression of women." These "traditional masculine values," therefore, "have served as justification for wife and child abuse."[19]

According to Linda Thompson and Alexis J. Walker, writing in the *Journal of Marriage and the Family,* our society's "enduring image of fatherhood" consists of "a breadwinner who does not have the ability or the desire to nurture his child day-by-day, so he funds the family but keeps his distance."[20] This "narrow rigidity," according to the theologian James Dittes, means that "the father renounces his innate tenderness, vulnerability, and wish for intimacy, 'acting' instead as though he is in charge—the boss—the manipulator."[21] No wonder no one likes the guy.

Indeed, for the poet Adrienne Rich, fatherhood is nothing less than the ultimate metaphor for evil. Our unjust society is best understood as the Kingdom of the Fathers, which to her means "rapism and the warrior mentality."[22] This idea increasingly influences our popular culture as well. In ABC's 1993 television miniseries "Wild Palms," produced by Oliver Stone, Los Angeles in the year 2007 is riven by a struggle between liberal humanists and malignant totalitarians. The former call themselves "Friends." The latter are called "Fathers."

To Catharine R. Stimpson of Rutgers University, the essential identity of fathers is threefold:

First, they earn money in the public labor force and support their families through that effort. Next, they have formal power over women and the children in those families. Finally, they are heterosexual. They sleep with the women whom they dominate and bully the homosexuals whose desires openly surge elsewhere.[23]

Accordingly, Ursula Owen urges us to overthrow "the institutionalized power of the fathers."[24] On a more personal level, Sara Maitland, tormented by "every dark thing that father means," seeks to

cast out the Father in my head who rules and controls me.... This frightens me; I want to protect my father and my love for him. I do not want to kill him, to see him dead. I want to set the man free from having to be a father.[25]

Until recently, at least, the Old Father appeared frequently in poetry, plays, and novels. Walt Whitman knew him:

The father, strong, self-sufficient, manly, mean, anger'd, unjust,
The blow, the quick loud word, the tight bargain, the crafty lure.[26]

Dylan Thomas beautifully evokes the forbidding distance, the "sad height," of the Old Father:

And you, my father, there on that sad height,
Curse, bless me now with your fierce tears, I pray.[27]

A century ago, August Strindberg both revealed the Old Father's misogyny and foreshadowed his demise in the character of the Captain in *The Father.*[28] In 1955, Tennessee Williams perfectly captured his dark essence, especially his way of bullying and damaging his children, in the character of Big Daddy in *Cat on a Hot Tin Roof,* just as Clarence Day in 1939, with a lighter touch, had exposed and teased him in the character of Father in *Life with Father.*[29]

To the novelist and short story writer Donald Barthelme, these Old Fathers are "like blocks of marble ... placed squarely in your path. They block your path." He warns us darkly about "the rage of the king-father." Indeed, sometimes these guys grow fangs:

If you can get your lariat around one of his fangs, and quickly wrap the other end of it several times around your saddle horn, and if your horse is a trained roping horse and knows what to do, how to plant his feet and then back up with small nervous steps, keeping the lariat taut, then you have a chance. Do not try to rope both fangs at the same time; concentrate on the right. Do the thing fang by fang, and then you will be safe, or more nearly so. I have seen some old, yellowed six-inch fangs that were drawn in this way, and once, in a whaling museum in a sea-port town, a twelve-inch fang, mistakenly labeled as the tusk of a wal-rus. But I recognized it at once, it was a father fang.[30]

In Peter Taylor's novel *A Summons to Memphis,* Phillip Carver sadly recalls his father's cruelty in preventing his children from marrying. For George Carver was "a man with such natural or assumed authority that his children could never even contemplate an important step like mar-riage without receiving *his* advice and consent—or, rather, without accepting his inevitable rejection of the loved one." His daughters, espe-cially, "were made to feel that their conformity, their obedience, their moral support was the most important matter in their father's life. And they did conform, they obeyed, they supported—they did not marry."[31]

Phillip Carver is at the Memphis airport, about to step off the plane to see his father:

And suddenly I dreaded him—dreaded him as I used to dread him sometimes when coming home from Army camp, on leave. My impulse when I stood in the plane's exit hatch was to duck back inside, to let him feel if only momentarily that he had been wrong in his certainty that I would be watching him through the window.[32]

In *The Three Sisters,* Mary Sinclair writes movingly of a daughter who

hated it. She hated the whole house. It was so built that there wasn't a corner in it where you could get away from Papa. . . . He was aware of everything you did; of everything you didn't do. He could hear you in the dining-room; he could hear you overhead; he could hear you going up and downstairs. He could positively hear you breathe. . . . She drew in her breath lest he should hear it now.[33]

These powerful accusations pinpoint the core of the Old Father's identity. The Old Father wields power. He controls. He decides. He tells other people what to do. He has fangs. This aspect of his character gener-ates suspicion and resentment: sometimes from his wife, frequently from his children, and, increasingly, from the larger society as well.

This is the heart of the matter. Many contemporary critics do not view authority simply as one component of the Old Father's identity. They view authority—or, more accurately, domination—as synonymous with male identity itself. The power of the father thus derives less from culture than from nature, less from certain ideas about paternity than from inher-ent qualities of paternity and male sexual embodiment. In many respects, this view reflects a more intellectually serious analysis.

These critics do not object to one aspect of the Old Father's paternal identity. They object to paternal identity. More precisely, they object to the father's transmission of gender identity to children. For they identify the father-infant bond as the essence, the trigger, of a social malignancy that Jessica Benjamin and others call "splitting"—the division of humankind into masculine and feminine, dominant and submissive. This fundamental-ist critique of paternity thus recalls Jean-Paul Sartre: "There is no good father, that's the rule. Don't lay the blame on men but on the bond of paternity, which is rotten."[34]

In *The Bonds of Love,* Benjamin identifies "gender polarity"—the split-ting of human potentiality into male and female—as "the deep source of discontent in our culture."[35] Moreover, confronting this discontent "requires us simultaneously to acknowledge and criticize the father's power."[36]

Why the father? For Benjamin, "the route to individuality" for the human infant "leads through identificatory love of the father."[37] Infants and toddlers, who begin the process of individuation by recognizing that they are separate from the mother, are "looking for an attachment figure who will represent their move away from infant dependency to the great outside. This figure is the father."[38]

Even before "symbolic consciousness of gender" begins to emerge, "the father is experienced in his total physical and emotional behavior as the exciting, stimulating, separate other." Thus "from the beginning, fathers represent what is outside and different—they mediate the wider world."[39]

Accordingly, "separation and desire are thus joined in the father," so that paternity itself imprints upon the child "the split between a father of liberation and a mother of dependency."[40] Father becomes freedom. Mother remains necessity. Father, outside. Mother, inside. Father, agency. Mother, victimhood. Father, desire. Mother, denial of desire. Father, domi-nation. Mother, submission.

For a son, "identificatory love for his father is the psychological founda-tion of the idealization of male power and autonomous individuality." A daughter, by contrast, suffers from "the missing father": the absence of a same-sex parent who embodies desire. For her, as for her brother, "the privi-lege and power of agency fall to the father." For both, therefore, "the reac-tion against dependency can turn into ideal love of paternal power," thus marking "the entry into a gendered reality" which tragically "precludes the necessity of dealing with the contradictory tendencies within the self."[41]

What is to be done? For Benjamin, the task is nothing less than eradi-cating gender divisions and restoring omnipotentiality to the human child. Certainly a large task. To achieve it, Benjamin recommends for parents a process of "crossing over," in which "gendered self-representation coexists with a genderless or even opposite-gendered self-representation." To cross over, of course, the father-child relationship must be radically transformed.

For crossover fathers must embody and transmit to children "both male and female aspects of selfhood."[42] In this way, splitting is transcended; tension and paradox are sustained.

Here is the essence of the transformed father-child relationship: the virtual elimination of gendered content from fatherhood as a social role. In short, paternity without gender. Fatherhood without manhood.

But that is only the beginning. The mere "reorganization of parenting" cannot "wholly eliminate the effects of binary opposition," since these effects, it turns out, define all of modern society's "psychic and cultural representations." Thus, for example, a

> father's primary care of the infant does not detract from the boy's readiness to identify with the standard cultural representations of masculinity and to locate his fantasy play "outside" the parent-infant relationship, not with dolls but with space ships.... At times it even seems that regardless of what real parents do, the cultural dualisms sustain the splitting of gender.

Faced with a societal crisis of these dimensions, Benjamin can only conclude with a sigh of profound pessimism, importuning us, even as we might never fully transcend "the deep structure of gender," at least to "face the enormity of this loss."[43]

Benjamin's basic understanding of paternity is widely shared among contemporary feminist authors.[44] The family therapist Olga Silverstein, for example, urges us to seek "the end of the gender split," since "until we are willing to question the very idea of a male sex role ... we will be denying both men *and* women their full humanity."[45] Similarly, Susan Moller Okin, approaching the topic as a political scientist, urges us to adopt a "genderless model of marriage and parenting." She concludes:

> A just future would be one without gender. In its social structures and practices, one's sex would have no more relevance than one's eye color or the length of one's toes. No assumptions would be made about "male" and "female" roles; childbearing would be so conceptually separated from child rearing and other family responsibilities that it would be a cause for surprise, and no little concern, if men and women were not equally responsible for domestic life or if children were to spend much more time with one parent than the other.[46]

Judith Lorber's work, moreover, while less nuanced than Benjamin's, not only builds on Benjamin's critique of splitting, but also seeks more explicitly to define the contours of a society free of gender complementarity. Lorber urges us, in a striking metaphor, to "dismantle Noah's Ark." No more splitting. To Lorber, this means "the eradication of gender as an organizing principle of post-industrial society" and the "restructuring of social institutions without a division of human beings into the social groups called 'men' and 'women.'"[47]

What about families? In postindustrial society, Lorber concludes, "kinship is no longer necessary" for child rearing. Thus she strongly endorses a trend that, in the real world, especially regarding fathers, is already occurring: "the separation of sexuality and procreation, and biological and social parenting." She urges the further proliferation of

> social categories of parenting other than "mother" and "father"—child bearers and child rearers, professional caretakers and educators, sperm and egg donors and gestators, legal kin and emotional supporters. . . . In short, the social roles of mother and father in a non-gendered society would not be indicative of the connection between "parent" and "child."[48]

In important respects, Benjamin's and Lorber's feminist analysis of the culture parallels Marx's analysis of the economy. Each analysis focuses essentially on the problem of authority: who has power and who does not. Each offers what might be termed a total theory, positing one social evil as the driving force behind all of reality, including all social injustice. Marx locates the evil in the organization of the economy, or the means of production. Benjamin and Lorber locate it in the organization of the family, or the means of reproduction. For Marx, the central dynamic of society is class conflict. For Benjamin and Lorber, it is gender conflict.

For Marx, the main antagonist is the capitalist. For Benjamin and Lorber, it is the father. In both cases, the enemy is described with deep respect. Marx freely acknowledges, even celebrates, the generative power of the capitalist. Benjamin similarly recognizes and at times even idealizes "the father's power" to shape the character of his child.

Each analysis demands radical transformations. One would destroy the link between capitalist and worker. The other would realign the relationship between parent and child, especially father and child. Indeed, as Marx would eradicate capitalism as a social idea, Benjamin and Lorber would largely eradicate fatherhood as a gendered social role.

Finally, both theories overrun the normal boundaries of science and the academy. Both adumbrate a utopia that lies at the end of history: in one case, a classless society; in the other, a genderless society. Both call for social struggle. Each is driven by a transcendent moral idea: equality. Each provides a coherent intellectual underpinning for a powerful social movement: in one case, socialism; in the other, feminism.[49]

Benjamin's and Lorber's essentialist, feminist critique of paternity represents our cultural script's most radical assault against the Old Father. At the same time, the animating core of this critique—a deep suspicion of paternal authority—is widespread and spreading in our society, especially within elite culture.

Surely, this critique is powerful. Much of it is accurate. Yet just as surely, and more fundamentally, our culture's increasing hostility toward even the idea of paternal authority also reflects the spreading belief that fatherhood itself is superfluous. An androgynous or ungendered paternity, after all, is incompatible with fatherhood as a social role. To seek the former is to give up the latter. Even more fundamentally, our growing uneasiness with paternal authority may also simply reflect the fact that we are a society increasingly without it.

The Kingdom of the Fatherless

Consider this dilemma of the father's power. It is a fundamental human problem, shaping psyches and cultures. The anthropologist Weston La Barre, for example, probing for the origins of religion in human societies, finally views the "anguish" produced by paternal authority as "the root of religion" and "the secret of who we are."[50] Certainly the fear and resentment of paternal authority appear to be an inherent outgrowth of fatherhood in virtually all human societies. In short, antagonism toward paternal power seems to go with the territory of fatherhood.

More than the mother-child bond, the father-child bond is frequently charged with distance, tension, and even hostility, all stemming, at least in part, from the typically distinctive content of paternal authority. Of course, maternal authority is also a source of profound tension and conflict for both sons and daughters, especially for daughters. Similarly, the father-son relationship can be heavily weighted with conflict, even tragedy, based in part on primitive male rivalries (your strength versus my strength) and unconscious feelings, including sexual jealousy, famously described by Freud as the Oedipus complex.

Yet, despite the obvious importance of maternal authority as an influence on children and despite the frequently heightened tension found in same-sex parent-child relationships, the father's power, as a general anthropological proposition, is more conflictual than the mother's: more rule-oriented, more emotionally distant, more aggressive, more physically coercive, more instrumental, and therefore more overtly severe. Thus, while La Barre can describe the tendency of the mother to be "anxious, uncertain, overprotective," he warns of the father's darker tendency to be "vengeful, angry, frightening."[51] Similarly, to Walter J. Ong, the primary threat posed by the father "is not clutching or smothering or swallowing but brutal domination."[52]

This more conflictual relationship produces a necessary but potentially explosive tension between father and child. Much of this tension is rooted in the fact that the child both craves and resents authority. So does a culture. Accordingly, for the infant—and, more broadly, for the culture—the entire dilemma of authority evolves prototypically as conflict with the parent: especially and typically the father. Paternal authority, then, emerges as a deeply problematic, but also essential, drama of both individual identity and social life.

Freud describes this phenomenon as the "father-complex": the "ambivalent emotional attitude" of the child toward the father, which in turn forms the phylogenetic basis of later, more generalized attitudes toward authority, including "a powerful unconscious element of hostility."[53] Certainly, this combustible contradiction inherent within fatherhood—closeness partly through distance, affection partly through coercion—helps explain why fatherhood constitutes such a problematic contrivance in human societies.[54]

Especially in modern societies. The modern temperament is largely defined by its ambivalent, skeptical view of authority, particularly those primary forms of authority, such as paternal control, that remain essentially discretionary, or unregulated by law. Accordingly, in societies in which all authority is increasingly suspect, the authority of the father, in particular, is likely to be understood, in some ways correctly, as arbitrary and dangerous.

Especially in America. This nation, after all, originated in revolt against the authority of the king. We are the inheritors of regicide, the jealous guardians of power stolen from a societal Old Father. We are the sons of liberty. Throughout our society, from the Mayflower to Ellis Island, the freedom-seeking rebellion of youth against the ways of the Old Father emerges as a master theme in our art, our politics, and our choice of folk heroes: an enduring aspect of our national myth and of popular understanding of our national character.

The Old Father says: Stay at home. Obey me. Learn my trade. Marry one of our kind. Do not forget your faith. Cut your hair. Much of the American answer is: I will go West. I will marry whom I please, do as I wish. You do not understand. Your ways are not mine. I will not obey you. Even: I do not trust you.

Especially in fatherless America. The United States is becoming an increasingly unfathered society. Consequently, our spreading mistrust of fatherhood—and, indeed, our spreading cynicism toward all authority—almost certainly stems not primarily from any particular quality of the father-child bond but more from the increasing absence of any such bond at all. In the case of fathers, absence does not make the heart grow fonder.

For the generalized mistrust of children toward fathers is not simply the result of what fathers do. It can also, and especially, be the result of what fathers do not do. Our intense resentment of the Old Father is probably less a result of his presence than of his absence. We abhor him in part because we no longer know him.[55]

Robert Bly describes widespread fatherlessness as a societal "hole" that "fills soon with hostile suspicions." Thus "the father is truly evil, he loves no one, he cares only for himself, he is pitiful, he is a fascist, he's completely incompetent, like all older men he is corrupt, he is selfish, he only wants to control, he wants me to die in war, he takes bribes, he is a Nazi."[56]

Here is a core irony of fatherhood. If having a father fosters anger in children, having no father fosters greater anger. If fathers generate tension and ambivalence in children that is hard to resolve, fatherlessness generates cynicism and confusion that is much harder to resolve.

If paternal authority is problematic, abdication of paternal authority is tragic. Yes, a fathered society must struggle with the inherent tensions of domesticated masculinity. But a fatherless society must accept the consequences of undomesticated masculinity: mistrust, violence, nihilism.

Adrienne Rich is wrong. Ultimately, rapism and the warrior mentality represent the kingdom of the fatherless, not the fathers. Male predation is not the synonym, but rather the necessary antonym, of encultured paternity.

This understanding of the father constitutes faint praise indeed. Such a father can only reflect, but not transcend, the fundamental human problems deriving from procreation and sexual embodiment. In this sense, a father is only good enough to be better than the alternative. In this same sense, however, perhaps the dramatic fracturing of fatherhood in our society leads us to protest too much. Perhaps our cultural demonization of the Old Father largely reflects the fact that, for the most part, he no longer lives among us.

CHAPTER 6

The New Father

If the Old Father is a destructive, overbearing fellow whom we would never want to marry our daughter, the New Father is fast becoming our best friend. He is the answer to our worries about what it means to be a man, the answer to our concerns about how to care for children, the answer to our dreams about social justice, personal happiness, and equality between the sexes. Among the stars of today's fatherhood script, he is the one good man.

The Old Father is bad. He is the way things used to be. The Unnecessary Father is irrelevant. He is the way things are. The New Father is good. He is the way things ought to be. He is our hope, the wave of the future. He is fatherhood, finally, with a human face.

He is nurturing. He expresses his emotions. He is a healer, a companion, a colleague. He is a deeply involved parent. He changes diapers, gets up at 2:00 A.M. to feed the baby, goes beyond "helping out" in order to share equally in the work, joys, and responsibilities of domestic life. Because he is a favorite of the media—he is the one required guest on every television show that devotes a special segment to Father's Day—his influence goes far beyond his number. Fathers like him are

> finding that "equal sharing" is more satisfying and fair-minded than just doing the token chores they once considered "dad's work." Men who used to "help out" their wives by babysitting now see child-rearing as an important part of their lives, and in many homes both parents share this responsibility, the work and decision-making as well as the fun of parenting.[1]

In *How Men Feel,* Anthony Astracham succinctly defines the "new father" as one who performs "half the work of child raising from the moment of birth" and who has "abandoned or transcended most traditional male sex roles and the male attempt to monopolize power."[2] Similarly, to David Giveans and Michael Robinson, the New Father transcends the role of "aloof breadwinner" and is thus "apt to be as comfortable pushing his child in the supermarket as he is seeking success for himself in the job market."[3]

Letty Cottin Pogrebin devotes a chapter of her book *Family Politics* to celebrating the "New Fathers" who "do not have to pretend":

A man in Albuquerque, for example, loves being a father so much that he wanted to share his enthusiasm with a father-to-be. He gave his best pal a baby shower at which men friends gathered to toast the forthcoming baby with good will, good food, and a rap session about father feelings. All over the country, men are materializing in childbirth courses, child-care centers, and early childhood education; they are staying home to care for their own children, braving the quizzical stares of cops and mothers as they push a baby carriage or watch their children in the playground; asking for joint custody; demanding paternity leave; and taking baby-care classes to prepare to be more skillful, better prepared fathers.[4]

To advance this ideal, she argues, our culture is "breaking the absurd linkage of Father with Breadwinner, understanding that one role is not dependent on the other and that neither role determines 'masculinity.'" We are also eliminating "sex specialization" within the family: "Sex-specialized caring imperils children because it is contingent on parents' sex role choreography rather than children's needs."[5]

In today's specialized discourse on fatherhood, the New Father is not only the most popular fellow. He is the only popular fellow. On the ground, in real life, he may be hard to locate. But he has captured our hearts.

Especially, it seems, our academic hearts. Indeed, I can discover very little academic writing on fatherhood during the past twenty years that questions, or even probes beyond, the confines of what might be termed the New Father paradigm. To review this scholarship is to be struck time and again by the fervency—indeed, the sense of moral urgency—with which contemporary scholars seek both to define and to applaud the New Father as a cultural ideal.

The depth of this consensus is illustrated by special issues of two scholarly journals, one in 1979 and one in 1993, focusing on fatherhood. The earlier one, *The Family Coordinator,* sponsored by the National Council on Family Relations, devoted its special issue to "Men's Roles in the Family." The "keynote for this issue," the editors tell us, is "Strategies for Changing Male Family Roles," including "strategies which women are using to effectively produce changes in men's role behavior" and "reciprocal role changes for husbands and wives." This issue also focuses on the shortcomings of the "breadwinning role" for fathers, the equal capacity of fathers to nurture infants, "Appalachian males who wish to modify and modernize their family roles," and "the difficulties which confront men who would like to adopt less conventional sex roles in their families."[6]

Jump to 1993, when *Families in Society,* sponsored by Family Service America, devotes a special issue to fatherhood, entitled "Half Full or Half Empty?" The answer, of course, is both. On the one hand, says the editor, "we need to create 'diaper changing men' who will embrace a more nurturing, hands-on parental role." On the other hand, since "many fathers are already more involved and more nurturing," we need to "build on the progress that has been made."[7]

The core assumptions of all the articles in both issues are virtually interchangeable. Both publications operate almost solely within the New Father paradigm. Moreover, the philosophy and range of topics found in these two journal issues, separated by fourteen years, provide a surprisingly representative sample of all scholarly output on the subject of fatherhood published between those two dates.

A survey of the current leading high school and college textbooks on family life confirms this finding. What might be termed the textbook story of fatherhood typically stresses, on the one hand, the importance of "choice and change" in family life and, on the other, the problems stemming from male resistance to needed change. For example, men do not seem to understand, as one textbook puts it, that "[a]ndrogyny would be especially beneficial to men. They could stop being workaholics ... stop killing one another in wars, and stop worrying about being a 'real man.'"[8] Another textbook points to the same problem: "Boys, especially, continue to think about sex and gender in terms of traditional gender roles."[9]

Especially among the experts and in the media, this message is ubiquitous. "The American family is changing, and men are dragging their feet," warn the family scholars Janet G. Hunt and Larry L. Hunt. Specifically, un-new fathers are dragging their feet regarding "a less gendered society" with "more symmetrical families and more androgynous personalities— free of negative and distorting personality characteristics and internal blocks to self-esteem."[10]

The family therapist Augustus Napier urges us to find "a new kind of male hero," since

> our culture is awash with cynicism and disillusionment with men, and for good reason. . . . What, for God's sake, would the ideal version of the man designed for something other than warfare, or for the conquest of the world's diminishing rain forests, or for staring into a computer screen, be like?

To Napier, such a new version must center on the recognition by fathers that "the basic pathology of the father's response is driven by his emotional distance from the inner circle of the family," and that, accordingly, he must obtain, perhaps from family therapy, a "new map for masculinity" that can "direct him toward the new behaviors which society needs him to learn."[11]

The author Clayton Barbeau agrees: "If the men of our time are to live up to the women of our time, then I think that they must take a long, hard look at their upbringing and their assumptions as men." Fathers are victims of "obsolete sex roles" and the "masculine mystique," resulting in the "miseducation of the American male." Men must begin to "drop our masks and our role-playing." They must begin "digging into themselves and seeing what historical baggage they can jettison, what chains from the past they can saw off, to bring themselves greater emotional freedom."[12]

James Garbarino, the president of the Erikson Institute for Advanced Study in Child Development, agrees:

> To develop a new kind of father, we must encourage a new kind of man. In *My Fair Lady,* Professor Higgins asks, "Why can't a woman be more like a man?" It's time to ask the opposite question. If we are to rewrite the parenting scripts to emphasize nurturing and the investment of self in children's lives, we need to ask, "Why can't a man be more like a woman?"[13]

To develop this new like-a-mother father requires the help of professionals. They stand prepared to offer this help. To Ronald F. Levant, founder of Boston University's Fatherhood Project, the main challenge facing "the new fathers" is not only to "fashion a paternal role different from that of their fathers, but also to prepare their children for flexible adult roles that are not predetermined according to gender." Thus: "To help fathers meet this challenge, educational programs are needed both for the current generation of fathers, and for the next generation." He urges "the providing of parenting knowledge and training to males" through "fatherhood educational programs that are currently emerging as needed instruments of change."[14]

Beth M. Erickson summarizes her main idea in the title of her book for therapists: *Helping Men Change.*[15] In a review of fatherhood for the journal *Family Relations,* Shirley M. H. Hanson and Frederick W. Bozett similarly pose this challenge to researchers and family service professionals: "how can males be better socialized early in life to be more active in nurturing and caretaking?"[16]

This question dominates contemporary journalism and popular writing on fatherhood. Writing in the *Boston Herald,* Beverly Beckham recalls the shortcomings of the Old Father: "[He] worked 10, 12, 14 hours, came home, sat down, read the paper, ate dinner, took out the rubbish, shoveled snow in the winter, cut grass in the summer, and gave the final word in all important decisions." But today: "The monarchy is dead." Instead, the emerging new fathers "get up at night to feed and change an infant. They comfort crying babies, they take toddlers for haircuts, they even push baby carriages. . . . This is the way parenting should be. Fifty-fifty."[17]

In *The Father,* Arthur D. Colman and Libby Lee Colman develop the metaphor of "earth" father as against "sky" father. Sky father: "providing and protecting" while remaining "cold, aloof, and competitive." Earth father: "dyadic parenting," or "equity in nurturance." Accordingly, in their parlance, sky is Old, earth is New. Their unsurprising recommendation for fathers: less sky, more earth.[18]

Popular magazines strongly agree. According to a 1993 *Child* magazine cover story: "Everybody's been talking about the 'new dad.' The one who does the dishes, reads to his kids, and takes paternity leave. But does the 'new dad' live in your house?" To find out, ask these questions. Does he rank being "emotionally available" as more essential to good fathering than "being a good provider"? Is he "as adept at fixing baby's formula as he is at fixing a flat"? Does he "minimize gender stereotypes" and transcend "the legacy of the traditional, aloof father"? If he has a daughter, does he take her on fishing trips, wash the car with her, and play basketball with her? If he has a son, does he shampoo his hair, plant flowers with him, and let the child see him cry?[19] These are the signs.

Similarly, *Redbook* magazine's 1993 story on "The Good Father" poses three key questions for American fathers. First: "Does he do diapers?" (Answer: "Yes, all across the nation, armies of fathers are waving the white flag of enlightenment: a clean diaper. But have they ever shopped for Luvs or Pampers?") Second: "Will men take paternity leave?" (Answer: No. Or, at least, not yet. However: "Paternity leave is becoming socially acceptable and politically correct.") And finally: Can men overcome traditional gender roles? (Answer: "Men have come a long way, certainly, but perhaps not far enough.")[20] Not surprisingly, a 1993 "Parenting Poll" in *Parenting* magazine features this question: "Did Dad change the children's diapers at least half the time?"[21]

Not to be outdone, a 1993 questionnaire for fathers in *Parents* magazine reflects precisely these same concerns: How active are you in infant care? Do you change diapers? Would you consider taking paternity leave? Staying at home full-time? Working on a flextime schedule? Is fatherhood more or less important than your career?[22] These, it seems, are not simply crucial questions for these magazines. They are the only questions.

In sum, defining and celebrating the New Father are by far the most popular ideas in our contemporary discourse on fatherhood. Father as close and nurturing, not distant and authoritarian. Fatherhood as more than breadwinning. Fatherhood as new-and-improved masculinity. Fathers unafraid of feelings. Fathers without sexism. Fatherhood as fifty-fifty parenthood, undistorted by arbitrary gender divisions or stifling social roles.

The Missing Father

I applaud much of the New Father vision. I admire hands-on, involved, off-the-sidelines fatherhood as good for children, good for society, and good for men. In my own life, I strive to be such a father.

But as a cultural model for men, as the happy ending in today's expert story, the New Father idea is deeply flawed. First, it insults our society's patrimony. As a cultural proposition, much of the New Father model depends upon denigrating or ignoring the historical meaning of fatherhood in America. Indeed, much of the New Father ideal is based explicitly upon belittling our own fathers.

Second, and more important, the New Father model opposes the needs of children by assaulting the requirements of parenthood. Recall Letty Cottin Pogrebin's remarkable claim that parental "sex role choreography" is destructive because it ignores "children's needs." In fact, the opposite is true: Gendered parental roles derive precisely from children's needs.

Attacking "sex role choreography" may serve the needs of autonomous, rights-bearing adults. But it does not serve children's needs. By shifting our focus from the dependent child to the freedom-seeking adult, the New Father model simply wishes away the central exigencies of parenthood. This intellectual failure is exposed with compelling clarity by the work of two important scholars.

In *Reclaimed Powers,* David Gutmann integrates psychological and anthropological evidence from a diversity of cultures, both traditional and modern, to set out a broad psychosocial model of parenthood and aging in human societies. The peculiar trait of our species, Gutmann reminds us, is the comparatively long period of time during which the human child is dependent on his mother and father for survival. During these years, which Gutmann terms the "parental emergency," the needs of the child compel mothers and fathers to specialize in their labor and to adopt gender-based parental roles. In doing so, parents necessarily "surrender a large piece of their narcissistic claims to personal omnipotentiality and immortality, conceding them instead to the child." The result, Gutmann concludes, is the "routine, unexamined heroism of parenting."[23]

The "parental emergency," of course, does not last forever. Children grow up. As it ends, moreover, gender roles across cultures tend to converge toward what Gutmann terms "post-parental androgyny." Men can become more expressive and affiliative, women more competitive and assertive. In midlife and old age, then, each sex can "reclaim" exactly those aspects of human potentiality that, during the parental emergency, were ceded to the other sex in the interest of the child. During the parental emergency, however, the role of culture is to guide adults—especially men—to restrict their narcissism through the adoption of family roles that serve the child.[24]

The New Father model is willfully blind to this fundamental characteristic of parenthood and the life cycle. Gutmann begins with the needs of the child, alerts us to the cross-cultural importance of gendered parental roles, and describes the psychosocial process of "having it all," not today, but in the fullness of a lifetime. The New Father model begins essentially with the desires of the adult, denigrates any conception of gendered parental roles, and offers a perspective on the adult life cycle that almost never extends beyond the period of diaper changing.

Alice Rossi's work amplifies this criticism of the New Father model. In a seminal presidential address to the American Sociological Association in 1983, she insisted that "none of the existing theories prevalant in family sociology" is "adequate to an understanding and explanation of human parenting." The reason for this failure of expertise, she concluded, is that current scholarly discourse on parenthood either ignores or denies biologically rooted differences between men and women. Rossi, who hardly won universal praise for this address, advised her colleagues:

> Gender differentiation is not simply a function of socialization, capitalist production, or patriarchy. It is grounded in a sex dimorphism that serves the fundamental purpose of reproducing the species. . . . Theories that neglect these characteristics of sex and gender carry a high risk of eventual irrelevance against the mounting evidence of sexual dimorphism from the biological and neurosciences.[25]

The New Father model is based precisely on the rejection of "characteristics of sex and gender" in parenthood. Indeed, its principal aim is the deconstruction of gender dimorphism within parenthood. To replace gender differentiation, the New Father offers a model of androgynous parenthood—fatherhood without gender—that Rossi clearly believes to be a contradiction in terms, ultimately an irrelevance.

Finally, then, the New Father model is a mirage. It purports to be about fatherhood, but it is not. There is no father there. The New Father is a missing father. For as a cultural model—a set of cultural cues for paternal behavior—the New Father reflects the puerile desire for human omnipotentiality in the form of genderless parenthood, a direct repudiation of fatherhood as a gendered social role for men.

For these reasons, our cultural wish for the New Father depends upon, and even presupposes, our growing cultural acceptance of fatherlessness. As a result, the New Father, hero of our contemporary cultural script, will only serve to erode further the possibility of effective fathering in our society. For the New Father finally becomes no father, a synonym for the belief that fatherhood is superfluous. He can be best understood as the Unnecessary Father of the future.

An Old Story

The most admirable theme of the New Father model—the importuning of fathers to act tenderly toward their children—is not new at all. On the contrary, the idea is almost as old as fatherhood itself.

The self-congratulatory needs of today's baby-boomer parents notwithstanding, paternal affection was not invented, like a new vaccine, by the post-1970 generation of "new" fathers. As both ideal and reality—as both elite cultural exhortation and kitchen-table practice—the idea of close-in, emotionally bonded fatherhood can claim a much more venerable lineage.

More than two centuries ago, Jean-Jacques Rousseau, in his famous evocation of the origins of human society and "the first developments of the heart," described the "establishment and differentiation of families" based on "husbands and wives, fathers and children in a common habitation," concluding: "The habit of living together gave rise to the sweetest sentiments known to men: conjugal love and paternal love." For Rousseau, the "sweet sentiment" of paternal love forms a fundamental basis of human societies.[26] Indeed, a father's tenderness is a classic component of the fatherhood script in virtually all societies.

In America, especially, New Fathers have thrived for many generations. More than a century ago, Tocqueville correlated the emergence of democracy in America with the emergence of a more affectionate fatherhood in America. As "manners and laws become more democratic," Tocqueville observed,

> the relation of father and son becomes more intimate and affectionate; rules and authority are less talked of; confidence and tenderness are oftentimes increased, and it would seem that the natural bond is drawn closer.

In the American "democratic family," Tocqueville finds that "a species of equality prevails around the domestic hearth." Though the father

> be not hedged in with ceremonial respect, his sons at least accost him with confidence; no settled form of speech is appropriated to the mode of addressing him, but they speak to him constantly, and are ready to consult him day by day: the master and the constituted ruler have vanished,—the father remains.[27]

In examining the advice literature to American parents written during the nineteenth century, the historian Stephen M. Frank also finds that "fathers were being urged by the 1850s to abandon an authoritarian posture in the family in favor of tender ties with children," and that "at no time during the nineteenth century did the normative pronouncements directed at men prescribe breadwinning as the father's exclusive family function."[28]

For example, centrally important to the nineteenth-century fatherhood script was the Christian fatherhood movement, "whose central premise was that fathers owed their children more than material support." To many of the clergymen and other writers, male and female, who celebrated the ideals of Christian fatherhood, "the authoritarian and distant fatherhood of the past was a grave error that should not be repeated."[29] One prominent author of the 1850s, writing sadly of children who grow up without knowing their fathers intimately, put it this way:

> Who is there in mid-life that has not experienced, or has not witnessed, at least, the unhappy effects of this error? To how many minds has it brought a cloud over the memory of a departed father! There was reverence, it is true, for that father; but love never entered the heart. We have the grand outlines of Christian character in the picture left of him. There are stern principle, unbending integrity, truthfulness, fidelity, and justice; but the delicate shades and softer tints of affectionate manners, pleasing tones, the ever-beaming countenance, that speaks of a childlike spirit,— these we miss.[30]

In an important sense, then, the nineteenth-century evocation of Christian fatherhood clearly presaged today's evocation of the New Father. More broadly, across time and cultures, it seems, one perennial piece of advice to fathers has been the importance of acting tenderly toward their children. The New Father, it turns out, is an old story.

True fatherhood, the cultural scripts repeatedly remind men, is more than breadwinning; aloofness and authoritarianism are inconsistent with effective paternity; true manhood, and true happiness, stem in large part from close ties to children. On the one hand, the prevalence of this message surely suggests the basic capacity and need of fathers everywhere to nurture their children. On the other hand, the urgency of the message also suggests that fathers, much more than mothers, require strong cultural guidance—in fact, constant reminding—on this matter.

Ironically, the period of recent U.S. history in which fathers probably received the strongest guidance on this point—and certainly in which an unprecedented number of fathers took the message to heart—is none other than the 1950s. In much of our current cultural discourse, of course, the 1950s are portrayed as a paternal wasteland: workaholic commuter

Dads in gray flannel suits; violence-prone tyrants who lorded it over women and children; materialists who thought fatherhood meant paying bills; and cold, emotionally remote Old Fathers who wounded their children through distance.

Doubtless there were such fathers in the 1950s. We know they existed in part because so many of their highly educated children have written books saying so. But as a group, the fathers of the 1950s did rather well by their children, at least compared to the fathers who preceded and followed them. They got and stayed married. They earned a lot of money, much of which went to their children. Many of them worked in physically demanding jobs, wearing blue collars and washing their hands with Lava soap. If these fathers sometimes fell asleep after dinner while reading the paper or watching TV, they did so partly because their work made them tired.

They spent more time with their children than their own fathers had with them, and also more than their sons, living in a divorce culture, would later spend with *their* children. They coached Little League, installed Sears swing sets in the backyard, took countless photos of the kids, attended games, practices, and school plays, interviewed boys who wanted to date their daughters, washed the car, puttered in the yard, took the garbage out, came home every night for dinner. They stayed around.

They were the most domesticated generation of fathers in modern American history. Of course, many of today's cultural critics prefer to believe the opposite. For example, many contemporary analysts take the title of Sloan Wilson's famous 1955 novel, *The Man in the Gray Flannel Suit,* as a metaphor for the work-obsessed, emotionally absent Old Fathers of the period. Similarly, William Whyte's important 1956 study, *The Organization Man,* has come to serve as a retroactive coda for a generation of fathers who placed loyalty to the corporation above loyalty to the family.

Yet these contemporary images deform the actual themes of these books. Family commitment is a core value of *The Man in the Gray Flannel Suit.* For example, in a moment of epiphany, Tom Rath, the novel's hero, refuses a work request from his boss. When he is old, Tom explains, he wants to be able to remember that he spent his time "with my family, the way it should have been spent."[31] As David Riesman put it in 1958:

> In a number of business novels, of which *The Man in the Gray Flannel Suit* is representative, it is taken for granted that a sensible fellow, and indeed an honest one, will prefer suburban domesticity and a quiet niche to ulcerous competition for large business stakes, despite the view from the top and the interesting climb.[32]

Much of *The Organization Man* is actually a critique of this turn toward familism among 1950s fathers. For example, Whyte brilliantly describes the child-centeredness of the new suburbs: "It is the children who set the basic design," since "what unites [residents] most are the concerns of parenthood."[33] But Whyte explicitly criticizes this trend. For him, the familistic norms of these new fathers reflects what he believes to be a decline of the Protestant ethic and thus an overall weakening of the American male character.

Indeed, Whyte specifically criticizes the fictional character of Tom Rath as an archetypal Organization Man, a "true product of his times" who "want[s] to work hard, but not too hard," so that he can have "plenty of time with the kids."[34] In the end, *The Organization Man* is less a description of 1950s Old Fathers than an indictment of 1950s New Fathers.

In David Riesman's famous phrase, the fathers of this period were less "inner-directed" and increasingly "other-directed": empathic, cooperative, responsive to the wishes of others. Riesman and other leading observers of the 1950s agrees that, despite the era's strong endorsement of maternal domesticity, male and female roles in the 1950s were less diverging than converging.[35] More than any previous generation, husbands of the 1950s believed in, and acted upon, the ideals of companionate marriage. A review of the parents' advice literature of the 1950s clearly shows that these values—emotional closeness, participation, physical affection—made up the culturally celebrated hallmarks of the 1950s father-child relationship.[36]

In their own time, these postwar "new" fathers won considerable praise from the family experts. After World War II, wrote Margaret Mead in 1959, "something did happen to men as fathers. The G.I.'s came home to be the best fathers—from the standpoint of their young children—that any civilized society has ever known."

This "new kind of fatherhood," Mead observed, because of its focus on fathers as caregivers for young children, "is a very extreme contrast to anything we have known before."[37]

In 1955, in a fascinating paper on "A Century of Declining Paternal Authority," J. M. Mogey defines this newly regnant ideal of fatherhood as one in which the father is "an active, sharing helper":

> The direction of the change is clearly toward the greater participation of the man in all the tasks of the household. Paternal authority of the jural type . . . is gone. In its place there has been a tendency to recognize the equalitarian family based on companionship.

To Mogey, this "newer father behavior" means nothing less than "the reintegration of fathers" into families. In light of this change, Mogey seeks to explain the two major family trends of the era: the declining divorce rate and the rising birthrate. His reason for both: the New Father. Thus: "A change in the position of the husband from a rigorous insistence on responsibility with a concomitant of social distance to a more active participation in domestic routines helps to explain these new developments." In short, "family stability" in the postwar era "rests upon a new base, the redefinition of the father role."[38]

The point is clear. Regarding the importance of involved fatherhood and paternal affection, the New Father of the 1990s is less a repudiation of 1950s fatherhood than an elaboration of it. Yes, the evidence clearly shows that many married fathers today are more closely involved with their children—more emotionally accessible, more demonstrably affectionate, more versed in the daily routines of child care, less punitive—than their own fathers were with them. But this trend in paternity reflects historical continuity, not discontinuity: less a sharp break with the past than the intensification of a long-term trend.[39]

On a more fundamental level, our contemporary celebration of involved fatherhood represents the re-creation and reiteration, for this generation of fathers, of a very old story: the need to bind men to the lives of their children, to constrain male tendencies toward detachment and instrumentalism, and to temper paternal authority with paternal tenderness.

This story is vital for men. Cultural scripts seldom importune mothers to bond with their children. Maternal tenderness is assumed, not recommended. Paternal tenderness, precisely because it is more problematic, is urged, demanded, insisted on. In this sense, our periodic cultural declarations of "new" fatherhood may serve an important purpose. Perhaps, in order to become good enough, each generation of fathers needs to discover a "new" fatherhood, even if it is less than new, just as they need to compare themselves favorably, if perhaps unfairly, both to their own biological fathers and to a forbidding cultural Old Father.

Here is the best of today's New Father message. Paternal tenderness is good. Yet over the past two decades, as this venerable message has been absorbed into the larger model of the contemporary New Father, the message has been stripped of its context and integrity. As a result, the old ideal of paternal tenderness has been transmogrified into a radical negation of fatherhood itself.

Fatherless Breadwinning

To illustrate this negation, consider the matter of breadwinning. Surely, one of the more significant social inventions in human history is the set of practices, largely inhering in the idea of fatherhood, whereby men voluntarily give money and other material resources to wives and children. In our public discourse, we typically refrain from describing this practice in gendered terms, but this father-to-other transfer nevertheless remains a key organizing principle of our economy and society. Indeed, it would be almost impossible to overstate its historical importance in all societies as a determinant of child and maternal well-being.

In my interviews with married fathers, I sought, above all, answers to this core question: What is a good father today? Sitting with groups of ten or twelve, I would turn to my easel, get out a Magic Marker, and make a list. We pushed and probed: What does it take to be a "good family man" today? In every group, the word that ended up at or near the top of the list—a primary, assumed denominator of good fatherhood—was *provider*. Interestingly, men with employed wives offered this answer just as unambiguously as did men with wives outside the paid labor force.

These 1990s fathers, even as they affirmed the satisfactions of involved fatherhood, were virtually unanimous in this conviction: To be the primary breadwinner of the family is a bedrock responsibility of the good family man. In these interviews, this belief was not debated, or even elaborated. It was stated plainly, without either self-congratulation or self-pity, as an unremarkable fact of family life.[40]

Paternal breadwinning is rooted in economics, of course, but it also extends well beyond economics. Consider the case of Xavier McDaniel, a basketball star with the Boston Celtics. In 1993, a reporter asked him how he had acquired his unusual competitive intensity. McDaniel talked about his father, who

> worked two jobs—one loading and unloading trucks for a food service company, the other as a janitor at the University of South Carolina—in order to support six kids. "Some days our family didn't even see our dad," he said. "I saw him in a situation where he didn't give up, so why should I give up?"[41]

Consider his words closely. Some days he "didn't even see" his dad. Yet he "saw him" in a certain situation. Not to be overly grand about it— McDaniel would claim no expertise as a philologist—but in these comments, McDaniel is proffering a philosophy about what it means to "see" a father.

He "sees" his father even when his father is away from home, out of sight, working two jobs. He sees what his father does in the world, and why, and for whom, and at what price. Indeed, this special way of seeing his father has shaped McDaniel's entire life, including his capacity to travel from the wrong side of the tracks in Columbia, South Carolina, to success as a professional athlete. Thus, McDaniel is not simply saying that he is grateful for his father's economic support, though clearly he is grateful. More fundamentally, McDaniel is insisting that his father, as he worked those two jobs, was being a good father.

Yes, those two jobs kept James McDaniel away from his children for much of the time, working for a boss, doing physical labor that offered little intrinsic satisfaction or chance for personal growth. During those hours, he was unavailable to his children, unable to be a hands-on nurturer, unable to be emotionally close.

But while James McDaniel was away from home, loading trucks and cleaning floors, he was not simply a working father. He was also working at being a father. Indeed, as his son now sees it, James McDaniel's work at those two jobs constituted the father's essential, irreplaceable gift to the son. James McDaniel was a breadwinner who gave his son more than bread. He was a work-driven father who, from a distance, wearing work clothes, shaped the character of his son. In the deepest meaning of the word, James McDaniel was a provider.

In short, Xavier McDaniel sees fatherhood in his father's work. His insight captures a crucial dimension of fatherhood: the problematic irony of proximity through distance. ("Some days we didn't see him. I saw him.") Compared to mothers, fathers tend to do more of their family work on the periphery, indirectly, away from the emotional center, sometimes out of sight. Compared to motherhood, fatherhood is much more strongly mediated by the demands of work and by the exigencies, as politically incorrect as this may sound, of male competition.[42] Herein lies the key to understanding what social scientists call the breadwinner role.

For studies repeatedly demonstrate that men, much more than women, tend to view breadwinning as part of parenthood, not as an obstacle to it. Robert Zussman studied married men employed as engineers at two New England corporations. For these middle-class fathers, he finds, "there is a rather easy harmony between the demands of work and the demands of family." To them, "work and family are part of a single whole. Work and family are not competing. . . . Rather, the engineers meet what they see as the obligations of husbandhood and fatherhood precisely by meeting their obligations as employees." Zussman himself does not applaud this way of thinking. He worries that this "conception of the 'good provider'" may make these men "strangers in their own homes."[43] Indeed, virtually no scholars who study this issue like what they find.[44] But Zussman tells us what these fathers believe.

Robert S. Weiss reports similar findings. In his study of occupationally successful middle-class fathers, he found that such men view marriage as "a partnership of equals, albeit one in which the man is the partner ultimately responsible for the provision of income and for the family's protection."[45] Weiss also found, as I did in my interviews, that fathers hold this view irrespective of whether their wives work outside the home and irrespective of whether their employed wives are holding jobs or pursuing careers.[46]

Numerous other studies confirm this distinctively paternal understanding of how work relates to family commitment. Fathers consistently view breadwinning and parenthood as overlapping domains. Just as consistently, mothers view them as conflicting domains. Even scholars who clearly wish these people would change their minds do not dispute the persistence of these divergent, gendered conceptions of parental obligation.[47] Teresa M. Cooney and Peter Uhlenberg, in their study of highly educated parents, found that "gender differences in the connection between work and family experiences remained substantial. . . . Marriage and parenting continue to be positively associated with work involvement and rewards for men, but are related to persistent employment disadvantages for women."[48] And in her study of employed wives, Jean L. Potuchek concludes: "Attitude surveys consistently show that both men and women attribute a greater responsibility for family support to men than to women."[49]

A recent survey of 21,000 Canadian workers similarly concludes: "female parents report significantly more work-family conflict than male parents."[50] For example, the survey asked workers whether, and why, they had ever considered quitting their jobs. The answers, presented in the accompanying chart, are revealing. The most frequently cited reason for fathers was that they were unhappy in the job. For mothers, by far the most important reason was that they did not have enough time with their children.

Reasons for Considering Quitting a Job

	Mothers	Fathers
	(Percentage)	
Not enough time with children	40.9	9.2
Unhappy in my job	20.1	27.7

Source: From Linda Duxbury, Christopher Higgins, and Catherine Lee, "Work-Family Conflict," Transition 23, no. 2 (June 1993): 12.

Similarly, Harriet Presser has surveyed employed married parents of preschool children who work nonstandard hours, such as night shifts and split shifts. When asked why they did it, by far the most frequently cited reason for fathers was "requirement of the job." For mothers, the most frequently cited reason was "better child-care arrangements."[51]

These studies reveal a core failure of the New Father idea. As a cultural model, the New Father's plea to American men on the subject of breadwinning could not be clearer. Lay down your tools. Consult your soul. This is not your special obligation.

The New Father does not seek merely to qualify or relativize paternal breadwinning but to discredit it. The New Father model bluntly warns men: Breadwinning erodes fatherhood. It constrains human potentiality. Thus, to the exact degree that a father adheres to the old "breadwinner role," he robs his children, undermines gender equality, and represses his own spirit.

A *Parents* magazine Father's Day feature on "The New Father" celebrates those fathers "who put fatherhood before work," recognize that "the workplace may be the staunchest enemy of the involved father," and use "their own fathers as models of what *not* to do."[52] *Child* magazine concurs: "The 'good provider' role is still what both mothers and fathers see as the primary factor limiting men's at-home involvement."[53] In *50-50 Parenting*, Gayle Kimball defines good fathers as those who "focus less on work and put less premium on work success," since "traditional breadwinners" typically "distance themselves from their feelings" and thus engage in "dehumanized behavior."[54]

The counselor and author Herb Goldberg worries that men are "in harness," psychologically choked, by "the breadwinner bind."[55] The writer Christopher P. Anderson puts it plainly: "Father's conventional role as provider is unquestionably the reason that he is regarded as an outsider not only by members of his own family but also by experts who have long since dismissed the possibility of his making any significant personal contribution to family life."[56]

Anderson is right about the views of the experts. In 1981, the influential sociologist Jessie Bernard offered a seminal critique of "the good-provider role" for fathers. For Bernard, this paternal role "delineated relationships within a marriage and family in a way that added to the legal, religious, and other advantages that men had over women." Because of it, the "wife of a more successful provider became for all intents and purposes a parasite, with little to do except indulge or pamper herself." The good-provider role hurt fathers as well, primarily by placing "constraints on emotional expression by men." As a result, male resentment of the good-provider role is "serious, bone-deep." Many fathers are "disillusioned with their jobs" and eager to "protest the repudiation of expressivity prescribed in male roles." Bernard wonders if men will shift toward a new fatherhood: "Will men find the apron shameful? What if we were to ask fathers to alternate with mothers in being in the home when youngsters come home from school?"[57] Each of these themes is now ubiquitous in our cultural celebration of the New Father.

The first idea is that male breadwinning burdens mothers. To the historian Robert L. Griswold, the "linkage between fatherhood and breadwinning" has "justified men's limited commitment to child care" and thus been "part and parcel of male dominance."[58] Similarly, to Kathleen Gerson, the "myth" that "breadwinning is a traditional or natural pattern" among men is threatening to mothers, since it undermines "equal parenting" and serves as "justification for male control over women and children."[59]

Moreover, male breadwinning burdens mothers by restricting men emotionally, thus crippling them as husbands. As one currently popular text-book insists: "traditional men are often confused about their spouses' expectations of intimacy; they believe they are good husbands simply because they are good providers."[60]

At the same time, male breadwinning burdens fathers. As Elaine Tyler May put it in her critique of 1950s paternal breadwinning:

> The potential tragedy in this situation was that in spite of widespread prosperity, the provider role was a heavy burden, and not all men could be successful at it. Nor was the status of family breadwinner always adequate compensation for an otherwise monotonous or dissatisfying job.[61]

Finally, male breadwinning burdens children. In *Fathers and Families,* Henry B. Biller asks why a father typically has "little impact on a direct personal level in his child's life." His answer: "The influence the typical father does feel in the family is all too often based primarily on his ability to provide financially for his children."[62] Writing in *Family Relations,* Ralph LaRossa agrees that "the man-as-breadwinner model of fatherhood" erects harmful "structural barriers to men's involvement with their children." For LaRossa, the solution is to "alter the institutional fabric of American society" through extended paternity leaves, flextime jobs for fathers, and a cultural commitment to revising downward the "level of achievement in market work expected of men."[63] Anna Coote, Harriet Harman, and Patricia Hewitt summarize this point succinctly: "the traditional emphasis on men as breadwinners" has "effectively exiled them from their children."[64]

This theme—breadwinning thwarts fatherhood; doing the former means not doing the latter—brings the idea of male breadwinning full circle. James McDaniel stretched himself to work two jobs in the belief that doing so would, among other things, make him a good father. Mark Gerzon, in *A Choice of Heroes,* makes the exact opposite claim: "No matter how I stretched myself, I could not be a father *and* a breadwinner."[65]

The influence of this message surely helps to explain our contemporary cultural obsession with stay-at-home Dads, Daddy trackers, and fathers on paternity leave. Seen demographically, as a proportion of all fathers, these men are quite scarce. But seen culturally, as an elite image of the New Father, they are ubiquitous.

"I was invited here this morning because I am a father on paternity leave," explained a New York television producer to the U.S. House Select Committee on Children, Youth, and Families. He described "my tenure as 'Mr. Mom'" for his five-month-old daughter: "I am her full-time baby-sitter and bath giver, entertainer and audience, diaper changer and dance partner, not to mention chief cook, and, yes, bottle washer."[66] In the same spirit, the *Chicago Tribune* featured a story on "A real 'Mr. Mom'": a sportswriter who became an at-home Dad and, among other things, wrote a book about it, *From Deadlines to Diapers.*[67]

Asked why more fathers of infants do not stay at home or take paternity leave—one study found that, while some 31 percent of employed men are eligible for paternity leave, only about 1 percent of them take it—Joseph H. Pleck of the Wellesley Center for Research on Women explains to the *Washington Post:* "The attitude is actually out there—yes, fathers should be involved. But there is also the attitude out there that fathers should not reduce their commitment to the job, never forget that their primary responsibility is to earn an income."[68]

This attitude, it seems, is not good. Even worse, complains William Pollack of Harvard Medical School, some men assume that "as new fathers, they should elevate their income or career status." Such negative paternal tendencies, warns James A. Levine of the Families and Work Institute, can "protect and reinforce traditional roles—no matter how enlightened or progressive or rational or aware the couple is."[69]

What, then, is a progressive, rational New Father to do? He must change his behavior. He must work less. The New Father must also change his mind. He must embrace a new philosophy of employment. The bad old idea for fathers is that work and family are overlapping domains. The good new idea is that work and family are conflicting domains. Consequently, the core task of the New Father is to abandon the view of employment typically held by fathers and embrace the view of employment typically held by mothers.

To try to perform two roles that directly conflict can, and generally does, produce what sociologists term "role strain." Employed mothers of young children frequently experience this form of stress. Indeed, this maternal stress helps explain why mothers typically display a more negative, or at least a more ambivalent, attitude toward paid employment than fathers do, resulting in their decidedly more sporadic, contingent commitment to work outside the home. For example, among married couples with preschool children in 1991, 77 percent of all fathers were employed full-time, year-round, while only 28 percent of all mothers were employed full-time, year-round.[70]

Yet this typically maternal ambivalence and stress about employment are exactly what the New Father model prescribes for men. The New Father's plea is: role strain for me, too. The scholarly literature is clear on this point. In *The Myth of Masculinity,* Joseph H. Pleck urges us to reject the divergent, gendered perspectives on paid employment widely reported by real-world mothers and fathers. Instead, he urges this "proposition" for fathers seeking an "alternative paradigm": "Each sex experiences sex role strain in its paid work and family roles."[71] As Leigh A. Leslie, Elaine A. Anderson, and Meredith P. Branson put it in the *Journal of Family Issues:*

"women [who were studied] experienced more strain in the parental role than did men. . . . A true indication of shared parental roles may be an equalization of the parental strain men and women experience as they take responsibility for their children."[72]

From role complementariness to role strain. From work/family synergy to work/family conflict, or what is frequently called work/family "juggling." From a gendered understanding of a father's work to a genderless conception of a parent's work. These are the premises of the New Father at work.

Such ideas are compelling. But they are inadequate. Consider the matter of child well-being. With each passing year in our society, fewer and fewer children benefit from the economic provision of their fathers. The growing number of children in poverty, the tightening link between family poverty and fatherlessness, our national frustration at our seeming inability to squeeze even meager child-support payments out of an ever-expanding army of "deadbeat dads"—these are only the most obvious signs that child well-being in our society is now directly endangered by a mass refusal of fathers to provide economically for their children. Fathers have apparently grown weary of feeding others.

In these circumstances, there is something odd, even perverse, about importuning fathers to disconnect breadwinning from fatherhood. At a time when paternal provision is declining in our society, at great cost to children, along comes the New Father model to implore men to cease to view breadwinning as a father's special task. Lighten up. Think about yourself. The breadwinning role, after all, may be a sucker's game, something to feel resentful about. Or, even worse, it may be a bully's game, something to feel guilty about—an activity that makes you not more of a father but less of one.

Perhaps this message contains virtues. But surely it will do nothing to motivate fathers to provide for their children. It offers no reason to praise fathers who provide for their children, no reason to blame fathers who do not. This message does nothing to remedy, or even recognize, the declining economic security of children due to the loss of paternal provision. This message may even harm children by disparaging the idea and thus reducing the incidence of paternal breadwinning.

Look around. If the New Father strategy hopes to ungender breadwinning by detaching it from fatherhood, then its proponents should be well pleased. The strategy is working. Disrespect for paternal provision. Less paternal provision. The result, however, is the weakening of fatherhood as a social role and the growing material impoverishment of large numbers of children.

More fundamentally, the New Father philosophy of breadwinning is antithetical to the basic psychosocial dynamic of fatherhood. The onset of the "parental emergency" requires a dual mobilization. The mother mobilizes to nurture the child. The father mobilizes to nurture the mother and provide for his family. By explicitly opposing this mobilization, the New Father model frustrates this classic redirection of male narcissism toward meeting the needs of the newborn child.

Does the ideal of paternal breadwinning burden mothers? In some instances, of course, yes. Surely some mothers today want to hold a job, or devote more hours to a career, only to find themselves thwarted by domineering husbands who brandish their "breadwinner roles" as weapons against their wives' desires. However, I have not met many such mothers. Indeed, survey data and interviews with parents demonstrate that this phenomenon, so central to the New Father rationale, is now relatively rare in our society.[73]

What is common, on the other hand, is mothers who suffer from economic insecurity, even poverty, due to the loss of paternal breadwinning. The popular phrase "feminization of poverty" properly underscores the fact that poverty in the United States is increasingly concentrated among female-headed households.

But the feminization of poverty stems largely, in Michael Novak's phrase, from the masculinization of irresponsibility: the refusal of fathers to provide economically for their children. For this reason, many poor mothers in our society would not resent being burdened by a little more male breadwinning. At least for these mothers, the New Father's assault on the ideal of paternal breadwinning cannot be seen as either liberating news or a harbinger of less burdened times to come.

Moreover, for every married mother in our society who wishes to work outside the home, or work longer hours outside the home, only to be opposed by her husband, there are many more who wish to reduce or eliminate their commitment to paid employment, only to be opposed by their husbands. I am unaware of scientific data measuring this issue with precision. But interviews with married parents suggest that what frequently burdens young mothers today is not the ideal of paternal provision, but rather the erosion of that ideal.

Heidi Brennen is a co-director of Mothers at Home, a volunteer-run national support group for mothers. She summarizes the type of letter that she often receives from new members:

> I am on maternity leave from a good job. I have a six-month-old baby. We could afford to live on his salary, but my husband is pressuring me to return to work. He thinks it is a waste of time for me to stay home because we could afford decent day care and get ahead financially with my income. It is hard for him to understand how I feel or what I do all day—he can't really see the results in the way that I do. How do other mothers handle this?

In her talks and correspondence with new mothers on this subject, Brennen, a mother of four young children, has arrived at this view:

> Now, when I hear a mother sigh that she would like to be at home but that they can't afford it, and I know that her husband's income is possible to live on, I begin to wonder if there isn't this tension going on between them. I especially question it when I hear the husband rave about the child-care arrangements while the wife remains silent. . . . It seems that many of today's fathers no longer have any pride in, and willingness to accept responsibility for, breadwinning. . . . We have received letters from women [at home] who say that their husbands are sometimes mocked at work for "having a wife that lives off them." Today it seems that men are congratulated for finding a high- or consistently income-earning wife.[74]

A generation ago, a man might brag to other men: "I would never let my wife work." But today, it seems, due in part to the New Father idea, a much more typical boast might be: "I would never let my wife not work." Both views, of course, veer toward a form of sexism and male coercion. But only one—the New Father view of who should win bread and why—repudiates the notion that fathers have a special, unequal obligation to provide for their families.

Does paternal breadwinning burden men? In some ways, of course, yes. A man who embraces the New Father philosophy of employment does indeed unburden himself. He frees himself up to make more choices, perhaps to express more emotions, certainly to discover himself apart from externally defined "roles." Certainly there is much to commend in this aspiration. Freedom is good. Especially in America, freedom is hard to argue against. But in this case, let me try.

For in liberating fathers from the breadwinner role, the New Father model also seeks to liberate fathers from widely held norms of masculinity. At the same time, our elite cultural script notwithstanding, most men in our society simply do not wish to be liberated from their masculinity. This viewpoint is a key to understanding their unprogressive, lopsided commitment to the provider role.

Paternal attachment to breadwinning is neither arbitrary nor anachronistic. Historically and currently, the breadwinner role matches quite well with core aspects of masculine identity. Especially compared to other parental activities, breadwinning is objective, rule-oriented, and easily measurable. It is an instrumental, goal-driven activity in which success derives, at least in part, from aggression. Most important, the provider role permits men to serve their families through competition with other men.[75] In this sense, the ideal of paternal breadwinning encultures male aggression by directing it toward a prosocial purpose.

For these reasons, the breadwinner role has always been, and remains, a basic cultural device for integrating masculinity into familism—the clearest, simplest means for men to act out their obligations to their children. Faced with these stubborn facts, our society can respond in one of two ways. We can, through the New Father model, continue to assault male breadwinning in a root-and-branch attempt to reinvent men and deconstruct traditional masculinity. Or we can endeavor, however imperfectly, to incorporate men as they are into family life, in part by giving them distinctive, gendered roles that reflect, rather than reject, inherited masculine norms—such as, for example, the breadwinner role.

The New Father model does not merely unburden men of breadwinning as a special obligation. Ultimately, it unburdens them of fatherhood itself. For, as the example of breadwinning demonstrates, the essence of the New Father model is a repudiation of gendered social roles. But fatherhood, by definition, is a gendered social role. To ungender fatherhood—to deny males any gender-based role in family life—is to deny fatherhood as a social activity. What remains may be New. But there is no more Father.

Why Can't a Man Be More Like a Woman?

Ultimately, the ideal of androgynous fatherhood—fatherhood without the masculinity—emerges as the animating principle of the contemporary New Father model. Michael Lamb roots his advocacy of the New Father model in the basic premise that "very little about the gender of the parent seems to be distinctly important. The characteristics of the father as a parent rather than the characteristics of the father as a man appear to influence child development."[76] Similarly, Andrew M. Greeley urges society to administer a "dose of androgyny" to men. We should "insist that men become more like women."[77]

This view is widely shared among the experts. In *Fathers and Families,* Henry B. Biller urges basic changes in gender identity for fathers. They must become more sensitive, less rigid, much more flexible. They must "broaden their personal identities." They must avoid "rigid conceptions of masculinity." They must "defuse gender stereotypes." They must "overcome some entrenched misconceptions about fatherhood." Only if they implement these identity changes will they be able to "equitably share child-rearing responsibilities."[78]

Diane Ehrensaft agrees. In *Parenting Together,* she asks: "Can a man and woman mother together?" Her basic answer is, Yes, if they try very hard. Her book investigates "co-ed mothering," or "men and women who have embarked on the project of 'mothering' their children jointly."[79]

For her study, Ehrensaft interviewed forty fathers dedicated to "equal parenting" or "co-ed mothering." Her conclusions about these fathers are remarkable. "Central to their own childrearing philosophy," she finds, "was a disavowal of gender expectations." Why? Because these men, above all, "did not feel comfortable with the male culture they grew up in or had to live in now." These fathers, she finds, "grimace about maleness." She reports: "If being male meant fathering as their fathers had done, they wanted nothing of it. They would instead be 'mothering' men." As a result of this view of paternity, "the fathers in this sample did not express the desire for a same-sex child; there was not the same longing to re-create the self." Thus, "many of the fathers wished for a girl so as to avoid having a boy."[80] Ehrensaft strongly endorses this model of fatherhood.

Her approving portrayal of fathers who hope not to have sons is revealing, since it highlights a larger ethos that is impossible to ignore in so much of the contemporary literature on fatherhood: the ethos of malevolence toward men. Some of this malevolence is implicit; much of it is overt and perfervid.

Consider, in this regard, both the Old Father and the New Father. In the case of the Old Father—the fathers of those who are writing—the malevolence toward men is direct. They are the victimizers, the rapists, the oppressors. In the case of the New Father—either the writers as they see themselves or the desired partners of the writers—the animus toward men is more indirect. New Fathers are the last, best hope for rerigging men. In both cases, males are clearly defined as the problem to be overcome. The solution desired by Ehrensaft's new fathers—do not conceive male offspring—is extreme, but consistent with this larger ethos and the overall perception of the problem.

Closely related to the desire to avoid male offspring is the desire to remove masculine traits from male offspring. In one case, the goal is to eliminate the problem of maleness by avoiding the birth of males. In the other, the goal is to minimize the problem of maleness by transforming the sexual identity of male children.

Consequently, a prominent theme throughout the New Father literature is the urgent need to resocialize boys. As Letty Cottin Pogrebin succinctly puts it: "Childhood is where fatherhood must be changed."[81] The logic is simple: Rewire masculinity by rewiring little boys. The New Child is parent of the New Father. This logic informs a cascade of New Father recommendations. Mandate child-rearing classes for boys in the schools. Replace their toys. Rewrite their books.[82] Offer them nontraditional role models. Teach them that aggression is bad, gentleness is good. Discourage competitive sports. Discourage hunting. Discourage traditional gender roles. Teach them how to change. Teach them how to transcend masculinity.[83]

A third revealing aspect of the New Father ethos is the tolerant and even celebratory view of mother-headed homes embraced by many proponents of the New Father model. One might expect these fatherhood advocates to worry about, perhaps even criticize, the steady growth of fatherless homes in our society. But most do not. Many of the strongest advocates of the New Father model are also the strongest defenders of the viability of single-parent homes. Dorothy Dinnerstein of Rutgers University succinctly summarizes this viewpoint:

> we should be less concerned about the growing number of single-parent households in our society—as long as they can provide the child with an involved parenting figure of the missing sex—and more concerned about our many "traditional" families which dump all the child-rearing responsibilities on the mother.[84]

Let's see, now. Single-parent homes are just fine, thank you. But we desperately need the New Father model. What unites these two seemingly contradictory ideas in the head of one person? It is the belief that there is nothing special about a father, that there are no fundamental tasks in family life that are properly and necessarily his work. In short, what unites these two ideas is the belief that fatherhood is superfluous.

If fathers are superfluous, fatherless homes do not alarm us. And if fathers are superfluous, the main project for men in two-parent homes is to prevent things from being "dumped" on women, primarily by mimicking femininity and overcoming masculinity. In one instance, the final result is a fatherless home. No big deal. In the other, the final result is an extra set of hands via genderless paternity. Much to be desired.

At bottom, the New Father idea presupposes the larger thesis that fatherhood is superfluous. In this respect, the New Father is indistinguishable from the Unnecessary Father. In our current cultural discourse, the two are usually understood as opposites: one good, one bad. But in this larger sense, they are interchangeable characters in a single cultural narrative. Whether we look at the New Father or the Unnecessary Father, the underlying theme is the same: the irrelevance of fatherhood as a distinct male activity.

For this reason, undergirding the entire New Father model is the imperative of gender role convergence. The essence of this imperative is the removal of socially defined male and female roles from family life. Such roles should be replaced by two ideas. The first is the moral importance of personal choice—the belief that choosing freely among family behaviors is not simply a possible means to something good but is itself something good.[85]

The second is an ideal of human development based on a rejection of gendered values—especially those associated with traditional masculinity—and an embrace of gender-neutral human values. In part, the imperative of role convergence simply urges the reduction or elimination of sex specialization within the family. But in a larger sense, the imperative warns that any notion of socially defined roles for human beings constitutes an oppressive and socially unnecessary restriction on the full emergence of human potentiality.

Benjamin Spock, who has probably had more influence on American parents than any other person in this century, substantially revised his famous book, *Baby and Child Care,* in 1985 to incorporate this imperative of gender role convergence. Women, he tells us in the updated version,

> in trying to liberate themselves, have realized that men, too, are victims of sexist assumptions—sexual stereotyping. . . . When individuals feel obliged to conform to a conventional male or female sex stereotype, they are all cramped to a degree, depending on how much each has to deny and suppress his or her natural inclinations.[86]

More poetically but in exactly this vein, Mark Gerzon celebrates the new cultural narrative of family life:

> Couples may write their own scripts, construct their own plots, with unprecedented freedom. Whether the encounter is between strangers on a bus, colleagues in a meeting, or lovers in bed, a man and a woman are free to find the fullest range of possibilities. Neither needs to act in certain ways because of preordained cross-sexual codes of conduct.[87]

This is a vision, ultimately, of freedom. In many ways, it is a bracing, exhilarating vision, bravely contemptuous of boundaries and inherited limitations, distinctly American in its radical insistence on self-created identity. It draws upon the American myth, the nation's founding ideals; it echoes much of what is best in the American character. It is the vision of Whitman in his "Song of the Open Road":

> *From this hour I ordain myself loos'd of limits and imaginary lines,*
> *Going where I list, my own master total and absolute.*[88]

There is so much to commend in this vision. It is the reigning ethos of much of contemporary American culture. But as a social ethic for fatherhood, I dispute it.

I dispute it because it demands the obliteration of precisely those cultural boundaries, limitations, and behavioral norms that valorize paternal altruism and therefore favor the well-being of the human infant. I dispute it because it denies the necessity, and even repudiates the existence, of fathers' work: irreplaceable work in behalf of family that is essentially and primarily the work of fathers. I dispute it because it tells an untrue story of what a good man is, and of what a good marriage is.[89] In addition, I dispute it because it rests upon a narcissistic and ultimately self-defeating conception of male happiness and human completion. Thus it cannot be, at bottom, the vision of the good father. It is finally the vision of Huckleberry Finn, the boy who ran away from society, and of Peter Pan, the boy who would never grow up.[90]

Fundamentally, the New Father's imperative of role convergence is based on the sexual equivalent of what some political scientists term the "end of history."[91] Politically, the end of history refers to the ending of the historical contest between communism and capitalism, between the two political ideologies whose struggle, now over, shaped the politics of the modern era. The struggle is over because one side won everything. The losing side not only lost but now seeks to emulate the victor. Thus, in world political terms, consensus replaces conflict; sameness replaces difference; universalism replaces particularism.

Sexually, the end of history would refer to the ending of any historically inherited and socially important differences between males and females. Unlike past sexual history, which was based on differences and complementarities, the end of sexual history would denote the fundamental social irrelevance of sexual roles—a new fusion of previously divided components of humanity.

Moreover, the end of sexual history also suggests the end of a tension or struggle. As in the political analogue, the struggle ends because, at least within the home, one side wins everything. The losing side not only loses but also seeks to emulate the winning side. Sexually, the losing side is aggression, instrumentalism, competition, toughness, and other historically masculine norms. The winning side is nurture, cooperation, empathy, and other historically feminine norms. Accordingly, in the realm of domestic life—in public life, the trend is the same but the other side wins—the historical tensions rooted in sexual complementarities are replaced by a new consensus rooted in sexual universalities. Independence replaces dependency. Sameness replaces difference. Particularisms evaporate into the whole. History ends.

I will leave it to others to debate the end of political history. But I decline to accept the end of sexual history, either as an empirical fact or as a utopian goal.

For as David Gutmann and Alice Rossi remind us, the sexual division of labor within the family is a common trait in human societies, occurring across history and cultures, precisely because it is integral to the survival and reproduction of the society. The parental emergency requires—indeed, is defined by—the adoption of gendered parental roles. The human child does not know or care about some disembodied abstraction called "parent." What it needs is a mother and a father who will work together, in overlapping but different ways, in its behalf.

The sexual division of labor is not, at bottom, the result of social conditioning or cultural values. Nor does it have anything to do with fostering the desire for omnipotentiality that is present in all humans. As Gutmann pointedly insists: "the parental transformation is not aimed at forging the adult self but is instead aimed at bringing about the psychological formation, the selfhood, of the offspring."[92] Ultimately, the division of parental labor is the consequence of our biological embodiment as sexual beings and of the inherent requirements of effective parenthood.

These basic facts have not disappeared and will not disappear. History continues. Moreover, the necessity and irreplaceability of a father's work have not disappeared and will not disappear. In service to the child and to the social good, fathers do certain things that other people, including mothers, do not do as often, as naturally, or as well. When fathers do not do this work—as is increasingly the case in our society—child and societal well-being decline.

Historically, the good father protects his family, provides for its material needs, devotes himself to the education of his children, and represents his family's interests in the larger world. This work is necessarily rooted in a repertoire of inherited male values: historically and socially mediated understandings of what it means to be a good father. These values are not limited to toughness, competition, instrumentalism, and aggression—but they certainly include them. These "hard" male values have changed and will continue to change. But they will not disappear or turn into their opposites. Nor should we wish them to.

Finally, I dispute the New Father's imperative of gender role convergence because I do not credit its promise of greater human happiness. The desire for omnipotentiality—including the wish to be both sexes at once—is part of the human condition. Indeed, Lawrence Kubie calls this infantile desire "one of the deepest tendencies in human nature."[93] But as a governing ideal of human completion, androgyny and gender role convergence reflect the ultimate triumph of radical individualism as a philosophy of life.

Indeed, androgyny constitutes the most radical conception of expressive individualism that a society can imagine. It is the belief, quite simply, that human completion is a solo act. It is the insistence that the pathway to human happiness lies in transcending the old polarities of sexual embodiment in order for each individual man and woman to embrace and express all of human potentiality within his or her self. No longer, in this view, do we accept otherness as a biosocial fact. Instead, we appropriate otherness into the self. No longer would a man alone consider himself in some way to be incomplete. The fractured moieties of male and female, child and adult, reside together as part of the omnipotentiality of the individual man. Now each man, within the cell of himself, can be complete.

This idea, so deeply a part of our culture, is fool's gold. It is a denial of sexual complementarity and ultimately a denial of generativity—particularly male generativity, which is, much more than the female's, largely a social construction. Especially for men, this particular promise of happiness is a cruel hoax. Like all forms of narcissism, its final product is not fulfillment but emptiness. If fatherhood has anything to say to men, it is that human completion is not a solo act.

CHAPTER 7

The Deadbeat Dad

The Deadbeat Dad is a bad guy. He is morally culpable. He is a criminal, he belongs in jail. He is the reigning villain of our contemporary fatherhood script. His visage, framed by a Wanted poster, makes the cover of *Newsweek:* "Deadbeat Dads: Wanted for Failure to Pay Child Support."[1] At the Child Guidance Center in Akron, Ohio, a little girl writes this imaginary letter to her dad:

> Dear Dad,
>   I wish you the worst Father's Day ever. And if you don't pay, you don't get love. Oh yeah, by the way, my mom makes less money than you. . . . I hate you.[2]

The Deadbeat Dad is a bad guy because he refuses to pay. Of course, he has also abandoned his children and the mother of his children. Yet in contemporary cultural terms, that character trait is secondary. The main issue is not abandonment. The main issue is payment. Accordingly, the main societal imperative, as Senator Daniel Patrick Moynihan succinctly puts it, is to "make the daddies pay."[3]

If we cannot enforce good fatherhood, the script goes, we ought to enforce child-support payments. Besides, for children, money is the true bottom line. Testifying before the U.S. House Select Committee on Children, Youth, and Families, Andrew J. Cherlin of Johns Hopkins University concludes that "the major problem the children have in a single-parent family is not the lack of a male image, but rather the lack of a male income."[4]

In our cultural model of the Deadbeat Dad, the core issue is money absence, not father absence. This belief is widely shared among the experts. In July 1993, for example, the Census Bureau reported a 60 percent increase in out-of-wedlock childbearing since 1982. To the *New York Times* editorial board, the deeper meaning of this trend was clear: "As the number of unwed mothers grows, so does the number of deadbeat dads." Accordingly, our society's principal response to unwed childbearing must be "a more vigorous effort to track down fathers who refuse to pay support."[5]

Meet the Deadbeat Dad of the 1990s: the last traditional breadwinner in the experts' story of fatherhood. For him only, fatherhood is measured in dollars. For the New Father, of course, that old breadwinner role is a thing of the past. But for the Deadbeat Dad, the breadwinner role is alive and well: the one role that society demands that he play, even as he resists. For the New Father, breadwinning thwarts fatherhood. For the Deadbeat Dad, breadwinning defines fatherhood.

In several respects, the Deadbeat Dad and the New Father are opposites. One is the best, the other is the worst. One lives with his child, the other does not. One repudiates the traditional male role, the other is a caricature of the traditional male role: absent, but expected to pay.

Yet underneath these differences, the Deadbeat Dad and the New Father share this fundamental trait: as cultural models, both derive from the idea that fatherhood is superfluous. The essence of the New Father model is the erasure of fatherhood as a gendered social role for men—fatherhood reduced to genderless parenting skills. The essence of the Deadbeat Dad model is that absent fathers can be fathers by writing checks—fatherhood reduced to the size of a wallet. Neither model incorporates fatherhood as a distinctive social role. Both models view men as problems to be overcome. At bottom, both models presuppose an increasingly fatherless society.

In this sense, the Deadbeat Dad is less a new departure than a variation on a theme. In cultural terms, he is the next-door neighbor of both the New Father and the Unnecessary Father. Despite the differences, these three guys all recognize one another. Here is the basis of their mutual recognition: None of them, as men and fathers, is an irreplaceable caregiver for his children. Indeed, here is the most concise definition of the Deadbeat Dad: the Unnecessary Father who refuses to pay.

The Bad Understudy

The Unnecessary Father, the Old Father, and the New Father are the three leading characters of our contemporary fatherhood script. They are the stars. They get most of the attention.

The Unnecessary Father is a star because he is the chorus. He comments on every scene, he explains all the action. Both the Old Father and New Father are biological fathers. Moreover, both live with their children and thus can perform the daily tasks of fatherhood. In short, they qualify as leading characters in the script largely because both of them combine biological fatherhood with social fatherhood.

The remaining five characters in the script do not meet this threshold test. They are the fatherhood understudies. They are either biological but not social fathers, or social but not biological fathers. They are almost-fathers, sort-of fathers. The three biological fathers—the Deadbeat Dad, the Visiting Father, and the Sperm Father—do not live with their children and thus cannot care for them on a routine, daily basis. The Stepfather lives with children, but not his children. The Nearby Guy—the boyfriend, the friend—is not a biological father and he may or may not live with children, though he increasingly finds himself playing what passes for a fatherly social role.

Accordingly, each of these understudy roles represents the growing disembodiment and dispersal of fatherhood in our society. Each embodies the splitting apart of fatherhood from father. More specifically, as cultural models, each of these fathers has lost, or failed to attain, the core prerequisites of good-enough fatherhood. The evidence is overwhelming: To be a good-enough father, a man must reside with his child and sustain a parental alliance with the mother of his child. In cultural terms, these five minor fatherhood roles are understudies, almost-fathers, precisely because their fatherhood is unsupported by these twin foundations.

At the same time, however, all five of these roles are growing in social importance. They characterize increasing proportions of men. With each passing year, these understudy fathers become more present, more vital, in the lives of children. In this sense, they are becoming the fathers in our increasingly fatherless society.

Of these five understudies, the Deadbeat Dad role is by far the thinnest, the most widely known, and the most vilified. It is a small role for bad men. It is a specialty role, defined by minimal expectations and severely limited possibilities. To date, it is not even a speaking role. The point is not to say something but rather to do something: pay. Finally, our culture's view of this role is governed by an assumption of bad faith. As a phrase of speech, a "Deadbeat Dad" is our society's only popular label for parents that is overtly pejorative.

No other family behavior, and no other family policy issue, has generated such an urgent societal consensus on what is to be done. Extracting payments from Deadbeat Dads is now a regnant priority in our society, uniting liberals and conservatives, Republicans and Democrats, elite opinion and popular sentiment. In the 1992 presidential campaign, for example, applause lines about Deadbeat Dads emerged in the stump speeches of both George Bush and Bill Clinton, constituting arguably the only issue in the campaign on which they publicly agreed.

The Deadbeat Dad is also increasingly visible in the popular culture. He is the subject of popular books, magazine features, and made-for-television movies.[6] Even the *National Enquirer,* ever alert to its social responsibilities, has launched a Deadbeat Dad series—"Help find the cruel louse who deserted his four children"—which enlists the participation of readers in "hunting down and capturing some of the most wanted deadbeat dads in America."[7]

The Deadbeat Dad has emerged as our principal cultural model for ex-fathers, for obviously failed fathers. As a cultural category, the Deadbeat Dad has become our primary symbol of the growing failure of fatherhood in our society. We demonize him in part because he reminds us of our fatherlessness. He represents loss. He forces us to reduce our expectations. Consequently, we vilify him, we threaten him—we demand that he pay—largely because he so clearly embodies the contemporary collapse of good-enough fatherhood.

Yet the content of our demand illustrates both the depth of our pessimism and the lowering of our standards. We do not ask this guy to be a father. That would be utopian, impossible. We ask him to send a check. Instead of demanding what is owed, we demand money.

We respond to the Deadbeat Dad by denying and pretending. If only we could get tough with these guys, that would fix what is broken. Get them to pay. That would help the children. That would relieve the taxpayer. Here, finally, is a family policy we can all agree on.

But this strategy is a fantasy. It is based not on evidence but on wishful thinking. To date, the strategy of tracking down Deadbeat Dads has failed even on its own terms: It has not improved the economic well-being of the typical fatherless child. Yet the real failure runs far deeper. From the child's perspective, child-support payments, even if fully paid, do not replace a father's economic provision. More fundamentally, they do not replace a father.

Our current Deadbeat Dad strategy fails even to acknowledge our society's spreading crisis of family fragmentation and declining child well-being. For what is broken in our society is not the proper police procedures to compel small child-support payments from reluctant men. What is broken is fatherhood.

Andrew Cherlin, then, muddles the issue completely. First, he imagines that, in the home, "a male income" and "a male image" are two separate things. Fundamentally, they are not. Consequently, his preference for the former over the latter is all but meaningless. But let us imagine, with Cherlin, that the two could be separated. He still gets the issue backward. The "major problem" in fatherless homes is not "the lack of a male income" (though that certainly is a problem). The major problem is "the lack of a male image"—that is, the lack of a father. To pretend otherwise is simply to pretend that money is important, but fathers are not.

Ultimately, the solution to the growing problem of Deadbeat Dads is not jail cells, Most Wanted posters, job-training programs, interstate computer networks, or IRS agents. At best, these are Band-Aids on an infected wound. At worst, they are a form of denial—a self-defeating strategy intended to excuse our drift toward fatherlessness. The only solution to the problem of Deadbeat Dads is fatherhood.

Follow the Money

How much does the Deadbeat Dad owe? How much can we force him to pay? The essential questions are mathematical, not sociological. Let us calculate the answers.

Prior to the 1970s, requiring and enforcing child-support payments from absent fathers was almost exclusively a local matter. Compared to today, caseloads were much smaller, comprising mostly instances of divorce or paternal abandonment. Operating under broad guidelines set by state statute, local judges typically exercised considerable authority and discretion in both awarding payments and monitoring compliance.[8]

By the early 1970s, however, an emerging demographic earthquake was beginning to command the attention of federal policy makers. The initial sign was the growth of federal welfare expenditures, as rapidly growing caseloads began to increase the scale and cost of Aid to Families with Dependent Children (AFDC), the federal government's major assistance program for poor mothers and their children.[9] More important, AFDC was enacted in 1935 primarily to aid widows and orphans; yet by the 1970s mothers receiving welfare were much less likely to be widows and much more likely to be divorced or, even more likely, never to have married.[10]

As a result, with remarkable speed and little debate, the government's basic social contract was redefined by the new demographics of fatherlessness. The federal government was no longer primarily aiding the mothers of children whose fathers had died. Now the government was primarily aiding the mothers of children whose fathers had left them. Moreover, what was true of the AFDC caseload was also true of the larger society. These fathers were not dead. They were just gone. And with each passing year, more of them were gone.

The explosion of father absence in the 1960s and 1970s was essentially voluntary—not the result of acts of God or of fate, but the result of human decisions, of choices. Between 1960 and 1980, the proportion of children in the United States living apart from their fathers nearly doubled, from 17.5 percent to 32.2 percent. During this same period, moreover, the proportion of father-absent children living with widows dropped sharply, while the proportion living with divorced or never-married mothers rose dramatically (see tables 1.2 and 1.3). Consider, for example, the case of black children. According to William Julius Wilson and Kathryn N. Neckerman, the "number of black children growing up in fatherless families increased by 41 percent between 1970 and 1980, and most of this growth occurred in families in which the mother had never been married."[11]

Policy makers thus confronted a simultaneous growth and transformation of fatherlessness. This recognition led directly to the creation during the 1970s and 1980s, for the first time in our nation's history, of a large federal and state bureaucracy devoted to enforcing private child-support payments from absent fathers. No longer would child-support issues remain local, while the federal government assisted widows and orphans. Now these two domains of public concern—public assistance for poor mothers and the volitional absence of fathers—had become inextricably linked. These fathers could be found and made to pay.[12]

Moreover, these new men were becoming a mass phenomenon, a new social type—not just among the poor but across society. They could be studied and counted. And counted on. The issue was fairness. These men were wrongly forcing other people to support their children. They obviously were reluctant to pay, but just as obviously, they could and should pay. But the new men required a name. How about, well, deadbeat dads?

In 1975, the U.S. Congress began to federalize the issue of child support by passing the Child Support Enforcement Amendments and establishing a federal Office of Child Support Enforcement. Irwin Garfinkel describes this legislation as "the federal government's first step toward paying for and overseeing enforcement of private child support."[13] In 1979, the U.S. Census Bureau first began to collect national data on child-support payments.

Congress passed additional child-support legislation in 1984, containing three basic goals: to establish more uniform standards for the size of child-support awards, to require states to withhold wages from absent fathers who owed child support, and to increase the proportion of legally identified absent fathers—the essential first step toward collecting child support. In the 1988 Family Support Act, the Congress went much further, establishing stricter guidelines in each of these three areas and devoting more federal and state resources to paternity identification and to monitoring and enforcing child-support payments.[14]

The phrase "deadbeat dad" first began to appear in the media in the early 1980s. By the late 1980s, it had become a staple of our cultural and public policy discourse on fatherhood.[15]

Today, child-support enforcement remains a major priority for U.S. social policy. The federal-state child-support program has become a large and growing public bureaucracy, employing, as of 1992, about 230 federal officials and some 38,000 state officials. In recent years, virtually all states have launched new efforts to identify nonresident fathers and to collect more child-support payments. In 1990, state-level expenditures on these efforts totaled approximately $1.6 billion.[16]

These massive and expanding programs constitute our society's central response—indeed, virtually our only response—to the rapid rise of volitional father absence. In our current cultural story, the main problem in fatherless homes is, as Cherlin put it, "the lack of a male income." To date, our only solution is tracking down Deadbeat Dads.

Let us examine the results of this approach. Tables 7.1 and 7.2 tell the central story. They present data detailing both the changing dimensions of the problem and the effectiveness of our strategy for solving it.[17] The tables compare two moments in time, separated by eleven years. The first is 1978–79, shortly after Congress began to federalize the issue of child-support enforcement and the first period for which national data are available. The second is 1989–90, the most recent year for which data are available. Analysis of these data yield three basic conclusions.

1. *In only eleven years, the problem itself grew radically larger and more intractable.*

In 1990, fathers were absent in 27.5 percent of all homes with mothers and children, up from 21.6 percent in 1979. Approximately 10 million

TABLE 7.1
Mothers Living with Children Whose Fathers Are Absent
(*in millions*)

	1979	1990
Mothers living with children under age 21	32.8	36.2
Mothers living with children under age 21 whose fathers are absent	7.094 (21.6%)	9.955 (27.5%)
Mothers living with children under age 21 whose fathers are absent	7.094 (100%)	9.955 (100%)
divorced	2.390 (34%)	3.056 (31%)
never married	1.374 (19%)	2.950 (30%)
remarried	2.006 (28%)	2.531 (25%)
separated	1.257 (18%)	1.352 (14%)

TABLE 7.2
Child-Support Payment from Absent Fathers

	1978	1989
Percent of mothers living with father-absent children who are supposed to receive payments	48.3% (3.424 million)	49.8% (4.953 million)
Received full payment	48.9%	51.4%
Received partial payment	22.8%	23.8%
Received no payment	28.3%	24.8%
Mean payments received by all women who received payments (1989 dollars)	$3,305	$2,995
Mean payments received by all divorced women who received payments	$3,584	$3,322
Mean payments received by all never-married women who received payments	$1,793	$1,888
Mean payments received by all women with four or more children who received payments	$5,056	$3,226
Mean payments received by all women who were supposed to receive payments	$2,370	$2,252
Percent of aggregate due actually received	64.3%	68.7%

Tables 7.1 and 7.2 Sources: Gordon H. Lester, "Child Support and Alimony: 1989," Bureau of the Census, Current Population Reports, series P-60, no. 173 (Washington, D.C.: Government Printing Office, September 1991), pp. 3–4, 9. The numbers of mothers living with children under age 21 for 1979 and 1989 are derived from the Bureau of the Census, Current Population Reports, series P-20, no. 352 (March 1979) and no. 447 (December 1990). In 1979, there were 30.5 million married-mother and mother-only homes in the U.S. with children under age 18, and a (Census Bureau estimated) 35.1 million such homes with children under age 21. For 1990, the figures were 33.3 million and 39.1 million, respectively. My estimates for the numbers of these households in 1979 and 1989 with children under age 21—the relevant age for measuring child-support payments—come from halving the difference from these two sets of numbers.

homes in 1990 consisted of mothers living with children whose fathers were absent.

Moreover, apart from the overall increase in fatherlessness, the underlying demographics of father absence—the salient characteristics of the pool of fatherless families—shifted dramatically during these years. As a proportion of all fatherless homes, three of the four categories of father absence declined during this period. Thus divorce, remarriage, and separation each account for a currently declining proportion of all father-absent homes.

But fatherlessness due to nonmarriage has skyrocketed. Unwed parenthood accounted for 19 percent of all fatherless homes in 1979. Eleven years later, it accounted for 30 percent. Unwed parenthood has thus become, by far, the nation's fastest-growing family structure trend and the primary engine of the current growth of father absence in our society.

Moreover, there are no signs that this trend is slowing down. Indeed, the most recent available data from the Census Bureau and the National Center for Health Statistics suggest quite the opposite. By 1992, nonmarital childbearing had reached virtual parity with divorce as a social generator of female-headed homes.[18] Sometime during the mid-1990s, if current trends continue, the total number of father-absent homes created by unwed childbearing will surpass the number created by divorce. In this respect, unwed parenthood will soon become the nation's principal cause of fatherlessness.[19]

This demographic shift profoundly alters the meaning of the Deadbeat Dad as a cultural category. Close your eyes and picture a Deadbeat Dad, circa 1960 or even 1970. The image that will likely come to mind is one of a married guy who has deserted his wife and children.[20] A guy who has wronged his family. A guy who has broken his promise, run away from his responsibilities. A guy who has moved out of the house he once lived in, and where his wife and children still live.

Now picture a Deadbeat Dad, circa 1995. He is much more likely to be a guy like the one who fathered Sam, the little boy whose mother, Anne Lamott, wrote a best-seller about her experiences as an unmarried mother. For "a while," she tells us, Sam's father "was my friend."[21] Later, she elaborates:

> I had known this guy, in the Biblical sense, for three months. We did not have a romantic relationship as such. For instance, I did not sit around singing "Let it please be him" whenever the phone rang. And we certainly did not expect to have a future together.[22]

This type of father is the wave of the future. He is the new-style absent father, the emerging Deadbeat Dad of the 1990s. He may have once lived with the mother and child. Or maybe not. Maybe he never had to move out because he had never moved in. Maybe he was just around, nearby.

Maybe he had, or hoped to have, a serious relationship with the mother. Or maybe not. Maybe the mother included him in her thinking about conceiving and bearing a child. Or maybe not. Maybe he never even learned about the child. Maybe the mother still wishes he would come around, spend time in the home, try to be a father to the child. Or maybe not. This guy may be the last person on earth she would want to see, or would want her child to see.

Either way, there have never been any chains on this guy. Nothing formal, nothing legal. Nothing to tie him down. No promises, no piece of paper, no big commitments.

Except one. Every month for at least the next eighteen years, we tell him, he is supposed to give a child-support payment to the mother. If he does not, he is a Deadbeat Dad. He is a criminal. If he does not, we need to track him down. Give him a blood test. Get tough with this guy. Make him pay.[23]

What is wrong with this story? What is wrong is that, in the case of the Deadbeat Dad, our current cultural script wants it both ways. On the one hand, as Frank Mott puts it, fathers are "not that important." For children and for society, fatherhood is nonessential. Consequently, we should refrain from becoming alarmed as increasing numbers of women want children, but not husbands. Or as increasing numbers of men father children without any intent to live with them, or to raise them, or to marry the mothers.

On the other hand, there is a fixed ethical and legal rule: The minimum requirement for every biological father in the United States is eighteen years of regular child-support payments.[24] Do anything else you want, we don't mind. Don't get married if you don't want to. The same goes for the mother. The only rule is that the guy should make those payments. We do not care about the "male image." But we are serious about the "male income."

To put it mildly, the two sides of this story are incompatible. To put it a bit more sharply, the entire story is morally unserious. Half of it is based on denial. (Fathers are not that important.) The other half is based on wishful thinking. (Make the fathers pay.)

We should make up our minds. If we expect these new men to be fathers, we should start telling them so. If we do not, we should admit it and stop kidding ourselves. For there is no such thing as the male income that can be systematically detached from the male image, any more than there is some shard of fatherhood called child support that we can preserve, like a tiny dried flower, while we consciously throw the rest of fatherhood away.

If, as a cultural proposition, we insist on child support, we must also insist on fatherhood. But to require the former while deconstructing the latter is to insult logic and reduce our cultural discourse on fatherhood to the level of parody.

Not surprisingly, then, child-support payments from absent fathers to never-married mothers are, in practical terms, virtually meaningless. For example, while 77 percent of divorced mothers in 1989 were awarded child-support payments, only 24 percent of never-married mothers received an award.[25] As Jay D. Teachman and Kathleen Paasch conclude: "Perhaps the most important factor in determining whether an award is made is marital status—the effects of which remain after socioeconomic and legal characteristics are controlled."[26] Moreover, within the minority of never-married mothers who actually received any payment in 1989, the mean payment per mother was only $1,888—far lower than the payment received by any other group of eligible mothers.

Payments from never-married fathers are negligible because they derive from a negligible foundation of fatherhood. Ultimately, meaningful child-support payments will come only from men who see themselves as fathers. For, despite our cultural script's unusual insistence in this instance on strategies of coercion and vilification—calling them deadbeats, circulating Wanted posters aimed at humiliating them—the evidence clearly shows that the nature of child-support payments depends primarily upon the nature of the father-child bond. Typically, a stronger relationship equals more payments.

In short, the more fatherhood, the more money. But the current trend within today's growing pool of absent fathers is exactly the opposite: less fatherhood, less money. The new-style absent fathers of the 1990s are much less likely to pay child support precisely because they are much less likely even to attempt to act as fathers toward their children.[27]

For example, according to Census Bureau data, about 78 percent of all absent fathers in 1990 who had visitation privileges with their children were also obligated to specific child-support payment schedules.[28] Again, more visits, more payments. Yet, while 67 percent of all divorced fathers had visitation privileges in 1990, only 33 percent of all the new-style absent fathers—those who had never married the mother—had visitation privileges.[29] More tellingly, of those 33 percent with visitation privileges, about 73 percent did not visit their children even once during 1989.[30]

Similarly, Judith A. Seltzer's study of absent fathers reports "striking differences in levels of paternal involvement for children born in and outside of marriage." Among absent fathers, she concludes, those "whose children were born outside of marriage are less involved with their children on all dimensions—paying support, visiting, and decision-making—than those whose children were born in marriage."[31]

Consequently, many of these new men do not consider themselves to be Deadbeat Dads at all. Their reasoning may be sad, but at least it is consistent. They do not think of themselves as deadbeats precisely because they do not think of themselves as dads. These guys never signed on to anything. They never agreed to play by any fatherhood code. They do not have—they have never had—any explicit obligations to either their children or to the mothers of their children. By what reasonable principle do they owe anybody anything?

Moreover, the mothers of their children increasingly affirm this same view of fatherhood. Many of the mothers simply do not want these guys around. And if the price tag for this peace of mind is, say, $1,888 in potentially obtainable child-support payments, then so be it. For example, compared to divorced mothers, never-married mothers, when asked by the Census Bureau why they receive no child-support payments, are more likely to say "did not pursue an award" or "did not want an award."[32] Why bother? For these mothers, the father did not leave. He was never there in the first place. As a result, he is an improbable source, indeed, for child-support payments, just as he is an improbable source for fatherhood.

In sum, from 1978–79 to 1989–90, the social phenomenon of Deadbeat Dads changed fundamentally. The change was twofold. First, the problem grew much bigger. Second, the problem grew much more intractable, as nonmarriage reached parity with divorce as a generator of contemporary fatherlessness. Unwed fathers are rapidly becoming the typical Deadbeat Dads of our era, the emerging absent fathers of an increasingly fatherless society.

2. Since 1978, a continually intensifying national campaign against Deadbeat Dads has failed to produce any net improvement in the economic well-being of the typical father-absent child.

Since the late 1970s, two theses have come to dominate our periodic attempts to assess our progress in tracking down Deadbeat Dads. The first is that our efforts are paying off. We still have much to do, but there is reason for optimism: With each passing year, we collect more money from these guys. Getting tough works. The second thesis is that some new, tougher step—soon to be mandatory across the nation—will succeed in extracting more payments from Deadbeat Dads. We have not yet gotten tough enough, but we will soon. The check will be in the mail tomorrow.

Consider, for example, several typical assessments from 1987–88, during congressional debate over the Family Support Act. As the *Christian Science Monitor* put it in 1987: "During the 1980s American society—and its government—has put more emphasis on forcing absent fathers to pay child support. As a result child support payments to the mothers have been rising steadily."[33] The next year, the *Monitor* was more specific: "Since 1984, the Child Support Enforcement Program (a partnership of local, state, and federal governments) has nearly doubled the amount of court-ordered child support it collects each year, recovering $3.9 billion in 1987."[34]

"Child-support collections continue to increase each year. From 1984 through 1987, collections increased approximately 70 percent," reported Ann Schreiber of the U.S. Office of Child Support Enforcement in 1988.[35] According to *Governing* magazine that year, "research continues to show that dollars put toward child support enforcement—particularly toward early establishment of paternity—can reap large harvests in saved welfare costs."[36]

The following year, after the passage of the Family Support Act, the *Washington Post* reported that the federal-state child support enforcement program "collected $4.6 billion in fiscal 1988, a huge jump over the past few years." Congressman Thomas J. Downey told the *Post*: "The good news is that the program seems to have improved since the mid-1980s." At the same time, the *Post* continues, "Downey said improvements can be expected as states implement changes in the program authorized by [the Family Support Act]."[37]

Five years later, in 1994, the Office of Child Support Enforcement reported the same good news: "In FY 1992, State support collections reached a high of $7,964,522,000, an increase of almost 15.7 percent over the prior year and 73 percent over the total of 5 years ago."[38]

Indeed, this notion among policy makers and opinion leaders that we are now successfully cracking down on Deadbeat Dads may be the single most widely shared and celebrated idea in today's family policy debate. But this idea suffers from one flaw. It is not true.

Repeated claims that "the program seems to have improved" are based largely on a statistical mirage, unrelated to the economic well-being of specific children. The mirage has two components. First, as the problem grows, the total caseload increases. As a result, the total number of dollars collected can increase substantially without producing any increase at all in the dollars collected per child.

Second, and more important, child-support cases are now less and less likely to be handled by local courts and more likely to be handled by state and federal bureaucracies. As with the expansion of the caseload, this transfer means that state and federal agencies can collect "more" child support without producing any real gains for the typical father-absent child.[39]

As a result of this phenomenon, most of the publicly disseminated data on child-support enforcement obscure more than they reveal. They help us to deny rather than understand. They permit the state of, say, Virginia to issue regular press releases boasting of huge increases in child-support collections. Meanwhile, from the perspective of a typical fatherless child in Roanoke or Falls Church, nothing much has changed.

Examine the data from Tables 7.1 and 7.2. Child-support payments from absent fathers in 1989, after eleven years of intensive efforts to improve collections, were virtually unchanged from those in 1978. For example, the proportion of single mothers who were supposed to receive payments—as well as the proportion who actually received payments—was basically the same in 1989 as it had been eleven years earlier. Similarly, the mean payments received by all women who were supposed to receive money remained essentially stagnant during this period. In fact, according to several key indicators, we are doing a worse job of collecting child support today than we were in 1978. For example, among mothers who received support, mean payments per mother actually declined slightly in real terms from 1978 to 1989. So did mean payments per divorced mother. Mean payments per mother with at least four children declined sharply.

Not only did payments received decline, but so did payments due. In 1978, the mean payment owed per mother was $3,680. By 1989, it had dropped to $3,293.[40] Indeed, the reason for the improvement in the total child-support collection rate during this period—from 64.3 percent in 1978 to 68.7 percent in 1989—is not a happy one. The collection rate improved only because mean payments due decreased more rapidly than mean payments received.[41]

Overall, here is the best that can be said about our national child-support enforcement program from 1978 to 1989: During a time when the problem of absent fathers grew far larger and more ungovernable, the program did succeed in preventing a large decline in per-child support payments. In this respect, our continually escalating efforts did keep us roughly even with the continually escalating scale of the problem. In other words, our best exertions were enough to keep things from getting much worse, much faster—faint praise, indeed, for a gamble on which we have bet the entire farm.

3. *Even when awarded and paid, child support typically reflects the loss, rather than the continuation, of a father's economic provision.*

In 1989, among the minority of mothers living with father-absent children who were supposed to receive child-support payments, the mean payment received was $2,252. Similarly, among all mothers who actually received payments, the mean payment was $2,995. Among divorced mothers who actually received payments, the mean payment was $3,322. In real terms, these figures are roughly equivalent to those from 1978.

From these data, we may reasonably derive a generalization. Among all mothers in 1989 who either did receive or should have received child-support payments, the mean total of the payment in question was somewhat less than $3,000. To simplify, call it $3,000 in child support per participating family.

Here, then, are the actual dollar stakes of child-support enforcement in the United States: Under optimal conditions, the typical mother may expect to receive about $3,000 per year from the absent father.

According to quite conservative estimates from the U.S. Department of Agriculture, the direct annual expenditures on a single three-to-five-year-old child in a two-parent middle-income family during 1990 totaled approximately $8,000. For two children under age seventeen, expenditures totaled about $14,000, and for three children, about $17,000.[42]

These are no-frills budgets. No summer camps, no special vacations, no savings plans, no extras. Some health care costs, such as childbirth and prenatal care, are not included. The costs of current or future college educations are not included. No costs of children over the age of seventeen are included. No indirect costs are included, for example, the costs of taking time off from work to care for children or of adjusting or reducing work hours to fit children's needs.[43]

Compare these baseline costs of child rearing to the income data presented in Table 7.3. In 1990, the median income for married couples with at least one child under age eighteen was $41,260. For female-headed households with at least one child, the median income was $13,092. To simplify, let us say that a man working full-time in 1990 earned about $30,000 and that a woman working full-time earned about $20,000.

These numbers tell us that a married father in 1990 typically contributed about $30,000 to what we might term a family fund. (Note that $30,000 not only roughly equals the median male wage but is also roughly equivalent to the income gap between married-couple households with children and female-headed households with children.)

For lack of a better term, call this guy the $30,000 father. Of course, not all of the $30,000 went to his children. Certainly, some of it was spent on

TABLE 7.3
Median Incomes in 1990

Married couples with children	$41,260
Female-headed families with children	$13,092
Married males working full-time	$31,714
Males working full-time	$29,172
Females working full-time	$20,586

Source: "Money Income of Households, Families, and Persons in the United States: 1990," Bureau of the Census, Current Population Reports, Consumer Income, series P-60, no. 174 (Washington, D.C.: Government Printing Office, August 1991).

his own personal needs: his hobby, his lunches, his shaving cream. But just as certainly, the great majority of that $30,000 was spent on the creation and maintenance of what might be called a common family residence.

Begin with direct expenditures on children—in 1990, about $8,000 for one young child and $14,000 for two children. His $30,000 can cover those expenses. But from his children's perspective, the actual child-raising purchasing power of that $30,000 certainly surpasses the sum of these direct expenses. For this $30,000 father is not simply doling out some carefully circumscribed payments. He is helping to create a home for a family. He is not a contributor. He is a participant. There is no "them." There is just "us."

The house he lives in also houses the other members of his family. The food he puts in the refrigerator, the garbage can he takes out at night, the Christmas tree he decorates, the TV he watches, the car he drives, the insurance he buys, the vacation he plans for—all these ways of spending that $30,000 contribute directly to the economic well-being not just of him as an individual but also, and probably primarily, to the economic well-being of his spouse and children.

If he puts some of that $30,000 in a savings account, those savings will ultimately benefit not just him but also his children. If he gets a raise at work—up to, say, $32,500 —that extra $2,500 may be frittered away in poker games, of course, but typically most of that raise will go directly, without any court order requiring it, toward improving the economic well-being of the entire family. If a sudden crisis strikes—for example, if a child becomes seriously ill—the entire $30,000 is likely to be mobilized, as much as possible, in response to the crisis.

Moreover, the $30,000 father typically does not cease to contribute to the family fund at some specified moment. In most states, for example, child-support payments are usually no longer required after children reach age eighteen. But the $30,000 father is quite likely to help pay for college educations for his over-age-eighteen children. Just as frequently, he will help his over-age-eighteen children purchase a first used car or rent a first apartment. Perhaps his children will continue to live in the home after age eighteen, or will return home after being on their own for a while, in the aftermath of a lost job or an ended marriage. In all these instances, this guy's contributions are likely to continue uninterrupted.

In sum, this father typically makes all, or almost all, of that $30,000 available to his family's common fund and to the common family residence. He does so not because the sheriff makes him, but because he wants to. His attitude is not, How little can I do? but, How much can I do?

Compare this $30,000 father to a reformed Deadbeat Dad—a guy who now sends in his child-support payments on a regular, or fairly regular, basis. Call this guy the $3,000 father. (As we have seen, $3,000 is the approximate mean payment received by mothers who received or should have received child-support payments in 1989.)

This guy's $3,000 represents about 10 percent of the median male wage. Viewed differently, this $3,000 represents slightly less than 40 percent of the yearly estimated direct costs of raising a single three-to-five-year-old child. In the case of two children, the $3,000 represents about 20 percent of direct yearly costs.

Consequently, even if the absent father pays his $3,000 in child support, the single mother must still come up with about $5,000, or more than 60 percent of all direct expenses, for her one young child. In the case of two children, she must provide about $11,000, or almost 80 percent of all direct expenses. If she cannot afford to do so—recall that her 1990 median family income was about $13,000—she must do what millions of mothers in her position do. She and her children must do with less. She must lower their living standards. She and her children must leave the broad middle class and accept the reality of economic vulnerability.

Now, if this father earning $30,000 is paying only $3,000 to support his children, where is the rest of that money going? The simplest answer is that it is not going to a common family fund or a common family residence for his children. It is going to a separate fund and a separate residence.

The house he lives in does not house his children. The food he puts in the refrigerator, the garbage can he takes out at night, the Christmas tree he decorates, the TV he watches, the car he drives, the insurance he buys, the vacation he plans for—none of these ways of spending that $27,000 contributes directly to the economic well-being of his children.

Put another way, for the $30,000 father, the child-support ceiling—the most he can be reasonably expected to do—is somewhere near $30,000. For the $3,000 father, the very structure of his situation means that his child-support ceiling is exactly $3,000. For this $3,000 father, then, the basic idea is not, How much can I do? Especially if he marries another woman and has new children to support—or even if he moves to another state, or loses his job, or gets sick, or perhaps simply takes up an expensive hobby—he will be inclined to seek to pay less, not more. He is no longer a participant. He is a funder, a taxpayer. He no longer gives his income to his family; instead, he gives child-support payments to a mother. As a result, $27,000 of his $30,000 is simply no longer available for the creation of a home for his children.[44]

Of course, if the $3,000 from the absent father is not available to the mother—if the guy misses a payment or decides to become a Deadbeat Dad again—she and her family will suffer a further decline in living standards. But either way, the $3,000 in child support does not even begin to match the value of the economic provision of a typical married father. In blunt economic terms, the $3,000 father is worth about 10 percent as much to his children as the $30,000 father. Here we see the difference, in the economic sphere, between child support and fatherhood.

Falling Down

In contemporary cultural terms, the Deadbeat Dad problem is essentially a monetary problem. Yet despite the ubiquity of this theme in today's discourse, the deepest tragedy of the Deadbeat Dad as a cultural model has nothing to do with money. Forget the fact that our intensive national campaign to extract more money from these guys is, according to most measurements, simply not working. Forget the fact that even a reformed Deadbeat Dad—one who never misses a child-support payment—is doing precious little of what a father does to provide financially for his family.

The deepest tragedy of the Deadbeat Dad is not the loss of money. It is the loss of fatherhood. Today's cultural script notwithstanding, the loss of money, for children and for the society, is trivial compared to the loss of fathers. Consequently, to comprehend the true societal meaning of the Deadbeat Dad, we must not simply follow the money. We must also follow the men.

Consider, for example, the disturbing fact that growing numbers of real-life estranged fathers—including many Deadbeat Dads—are, almost literally, going crazy. As their fatherhood decomposes, or is threatened, they lose self-control. Some pick up guns and start killing people. Typically, the people they kill are children, ex-spouses, and government officials who seem to stand between them and their former lives, especially social workers, judges, and child support–enforcement officers. As fatherhood fragments in our society, this species of violence is spreading.

As a result, across the country, a new type of crime story is popping up in newspapers and on local television news. Call it the story of the Killer Ex-Dad. Or, more specifically, in many instances, the story of the Crazed Deadbeat Dad.[45]

A popular 1993 movie, *Falling Down,* perfectly captures this underlying relationship between fragmenting fatherhood and male violence. The movie generated widespread public discussion, including a *Newsweek* cover story. But virtually all the discussion centered on the current politics of race and multiculturalism, especially the threat, as represented by the movie, of "white male backlash" against growing cultural and ethnic diversity.

These themes are certainly present in the film. Bill Foster, played by Michael Douglas, is a crew-cut, middle-class white guy who suddenly loses his grip and erupts into violence. He shoots a young Latino man. He assaults a Korean grocer. During the course of a day, we watch him become progressively unhinged. It's hot outside. His car is stuck in traffic.

Everything has gone wrong for this fellow. Modern urban life, we sense, has driven him crazy. In the end, he tries to kill his wife and daughter. Is this the coming urban dystopia? Is this how white men feel about America? These questions preoccupied the film's reviewers and critics.

But underneath these political themes, this movie is about fatherhood. Or, more precisely, the movie seeks to examine the connection between coherent fatherhood and male sanity. For just like the Captain in August Strindberg's *The Father*, Bill Foster loses his balance—and finally his life—precisely because he loses his fatherhood.

Foster's wife has divorced him. (He was no prize as a husband and father.) She is afraid of him; he has a terrible temper. She has a restraining order to keep him away from his former home and away from their daughter. He does not pay child support. He is a Deadbeat Dad.

The day that Bill Foster falls down—the day that he loses control—is his daughter's birthday. But he cannot attend the party, cannot give his little girl, Adele, a gift. He phones Beth, his ex-wife, to tell her: "I have to come home. I have to bring her a present." She answers: "This isn't your home anymore." Foster: "How is Adele?" Beth: "She's doing just fine without you."

The birthday party he cannot attend is what finally pushes him over the edge. Repeatedly in the movie, when people ask where he is going, he says simply: "I'm going home." When someone praises him as a political reactionary, an urban vigilante, he disagrees: "I'm not a vigilante. I'm just trying to get home to my little girl's birthday."

But he cannot go home, and this fact, above all, is what drives him crazy. Removed from his home, estranged from his child, denied the role of husband and father, his life ceases to make sense. He is lost. He feels castrated, unmanned, unfathered. He lashes out. He becomes a Crazed Deadbeat Dad. He picks up a gun and decides, just like the real-life estranged fathers in the news stories, to murder his ex-wife and child.[46]

Ultimately, then, we misunderstand *Falling Down* if we see Bill Foster primarily in political terms. His story is not simply a scary metaphor for white male backlash. It is not, at bottom, the story of a xenophobe, or a racist, or an armed critic of American liberalism, a sort of embittered Rush Limbaugh with a gun. *Falling Down* is about the violent decomposition of a man's life. The central dynamic of that decomposition is the fracturing of fatherhood.[47]

These are the ultimate stakes in the story of the Deadbeat Dad. The core problem is not that these men are failing to send in their child-support payments. Nor is it simply that child support, even when paid in full, largely deprives children of the economic support of their fathers. These issues are certainly important, but they are merely derivative. They are among the milder symptoms of the disease.

Our prevailing understanding of these guys simply misses the point. For children and for society, the decisive question is not whether men will pay child support but whether men will be fathers. When the answer is no, the social consequences extend far beyond household finances. What are the level and nature of violence in our society? What shapes the character and competence of our children? What is a man? What kind of society are we? When we consider the Deadbeat Dad, these are the real questions.

What is the best strategy for reducing the number of Deadbeat Dads? There are three possibilities. The first approach is to do more of the same. Get tough. If that fails, get tougher. Pass stricter laws. Crack down harder. Squeeze it out of these guys. Maybe there is a breaking point, some yet-to-be-reached level of legal and societal pressure that will finally crack the resistance of these men. Currently, this strategy enjoys overwhelming bipartisan support in Washington, in state legislatures, among policy analysts, and among opinion leaders in the media. Let us call it the "get tougher" strategy.

In Massachusetts in late 1992, Governor William F. Weld proposed new child-support legislation that was praised by advocates as "the toughest in the nation." The proposal would give state officials new powers to pressure Deadbeat Dads by revoking their driver's licenses, revoking their business and professional licenses, garnisheeing insurance reimbursement checks, and jailing them for up to five years for nonpayment. Under this proposal, according to the *New York Times,*

> a broad spectrum of society would be enlisted to help in child-support collection, including hospitals, insurers, employers and state licensing agencies. The Department of Revenue, which oversees child-support collections, would be given the power to subpoena records from telephone companies, utilities and trade groups to track down parents.[48]

In New Jersey in 1993, posters began appearing in train stations and bus stops, on the sides of buses, and in public schools. Next to a photo of a blue-eyed toddler, the caption reads: "It's amazing how many guys disappear when one of these shows up." The poster displays the phone number of the state's new "child support hotline." The Trenton *Times* described the new advertising campaign as "the latest high-profile step" by Governor Jim Florio aimed at "targeting deadbeat dads."[49]

Across the country, states are currently debating and testing a variety of additional "get tougher" techniques. Intercepting tax refunds. Attaching funds from workers' compensation and unemployment compensation. Seizing lottery winnings. Seizing and selling cars and other assets. Revoking hunting and fishing licenses. Suspending teaching certificates. Seizing settlements from civil suits and from class-action lawsuits. Telling credit agencies about Deadbeats. Pressuring unmarried fathers-to-be in hospital waiting and delivery rooms to acknowledge paternity by signing legally binding documents.[50] Making new wives and grandparents responsible for child-support payments. Staging highly publicized police "arrest round-ups" and undercover "sting" operations. Televising the names and photographs of "Most Wanted" local Deadbeat Dads. Establishing interstate computer networks and tracking programs. Requiring some or all employers to report the names of new employees to child-support officials, so that the new hires can be cross-checked against a list of Deadbeats.[51]

Maybe all of this will work. If all goes well, perhaps mean child-support income per participating family could reach, say, $4,000 per year by the end of this decade.

But don't count on it. So far, the problem has continued to grow faster than any of our efforts to solve it. With each passing year, more and more children do not live with their fathers, just as more and more men father children without feeling even the slightest sense of paternal obligation. Apart from wishful thinking, there is little evidence that any of our new-and-improved collection techniques will do much to reverse, or even keep pace with, this core demographic trend.[52]

Consider the case of Wisconsin. Wisconsin does far better than most other states in collecting child support. According to a study by the Children's Defense Fund, for example, Wisconsin's 1990 child support–enforcement rate—the proportion of state-initiated cases in which absent fathers actually pay at least some child support—was about 33 percent, a success rate matched only by Vermont.[53]

Within Wisconsin, consider the case of Racine. As part of a welfare-reform pilot project initiated in 1989 by Governor Tommy Thompson, two counties in Wisconsin have launched an especially intensive, coordinated effort to improve child-support collections. One of those counties is Racine.

Racine's population is about 175,000. By most standards, it is a pleasant, largely middle-class community, relatively unscarred by the worst problems facing urban America. In 1992, Racine initiated 972 actions against child-support noncompliance, occupying the full-time attention of 35 government employees and generating a total of about 350 court hearings each week. The county has acquired a sophisticated computer system to track down absent fathers and monitor payments. Racine can also rely on a strict state law that permits the automatic garnisheeing of wages for child support. Finally, if a man refuses to participate in Racine's child-support program, he can wind up in jail. If the "get tougher" approach can succeed anywhere, it ought to succeed in a state like Wisconsin and a locality like Racine—stable, well-run places that are trying very, very hard to make Deadbeat Dads pay. Yet it is not succeeding.

Two-thirds of the absent fathers comprising Wisconsin's child-support caseload do not pay any child support at all. Moreover, most unmarried fathers never become a part of the state caseload, since most of them are never even identified. Yes, the Racine pilot project has produced some increases in child-support payments from absent fathers whose families are on AFDC. Still, as Joe Klein of *Newsweek* puts it:

> the out-of-wedlock birthrate is soaring and there is a sense of swimming against the tide. The welfare system pays for one of every three births in Wisconsin; a recent study of major welfare hospitals showed that paternity was established in less than 40 percent of the births. Remember, the state collects from only a third of the fathers it can *find:* one-third of two-fifths is, hmm, very depressing—maybe 13 percent of all "welfare fathers" in a state that really works at making the daddies pay.

Even if more of these fathers could be tracked down, Klein reasons, "the hordes of public employees necessary to bring a program like [Racine's] to a city the size of, say, Milwaukee, would be staggering."[54]

Most states, of course, do not do as well as Wisconsin. Nationally, for example, legal paternity is established in fewer than one-third—perhaps as few as one-quarter—of all cases of babies born to unmarried mothers.[55] Overall, the growing pool of absent fathers in our society is increasingly dominated by men who have never felt or experienced much of an obligation to their children. In such circumstances, to seek to increase child-support payments is certainly, even in a place like Racine, to swim against the tide.

The second strategy is to recognize reality and stop trying to make soup from stones. Figure out a better, more workable way to support the children. From different perspectives and at different moments in recent history, two of the nation's leading scholars in this area have come quite close to recommending exactly this strategy.

In 1979, just as the nation was beginning to federalize the problem of child support, David L. Chambers published *Making Fathers Pay,* an influential analysis of contemporary child support–enforcement procedures. Chambers argues against using the threat of jail as a primary means of enforcing child-support orders. Instead, he urges wage withholding—precisely the strategy that policy makers increasingly adopted during the 1980s and early 1990s. However, Chambers is also a realist. Ultimately, he suggests, no enforcement strategy will prevail in counteracting the steady decomposition of fatherhood in our society.

In the future, Chambers speculates, long-term child support from an absent father may become "an anachronism." Even in cases of divorce, he reasons, the best option for society might be to require child support from the father "for only a few years after separation," after which time he "would have no enforceable rights in or duties to the child." Like alimony, child support "might similarly come to be viewed as transitional, with the overt recognition that after some period the noncustodial parent might well cease to have much contact with his children." In short, as fatherhood collapses, the society might simply cease the practice of "fixing for men and women the terms of their relationship well after their lives have settled into other patterns."[56]

In 1992, just as the nation was completing the federalization of the child-support problem, Irwin Garfinkel published *Assuring Child Support*. Garfinkel has clearly influenced many scholars and policy makers, including several members of Congress who developed a major legislative initiative, the "Child Support Enforcement and Assurance Proposal," deriving largely from his recommendations.[57]

Garfinkel's core proposal is twofold. First, he urges us to complete the federalization of child-support enforcement in order to collect more and larger payments from absent fathers. (Get tougher.) But Garfinkel, like Chambers, is also a realist. No matter how tough we get, he suggests, many absent fathers—indeed, currently growing numbers of absent fathers—simply will not support their children. No enforcement strategy, he recognizes, can fully empower us to swim against this demographic tide.

Accordingly, whenever fathers do not pay child support, Garfinkel recommends that the government pay it. In this way, child support is "assured," irrespective of the success or failure of the "get tougher" approach. Call it a Deadbeat Dad insurance program. If the father does not pay, the society will.[58]

The appeal of Garfinkel's idea is clear.[59] Unlike our current approach, a federal assurance of child support would, indeed, guarantee the delivery of more money to fatherless children and their mothers. These families are vulnerable; they need support. The drawback, of course, is equally clear. Garfinkel's proposal would shift much responsibility from fathers to the state. It would effectively subsidize fatherlessness. The "assurance" component of his proposal would provide economic incentives for precisely the behavior—fathers declining to support their children—that the "enforcement" component of his plan seeks to discourage.[60]

As a result, millions of mothers would ultimately come to rely on government, not on fathers, for help in raising their children. In this sense, the proposal would facilitate the further dispersal of fatherhood in our society. Providing for a child would become less the specific responsibility of one father than the general responsibility of the society. For what is "assured" in Garfinkel's plan is not fatherhood, nor even a father's economic provision, but a societal substitution for a father's economic provision.

From differing vantage points, then, both Chambers and Garfinkel urge us to abandon our current strategy of relying solely on a "get tougher" approach to child support. Chambers suggests that we simply cut our losses, getting what we can, but finally permitting these effectively child-free fathers to get on with their new lives. Garfinkel suggests that, as we get tougher, we also establish a guaranteed replacement for paternal provision.

Sure, they both tell us, try hard. Be creative, be tough. Get whatever we can from these guys. But also be realistic. Fatherhood is decaying in our society. A lot of these guys will never pay. Therefore, we must make other plans.

But consider for a moment a third idea—essentially absent from today's debate on child-support enforcement, but worth pondering. That idea is fatherhood. What if this issue is not really about court orders or police procedures at all, but about the meaning of manhood in our society? What if child support finally has almost nothing to do with the male income and almost everything to do with the male image?

Perhaps, as Chambers and Garfinkel suggest, it is ultimately futile for society to insist on this new sort-of father: the $3,000-per-year father who does not live with his children. But instead of lowering our standards, what if we raised them? What if the society insisted on more of the real thing: the $30,000-per-year father who lives with his children? What if the whole idea of "child support," understood as a viable and enforceable way of life for millions of detached men, turns out to be largely a mirage? What if there is simply no sustainable cultural model—no prosocial halfway house—between fatherhood and fatherlessness? What if we have only two choices?

CHAPTER 8

The Visiting Father

The Visiting Father is hard to see. He is a shadow dad, a displaced man trying not to become an ex-father. He is a father who has left the premises. He still stops by, but he does not stay. He is on the outside looking in. No longer the man of the house, he has been largely de-fathered. He is a father once removed. He has become a visitor.

As a visitor, he is part father, part stranger. Physical distance, combined with estrangement from his children's mother, has radically diminished his paternity. Now a weekend and holiday dad, a treat father, a telephone father, he is frequently filled with resentment and remorse. He mourns the loss of his fatherhood much as one would mourn the loss of health.

He loves his children, but he did not stay with them. He wants to be a good father, but in ways that matter most, he cannot be. He cannot raise his children. He can only visit them.

In today's prevailing cultural story, the Visiting Father, unlike the Dead-beat Dad, is not viewed as a bad guy. Certainly, of the three biological understudies in our fatherhood script, the Visiting Father is by far the best father. He is responsible, he tries hard, he cares. He stops by. He makes payments. He does not make trouble. He does not forget birthdays. In this sense, a reformed Deadbeat Dad can aspire to become a Visiting Father.

The cultural category of Visiting Father represents a large and growing number of men. Of the approximately 10 million father-absent homes in 1990, about 55 percent of the fathers had visitation privileges and about 7 percent had joint custody.[1] Another way to gauge visitation is to measure child-support payments, since each of these indicators is an important predictor of the other. As shown in table 7.2, of the approximately 5 million single mothers who were supposed to receive child support in 1990, about 75 percent, or about 3.75 million, re-ceived either some or all of the support that was owed. Another reasonable measure of visitation is residential proximity. In 1990, about 64 percent of absent fathers lived in the same state as their children.[2]

A reasonable estimate, then, is that in the United States in 1990 there were between 4 million and 6 million fathers who did not live with their children, but who visited them on an occasional or a regular basis. Put another way, if we assume 6 million visiting fathers to be a roughly accurate count, there is now one visiting father for every four married fathers in the United States. If current trends continue, of course, this ratio will increase.

What is the prevailing view of the Visiting Father in our contemporary elite discourse? Who is this guy? What does he do? What are the consequences of his actions for children and for society?

Here is the first and most important answer: Our culture simply does not have much to say about this fellow. Indeed, compared to most of the other roles in today's fatherhood script, the Visiting Father seems to play a small, ambiguous part, mostly in the shadow of others. In cultural terms, this father remains largely invisible.

In truth, he does not even have a proper name. Some divorced fathers, especially those active in the fathers' rights movement, vehemently object to the term Visiting Father. More important, while this term is used by many (but certainly not all) scholars who study divorce, it is not a widely used or even well-understood term even among opinion leaders, much less the wider public. Thus, while journalists, television commentators, and policy makers all routinely discuss Deadbeat Dads and New Fathers, the large and growing phenomenon of the Visiting Father almost never commands their attention or excites their curiosity.

Yet visiting fathers now outnumber welfare mothers. They outnumber unemployed men. In 1990, they outnumbered unemployed married fathers by a ratio of up to 7 to 1.[3] They greatly outnumber both the stay-at-home dads and the dads-with-sole-custody who have become staples of our media discourse on family change. They dramatically affect the lives of millions of women and children. Their emergence as a mass male trend has been quite sudden. Historically, they represent a radical departure from all previous models of effective paternity.

Yet how many blue-ribbon commissions have been formed to study this phenomenon? How many congressional committees have held hearings? How many opinion leaders today discuss the meaning of the Visiting Father? Almost none. No one seems to hate these guys. No one seems to worry about them or feel sorry for them. No one seems to pay much attention at all.

What explains this odd lacuna? If the Visiting Father is viewed primarily as a benign version of the Unnecessary Father, then he is nothing new.

He is just another father who does not matter very much. For our society's view of the Visiting Father, like our view of each of the other cultural models of fatherhood, is shaped largely by the belief that fatherhood itself is essentially superfluous.

If fatherhood is superfluous, why be fearful or worried about this Visiting Father? What has he done wrong? What harm can he do? He is responsible. He is not a criminal. He does not offend our sense of propriety or normality. He is not a Deadbeat Dad. He is only a defanged father—a father with no bite left.

Indeed, in light of the alternatives—and especially in light of our society's profound ambivalence about paternal authority—this Visitor Father, this sort-of father, carries distinct advantages. He sends in the payments. He exercises certain limited rights. But he no longer wields authority. He no longer has a key to the house. In short, he is no threat. Whatever success he can salvage from his fatherhood now depends, to a remarkable degree, upon the kindness of his estranged spouse and the forbearance and forgiveness of his abandoned children.

As a result, in a society that no longer deems fatherhood to be essential, the Visiting Father can be viewed, when we bother to view him at all, as essentially harmless, potentially even a mildly positive influence in the life of his children. For what remains of his fatherhood constitutes a kind of fatherhood lite—a modern, stripped-down version of paternity that can well pass for fatherhood in an increasingly unfathered society. The Visiting Father is an Unnecessary Father who pays child support and does not make trouble.

Can Visitors Be Fathers?

Despite our society's increasingly casual acceptance of the idea of the Visiting Father, the reality on the ground, especially from the perspective of children, is quite bleak. The nub of that reality is that visiting fatherhood is a contradiction in terms. Because "visiting" and "fathering" simply do not go together, the whole idea ultimately collapses.

The evidence shows that the great majority of visiting fathers are not—indeed, cannot be—good-enough fathers to their children. The deck is stacked against them. Too much has changed, too fast; too much will continue to change. In theory, it may be possible to restructure everything else about a family while maintaining fatherhood as a constant. In practice, it is hardly ever possible. Visiting fathers have lost the bases of their fatherhood. As Bronislaw Malinowski put it in his classic cross-cultural analysis of parenthood, "the child is linked to both its parents by the unity of the household and by the intimacy of daily contacts."[4] But for the Visiting Father, both aspects of this linkage are irrevocably shattered.

Yes, some visiting fathers may be able to leap over the barriers that separate them from their children. But most men, even good men, are not supermen. Yes, a few divorcing couples may be wise or lucky enough to transact a "good divorce" in which they continue to "co-parent" their children after they separate. But the vast majority of divorcing couples are not so wise or lucky.

For most divorcing couples, the marriage ends in bitterness, guilt, and pain. A small civilization has died. The children stay with the mother. The man moves out and tries to move on. When he does so, he may suffer enormously. He may have the best of intentions about not divorcing his children. But despite these feelings, most of these men lose the essence of their fatherhood. They drift away from their children almost as surely as they move away from their former homes and drift away from their former wives. This is sad. But it is the pattern.

It is the pattern not necessarily because anyone prefers it that way, but more because the very structure of the situation—the largely unavoidable meaning of the decision to divorce—permits no other way. In most cases, a man can be either a visitor or a father, but not both at the same time.

Consider the problem from the bottom up, as seen by children. Jill Krementz has sensitively interviewed children of divorced fathers. Ari, for example, visits his father every weekend:

> I really look forward to the weekends because it's kind of like a break—it's like going to Disneyland because there's no set schedule, no "Be home by five-thirty" kind of stuff. It's open. It's free. And my father is always buying me presents.

Now that his Dad has remarried, Ari, age fourteen, feels

> left out a lot of times. And one thing I really worry about is that I think they want to have a baby, and I know that if they do, it will be just like a replacement for me. That's because I only see my Dad on weekends, and since he would see the baby more than he'd see me, he'd probably grow to like it more than he likes me.[5]

Tracy, age sixteen, is the youngest of six children. Her father now "visits us about once a year," and her relationship with him "hasn't worked out very well." Though Tracy "thought the divorce was a good idea," she recalls that her parents' separation

> still made me feel sick inside for the first few years. I cried a lot—like whenever I would see my Dad I would come home afterward and cry hysterically. I was so sick that I'd throw up.

Overall, Tracy now feels that the separation from her father has "made me more understanding" and also "made me toughen out a lot." She had

> suggested to my Dad that we try to make something consistent—like writing to each other once a month —but he just said "Sure," and then he never did it. Now I finally realize that I'm probably better off settling for a limited relationship.[6]

Consider also the growing children's literature on visiting fathers. Written for the children of divorce and nonmarriage, these stories are both disturbing and significant. Indeed, in most bookstores and libraries, these new books for children probably constitute the most revealing bibliography available on the subject of fatherlessness.

In Eda LeShan's *What's Going to Happen to Me?* for example, the little girl Kathy

> feels shy and funny when her father comes to pick her up on Saturday mornings. He *looks* like Daddy and *sounds* like Daddy, but she still feels as if she is going out with a stranger. . . . He keeps asking her what she wants to do, where she wants to go. He keeps buying her all kinds of things that he never used to buy. Before the divorce, when Kathy went to the zoo with her father she had to nag and nag for Crackerjacks and balloons. . . . Now, all of a sudden, he buys her stuff she doesn't even want.

Making the point directly, the author warns the children:

> Sometimes visiting a parent gets harder instead of easier. At first you can still share all the things that happen when people live together. But as time goes by there are so many things you don't share. There seems to be more and more distance between you. Many children become frightened by this feeling of strangeness.

Not surprisingly, she continues, many children "begin to dread these visits."[7]

In *Why Are We Getting a Divorce?* children are told bluntly: "You have to get used to living with one parent and visiting the other one." Why is it usually the father who leaves? There are several good reasons:

> First, the family home should be for the family. It would be very unfair if your father kept the home for himself and made the rest of you go and look for another place to live.

But here is how this new situation, at best, can work:

> Let's say you're living with your mother and you visit your father on weekends or during vacations. Even though you've known him all your

life, those first visits are bound to feel strange. It's strange to see him living in a different place, maybe with somebody else, and it's strange to
have to say good-bye at the end of your visit. After a while, though, you
get used to the idea that divorce doesn't mean good-bye forever. And
then, little by little, visit by visit, you'll begin to find that maybe life isn't
so sad and bad after all.[8]

What do these children's books tell us about the Visiting Father as a
cultural model? First, these are sad stories. Despite the strained reaching
for not-unhappy endings that is so characteristic of this genre—"maybe
life isn't so sad and bad after all"—these stories are obviously about coping
with loss.[9] In the deepest sense, these stories suggest, a Visiting Father is
no longer a part of the family. ("The family home should be for the family.") Your father has left. Everything will change. Seeing him may come to
feel like seeing a stranger. He may look like your father and talk like your
father, but in most of the ways that matter to you, he will be more of an ex-
father than a real father. Underneath the artificial boosterism, this is the
no-nonsense moral of these new children's stories.

Moreover, even the boosterism in these books is fascinating. For despite
the phoniness, the upbeat endings of these stories are profoundly diagnostic of the spread of fatherlessness. Generally, these endings convey two
ideas to children. First, you can adjust. It may be hard, but you can learn
to cope. Second, and even more important, Daddy still loves you. Much
may have changed, but you can still count on Daddy's love. Presented as
the final interpretations of otherwise bleak narratives, these concluding
passages are clearly intended to comfort and reassure the children.

In Linda Walvoord Girard's *At Daddy's on Saturdays,* Katie has been
scared and sad since "Daddy moved away because of the divorce." But at
the end of the story, while Katie is visiting Daddy on a Saturday, a good
thing happens. They are eating pizza in Daddy's new apartment. ("Daddy
put a silly candle on the pizza, as if it were a birthday cake.") Daddy tells
Katie:

> Even though I can't be with you every day anymore, I love you. I'll never
> fool you, Katie. When I say I'll see you, that means I'll be there.

Afterward, even though Katie "still felt hurt about the divorce," she
finally realized that "in the world, there were things she could count on."
The story ends:

> What happened to Mommy and Daddy was sad. But Katie's daddy
> didn't disappear, poof, when the divorce happened. When his blue car
> pulled into the driveway, bringing her home, he always said the same old
> thing. "I'll be seeing you," Daddy said. And Katie knew he would.[10]

The basic idea here is poignant and clear. What matters most is that Daddy loves you. Other things have changed ("I can't be with you every day anymore"), but Daddy's love remains constant. You can count on it.

But can these children count on it? Should they? More crucially, is it fatherhood that they are counting on? In fact, a great many divorced fathers do indeed "disappear, poof," when the divorce happens. Katie, for example, knows what happened to her friend Mary: "Mary never sees her daddy."[11] But even in the case of well-intentioned visiting fathers, can children like Katie actually count on Daddy's love as a reliable foundation for the fathering they crave?

Maybe in the storybooks. But in real life, love is rarely enough. Love is good, of course, but on most days, love cannot conquer all. Especially in the realm of fatherhood, it is not the thought that counts. From the child's perspective, the crucial issue is not how Daddy feels. The issue is what Daddy does.

In the movie *Midnight Run,* a divorced father unexpectedly shows up at his former home, hoping to borrow money from his ex-wife. He sees his daughter. She obviously loves and misses him. She offers him her baby-sitting money. Overwhelmed with emotion, he refuses the money. He loves his daughter. The daughter knows that her father loves her. The father then gets into his car and drives away. Now, compare this emotionally aware divorced man to, say, an emotionally inarticulate married guy in Omaha who is taking out the garbage while telling his daughter that she cannot have the keys to the car. Which one of these men is a father?

Effective fatherhood is a way of living, not an emotion. When it becomes an emotion, detached from daily life and stripped of any empowering context, it is no longer fatherhood. It is an adult sentiment, and it amounts to very little for a child to count on. For this reason, despite the new storybooks, the fact that Daddy loves you—and that you know Daddy loves you—is simply not enough to make Daddy a good-enough father.

Moreover, here lies the ultimate tragedy of the Visiting Father: From the child's perspective, paternal love without paternal capacity is primarily a reminder of loss. This fact, more than any other, explains why postdivorce visits between father and child are so frequently painful, even traumatic. For the child, those visit-sized doses of father-love do not serve as a vaccine, as a protection from anguish. Quite the opposite. When you have been left, nothing reopens the wound like a small dose of kindness from the one who left you. For the child, this well-intentioned, ritualized wounding—this every-other-Saturday reminder of what has died—frequently becomes the central emotional dynamic of father-child visitation after divorce.

But what about the Visiting Father as seen by adults, by fathers and mothers? To view the problem from this perspective, consider again the primary activity of the Visiting Father: the visit. Many visiting fathers detest this word, for understandable reasons.

In *Single Father's Handbook,* Richard H. Gatley and David Koulack routinely use the word *visit.* Yet they describe it as "a galling term" that by implication reduces fathers to "mock parents." "Visiting," they worry, suggests that a father "has become an uncle or grandfather to his own kids."[12] More pointedly, Anna Keller insists that the terminology of visiting "underscores the demotion of one parent to the status of a guest in their child's life (and vice versa)." She continues:

> A "visitor's" intrusions in the family are those of an outsider; "visits" by "visitors" are generally at the invitation, or with the express permission, of the family; the term "visitor" carries none of the moral or legal weight that the parent-child relationship deserves.[13]

Keller is right. But the problem, of course, is structural, not linguistic. The problem is not the name we give to what this fellow does. The problem is what this fellow does.

He visits his children. His children visit him. The visit, then, constitutes the structural foundation—the defining act—of this parent-child relationship.[14] More often than not, these visits also constitute what Joseph Epstein describes as "the keenest torture that divorce has to offer" for fathers and children.[15] It is torture because, as Alexander Hillery puts it: "The visitation parent is no longer a real parent to his or her child."[16]

Visitation unfathers men. This phenomenon gradually strangles the father-child relationship. Indeed, the ultimate result of such not-like-a-father visiting is nothing less than the ending of fatherhood. Faced with the inherent falseness of their situation, many of these fathers, as Frank Furstenberg and Andrew Cherlin report, "start feeling like strangers to their children, like impostors."[17]

As a result, a great many visiting fathers, angered and ultimately defeated by the realization that they are becoming impostor-fathers, simply give up the effort and withdraw completely from their children's lives.[18] As Richard A Warshak, a clinical psychologist, observes: "Cast in the peripheral role of visitor, it is no wonder that some men fail to appreciate their importance to their children, and gradually drift out of their lives."[19]

What is it about the visiting relationship that produces this result? What explains the common, virtually predictable, failure of this attempt at continuing fatherhood? Many factors contribute, of course, but the underlying source of the failure is twofold.

First, most of these visiting fathers, not surprisingly, do not get along with their ex-wives. They are no longer members of a unified parental team. Indeed, Furstenberg and Cherlin report that a "major reason why fathers stop seeing their children is that they want to have nothing to do with their former wives."[20] Many single mothers, of course, feel exactly the same way about their former husbands.

Accordingly, Furstenberg and Cherlin estimate that fewer than one of every ten divorced fathers is able or willing to embrace the much-touted ideal of "co-parenting"—the maintenance of a cooperative parental alliance with the mother after divorce.[21] By contrast, the great majority of visiting fathers engage in what Furstenberg and Cherlin call "parallel parenting"—the establishment by the father of a separate relationship with his child, involving little or no contact with the child's mother. Remarriage, of course, typically reinforces this tendency toward parallel parenting.[22]

Yet, for the visiting father, parallel parenting is almost always a loser's game. It is a mass-tested recipe for paternal failure. It fails because whenever a mother becomes indifferent or hostile to a father's fatherhood, whenever she becomes less of a supporter than a bystander or even an opponent, that man's fatherhood is in trouble. Indeed, with all respect to the point that Furstenberg and Cherlin are making, there is almost nothing parallel about parallel parenting. Virtually all parental control resides with the custodial parent. Compared to the mother, the visiting father is largely without power or even knowledge.

Even when he was married, his wife was almost certainly the "lead" parent—the parent most involved in the day-to-day care and nurture of the children. Yet when he was married, however, he could rely upon his wife both to support and to complement him as a father. In a thousand ways, married mothers help their husbands to be good-enough fathers—sometimes by representing them to the children, other times by guiding and encouraging their husbands as fathers, still other times by deferring to their leadership.[23]

Divorce, almost by definition, destroys this basis for effective paternity. Indeed, in most cases, divorce does not simply end the parental alliance. Divorce inverts the alliance, turning mutualism into adverseness. For after divorce, according to Robert Weiss, "most custodial parents find non-custodial parents more nearly a burden than a resource." The visiting father becomes "someone to worry about, an obligation that limits what can be done on a weekend, a source of distraction and disturbance to the children." Because visits with divorced fathers can be very upsetting to children, many of the mothers Weiss interviewed "anticipate that an extended visit with the father means a week or so of conflict after the child returns."[24]

Weiss nicely captures the core issue. "Before the marriage ended," he observes, "the father would have been responsible for helping make the family work." But after the divorce, the "ways the other parent can be useful to the single parent are limited."[25] Put differently, in one case, he is viewed as a father. In the other, he is viewed as a guy who cannot help much and who may cause problems. This transmogrification of the parental alliance radically erodes the possibility of fatherhood.

The second debilitating feature of the visiting relationship is the absence of co-residency with children. To be a good-enough father—to sustain the dailiness of effective parenting—a man needs to live with his children. When he does not, he literally becomes an outsider.

If he vacates the house his children live in—particularly if his nonresidency is voluntary, something that he and his former wife have chosen—he vacates the only headquarters available to him for effective fatherhood. For good reason, Joseph Epstein concludes that the difference between "a father on the premises" and "a father with visitation rights" constitutes "a difference not of degree but of kind."[26]

As with the rupture of the parental alliance, the father's physical absence from the home makes postdivorce fatherhood a radically different—and much more problematic—idea than postdivorce motherhood. For this reason, fatherhood after divorce is not even remotely "parallel" to motherhood after divorce.

For the mother living with her children, the postdivorce challenge is to keep her family together, minus the father. But for the visiting father who has left the premises, there is no more family to keep together. He is all alone. The children and the mother are in. He is out.

Accordingly, the challenge facing the visiting father is to devise, essentially unassisted, an entirely new family household for those occasions when his children come to visit. He must start over, reinvent everything, construct an alternative family life for his children—complete with new rules, new routines, new expectations, and new father-child relationships. Most crucially, he must accomplish this feat in a home in which his children do not live, during arbitrary time fragments of, say, two days every other week.

Not surprisingly, this arrangement works very poorly for most men.[27] At best, it produces a weak, simulated version of fatherhood. It syncretizes fatherhood, transforming it from a coherent way of life into a disjointed series of highly self-conscious, highly pressured experiences. It amounts, in short, to fatherhood without context, which helps explain why it feels strange and inauthentic to everyone involved. Lots of activities outside the home, not many inside. Going to the movies. Eating out. Buying gifts. Not much continuity. Not much structure. Not many rules. Lots of pizza, not much homework. More like a vacation than day-to-day life in a home. More like visiting an acquaintance or a relative than living with a father.

Here is the bottom line for the Visiting Father: The end of co-residency and the rupture of the parental alliance mean nothing less than the collapse of paternal authority. Visiting fatherhood almost always becomes disempowered fatherhood, a simulacrum of paternal capacity. As Furstenberg and Cherlin remind us: "Americans think of parents as people who live with their children and whose business it is to know what their children are doing. Their authority arises from their role as protector and caretaker."[28]

Precisely. Yet the Visiting Father cannot meet these criteria. As a result, only wishful thinking permits us to continue viewing him as a parent at all. At bottom, he is no longer a father. He is an ex-father, a stranger-father, a guilty entertainer, a defanged father who has been granted permission to visit.

Better Divorce

To improve upon the model of the Visiting Father—to help divorced fathers become more than peripheral visitors—our contemporary cultural script's regnant idea is better divorce. Indeed, better divorce, or divorce reform, is not simply our culture's main prescription for the Visiting Father. It is virtually the only prescription.

Better divorce is to the Visiting Father what child support is to the Deadbeat Dad: an almost universally endorsed idea for making a very bad situation slightly less bad. It is an attempt less to strengthen fatherhood than to regulate—and thereby both moderate and institutionalize—the decline of fatherhood. Both better divorce and child support are ideas for preserving a shard of fatherhood within the context of an increasingly fatherless society. Both are intended as rescue operations aimed at sinking fathers. Both accept and even presuppose a societal lowering of standards: We no longer define fatherhood as the norm, but we struggle to salvage something called child support; we no longer count on marriage, but we strive to improve our procedures for divorce.

In part, the idea of better divorce reflects a faith in the primacy of process: the belief that *what* we do is sometimes less important than *how* we do it. In this view, the main problem we face is not divorce itself but rather how we transact divorce. The main challenge is to improve the process—to do divorce better. According to this perspective, improving the process of divorce will improve the meaning and outcome of divorce.

More fundamentally, the idea of better divorce reflects the conviction that a divorced father can still be a good father. How can he achieve this goal? Partly, of course, through personal commitment. He must have the motive. But our society can also create for him the means.

The means is divorce reform. In general, divorce reform seeks to create divorces that are less adversarial, less influenced by traditional gender roles, and more responsive to the idea that children need both of their parents, regardless of whether the parents remain married. Fewer lawyers, more mediators. Less anger, more cooperation, especially for the sake of the children. More training and information for divorcing couples, especially about postdivorce parenting. More recognition of the importance and rights of divorced fathers. More encouragement, whenever feasible, of joint custody.

In a larger sense, better divorce means mothers and fathers ending their marital partnership without ending their parental alliance. To achieve this goal, proponents of divorce reform envisage a sharp shift in both law and custom toward the expectation of equal co-parenting after divorce.

Melinda Blau's 1993 book, *Families Apart,* succinctly captures all the main components of the better-divorce idea. Blau is a contributing editor for *Child* magazine, where her regular column on the "New Family" won a 1993 media award from the American Association for Marriage and Family Therapy. We also learn from the book jacket that "she and her ex-husband are successful co-parents."[29]

Families Apart is based on the proposition that "parents could be taught to do divorce better." To Blau, "co-parenting after divorce" is "an idea whose time has come." She describes the essence of this idea as "divorce family style" and believes that such an improved style of divorce is "the least we can do for our kids."[30]

Blau begins by insisting that we stop "romanticizing marriage and the nuclear family." Divorced families are not worse than married-couple families, just different. Consequently, the challenge for both parents and policy makers is to "look at the *relationships* that shape a family, not the structure." For this reason, it is "time to 'normalize' divorce and to offer different kinds of postdivorce alternatives" to families.[31]

Done badly, of course, divorce can end a family. But done properly, according to the principles outlined by Blau, divorce can create a new family: one that spans two households. To describe these new families, she uses the term "families apart." Concretely, a family apart is a family in which the parents do not live together. Philosophically, a family apart is a family in which each parent views the other as a "bad spouse" but a "good parent"[32]—as no longer good enough to remain a marriage partner but still able to be a successful co-parent.

Creating a family apart requires effort and a willingness to change, especially for fathers. For example, fathers in families apart must learn to "step outside traditional gender roles" and become "a 'mix-'n'-match' parent—moving beyond the gender stereotypes toward newer, freer, more practical roles." A married couple may still choose to "[divide] some responsibilities along traditional lines." But after divorce, the old gendered divisions of labor—inherently undesirable in any case—are no longer even possible. In successful families apart, then, fathers have "discovered the virtues of androgyny."[33]

Overall, Blau's core message is upbeat: "With time, effort, attentiveness and, literally, 'response-ability,' you can create a new family form—a functional, healthy family apart." She has interviewed divorced couples who seek to build these new families apart. The main goal of her book is "to trumpet the accomplishments of parents who are doing it right."[34]

As she and her ex-husband are. Considering the importance of "doing divorce better," Blau is "proud that Mark and I have. We certainly did it better than my parents, who got divorced after thirty-five years of marriage. . . . Our children will also *be* different as a result of our joint caring and our commitment to their welfare."[35]

Blau's basic themes are ubiquitous in our contemporary discourse on the family. Certainly, the philosophy of better divorce guides the work of most family scholars who study divorce and offer recommendations to judges and legislators. For example, in *Joint Custody and Shared Parenting,* Susan Steinman recommends that policy makers contribute to the creation of a new parental model based upon "a reorganized family structure to best support the children's growth while allowing the adults to move on to a more satisfying life for themselves."[36]

Similarly, in *Nonresidential Parenting,* a 1993 volume of academic essays edited by James H. Bray and Charlene E. Depner, scholars seek to identify better "models of post-divorce parenting" based primarily on "a fundamental reassessment of the role of the nonresidential parent." Moreover, to achieve this goal, according to Bray and Depner, our society must rid itself of "biases about nonresidential parents" and thus finally "eradicate the stigma of the 'broken home.'" We must revise our current cultural understanding of the visiting parent:

> Positive and empowering images of their experience need to find their way into textbooks and the popular media. Public education and the media play a crucial role in their portrayal of the nonresidential parent and the possibilities for relationships between parents and children who do not live together.[37]

The widely respected family sociologist William J. Goode also urges us to adopt the philosophy of better divorce: "we should institutionalize divorce—accept it as we do other institutions, and build adequate safeguards as well as social understandings and pressures to make it work reasonably well."[38]

The better-divorce idea also increasingly informs our popular discussion of family matters, including advice literature for parents. An article in the *Washington Post* on divorce mediation is entitled "Making Divorce as Painless as Possible."[39] In *Helping Your Child Succeed After Divorce,* Florence Bienenfeld seeks to "help you, the divorcing parent, create a safe and nurturing environment for your children after divorce."[40] Similarly, Vicki

Lansky, a columnist for both the *Sesame Street Parents' Guide* and *Family Circle* magazine, bases her *Divorce Book for Parents* on her view that "[i]t's not divorce that makes a mess of your life and your kids, it's how you handle your divorce." Therefore: "For the sake of your children, make sure your divorce works well."[41]

Melvin G. Goldzband's *Quality Time* is devoted to an examination of "worthwhile activities shared between child and parent when their time together is restricted by separation or divorce." For if "one parent is not able to be with his or her children as frequently or as routinely as before, then the time spent with those kids is even more valuable to all of them than it was before the divorce."[42] In *Mothering* magazine, Barbara Wickell counsels divorcing parents to be "mature enough to make the shift from their . . . spousal relationship to a coparenting relationship."[43]

The literature on better divorce strongly reinforces the ideal of androgynous fatherhood. Indeed, if overcoming "gender roles" is vital for married New Fathers, it is even more imperative for Visiting Fathers. In *Single Father's Handbook,* for example, Richard H. Gatley and David Koulack devote a chapter to "Father as 'Mother'—The Evolution of a Houseperson."[44] For, as E. Mavis Hetherington and Margaret Stanley Hagan put it, "critical to the adjustment of the divorced father is his ability to participate in both 'father' and 'mother' roles."[45]

Better divorce also constitutes the animating premise of what is frequently termed the fathers' rights movement—grassroots organizations such as the National Congress for Men and Children and the Children's Rights Council that have sprung up in recent years to voice the concerns of the growing numbers of unhappily divorced fathers in the United States. Indeed, this movement is by far the nation's most interesting and politically potent expression of the better-divorce idea.

Between 1992 and 1994, I attended several annual meetings of leading fathers' rights organizations. I wanted to meet these fathers, learn how and why they formed these organizations, and hear their ideas. These men are not part of the cultural elite. Few of them are editors, authors, consultants, or business executives. Many more of them are guys who drive Federal Express trucks, process insurance claims, or work in airports. They seldom attend conferences.

These men are very angry. Indeed, their white-hot sense of injustice can sometimes produce in them the phenomenon of pressured speech, in which emotional intensity derails normal conversational rhythms. They are aware of this intensity.

Almost all of them are divorced and living apart from their children. Many of them, at least as they tell it now, never wanted the divorce. Their wives, for whatever reason, decided to divorce them—a decision that caused these men, suddenly and in many ways unexpectedly, to lose their children, their homes, a fair amount of their money, and a large amount of their pride and sense of worth. They feel irreparably aggrieved.

Most, to speak with moderation, do not get along with their ex-wives. Many are, or have been, involved in bitter disputes over custody and visitation. A surprising number, in the course of these disputes, have been accused by their ex-wives of child abuse. One man explained their general view of such charges by telling me that "whoever says 'child abuse' first, gets custody."[46]

At bottom, these men say, they are losing what matters most to them: their children. Moreover, they are all but helpless to do anything about it. For when push comes to shove between a custodial mother and a visiting father, the visiting father almost always loses. Even in legal terms, a father's right to visitation is more qualified and indeterminate than a mother's right to child support.[47] And in practice, if not by statute, if a custodial mother wants to turn her child against the father, or deny the father access to the child, she can frequently do so. In such cases, the father has almost no means of redress—except, perhaps, to join one of the newly emerging fathers' rights organizations.

In some respects, these groups are our nation's new fraternal organizations. With each passing year, in most communities, there are fewer and fewer men, especially younger men, who will join the Elks, the Kiwanis, the Masons, or the Lions clubs. But there are more and more unhappily divorced fathers who will join a local fathers' rights group. As a result, these organizations are becoming significant new vehicles of organized male purposefulness in our society.

These emerging groups of brothers are indefatigable workers. They write letters to local newspapers and state legislators. They prepare and circulate position papers. They phone in to the talk-radio programs. (One radio show in New England airs messages from these men to their children, such as "a kiss goodnight for Suzy from her father in Michigan.") They recruit other divorced fathers to join the movement.

The men of the old fraternal organizations saw themselves as civic leaders, living in a society that respected them for their service to others. Their concern was the local community, or what scholars term civil society. Essentially, these men sought to add something.

The men of the new fraternal organizations see themselves primarily as victims, living in a society that pays them no respect and almost no attention. Their concern is less communal than personal. They are seeking justice for themselves, redress for personal grievances. Essentially, they seek to salvage something.

The older fraternal organizations consisted primarily of married fathers. In this respect, these organizations were grounded in a marriage culture, expressing the aspirations of men in an essentially fathered society. The new organizations consist of divorced men on the verge of becoming ex-fathers. These new organizations are clearly grounded in a divorce culture, expressing the despair of men struggling against the odds to preserve a shard of their fatherhood in an increasingly fatherless society.

The slogan of the National Congress for Men and Children is Preserving the Promise of Fatherhood. The organization's mission is to help fathers "who desire to remain actively involved in the lives of their children regardless of marital status" and to seek a society "which validates and promotes the father as an equally strong role model, notwithstanding a divorce."[48] The bumper stickers for sale at their meetings say: Kids Need Fathers, Not Visitors.

David L. Levy, president of the Children's Rights Council, a coalition of fathers' rights groups in twenty-three states, summarizes the movement's core philosophy: "If divorce occurs, the model of two parents that the child had during the marriage should be what the child has after divorce. This means shared parenting or joint custody—with both parents sharing in raising the child after divorce." Shared parenting is easier if parents live near each other, "but even long-distance sharing can work, with a larger block of time in the summer, longer Christmas and spring breaks, and liberal phone access between parent and child."[49] Similarly, to Don Chavez, a fathers' rights leader who served on the U.S. Commission on Interstate Child Support, our society must come to recognize that "the rights, privileges, and opportunities of a father to know, guide, nurture and enjoy his children, presumed during marriage, MUST transcend the divorce process no more fettered than those of the mother."[50]

Demilitarized divorce. Mandatory parent training for divorcing couples.[51] A bias in state law toward joint custody. Shared parenting after divorce. These basic principles of the fathers' rights movement constitute the essence of the better-divorce idea. Better divorce, in turn, has emerged as our society's main—indeed, our only—proposal regarding the Visiting Father as a new cultural model for men.

Yet I refrain from embracing the idea of better divorce—not because it goes too far, or even because it goes in the wrong direction, but rather because it goes almost nowhere. As with child support, better divorce, although superficially reassuring, is largely an illusion, based less on evidence than on wishful thinking.

Probably the purest—and certainly the most entertaining—example of wishful thinking about better divorce is the popular and widely discussed 1993 movie *Mrs. Doubtfire*. Indeed, from start to finish, *Mrs. Doubtfire* constitutes a hymn dedicated to the promise of better divorce. In essence, the movie is a male fantasy of postdivorce fatherhood. If *Falling Down* portrays a dystopia based on the Deadbeat Dad, *Mrs. Doubtfire* summons a utopia based on the Visiting Father. In *Falling Down,* the unhappy ending is violent death. In *Mrs. Doubtfire,* the happy ending is better divorce.

For a number of weeks after its release, *Mrs. Doubtfire* was the top-grossing box office film in the nation. I saw the movie twice in New York, and young children accompanied by fathers constituted a large proportion of the audience. In this sense, *Mrs. Doubtfire* clearly succeeds as family entertainment for the 1990s. George R. McCasland of the National Congress for Men and Children called it "the greatest father's movie of all time." He urged his organization's leaders:

> Call the radio stations, the TV stations, the newspapers. Holler it from the mountain tops, this is the movie of the year, the movie of the decade. Every father who has faced the problems of access and visitation will see himself in this movie. Every father who has faced a judge and been told that loving his children is unnatural will see himself in this movie.[52]

Mrs. Doubtfire is a comedy about a visiting father in the midst of a divorce who will do almost anything—including pretending to be a woman—in order to be near his children. Daniel Hillard's wife is divorcing him. He is distraught. His children, we learn, mean everything to him. Yet a judge denies him custody and cruelly restricts his right to visitation. Desperate, he disguises himself as a nanny and is reborn as Mrs. Doubtfire. Unsuspectingly, Miranda Hillard, the estranged wife, hires Mrs. Doubtfire to clean house and care for the three children. The ruse is eventually uncovered, of course, first by the children, who are thrilled to be reunited with their dad, then by Miranda and her new boyfriend. The caper puts Daniel in even deeper trouble with the stern judge.

But in the end, everything works out fine. Miranda realizes that Daniel is a good father whose children love and need him. She agrees to rehire him—as himself this time—to care for the children each afternoon and to clean the house. The children are happy. Daniel is happy. Moreover, amid all this action, Mrs. Doubtfire has managed to become the star of a new children's television program. In the movie's last scene, Mrs. Doubtfire offers inspirational advice to children whose parents are divorcing.

Certainly, *Mrs. Doubtfire* is a funny movie. But from a philosophical perspective, the movie is self-consciously serious. It is an explicitly ideological movie, a movie with a mission: to affirm the possibility of better divorce. The star of the script is the divorced father who is a wonderful father.[53]

The movie incorporates all the main ideas animating the philosophy of better divorce for fathers. First, the divorced father is a victim. Typically, he is the victim of a brassy wife who would rather dump him and take the children than try to work things out. He is also the victim of a judicial system that is biased against him and of a society that does not respect or even care about him. In *Mrs. Doubtfire,* Daniel Hillard is a wonderful, lovable guy—even his wackiness is endearing—who clearly does not deserve to lose his children.

Second, the divorced father deeply loves his children. This is the movie's single biggest point. Pressed by the skeptical judge to explain himself, Daniel pleads "insanity," since he's been crazy about his kids since the day they were born. He needs to be with them, he says, as much as he needs air.

Third, the divorced father must transcend masculinity. The central metaphor of this movie could not be clearer: To become a good Visiting Father, Daniel becomes a woman. This change is more than merely a comic device for Robin Williams. Daniel does not simply alter his appearance; he alters who he is. He describes his newly found parenting skills: "I cook, I bake, I sew." Indeed, in important ways, Daniel, as Mrs. Doubtfire, becomes a much better mother than Miranda. Miranda appreciates the change. Near the end of the movie, she admits to Daniel that Mrs. Doubtfire "brought out the best in you. I miss her terribly." In the end, of course, Miranda gets her/him back, as a happy Visiting Father.

Fourth, divorce can be good and necessary. Mrs. Doubtfire sanctimoniously repeats to Miranda the old cliché: "Marriage can be such a blessing." Miranda's knowing rejoinder conveys the movie's deeper epistemology: "So can divorce." The youngest child asks her father: "Can't you just tell Mommy you're sorry?" Daniel explains: "Grown-up problems are a little more complicated than that." Miranda sums up the case for their divorce: "When I'm not with Daniel, I'm better. And I'm sure he's better when he's not with me."

Fifth, the main problem is not divorce, but how we handle divorce. In *Mrs. Doubtfire,* judges, lawyers, and other court officers are the bad guys. They polarize; they misunderstand what the children need; they turn human relationships into legal contests. But in the end, the common sense and decency of the parents prevail. Daniel decides to act as his own attorney. Miranda finally decides to ignore the court altogether. She promises Daniel and the children: "No more supervised visits, no more court liaisons." For she has concluded: "I don't want to hurt our children." If they do divorce better—minus the disguises, minus the animosity, minus the lawyers—they will not hurt the children. This scene is the movie's turning point toward a happy ending.

Sixth, a divorced father can be a good father. Daniel Hillard is a pretty wonderful Dad. If he has a flaw, it is that he loves his children so much that he sometimes ignores other adult responsibilities, such as holding down a regular job. (In the movie's first scene, he loses his job as a cartoon voiceover artist rather than participate in a scene that might encourage children to smoke.)

In the end, he is still a pretty wonderful Dad. His children adore him. He will be spending every afternoon with them. His ex-wife is appreciative and cooperative, even fond of him. He lives nearby. In some ways, despite the divorce, not much has changed. (He tells his five-year-old daughter that, with the family living in two separate houses, things will be "the same as always," except that they will have "a really big backyard.") In just a few weeks, and with great skill, he has transformed his new apartment into a warm, nurturing environment in which his children can visit him on weekends.

Indeed, divorce makes Daniel an even better father. Becoming Mrs. Doubtfire for a while has made him more sensitive and able to overcome traditional masculinity. By the end of the movie, Daniel has finally realized that living apart from Miranda ultimately makes him a better person and a better father.

And finally, what matters most for children of divorce is that Daddy loves you. On this point, *Mrs. Doubtfire* precisely replicates the moral of the new storybooks for children. In the movie's final scene, Mrs. Doubtfire, now hosting a new television show for children, answers a letter from little Katie McCormick of Youngstown, Ohio, who is sad because her parents have separated. In answer to Katie's question—"Did I lose my family?"—Mrs. Doubtfire says:

> You know, some parents, when they're angry, they get along much better when they don't live together. They don't fight all the time and they can become better people. And much better mommies and daddies for you.

He/she then tells Katie the most important point:

> Just because they don't love each other anymore doesn't mean that they don't love you. There are all sorts of different families, Katie. . . . And some live in separate homes and separate neighborhoods in different areas of the country. They may not see each other for days, weeks, months, or even years at a time. But if there's love, dear, those are the ties that bind. And you'll have a family in your heart, forever. All my love to you, puppet. You're going to be all right.

Mrs. Doubtfire was a very popular, successful movie. It struck a chord in our culture. Fathers took their children to see it. People responded to its message. The movie constitutes more than simply an anthem for the fathers' rights movement or a cinematic interpretation of the literature on better divorce. In a larger sense, its popularity is culturally diagnostic.

On one level, the movie's popularity reflects our willingness, even desire, to indulge in comforting fantasy—in short, to deceive ourselves—about the impact of divorce on fatherhood. But more fundamentally, this movie's cultural resonance, especially in its portrayal of the happy ending, points to our society's growing acceptance of the evisceration of fatherhood and the steady displacement of a marriage culture by a divorce culture.

In a marriage culture, the happy ending is marriage. Boy meets girl, boy gets girl, boy and girl triumph over adversity—this was the classic Hollywood formula. But the happy ending today is more likely to be the good divorce.[54] Boy and girl grow up by growing apart. As Miranda says, when she's not with Daniel, she's better. In the end, their divorce, although painful, makes them better people and "better mommies and daddies" for their children. Divorce becomes a metaphor for adult rebirth and renewal.[55]

This theme is important in America. For the idea of better divorce, while certainly not confined to the United States, is so prevalent in this nation precisely because its roots run so deep in American history and in what might be termed the larger American narrative. The vision of the good divorce—a vision of personal freedom—captures much of the essence of the American character. Our nation's founding document is a divorce document. It is a declaration of independence: an enumeration of the reasons for which people may justifiably dissolve the bonds that have connected them to others. In no other nation is the idea of "starting over" invested with such optimism and hope.

Like the rejection of the Old Father, this affirmation of the good divorce—the faith in separation as a means of personal renewal—constitutes a defining theme of the American story. This vision has much to commend it. Yet it has also given birth to the collapse of fatherhood in our society.

For when individual freedom becomes the reigning ethos not only of political life but also of sexuality and procreation, the primary result for children is the loss of their fathers. As a political and civic ideal, "starting over" has been a potent American strength. But as an ideal of family life, it constitutes our most disabling weakness: the animating cause of contemporary fatherlessness and thus the propeller of our most urgent social problems.

Whatever its other merits, the idea of the good divorce is inherently divergent from the idea of good-enough fatherhood. The two epistemologies are separate and incompatible. A Hollywood movie can fairly choose to celebrate one or the other, but it cannot honestly uphold both simultaneously. *Mrs. Doubtfire,* however, wants it both ways: better divorce, wonderful father. For this reason, it is a fundamentally dishonest movie, a comforting fantasy premised on a lie about the nature of fatherhood.

First, better-divorce literature notwithstanding, most real-life divorced fathers lack both the ability and the desire to transcend masculinity. Even after seeing *Mrs. Doubtfire,* very few visiting fathers will strive toward androgyny, what Melinda Blau calls a "mix-'n'-match" parent. According to the family scholars Greer Litton Fox and Priscilla White Blanton, since the necessary shift toward androgynous fatherhood is currently "achieved by only a minority of noncustodial fathers," our society must pursue nothing less than "reformulations of how men have been socialized to view both their masculinity as well as their role as fathers."[56] Meanwhile, the great majority of noncustodial fathers will continue to drift away from their children.

Second, most real-life divorcing couples do not direct their deepest resentments at judges or lawyers, or at something called the divorce process. Their deepest resentments are reserved for each other. What hurts most is not the process, but the divorce. The process can be better or worse, of course, but as regards both individuals and society, the primary issue is the decision to divorce. The method of carrying out that decision is not only secondary but largely derivative: process does not shape the divorce nearly as much as divorce shapes the process.

Consequently, unlike Miranda and Daniel Hillard, and contrary to the recommendations contained in the better-divorce literature, most divorced parents do not achieve postdivorce relationships based on good humor, warmth, mutual respect, rationality, and a commitment to cooperative coparenting. On the contrary, they usually do not get along very well at all. While this phenomenon weakens postdivorce motherhood, it tends to destroy postdivorce fatherhood. As Fox and Blanton report in their study of divorced fathers: "The one factor identified consistently across studies as most salient in constraining their relationship with their children . . . is the nature of the relationship with the former wife."[57] Similarly, Paul R. Amato identifies continuing "interparental conflict" as the reason why many studies of outcomes for children have "failed to find beneficial consequences of father involvement after divorce." Father-child visitations after divorce, Amato concludes, frequently serve primarily to "exacerbate conflict between parents, which is bad for children."[58]

Here we approach the ultimate futility—and irony—of the better-divorce idea. Its central recommendation to divorcing parents can be summed up simply. Get divorced, but not too divorced. Divorce each other, but keep your child's life as undivorced as possible. Break the bond with your spouse, but keep the bond with your co-parent. The trick for men is to split themselves psychologically into two parts. The husband part moves out, frequently to be replaced by another man, while the father part seeks, as best he can, to remain.

Except in the realms of theory and entertainment, this approach simply does not work for the great majority of divorced men. The empirical evidence shows that for every cooperative, co-parenting divorced father in our society, there are at least eight or nine divorced fathers whose links with their children and ex-wives range from minimal to nonexistent.[59]

Even in the realm of theory, consider the futility of Anna Keller's recommendation that noncustodial fathers engage in "visitation which is structured so as to reproduce the qualities of normal parent-child contact in the intact family."[60] Good idea, but Keller ducks the main point. No "structure" of visitation can possibly "reproduce the qualities of normal parent-child contact in the intact family." The only way for a father to achieve that goal is to live in an intact family.

Here is the ultimate irony. The "better" a divorce looks, the more it looks like, well, marriage. Living near each other. Cooperating. Communicating. Sharing the joys and responsibilities of parenthood. Making sacrifices and compromises for the sake of the family. Reproducing for children what exists in intact families. It all begins to sound like a good-enough marriage, minus the sex.

Yet a good-enough marriage is precisely what these couples have decided is no longer possible for them. They have decided to end their marriage—not simply part of the marriage but all of it, or at least as much of it as possible. For most fathers, this decision means moving out and moving on. It means the collapse of their fatherhood.

This sad irony—envisioning amicable half-marriages as the solution for estranged parents intent on divorce—reaches its most poignant expression in the men of the fathers' rights movement. Publicly, these divorced fathers fervently testify in favor of nonadversarial divorce, gender equality, and cooperative parenting after divorce. Yet these same men's private lives are frequently, perhaps even typically, scarred by bitter, adversarial divorces, including prolonged legal disputes with ex-wives over custody, visitation, and child support, and frequently including personally devastating charges of child abuse. Their key recommendation to the larger society—salvage fatherhood through better divorce—thus reflects precisely what they could not attain in their own lives.[61]

The uncomfortable truth is that, regardless of whether or how we change our divorce laws and customs, there is very little reason to believe that the swelling ranks of divorced fathers in our society can be good-enough fathers to their children. Yes, there are exceptions, even an occasional bit of hopeful news. But the hard facts remain.

For this reason, a seemingly utopian prescription for better divorce is less a solution to our fatherhood problem than a sign of our unwillingness to confront the problem. It represents less our demand for cultural progress than our acceptance of cultural regression. Despite its reformist rhetoric, the better-divorce idea is rooted less in optimism about the potential for on-the-ground fatherhood in our society than it is in a profound pessimism.

Perhaps, as Melinda Blau urges, parents can indeed learn to "do divorce better." Surely they could try. (Does anyone favor doing it worse? Would that even be possible?) But for children, as well as for fathers and for society, better divorce does not produce good-enough fatherhood. In our minds, this basic fact can be obscured by a futuristic theory called better divorce. But it cannot be avoided in the real world—not even with the aid of good intentions, sensitive divorce mediators, mandatory parenting classes, and new divorce laws.

Divorce is the problem. Pretending that better divorce is the solution amounts to little more than a way of easing our conscience as we lower our standards. As fatherhood fragments, children's well-being declines. But children need some ephemeral hope called better divorce about as much as they need some lifeless reminder of their father called child support. Both, for children, are only slightly better than nothing. What children need is a father.

Our society's ready embrace of better divorce reveals our willingness—indeed, our desire—to institutionalize an obviously degraded form of the father-child relationship. Ultimately, it amounts to our further acceptance of the idea that fatherhood in our society—not near-beer fatherhood, but the real thing—is no longer necessary or possible for all or even most of our children.

CHAPTER 9

The Sperm Father

The Sperm Father completes his fatherhood prior to the birth of his child. His fatherhood consists entirely of the biological act of ejaculation. He spreads his seed, nothing more. He is a minimalist father, a one-act dad.

Neither a New Father nor an Old Father, he is an unfather, leaving no footprints or shadows. To his child, he is both an anonymous and an imaginary father. He is the male originator of fatherless children. He does not know his child. His child does not know him. He is a father of whom there are no expectations.

His is the fatherhood of the one-night stand, the favor for a friend, the donation or sale of sperm. His child is the unintended consequence, the result of the affair that did not work out, the reason for the paternity suit, the baby he never learned about. He is also a convenience father, the ideal solution for women who want to create manless families and for men willing or eager to embrace procreation without fatherhood.

Psychologically, the Sperm Father is also a fantasy father. For both men and women, he embodies powerful strands of human desire. For men, the Sperm Father can represent the fantasy of sex without obligation; for women, the fantasy of the little girl left alone to play with her dolls, no boys allowed. For children, the Sperm Father becomes someone to imagine, a Rorschach father. My dad, I bet he's a real big man.

In several ways, the Sperm Father is prototypically modern, even postmodern. He is a brave new father, the cutting edge of contemporary paternity. This is the high-tech father of sperm banks and artificial inseminations. His fatherhood increases our options, gives us more choices.

Consequently, more than any other father, the Sperm Father is a marketplace father: a father of the cash nexus and of short-term exchanges. His is a fatherhood that can be bought and sold as a commercial product, or sometimes obtained for free, no strings attached. It is a fatherhood that can fit in a vial and be purchased off the shelf, like aspirin. Or to use a closer analogy, his fatherhood can be purchased in the same way that dairy farmers purchase bull semen.

Moreover, the Sperm Father also perfectly embodies the modernist aspiration of paternity without masculinity. No gender roles, no "mascu-pathology," no "splitting." Here is a fatherhood that certainly transcends gender. Here is the perfect father for people who believe that men in fami-lies are either unnecessary or part of the problem.

For these reasons, the Sperm Father is probably the wave of the future. He already represents a weighty and rapidly growing minority of actual fathers in the United States—probably as many as 30 percent of all fathers of young children. With each passing year, more and more children in the United States are born to such fathers.[1]

Yet, paradoxically, the Sperm Father also represents a return to the father of the primordial past. In this respect, he is even older than the Old Father. He is a state-of-nature father. For his style of fatherhood fully re-capitulates what Don S. Browning calls "the original mammalian con-dition."[2] Males impregnate, then drift away. Females raise the young.

A more modern term for an attenuated version of this idea is "separate spheres." Women in one sphere, men in another. Of course, few ideas in today's expert discourse on marriage are more unpopular than the idea of separate-spheres. The concept is widely dismissed as a sexist anachronism, a reminder of the evils of the Old Father. Yet outside of marriage, in the van-guard of contemporary family change, a radically irredentist version of sepa-rate spheres ideology is alive and flourishing. Women and children inside. Men outside. Fatherhood, the primary link between the two spheres, reduced to "the original mammalian condition" of sperm donation.

As state-of-nature fatherhood, the Sperm Father's style of paternity can be viewed as biology without society. Male procreation without male respon-sibility—the ultimate iteration in our society of decultured paternity.

In short, the Sperm Father constitutes the tiniest fragment of father-hood imaginable. He is a scintilla of a father, no larger or more purposive than a drop of semen. Consequently, his is by far the smallest role in our contemporary fatherhood script. He is much less of a father, for example, than the Deadbeat Dad. Someone, somewhere, expects the Deadbeat Dad to pay. His children might recognize a picture of him. The Sperm Father is nameless and faceless. No one expects him to pay. He cannot even be properly described as an absent father, since the word *absent* implies some normative presumption in favor of presence. The Sperm Father cannot be absent because it was never deemed possible for him to have been present.

He is our society's most extreme embodiment of the idea that children do not need fathers. For him, fatherhood as a social role is not simply unnecessary or superfluous; it is nonexistent. By definition, it cannot be imagined. For this reason, the Sperm Father's very existence in our society eviscerates not only fatherhood but also the idea of fatherhood, the possibility of fatherhood. The Sperm Father is the logical culmination of fatherhood in a fatherless society.

Explaining Fathers Away

Every year, the Sperm Father becomes a bigger presence in our cultural conversation. Physically, this father is invisible; he occupies no space. But culturally, as an idea of male procreative behavior, he now looms large. He can throw his weight around.

For example, he is now a character in children's storybooks. The title of Jeanne Warren Lindsay's book for preschoolers is *Do I Have a Daddy?* The answer is no.

> "What about daddy? Didn't he want me?" asked Eric.
> "Your daddy was excited. He came to see you when you were very little. But then he went away."
> "Did he like me?" asked Eric.
> "Oh yes! and he was very proud of you," Mother replied.
> "Then why did he go away?" asked Eric.
> "Caring for a baby is a big job," said Mother. "Your daddy wasn't ready for that."
> "Oh," said Eric.[3]

The Sperm Father is a character in the movies. In the 1992 television movie *The President's Child,* based on a novel by Fay Weldon, campaign aides to a presidential aspirant become worried that the young child of an attractive single mother, a TV news reporter, was conceived during her secret affair with . . . guess who? In Lawrence Kasdan's highly acclaimed 1983 film, *The Big Chill,* a single woman in her thirties, a lawyer, spends a weekend with old college friends trying to decide which, if any, of the men in the group she should ask to impregnate her. By the end of the movie, one of the woman's friends has volunteered her own husband, who agrees to perform the task. Everyone seems happy with this solution.[4]

The Sperm Father is a character in contemporary literature. For example, in Mary Morris's 1993 novel, *A Mother's Love,* Ivy, the mother of a newborn baby, describes how she

> conceived a child on the one and only night I had ever, on drunken whim, been careless with Matthew, who had been my lover off and on for years; we had a tacit agreement that marriage and children were not a part of our carefully shaped pact with the world.[5]

As a result, she signed the baby's birth certificate alone, "the space for his father's name left blank." Did the birth of this baby have anything at all to do with any adult male? At bottom, Ivy doubts it. To her, the existence of her baby is mysteriously, almost miraculously, detached from any aspect of paternity, even the biological aspect:

> It seemed as if this child had come to me the way the Trobriand Islanders believe—not through intercourse, which serves only to pave the way, but rather as a spirit that swims to you while you are standing, receptive, in clear water.[6]

A similar theme runs through Barbara Kingsolver's 1993 novel, *Pigs in Heaven*. Here we are told the story of a woman, Taylor Greer, and her six-year-old daughter, Turtle. Mother and daughter first found each other three years earlier, not as a result of a pregnancy and birth but as the result of "the miracle."[7] One day Taylor, sitting in her car, simply looked down and there was Turtle, suddenly beside her, out of nowhere, with no history and no explanation. Taylor became the little girl's mother.

As the larger story makes clear, Kingsolver's account of this moment of spontaneous generativity—something of a secular equivalent to the idea of immaculate conception—becomes the guiding metaphor for fatherhood in the novel.[8] In Taylor and Turtle's world, there is no father-child bond at all. There are no fathers.

For Taylor is the third generation of a family of "women on their own." Her grandmother ran a hog farm by herself for fifty years. Her mother, Alice, is about to leave her second husband. She became estranged from her first husband, Foster, when she was pregnant with Taylor. Alice was relieved when Foster left her and the baby, since "she'd known Foster long enough to know a good trade when she saw one, him for a baby." Now she is about to leave her second husband, Harland, who does nothing but watch television. She confides to Taylor's boyfriend: "I think we could go on for thirteen generations without no men coming around to speak of. Just maybe to do some plumbing once in awhile."[9]

Jax, Taylor's boyfriend, is no tower of dependability. He is "a keyboard player in a band called the Irascible Babies. Taylor sometimes feels she could take Jax or leave him, but it's true he's an asset on trips."[10]

Taylor's life with Turtle is threatened when the Cherokee Indians discover that the little girl is a Cherokee, the abandoned daughter of a dead mother and an "unknown" father. The tribe wants the girl back. The law supports the tribe.

The ending, however, is a happy one. Everyone compromises. Legal custody of the girl goes to a Cherokee, her maternal grandfather. Physical custody will be shared jointly by the grandfather and Taylor. (Notice that, in some respects, this ending clearly reflects the epistemology of better divorce as applied to the issue of adoption, albeit fatherless adoption.) "Obviously," concludes the young attorney for the Cherokee Nation, "with joint custody, everything depends on how well the two custodial parties are willing to cooperate."[11]

Here is a rich, complex story of a little girl and her extended family, both biological and adoptive, complete with a happy ending, without a single father anywhere to be found. In *Pigs in Heaven,* fathers are unnecessary for children, irrelevant to family life.[12] All male procreation occurs through Sperm Fathers.

The Sperm Father has also emerged as an important character in advice literature to parents, since growing numbers of mothers and children today face the challenge of how to manage without a father and without the memory or the possibility of a father.

The central problem addressed in this new advice literature is that fatherless children frequently upset, and even startle, their mothers by persistently fantasizing or questioning their mothers about "my father." Andrea L. Engber, who edits the newsletter *Single Mother* and writes a regular column for *Working Mother* magazine, reports that: "Recently, I've been overwhelmed by letters from mothers requesting advice on discussing their family situations. . . . the mutual concern of most of these moms is what to say about 'Dad?'"[13]

Jane Mattes, a clinical social worker who is the director of Single Mothers by Choice, also reports that many mothers "said they were disturbed to hear their children create fantasies about their fathers since they bore little resemblance to the truth. Keep in mind this is normal—young children have a vivid fantasy life and they use it to provide themselves with what they need." Faced with these fantasies, Mattes advises mothers to "try adopting an interested and accepting attitude."[14]

More specifically, in their 1994 book, *The Single-Parent Family,* Marge Kennedy and Janet Spencer King point out that such fantasies

> can create a safe haven, a way of augmenting and strengthening their identities. It's important that kids be allowed to verbalize their imaginings (they're going to have fantasies whether or not they share them with you). Equally important is that their fantasies originate with them and that your reaction be limited to "that sounds like quite a dad (or mom)," or "I bet it's fun to think about your other parent." You can also share some positive, self-affirming information—"You have brown eyes and strong hands, just like your father"—which can give kids the connectedness they seek.[15]

It is an adult fantasy, of course, to suggest that the "connectedness they seek" can be achieved by telling them the color of their fathers' eyes, just as it is a fantasy to believe that "what they need" can be attained by "adopting an interested and accepting attitude" toward their imaginings. What these children "seek" and "need" is a father. Yet that is exactly what they can never have. To insinuate otherwise—to pretend that what really matters is the therapeutic value of fantasy—is not to recognize their yearning but to trivialize it. It is to shrink their child-sized father yearning to adult dimensions by denying its implacability.

Such dissembling highlights the inherent contradiction of this new advice genre. This literature cannot encourage or even acknowledge fatherhood. It must settle for explaining it away.

In part, explaining fatherhood away means offering reasons for its nonexistence. Accordingly, for children who ask "Do I have a daddy?" Engber offers this advice:

> You might respond to these questions with simple explanations such as: "Everybody has a daddy in the beginning because it takes a mommy and a daddy to make a baby. Lots of mommies and daddies live together if they like each other. Your daddy and I did not want to live together, but I wanted you very, very much. Your daddy likes you very much, too, but he went away because caring for a baby is a very big job. He was not ready for a job like that."[16]

From this perspective, the way to help fatherless children is to provide them with reasons, which substitute for fathers.

Explaining fatherhood away also means advising adults not to feel bad or guilty about the spread of fatherlessness. Currently, much energy in our society is devoted to this task. In John Rosemond's *Parent Power!* for example, we learn that our "perceptions" of fatherlessness may be distorted by "myths":

> There are many myths, but foremost among them is one that says raising a child (or children) is much more difficult if you are single than if you have a partner. That is simply not the truth. . . . If you are a single parent, you are as capable as any two parents of raising healthy, happy children.[17]

In the "Ask the Experts" column of *Single Mother,* Leah Klungness, a psychologist, warns single mothers about "the guilties." Such guilt, rooted in the mistaken notion that "a father would make things different," is "distressing and unnecessary." To prevent this unnecessary distress, Klungness advises, remember a few basic points. Problems exist in every family, regardless of structure. Moreover: "Just because there is a father in the house does not mean the child is being fathered." After all, lots of fathers are bad fathers. Your situation could be worse. Besides, some things just happen. You are doing your best. Do not feel bad or guilty.[18]

This philosophy is quite prevalent in today's cultural discourse. Much of it is based in wishful thinking, or what psychologists would call denial. (One parent is as capable as any two.) Some of it obviously reflects the intention to define deviancy down. (Some fathers are bad; some things are worse than fatherlessness.) But much of it is rooted in the demand that we simply switch subjects. To change the subject, we no longer focus on the objective situations of children. Instead, we discuss the subjective feelings of adults. Accordingly, the root concern is no longer fatherless children. What matters is how the adults feel about themselves.

Finally, explaining fatherhood away means fracturing and disembodying fatherhood as a social role. April Martin, advising lesbian and gay parents, employs this approach:

> "Why don't I have a daddy?" may also mean . . . "Why isn't the man who created me biologically one of my functional parents?" . . . If the biological father is known to the child and has some role in the child's life, you can tell her that "Joe is the man who gave sperms to the moms to make you." It can be made clear that Joe never intended to become a parent himself, only to help you make a baby. You can emphasize that Joe likes her, but that his role does not include caregiving or responsibility. The kind of relationship your family has with Joe will be apparent to your child, and she will grasp that making a child and raising a child don't have to be done by the same person.[19]

Philosophically, Martin is affirming the dispersal of fatherhood. First, fatherhood is deconstructed, broken down into its various elements. Over here, making a child. Over there, raising a child. Then the fragments of fatherhood can be spread around to different people. All the parts "don't have to be done by the same person." As a result, the word *father* ceases to be a noun. There is no such thing as a father. Instead, there are people who do various fatherlike things.

In practical terms, what Martin affirms can be stated much more simply. Fathers, understood as men who know and raise their offspring, do not matter. They are unnecessary. She affirms what she calls "the completeness of a family without a father."[20]

But this literature goes even further. To rationalize the spread of fatherlessness, it seeks to deny the importance and even the possibility of any effective fatherhood in our society. For, as the new literature reveals, the cultural acceptance of the Sperm Father depends in part upon hostility—or at least indifference—toward even the idea of fatherhood as a social role for men. To make room for the Sperm Father is also to insist upon the essential irrelevance of all fathers.

Brave New Fathers

In 1993, Whoopi Goldberg and Ted Danson starred in a popular movie called *Made in America,* a lighthearted comedy about a mix-up at the sperm bank. The mother, it seems, thought she had purchased the sperm of an intelligent black man with which to conceive her child. But in fact, she accidentally received the sperm of a silly white guy who sells used cars. Years later, mother and daughter learn the truth about father. Big surprise, lots of fun.[21]

Made in America is culturally diagnostic. For the movie's comedic resonance depends upon three revealing assumptions. First, sperm-bank fatherhood has arrived. We see it around us. We know what it is. It is not only a demographic fact but also a cultural fact that informs us and can even entertain us. Second, sperm-bank fatherhood is essentially a commercial product, something bought and sold in the marketplace. And finally, there is nothing wrong with it. It may cause confusion—this is the basis of the humor—and it certainly presents us with new challenges and options. But at bottom, there is nothing wrong with it. The moral of the story is choices, not restrictions. There is little ethical ambiguity or conflict. The tone is progressive and upbeat. Comedy, not tragedy.

These same assumptions underlie our broader discourse. Indeed, they shape our current understanding not only of sperm banks generally but also of the most father-absent version of sperm-bank paternity: the use of purchased sperm by unmarried women. Artificial insemination by anonymous donors now accounts for at least thirty thousand births each year in the United States. Of course, most of these births are to married couples experiencing fertility problems—certainly an ethically and socially separate issue, since these babies will be taken home by two parents. But up to 10 percent of all births resulting from artificial insemination by donors—some three thousand births per year—are to unmarried women. And these numbers are growing.[22]

What does our society think about the use of purchased sperm by unmarried women to create radically fatherless children? To date, our collective answer has been twofold. First, we do not think about it very much. A movie here, a magazine article there, usually focusing on the most exotic cases. But very little serious discussion of the trend. Second, to the degree that we do think about it, we either approve of it or consider it a purely private matter, beyond the proper reach of moral judgment or legal restraint.

Surely the most surprising aspect of the emergent sperm market for unmarried women is not the fact that some people are willing to buy and sell the product but the fact that the society as a whole, it seems, could hardly care less. For example, forty-eight states (Oklahoma and

Connecticut are the only exceptions) take a purely laissez-faire approach to this new market, granting unmarried and married women precisely the same consumer rights to purchase sperm for the conception of children. Unlike national governments in Europe, many of which confine the use of artificial insemination to married couples, the U.S. Congress to date has evinced no interest in limiting or regulating this growing phenomenon.[23]

John A. Robertson of the University of Texas Law School, testifying before Congress in 1987, perfectly captures the prevailing economistic approach of U.S. legislators. To Robertson, a consumer's right "to make contracts with providers of gametes" cannot be prohibited or limited, except to assure that such contracts "are knowingly and freely entered into." The sole policy objective is to expand personal reproductive choices. The fact that some people may find some choices "distasteful" is "not a sufficient basis for public action limiting the procreative choice of willing parties."[24]

Outside government, in the media and in the universities, especially in philosophy departments and in the literature of bioethics, the emergence of fatherless children due to artificial insemination has been greeted, on the whole, by profound silence. As Daniel Callahan, a notable but isolated exception to this rule, has put it:

> While the general topics of reproductive choices and artificial means of reproduction have had a central place in bioethics, the literature and debate have usually centered on women's choices or women's role in such things as surrogate motherhood and *in vitro* fertilization. Fathers and fatherhood are just absent from the discussion altogether.

He continues:

> I find it remarkable that, with hardly any public debate at all, the practice—indeed, institution—of artificial insemination by an anonymous male donor so easily slipped in. What could society have been thinking about?[25]

The answer to Callahan's question seems evident. Apart from "not much" and "it's just a business," most of us seem to have been thinking, as David Wasserman and Robert Wachbroit recently put it, that

> the role of reproductive technologies in facilitating alternative parenting arrangements may prove to be healthy and liberating. The flourishing of families will depend on the capacity of our legal and social order to accommodate new forms of parenting, and on the capacity of the nuclear family to survive and flourish without a legal monopoly.[26]

Of course, in the case of artificially inseminated single women, for "alternative parenting arrangements," read "parenting without fathers." Throughout the professional literature on this subject, one theme is dominant. Our primary object, as Anne Donchin puts it, is to be a society in which "women can shape their reproductive experiences to further ends of their own choosing."[27] Fathers simply do not matter.

The socially legitimated sale of sperm from anonymous men to create fatherless children, while currently affecting only about three thousand children per year, is a cultural fact of considerable size and meaning. The quiet emergence of this type of fatherhood in our society signals not simply that a few of us are acting in a new way but, more important, that most of us are thinking in a new way. Our casual acceptance of fatherhood in a vial—our willingness to traffic commercially in this radical evisceration of fatherhood—reflects our growing acceptance of the trend toward a fatherless society.

The State of Nature

The central paradox of the Sperm Father is that he is both postmodern and primeval. His brand of paternity—fatherhood as impregnation—is simultaneously new and archaic. It is the latest trend. It is also the earliest human pattern of procreation.

For, prior to the cultural invention of fatherhood in human societies, the model of the Sperm Father precisely defined the contribution of males to child rearing. In the language of political philosophy, this primordial era of human existence is called the state of nature. It is the period that predates both the emergence of social institutions, including families, and the creation of culture, or shared ways of living. In short, it is the period of presociety. It is also—not coincidentally, but definitionally—the period prior to the emergence of fatherhood as a social role for men.

Indeed, political philosophers, no less than anthropologists, have clearly recognized the socialization of males into the fatherhood role as a precondition for the rise of successful human societies. In what might be called the political philosophy of fatherhood in the West, the socialization of paternity denotes nothing less than the transition from a brutish state of nature, in which men are primarily Sperm Fathers, to encultured human societies, in which men know and care for their children.

Certainly the seventeenth-century originators of Anglo-American liberalism—the creators of the philosophy of the modern liberal state—were deeply concerned with the problem of the father. For in the foundational texts of liberal theory, the concept of social fatherhood emerges as a defining feature of liberal society. For these philosophers, to lose fatherhood would be to lose much of the possibility of civil society. To lose fatherhood would be to regress to the state of nature.

In much of liberal political philosophy, to live in the state of nature is to live a harsh, dangerous life. Thomas Hobbes, the great English philosopher of the seventeenth century, famously described the state of nature in *Leviathan,* his masterwork, as "a time of Warre, where every man is Enemy to every man; [and] wherein men live without other security, than what their own strength, and their own invention shall furnish them withall." It is a time, finally, of "no Society; and which is worst of all, continuall feare, and danger of violent death; And the life of man, solitary, poore, nasty, brutish, and short."[28]

What is the pattern of procreation and child rearing in the state of nature? Regarding children, Hobbes tells us,

> the Dominion is in the Mother. For in the condition of meer Nature, where there are no Matrimoniall lawes, it cannot be known who is the Father, unless it be declared by the Mother: and therefore the right of Dominion over the Child dependeth on her will, and is consequently hers.[29]

In this passage, Hobbes brilliantly adumbrates the fundamental social bases of fatherhood. For men, marriage is the precondition, the enabling context, for fatherhood as a social role. Why? Because marriage fosters paternal certainty, thus permitting the emergence of what anthropologists call the legitimacy principle. This is my child, not another man's child. In turn, paternal certainty permits and encourages paternal investment: the commitment of the father to the well-being of the child.

By contrast, in "meer Nature, where there are no Matrimoniall lawes," males simply impregnate females, then move on. All responsibility for children is "in the Mother." This argument leads the contemporary political philosopher Philip Abbott to observe that, for Hobbes, "paternity is absent in the state of nature."[30] Conversely, as Jean Bethke Elshtain puts it, Hobbes's philosophy clearly suggests that "fatherhood is a defining characteristic of civil society." For Hobbes, in short, the emergence of fatherhood as a social role for men signifies the transition from barbarism to society.[31]

A similarly provocative argument is developed by John Locke, the other great English political philosopher of the seventeenth century, who, along with Hobbes, largely fashioned the intellectual foundations of modern liberal thought.[32] Indeed, although Locke's major work, *Two Treatises of Government,* published in 1698, is regarded today primarily as an analysis of government, Abbott reminds us that this seminal book is "concerned with two topics: the family and political power."[33] Like Hobbes, Locke undertakes to describe the origins of human society: the transition from the state of nature to civil society. To do so, he describes the emergence of fatherhood.

First, Locke tells us that males naturally and strongly desire to copulate with females. Indeed, we can deduce from Locke's argument that this male sexual drive constitutes the baseline, the central dynamic, of male procreative behavior in the state of nature. Locke poses the question harshly:

> What Father of a Thousand, when he begets a Child, thinks farther than the satisfying his present Appetite? God in his infinite Wisdom has put strong desires of Copulation into the Constitution of Men, thereby to continue the race of Mankind, which he doth most commonly without the intention, and often against the Consent and Will of the Begetter.[34]

Here is male sexuality freed from societal norms. It is asocial copulation, impersonal impregnation. It is frequently predatory and violent. Call it unencultured male procreation: fatherhood in the state of nature. It is the original model of the Sperm Father.

Yet through society, there emerges another, and ultimately more important, component of male sexuality. Locke tells us that God made man into such a creature that "it was not good for him to be alone." Thus God "put him under strong Obligations of Necessity, Convenience, and Inclination to drive him into Society."

The "first and strongest desire God Planted in Men," Locke reasons, is "Self-Preservation." But "next to this, God Planted in Men a strong desire also of propagating their Kind, and continuing themselves in their Posterity."[35] In this way, the male "Necessity" and "Inclination" toward generativity ultimately become defined by more than the mere act of copulation. They become enlarged by the need for males to go "into Society" and to "continue themselves in their Posterity."

Thus the "first Society was between Man and Wife, which gave beginning to that between Parents and Children." Moreover:

> For the end of conjunction between Male and Female, being not barely Procreation, but the continuation of the Species, this conjunction betwixt Male and Female ought to last, even after Procreation, so long as is necessary to the nourishment and support of the young Ones.[36]

In short, as males go "into Society"—and especially the "first Society" of marriage—fatherhood becomes more than simple impregnation, or what Locke finely terms "barely Procreation." Instead, it becomes "Paternal Care" and "Paternal affection," or what Locke describes as "the Office and Care of a Father."[37]

Consequently, Locke repeatedly insists that paternal authority does not arise "only from Begetting." Instead, the authority of both fathers and mothers "arises from that Duty which is incumbent on them, to take care of their Off-spring, during the imperfect state of Childhood."[38] In a chilling piece of foreshadowing, Locke rhetorically asks: If "the bare act of begetting" entitles a man to the "Name and Authority of a Father," what will become of such "Paternal Power" in "those parts of America where when the Husband and Wife part, which happens frequently, the Children are all left to the Mother, follow her, and are wholly under her Care and Provision?"[39]

Three centuries later, Locke's question seems as fresh as the 1993 journalistic obsession with Baby Jessica, the two-year-old girl from Iowa whose biological father—a clear example of a Sperm Father—ultimately succeeded, after a tangled and highly publicized legal dispute, in blocking her pending adoption by a married couple in Michigan.

In 1990, Daniel Schmidt, the father of two children whom he seldom saw and did not support, got his girlfriend, Clara Clausen, pregnant. Then the couple broke up. Clausen did not tell Schmidt about the child. When she decided to put the baby up for adoption, she named another man, her current boyfriend, as the father. She and the boyfriend signed the adoption papers. The little girl went to a new home in Michigan, where her adoptive parents named her Jessica.

Meanwhile, the mother told the truth to Daniel Schmidt, who then initiated legal action to get custody of a daughter he had never seen. During the protracted legal proceedings, the court papers referred to the child as B.G.C., for Baby Girl Clausen. Schmidt won. The child, now a toddler, came back to Iowa. Schmidt and the mother, by then reconciled and married, named her Jane Schmidt, her third name in less than three years.[40]

All this may sound tortuously complicated, but John Locke would have recognized it immediately. When fatherhood decomposes in a society, this is what happens. Confusion and deception about who a child's father is. Increasingly nuanced distinctions between "biological" and "social" fathers, along with ugly contests pitting one against the other. Lots of new work for lawyers, social workers, and court-appointed psychologists. Titillating new program topics for *Geraldo* and *Donahue*. The fragmenting of adoption as an institution, since adoption can be a coherent idea only if motherhood, fatherhood, and marriage are coherent ideas. Growing numbers of children with either no father or too many "fathers." In short, the paternity of the Sperm Father: male procreation in a kind of postmodern state of nature.

In the Sperm Father, male procreation comes full circle, ending up exactly where it began. In this sense, the Sperm Father is less a model of fatherhood than a model of both pre- and post-fatherhood. For, as a prevalant mode of paternity, the Sperm Father can exist only on either side of fatherhood as a social role for men: either before society cares whether men know and nurture their offspring, or after society ceases to care.

Consequently, today's reemergence of the Sperm Father as a mass male phenomenon constitutes our society's clearest example of cultural regression. In political philosophy terms, the Sperm Father signifies a relapse from society to the state of nature. In anthropological terms, he embodies the deculturation of male procreation.

For the society, the largest consequences of Sperm Fatherhood are the decline of child well-being and the rise of male violence, particularly predatory sexual violence. A society of Sperm Fathers is a society of fourteen-year-old girls with babies and fourteen-year-old boys with guns.

For the culture, the rise of the Sperm Father constitutes nothing less than father killing, the witting enactment of cultural patricide. For the individual man, being a Sperm Father is not a style of fatherhood but a means of paternal suicide: the collaboration of the male in the eradication of his fatherhood. Toward the end of the fatherless society, the Sperm Father represents the final solution.

CHAPTER 10

The Stepfather and the Nearby Guy

The Stepfather and the Nearby Guy are substitute fathers. They are not fathers, but they serve as what are frequently called father figures—nonfathers who help to raise other men's children. In this respect, they are the polar opposite of the Sperm Father. For him, paternity is strictly biological. There is no social component. For the Stepfather and the Nearby Guy, paternity is strictly social. There is no biological component.

Growing numbers of biological fathers—Deadbeat Dads, Visiting Fathers, and Sperm Fathers—do not live with their children and have discontinued the parental alliance with their children's mother. The Stepfather and the Nearby Guy are expected to fill the fatherhood vacuum created by their absence. As cultural models, they are viewed essentially as replacement fathers, perhaps able to offer the functional equivalent of fatherhood to children whose fathers have departed.

In this sense, the Stepfather and the Nearby Guy constitute two natural consequences, twin by-products, of the trend toward fatherlessness. As fathers disappear, these men appear, offering not fatherhood but a simulation of fatherhood. Their ranks are swelling. Increasingly, these are the men who raise the children.

There are important differences between the Stepfather and the Nearby Guy. Because the Stepfather is married to the mother, his commitment to her—and thus indirectly to her children—is much more formal and probably deeper and more enduring. The most common example of a Nearby Guy is a mother's boyfriend. Almost by definition, his commitment to the mother is ambivalent, sporadic, and contingent. From the child's perspective, especially compared to either fathers or stepfathers, boyfriends often come and go without leaving much of a trace.

A Nearby Guy can also be a family friend, a neighbor, a teacher, a Little League coach, a Scout leader, a Big Brother, a Sunday School teacher, a school principal or counselor, a social worker, or the father of a class-mate—any adult male who is willing and able to take a fatherly interest in a child growing up without a father. Such relationships, of course, are highly diverse and have impacts ranging from good to bad, profound to fleeting.

Yet the differences between the Stepfather and the Nearby Guy are out-weighed by three underlying similarities. First, both the Stepfather and the Nearby Guy are biologically and legally unrelated to the children they help to raise. The legal nonrelationship—if a mother dies, for example, a step-father loses any legal claim to custody—stems directly from the biological nonrelationship. Much of family law derives from the anthropological proposition that, as the family scholar David Popenoe puts it, "the family is fundamentally rooted in biology and at least partly activated by the 'genetically selfish' activities of human beings." As a result, almost all human societies accept the principle that "childrearing by nonrelatives is inherently problematic."[1] For this reason, family law—with only rare and carefully circumscribed exceptions, such as adoption—typically does not recognize nonrelatives as parental figures or as members of a child's family.

Second, both the Stepfather and the Nearby Guy embody a model of fatherhood born of loss and defined by ambiguity, complexity, and fre-quent change. In both cases, one man's fatherly acts spring from, and are made necessary by, another man's abandonment of his child. Especially for the child, then, emotions are always mixed, loyalties always divided. If I call this guy "Dad," or even think of him as a father, am I being disloyal to my real father? Am I happy that my mother found someone new, or angry that she replaced my father? What makes this new person any better than my father?

In both cases, relationships and living arrangements tend to change often. Some boyfriends and other friends stay around for a while, but most do not. William R. Beer describes a stepfamily as "like a trolley car that rolls along the tracks, with people getting on and off."[2] In both cases, things tend to get very complicated, in part simply because more people are involved, but, more important, because the people involved have diver-gent family histories and inherently conflicting commitments—many of which surface as real or symbolic conflicts between the substitute father and the biological father.[3]

Accordingly, even the word *father* can acquire an unclear meaning. In one sense, a child in this situation does not have a father. But in another sense, this child has at least two—and sometimes three or four or more—"fathers": men who agree at certain points to perform certain fatherly tasks. As a result, even the most basic question—Who is this child's father?—can become difficult to answer.

Third, both the Stepfather and the boyfriend version of the Nearby Guy are cultural models premised not on fatherhood but on the search for adult companionship. Both of these identities emerge essentially from what Judith Wallerstein calls second chances—new opportunities for adults to find mates. Put simply, for both of these replacement fathers, the main object of desire and commitment is the mother, not the child.

For the married father, of course, this distinction hardly exists. The two go together. The married father says: my mate, my child. But for good reason, the stepfather and the boyfriend must say: my mate, her child. Or even more sharply: my mate, his child. From the child's perspective, the arrival of a boyfriend or stepfather does not represent a "second chance" nearly as much as it represents a foreclosure of the first and only chance.

Despite these obvious conflicts, much of our current discourse about these newly prevalent father figures is shaped by a strong desire to look on the bright side. In general, our society views these men with considerable hopefulness, even optimism. In today's fatherhood script, they are pretty good guys. The experts seek to understand and support them. They are almost never viewed as a special problem or threat.

For in a society where fatherhood itself is increasingly viewed as superfluous, substitute fathers constitute little cause for alarm and even some cause for praise. Indeed, in an increasingly fatherless society, these father figures may be our last, best hope for a male presence in the lives of many children. We would like to believe in them.

The Stepfather

In 1963, Walt Disney Pictures released *The Incredible Journey,* a story of three adorable pets, two dogs and a cat, who become separated from the family that loves them, but then manage against all the odds to find their way home again. Thirty years later, Walt Disney released a remake of this popular children's movie, called *Homeward Bound: The Incredible Journey.* In general, the two films are quite similar. Yet in one important respect, the 1993 movie differs from its predecessor. In 1993, the struggle of the three pets to "go home" to the children is echoed by a parallel struggle of the three children to "go home" to their new life with a Stepfather.

The first scene in the newer movie is a wedding. Bob and Laura are getting married, and her three children are members of the wedding party. (We learn nothing in this movie about Laura's former husband—a gap in the narrative that seems both glaring and calculated.)[4] The two youngest children are indifferent to the man they call Bob, who turns out to be a terrific guy. The oldest child, Peter, is more obviously suspicious of Bob.

Immediately after the wedding, the family departs for San Francisco, where Bob has a temporary job. During the course of this relocation, the three pets are dropped off temporarily with a friend who lives on a ranch. The pets quickly become fearful and homesick. They miss the children. Soon they find a way to escape, thus beginning their incredible journey home.

Meanwhile, in San Francisco, the children learn that their pets are missing. They are crestfallen. Although no one is at fault, Peter clearly blames Bob for uprooting the family. Peter goes to the police station to report the pets missing. When the officer, filling out a form, needs the names of Peter's "parents," Peter starts to say the word *dad,* but quickly stops himself, referring to Bob instead as "her husband."

But over the next several weeks, amazing things happen. The three pets, showing great courage and faith, manage to find their way home to the children who love them. At the same time, the three children, settling in to their new life, lovingly embrace Bob as their father. The key scene—only moments before the missing pets reappear—is when Peter first calls his new stepfather "Dad." The ending is a happy one.

The 1963 movie had one moral: When wonderful pets are separated from the most important people in their lives, they desperately want to, and can, find their way back. But the 1993 movie adds a second, quite contradictory, moral to this story: When wonderful children are separated from their father, they want to, and can, find a new father to love. In this sense, the 1993 moral for the children is the opposite of the moral for the pets. To find their home, the pets go back. To find their father, the children go forward.

The pets struggle fiercely to reunite with those who left them. The children, on the other hand, easily accept a replacement for the one who left them. A father can be replaced. In this movie, losing a pet is much harder than losing a father.

In essence, the 1963 movie was about the importance of fidelity—not only regarding a child's relationship to a pet but, more broadly, regarding all primary relationships. The 1993 movie is also about fidelity, but only with respect to pets. For people, the 1993 conclusion about primary relationships is that change can be your friend. For children, the message is quite specific: Changing fathers is easy. For this reason, *Homeward Bound* is not simply a fantasy for children about pets but also a fantasy for adults about children. The essence of this adult fantasy is that a stepfather is a father, and that children in a stepfamily do not need or care about their biological father.

Among married couples raising children, the growing prevalence of stepfathers is probably the most important transformation of U.S. family life in this generation.[5] During the 1980s, the number of stepfathers continued to increase at an astonishing rate. By 1990, about 5.1 million stepfathers were living with dependent children in the United States, up from

3.7 million in 1980. In 1980, about 15 percent of all married-couple house-holds with children contained a stepfather. By 1990, the figure had reached 21 percent—a 40 percent increase in ten years.[6]

Most current advice literature for remarried parents leans toward gen-der-neutral terminology, typically describing issues as they relate to "step-parents" and "stepfamilies." Yet as a daily presence in the lives of children, stepfathers are far more numerous and important than stepmothers. Up to 90 percent of all divorcing mothers maintain physical custody of their chil-dren.[7] In 1990, mother-stepfather couples with children outnumbered father-stepmother couples by a factor of more than 17 to 1. Among all stepchildren, the vast majority live with their biological mother and a step-father. In this sense, "stepparenting" in the United States has become an overwhelmingly male activity.[8]

Many analysts, guided by the same cultural ethos that informs *Home-ward Bound,* are quite optimistic about the rapidly growing number of stepfathers in the United States. In *Making Peace in Your Stepfamily,* Harold H. Bloomfield describes remarried parents as "the new wave of what family is all about in America." His conclusion is unequivocal: "There is no reason why stepparents cannot parent just as effectively as biological parents."[9]

Testifying before a congressional committee, the historian Tamara K. Hareven describes "blended families" as "a new source of adaptability and stability" in U.S. family life:

> As a result of the remarriage of one or both of their parents, children of divorce may have access to three or four sets of grandparents rather than just two. They also may have access to many more aunts and uncles and cousins, and new relatives. Thus, there is encouraging evidence that divorce, in many cases, is followed by a recovery and reconstruction, as well as expansion of family ties.[10]

In *Making It As a Stepparent,* Claire Berman offers similar praise:

> Countless boys and girls are finding their lives broadened and enriched by the presence of four caring parents and by an untold number of new relatives and friends. They are enjoying the opportunity to experience a variety of life styles and to select from each that which seems to suit them best.[11]

Among scholars, Ross A. Thompson agrees with several other research-ers who can find "no reliable evidence that children in stepfamilies differ significantly from children in other family structures in intellectual and cognitive development, personality and social behavior, adjustment, and family relationships." Consequently, Thompson suggests that "remarriage has no significant positive or negative effects on children."[12] Kyle D. Pruett goes further. In some ways, stepfathers may be better than fathers. For Pruett finds that

> stepfathers may be more attentive to the needs of their children and . . . less arbitrary in their parenting style than are fathers of many intact families, partly because their consciousness has been raised about the overriding significance of *two* parents in the lives of their children.[13]

This abstract language is revealing. Many of these authors insist on blurring or even erasing the distinction between relatives and nonrelatives. Consequently, to Berman, children in stepfamilies have "four caring parents." Pruett describes how stepfathers attend to the needs of "their" children. This same language is ubiquitous in books about stepfamilies written for children. In *The Wedding,* for example, a storybook, Mrs. Grant tells her son Robby that she has decided to marry Jack:

> "What's going to happen to my dad?" Robby asked.
> "Nothing. You'll see him just the way you do now," Mrs. Grant said.
> "Is he still going to be my father?" Robby wondered.
> "Sure he will. He'll always be your father," she answered. "In a way, you'll have two fathers."
> "Two fathers?" Robby repeated to himself, trying to understand.[14]

However they might "try to understand," very few real-life children actually believe that they have "two fathers." Or that stepparents "parent" just as well as biological parents. Or that living in a stepfamily constitutes a "new source of stability." Or that living in a stepfamily "has no significant positive or negative effects on children."

All these ideas reflect less the actual circumstances of children than the wishful thinking of adults. From a child's perspective, the truth about stepfamilies is more nearly the opposite of these feel-good descriptions. Stepfamilies comprise the most unstable and volatile family form in our society. They are inherently fraught with bad outcomes for children. More specifically, the great majority of stepfathers are not—cannot ever be—replacement fathers or even extra fathers. In almost all of the most important ways, they are not fathers at all.

Despite Ross A. Thompson's claim to the contrary, the social science data regarding outcomes for children in stepfamilies are remarkably consistent and almost uniformly bleak. In 1992, James H. Bray and colleagues presented findings from a seven-year study of approximately two hundred married-couple families, half of which contained a stepfather. The researchers found that the stepfamilies "reported and were observed to have more negative family relationships and more problematic family processes than nuclear families." Over the seven-year period, for example, "remarried husbands became more negative and less positive toward their wives than first-marriage husbands."

Children in these stepfather families had "more behavioral problems, less prosocial behavior, and more life stress." Moreover, stepfather-stepchild relationships "continued to be less positive and more negative and became more negative over time than did father-child relationships."[15]

Numerous studies demonstrate that children who live with stepfathers experience outcomes that are no better, and frequently worse, than children in mother-only homes. For example, does the arrival of an "additional adult" in a household reduce children's susceptibility to antisocial peer pressure and thus lower the risk of deviant behavior? The answer, it seems, is no. In his survey of 865 adolescents, Laurence Steinberg concludes that

> youngsters living in stepfamilies are equally at risk for involvement in deviant behavior as are their peers living in single-parent households. Although an additional adult is present in the adolescent's stepfamily, this may be a case in which two parents are not enough.[16]

Similarly, Nicholas Zill has documented some of the long-term consequences of parental divorce for children. Does remarriage, or the arrival of a stepfather, offer any protection against these harmful consequences? The answer, again, appears to be no:

> We found that remarriage, which usually brings a reliable second income to the family, did not appear to have an overall protective effect. It may be that any advantages in economic or parental resources are offset by the rivalry and increased conflict that stepparents and stepsiblings often bring with them.[17]

Frank F. Furstenberg, Jr., summarizes the current U.S. evidence: "Most studies show that children in stepfamilies do not do better than children in single-parent families; indeed, many indicate that on average children in remarriages do worse."[18]

These remarkable findings are reinforced by research from Great Britain and Australia. In Britain, results from a major longitudinal study of 17,000 children born in 1958 reveal that those in stepfamilies not only experienced far worse outcomes than did children who grew up with their two biological parents but also, on almost every measurement, experienced worse outcomes than did children from single-parent homes. For example, compared to girls from single-parent homes, girls from stepfamilies were more likely to drop out of school, to leave home early (frequently due to friction in the home), and to bear a child before reaching age twenty. Compared to boys from single-parent homes, boys from stepfamilies were more likely to drop out of school, to leave home early, to enter into a cohabiting relationship outside of marriage, and to become a father at an early age.[19] As the London *Daily Telegraph* described this study: "What emerges is the sad picture of young people becoming estranged from stepfamilies at an early age, and starting independent lives with little in the way of educational attainment and opportunities for work."[20]

In Australia, the Children in Families study, sponsored by the Australian Institute of Family Studies, conducted in-depth interviews with 402 children living in Victoria. Half of the children interviewed were age eight or nine years old; half were fifteen to sixteen. Children at both age levels "reported significantly less support from stepfathers than from biological fathers in intact families." Stepfathers were also "less likely than custodial mothers to play the role of disciplinarian." Indeed, some stepfathers, at least initially, "may even exercise no discipline at all in a policy of deliberate non-engagement."[21]

Comparing children from intact, single-parent, and stepfamily homes, the study concludes that "it appears to be children from stepfamilies that have a disadvantage. These children, compared with children in other family types, have lower levels of reading ability, self-control, and self-esteem. . . . These findings suggest that gaining a new parent can be more debilitating than losing an old one."[22]

What causes this special deprivation experienced by the children of stepfamilies? Certainly many features of stepfamily life, from its instability to its inevitable breeding of divided loyalties, contribute to this phenomenon.[23] But the primary underlying cause is fatherlessness. Indeed, unlike children in mother-only homes, children in stepfamilies commonly experience a twofold loss of fatherhood. In short, in the area of fatherhood, many of these children are twice cursed.

First, the remarriage of either parent typically means the further erosion, and at times the cessation, of the child's relationship with his or her biological father. When a custodial mother remarries, for example, visits from the biological father typically become less frequent. Child-support payments become less likely.[24] Similarly, when the father remarries, he typically concentrates his attention and resources on his new home, not his old one. In retrospect, for the biological father, his divorce only began the process of disengaging from mother and child. As Furstenberg puts it: "Remarriage by either former partner usually hastens this process of disengagement."[25]

Second, and probably more important, the stepfather, precisely because he is not a father, can become for the stepchild a reminder of fatherlessness, an embodiment of fatherlessness. This guy is doing what my father should be doing. He is sleeping in the bed my father should be sleeping in. In this sense, his presence constitutes a rebuke of my father, a denial of my father. Moreover, if I let him "father" me, or if I agree with my mother that he is a great guy, I am admitting my father's guilt. If I let him win my affection, I may further lose my father's affection.

The result of this dynamic is not fatherhood or even a rough approximation of fatherhood. Fathers strive above all to protect their children, supporting and reassuring them, especially regarding the primacy of parental love. But what commonly results from the stepfather-stepchild dynamic is more nearly the opposite of paternal protection. Even in cases of good people with the best of intentions, what often emerges instead is a relationship that introduces children to new sources of divisiveness and anxiety regarding the most important questions in their lives.

Faced with such a stressful and largely insoluble problem, many stepfathers understandably respond by simply disengaging. Accordingly, many studies describe the stepfather-stepchild relationship, as against the father-child relationship, as less warm, less communicative, and significantly more detached. One study documents "a pattern in which the stepfather functioned as a more distant and detached observer."[26] Another concludes: "Both stepmothers and stepfathers take a considerably less active role in parenting than do custodial parents. Even after two years, disengagement by the stepparent is the most common parenting style."[27]

The advice literature for stepfathers clearly acknowledges, and frequently recommends, this strategy of disengagement. Indeed, this literature is quite revealing. For in many cases, alongside the boosterism and reassuring happy-talk—why your second family can be better than your first—these authors provide practical advice to stepfathers that is soberingly realistic and anything but reassuring.

Recall Harold H. Bloomfield's ringing assertion: "There is no reason why stepparents cannot parent just as effectively as biological parents." Yet in an article for *Parenting* magazine, Bloomfield divides his advice to stepparents into two categories. The first is "Grappling with Guilt." Divorced fathers, Bloomfield says, are "especially prone to guilt's debilitating effects because their children usually live with their former spouse, while they themselves may have become stepfathers to their second wife's children." He advises these stepfathers to "stop chastising themselves for the pain they've caused their children."

Under the topic of "Rolling with the Punches," Bloomfield writes: "Few stepparents are prepared to face just how much it hurts to be repeatedly spurned by their stepchildren." It is

> only natural to feel overwhelmed and trapped when you're raising children who aren't yours and who resent your presence. But the best tack for dealing with such frustration is to accept it, without letting it take over your family life.[28]

In an article called "Happily Remarried" in *Working Mother* magazine, Sandi Kahn Shelton argues that the "secret to a successful stepfamily is helping a new husband learn to be a good father." Toward this end, Shelton proposes a set of "tips" for mothers to pass along to their new husbands. First: "Help him realize that acceptance by the children is going to take a lot of time":

> Older kids may take years to become adjusted to a new parent in the household, and some may never really get beyond thinking of the stepfather as "my mother's husband." But don't be shocked if even very young children are resistant at first.

Second: "The mother should be the main disciplinarian for awhile." Until "expectations are smoothed out" and "trust is formed," most psychologists agree that "it's probably best if the mother is the one who sorts out the temper tantrums and makes sure the rules of the household are followed."

Third: "Don't try to force a relationship to develop between your husband and your children." The main rule here is to "resist the urge to promote harmony." She quotes a psychologist: "Stepfathers and children have to respect each other, be civil to each other, and try to get along. But they don't have to love each other."

Shelton mentions four additional tips. Protect the stepfather's possessions. ("You can't ask the stepfather to make all the adjustments.") Make new traditions together. (But in doing so, remember to "drop anything that isn't working.") Try to patch up problems with your ex-husband. And make time for your marriage. (Although second marriages can be "complicated," they "really do provide a second chance at happiness.")[29]

Almost all the advice literature for stepfathers and stepchildren brings up the question of names. Here, as throughout this literature, the most frequently used word is *complicated*. For the child, there are two basic complications. First, what is my name?[30] Do I keep my father's last name or, as my mother has (probably) done, take on my stepfather's name? In fact, most stepchildren retain their father's name. Yet, as Bloomfield observes, stepchildren who keep their father's name "often feel embarrassed, particularly at school or church where the difference becomes conspicuous. The child suddenly finds himself or herself having to explain why he or she has a different name than his or her own mother!"[31]

Second, what do I call my stepfather? Unlike the children in *Homeward Bound*, who took only a few weeks to begin calling their stepfather "Daddy," most stepchildren do not call their stepfather "Dad" or "Daddy," or refer to their stepfather as their father. Recognizing this fact, the advice literature generally recommends that children either choose a nickname for their stepfather or simply address him by his first name.[32]

In general, the advice literature urges a practical, flexible approach to the problem of names. Talk things over. Consult the children. Do what feels best. In *What Am I Doing in a Stepfamily?* an advice book for young children, children are told: "Remember, it isn't what you call someone that's important. It's how you feel about the person that matters."[33]

This approach is understandable, but it is based on a false idea. As an epistemological matter, and especially as a matter of child development, "what you call someone" cannot be separated from, much less pitted against, "how you feel about the person." The two go together. Or at least, they ought to go together.

However well intended, adult casualness about the word *father* serves only to blur the main issue. For children, the core question is simple: Who is my father? The name matters because the father matters. Consequently, which man I call my father matters. Most children do not call stepfathers "Daddy" or "my father" precisely because they do not believe that these men are their fathers.

These children are right. Whatever their other virtues, these men are not their fathers. They are not even replacement fathers or second fathers. Remarriage may offer adults a second chance for happiness. But remarriage does not offer children a second chance for fatherhood.

The Nearby Guy

In Los Angeles in 1993, Kevin Thomas went to court to prove that he is the father of a little girl named Courtney. Courtney's biological father, her mother's former boyfriend, is a man Courtney has never met. But Kevin Thomas, who had a platonic friendship with the mother, helped to raise Courtney from the time she was born until she was four years old. Then Thomas and the mother had a falling out, and she stopped allowing him to spend time with Courtney. Thomas hired a lawyer and went to court, seeking the same rights as any other noncustodial father.[34]

Thomas won his case. Embracing what one local newspaper termed an "evolving definition" of "daddy," the judge named him as Courtney's legal father.[35] Thomas could tell reporters: "I'm the real father."[36]

Legally, Kevin Thomas faced an uphill struggle. Courts typically insist that paternal rights derive solely from kinship, marriage, or adoption. But by 1993, Kevin Thomas's lawyer, Glen H. Schwartz, had already won several other limited but potentially precedent-setting custody and visitation victories on behalf of nonbiological, never-married "fathers"—men who assert that they are fathers and who help raise children, but who lack both a biological relationship to the child and a formal relationship to the mother.[37]

So Kevin Thomas, and other "fathers" like him, do have some grounds for optimism. They are winning recognition. Legally, the tide may be shifting their way. Culturally, the tide is certainly shifting their way.

For Kevin Thomas represents a spreading and increasingly acceptable, even welcome, type of fatherhood in our society: the fatherhood of the Nearby Guy. As a cultural model, the Nearby Guy is a father who is better than nothing. He is not a biological father. He has never been married to the mother. Unless he is a live-in boyfriend, he does not live with the child. He is much more detached and peripheral, closer to being an acquaintance than a relative.

But he is there, at least sometimes, willing to pitch in. He is a possible role model, a father figure, a man who will help. Benjamin Spock once observed that "children know that they need a father figure and will create one out of whatever materials are at hand."[38] For a growing number of children in our society, the Nearby Guy is the only material at hand.

In our hearts, we realize that he is not a father. At the same time, our society increasingly describes him as one, hoping that he can offer a small but valuable piece of fatherhood to the children who are growing up without fathers. David Ray, whose father left when he was a child, writes movingly of his lifelong search for "potential fathers—and by father I mean not bearer of seed but bestower of human kindness and companionship, a man with some flicker of interest in a boy's future."[39] David Giveans and Michael Robinson describe the importance of the "psychological father," defined as any man who

> responds to and is a significant influence in forming a child's future. Psychological fathers include friends of the nuclear and binuclear (single-parent) family, men participating in organized groups for children such as PAL, Big Brothers, and foster grandparent programs, and male teachers.[40]

Maybe we should give this guy a chance, support what he does. Maybe he can help. In an increasingly fatherless society, perhaps the Nearby Guy represents part of the solution.

For this reason, family scholars frequently study the Nearby Guy, seeking to validate his contributions to child rearing. For example, when speaking of teenage mothers and their children, Harold P. Gershenson recommends that we "redefine" the word *father,* since the old definition, bound by biology and marriage, is "not very useful for understanding family processes" in these families. The new definition, according to Gershenson, must expand "the possible range of candidates for fatherhood," recognizing that "the experiences of most children of young mothers are not with one father figure but with many."[41]

In his study, Gershenson examines "four groups of fathers" who are "men other than the child's biological father." These groups are: "current husbands of the young mothers, former husbands or boyfriends who are not the children's biological fathers, current boyfriends (not the biological fathers), and the mothers' own fathers or stepfathers." Gershenson insists that this "multiple fatherhood" should "not be construed as having necessarily negative effects on the child." Indeed, Gershenson concludes that "neither kinship nor household membership is necessary for a male to perform those psychological and instrumental functions commonly associated with fatherhood in our society."[42]

Margaret Crosbie-Burnett, Ada Skyles, and Jane Becker-Haven recommend a similar "reconceptualization." Instead of focusing simply on "biological parents," our society "must validate and utilize all adults who are available and may already be helping to rear children."[43] Toward this end, James A. Levine, seeking ways to involve fathers in the Head Start program, recommends that researchers and program developers "define father to include father figures." Thus: "Broadening the definition of father to 'father figure' allows professionals to be more sensitive to family networks . . . by tapping into a larger pool of males."[44]

What is striking about these studies is their repeated insistence upon redefining the primary word: *father*. In the view of these scholars, this word simply does not, and ought not, convey a specific meaning. Instead, the word is broadened, thinned out, complexified to mean: *a Nearby Guy*.

The old definition was objective. Are you the biological father? Are you married to the mother? The new definition is subjective. How do you feel about this child? How does the child feel about you? Are you acting like a father? As a cultural category, the Nearby Guy is highly elastic and purposefully vague.

Indeed, if the Nearby Guy qualifies as a father, or at least as a sort-of father, even the simplest questions about fatherhood become impossible to answer with any precision. Do I have a father? Hard to say. For we must now grapple what Frank L. Mott calls

> the highly complex nature of paternal absence; the father's absence from the home (even for children whose fathers have *never* lived in the home) masks the contact that substantial proportions of father-absent children have with individuals—fathers or other father figures—who can potentially be fulfilling the fatherhood role.[45]

Mott seems to be saying that amid all this complexity, perhaps some fathering is taking place. If the idea of "father" is stretched far enough—if we can call the Nearby Guy a father—anything is possible.[46]

Why does our society increasingly look to the Nearby Guy as a father? Why are we redefining the word *father* to include him? As an empirical matter, his claim to fatherhood is almost self-evidently frivolous. Recall the basics. In all societies, fatherhood is a social role that obligates men to their biological offspring. The enabling foundations of fatherhood are co-residency with children and a parental alliance with the mother. Measured against any of these baseline criteria, the Nearby Guy does not even come close. Imagining that he does, or even that he theoretically can, is not analysis but wistfulness.

So the crucial question about the Nearby Guy is not empirical but philosophical. It is less about him than about us. For if this guy is clearly not a father, why are we beginning to call him a father? What is the cultural basis of his appeal?

In part, the Nearby Guy is a helpful fellow for scholars seeking to confirm the viability of the mother-headed home. If the Nearby Guy can be a father to these children, then father-absence "per se" constitutes much less of a problem. For example, in her essay on "Making Single Motherhood Normal," Iris Marion Young concedes that it is "plausible that parenting is easier and more effective if two or more adults discuss the children's needs and provide different kinds of interactions with them." Yet: "It does not follow, however, that the second adult must be a live-in husband." To Young, a "relative, lover or friend" would do just as well, or in some cases, even better.[47] In this instance, the Nearby Guy is a cultural idea aimed explicitly at the deconstruction of fatherhood, or what might be called making fatherlessness normal.

But more often, praise for the Nearby Guy in our society reflects less a denigration of fathers than a longing for them. In this sense, calling the Nearby Guy a father—hoping that he might be a father—constitutes a kind of cultural yearning, a cry for help. The tone is not angry or assertive, but poignant. We need some men to be around these fatherless children. We need more male teachers, more Scout leaders, more Big Brothers. In an article on male nannies, the *New York Times* reports that "men are more frequently hired as nannies by single mothers who are looking for a male presence in their children's lives."[48] The yearning is strong. We are running out of fathers. Maybe these guys can do something.

In a larger sense, however, this hopeful embrace of the Nearby Guy constitutes our ultimate acceptance not only of fatherlessness but of a culture of fatherlessness. For as fatherhood declines in our society, so does our idea of fatherhood. As fatherlessness spreads, fatherhood itself becomes harder even to recognize, much less to defend. As a result, we lose the will, and even the ability, to make distinctions. Definitions get stretched out. Standards get lower. Ideas get both weaker and more complicated. We get desperate. In a culture of fatherlessness, anybody can be a father.

PART III

FATHERHOOD

CHAPTER 11

The Good Family Man

The Good Family Man is a necessary father without portfolio. As a cultural model, he is largely missing from our current scholarly and expert discourse on fatherhood. In today's prevailing script, he is a character without a name, unheralded, often unrecognized. He plays his part off to the side, out of the spotlight, barely visible, increasingly overshadowed by others.

Despite this cultural imperceptibility, millions of men in the United States are Good Family Men. Yet their ranks are rapidly thinning. With each passing year, the Good Family Man represents an increasingly smaller proportion of actual men in our society.

As a father, the Good Family Man is not perfect, but he is good enough to be irreplaceable. He is married. He stays around. He is a father on the premises. His children need him and he strives to give them what they need, every day. He knows that nothing can substitute for him. Either he is a father or his children are fatherless. He would never consider himself "not that important" to his children.

It would never occur to him—or to his children or to his wife—to make distinctions between "biological" and "social" fathering. For him, these two identities are tightly fused. Nor would it ever occur to him to suspect that the "male income" is more important for children than the "male image." For him, the two fit together. Consequently, he seldom ponders issues such as child support, visitation, paternity identification, fathers' rights, better divorce, joint custody, dating, or blended families. His primary concerns lie elsewhere.

The Good Family Man is not what Melinda Blau calls a "mix 'n' match" parent. He has not transcended his masculinity or "moved beyond" male roles. It would rarely occur to him to call what he does "mothering" or even "parenting." To him, the key word is not a verb at all, but a gender-specific noun, "father," whose meaning is clear.

In today's expert story of fatherhood, brief appearances by the Good Family Man are frequently, and in many respects wrongly, labeled as re-appearances of the Old Father. A guy who remains too "traditional." Similarly, the Good Family Man is sometimes portrayed simply as a prospective New Father, a kind of father-in-progress, with the potential for becoming something better and newer.

Yet the Good Family Man is neither a resurgent Old Father nor a New Father in waiting. He wields authority. He believes that he is doing men's work in his family. He assumes that his fatherhood is necessary and irreplaceable. At the same time, he knows that his wife also wields authority. He knows that her work in the family, while not identical to his, is equally important and also irreplaceable. He aspires to the ideals of paternal tenderness and companionate marriage. He believes that men who lead are men who serve.

Ponder the three words. *Good:* moral values. *Family:* purposes larger than the self. *Man:* a norm of masculinity. As a phrase of speech, *good family man* was once widely heard in our society, bestowed on men deserving it as a compliment and a badge of honor. Rough translation: He puts his family first.

Yet today, this phrase sounds antiquated, almost embarrassing. The phrase sounds old-fashioned in part because, as each year passes, there are fewer such men. As one father told me, today's good family man is increasingly likely to have "gray hair or no hair."[1] Another observed that

> they're just not there. They've either run away, or things have shifted where it's just really hard to be that way. And it shows up in what the kids are getting into now. So that a good family man is hard to find. And if you're trying to be it, you're in the minority.

Moreover, the phrase sounds old-fashioned because today's prevailing cultural narrative pays almost no attention to this guy. He has little cachet, and he is no favorite of the experts. Demographically, the Good Family Man constitutes a significant but shrinking presence in our society. Culturally, he is nondescript, almost invisible.

Despite these weaknesses, the Good Family Man has one distinctive strength. He is not simply one more version of the Unnecessary Father. As a cultural model, he constitutes the best evidence available that fatherhood is not superfluous. In an increasingly fatherless society, the Good Family Man stands for fatherhood. Consider his story.

Good-Enough Fatherhood

In 1992 and 1993, several colleagues and I conducted two-hour focus-group interviews on the subject of fatherhood with approximately 85 married fathers in four cities: Denver, Colorado; Jackson, Mississippi; Teaneck, New Jersey; and Cleveland, Ohio. In Cleveland, we also interviewed 12 married mothers on the subject of fatherhood. In addition, we interviewed approximately 150 parents in five localities—San Francisco, California; Chicago, Illinois; Towson, Maryland; Teaneck, New Jersey; and Austin, Texas—on the broader subject of contemporary parenthood and family life.

All together, we reached about 250 parents in eight states for these in-depth, in-person interviews, conducted in small groups ranging in size from nine to twelve. We sought to reach a broad cross-section of married, middle-class America. To fit our interview criteria, a person had to be currently married, have at least one child at home under age eighteen, and have a family income that was higher than poverty and lower than affluence, usually between $20,000 and $50,000 per year. Regarding race, ethnicity, and the labor-force participation of mothers, the parents we interviewed mirrored the diversity of the local populations.

In interviewing these men, and in asking these women about their husbands, I sought to explore one basic question: What does it mean to be a good father today? Our prevailing expert discourse, dominated by the idea of the Unnecessary Father, provides flawed and even hostile answers to this question. So I decided to look to fathers themselves. More specifically, I looked to the men most likely to be good-enough fathers: stably married men living with their biological children. I asked them, What is a good father? Is a good father different from a good mother? What is happening to the good father in our society?

These interviews revolved around lengthy discussions of a single phrase: Good Family Man. One hour into the interviews, after introductions and preliminary discussions of "what it's like to be a father today," I would write the phrase with a Magic Marker on a large sheet of easel paper. Have you heard this phrase before? Under what circumstances? What does it mean to you? What is the definition of a good family man today? I pushed these groups of fathers to work together, expanding and clarifying their definition, struggling to get the right traits listed in the right order.

To appreciate the essential story of these encounters, consider what happened in the course of one evening during the summer of 1992 in Denver. Listen to twenty married fathers, two groups of ten each, take up the challenge of defining the Good Family Man. The way they reason and the words they choose—not simply their conclusions, but their specific words—merit close attention.

With the first group, I moved toward a consideration of the Good Family Man by asking these men to summarize the two or three most important things they do for their children. Omitting repetition and extraneous comments from the transcript, here are the key words and phrases they used to answer this question: *Sports.* (Laughter.) *Lots of sports. Lots of athletics.*

Playmate. Tour guide. ("I mean, not just to the zoo, but trying to, parts of their life.") *Education and teaching. Practice.* ("Just helping with home-work.") *Career guidance. Motivation. Goal orientation. Dealing with vio-lence.* ("I hesitate to say getting them to associate with the right people, but it's more like trying to keep them from associating with the wrong people. . . . It's like, 'Don't hang around them jerks.'")

After each of them had answered, I asked these fathers whether they had ever heard the phrase *good family man.* Most of them had. How had they heard it? What did it mean to them? Here are five answers that cap-ture their collective response:

> You'd hear it, like, at a funeral.
> Church-related: "He was a good family man."
> I guess somebody with strong ties with the family and spouse.
> I heard it at school—his school, see, school was overloaded with women teachers and, you know, you can hear them talk about friends or another male teacher in the building, and they'll say he's a good man. You know, referring to his family. He takes care of them.
> I go to school in the evenings and I was getting a study session together. And I told this study session I couldn't attend, you know. One of the individuals said, "Oh, you're a good family man, huh?" And I said, Yeah, I have to take care of some deals with my children.

Turning away from their recollections of the phrase, I then asked them to begin working together on a modern definition. What does it mean to be a good family man today? What if the phrase were to be included in a new dictionary? What would the dictionary say? Distilled from the tran-script, here are the specific words they selected: *Responsibility to your fam-ily. Love. Genuinely cares for his family.* ("Well, I was going to say that all of his decisions are made in terms of what's best for the family, not neces-sarily for his own personal wants.") *Family first. Willing to sacrifice. Good provider.* ("At least a steady provider. Didn't make a fortune, but he went to work every day.") *Spends time doing family activities.* ("He's also a *busy* family man." [Laughter.] *High moral character. Sharing. Being there for the sad times as well as the good. Sets a good example. Admits mistakes.*

Then I asked: "Now, talk to me a minute about what's happening to this guy today. Compared to, say, twenty years ago, are there more people like him, or fewer?" The first response came from a guy who simply said: "Dinosaur." Here are three other comments that convey the basic sense of the discussion:

> Probably fewer, because we're having more divorces and they seem to be a little bit more violent than they used to be.
> I think it goes back to the morals, kind of. The young men that get

married today, they don't seem to have some of those qualities. Or at least be striving for that, you know. It seems like, you know, it's easy to lie, not to tell the truth. It's easy just to run off and leave a young lady with a baby.

The results of living high and running fast haven't made people happy, and they're looking for what they missed. And seeing what they missed is a strong relationship with family. And that was lost for a while, but I think it's coming back some.

Again shifting the topic, I asked them to return once more to the Good Family Man traits listed on the easel paper: "It's a long list, right? What are the one or two main things? What's the heart of it and what's peripheral?"

They reorganized and consolidated, searching for ways to present only the essential traits, and in order of priority. Here is their final definition of a Good Family Man:

1. Puts his family first
       is responsible for his family
       cares for his family; makes sacrifices for family, not self
       spends time on family activities

2. Good and steady provider

3. Sets a good example
       high moral character
       "being there" for family; steadiness; won't bail out
       admits mistakes.

They went home. Ten more fathers arrived. With this second group, I similarly approached the main topic by asking them to describe the "two or three most important things you do" for "your wife and children." A rich discussion followed, yielding this group's preliminary definition of the Good Family Man. These seven comments convey the basic themes of this conversation:

I think first you have to provide for your family financially. Probably everybody will agree on that one. The other one is the positive role model.

Protector—protect your family. They need somebody to run to when they're in trouble. They need you there and you need to be there for them. And that's basically what I mean by protecting them. Making sure that no outside forces hurt them.

I agree with the guys, what they're saying, the first and second one. [Another one should be] reassuring or reestablish their confidence in themselves and what they can do . . . because they have to have self-confidence enough that somebody else won't influence them to do something they shouldn't do.

Self-esteem is so important, especially in minority kids. I also, I try to give them a lesson learned in life. . . . [I say to my kids:] I'm going to pass this on to you. It cost me, but I'm going to give it to you to put in a paper bag to take with you for life. And if you can use it, but it's a lesson learned—I've paid for it. I want to give it to you so you don't make the same mistake. And I try to build a foundation of common sense and mother wit that my grandfather gave me.

I think one of the strongest roles that the father can have is the spiritual leader in the house.

I agree with that. Spiritual, moral. Imparter of wisdom to your kid. And then I'd add one: Your kid's got to see a right relationship between you and your wife, because they're going to base their relationship with their wives or husbands in the future on what they see in you.

And I tell my daughter, I've been stressing to her since she was small . . . you lead, don't follow. You get out in front and stay out in front. Anybody else come to you, you say, look, there ain't no choice. I'm in front. . . . The boy, I try to instill the same thing. Lead a ship. You be the leader. Volunteer. Get out front. You manage. Say who's going to be in charge of being in charge.

When they seemed satisfied that they had answered this question, I went to the easel and wrote down the phrase Good Family Man. "You don't hear it often," said one man. Another said: "You know, it sounds like it comes from a eulogy." And another:

No, you just don't hear it anymore. Long years ago it was familiar to hear it, you know, back in the coal mines and in the mountains and little farming communities and little-bitty towns. The city, you never hear it. You've got to go out in the country to hear it. Little churches, like at church, maybe.

Another father argued that the usage has declined in part because the definition of the phrase has changed. In modern society, the ideal of the Good Family Man is much more complex and multifaceted. As he put it:

I think what's going on is the definition of what we're trying to do now. Maybe before, a good family man was a guy who brought home enough money to take care of the family. Now, we are defining that cliché much more rigidly. And we are saying a family man is someone who spends time with their family, takes them to church, whatever you feel is important as a good family man. And the reason it's not being said now as much as it was before is that, before, it was easier to identify and easier to see somebody who just brought home enough money.

They had a nice house. Now, you are looking at their children, you are looking at how well behaved their children are, and how active the father is in that position.[2]

I asked them to turn these ideas into a list, to pick the key words. Here are the words they selected: *Provider. Demonstrates love of wife and children through actions. Good role model. Spiritual leader. Biblical values. Makes time for his family. Knows and balances his priorities. Community leader and volunteer.* ("Boy Scout leader . . . coach, stuff like that.") *Protector. Teacher. Problem solver. Good listener. Guidance counselor. Reliable. Knows the value of money.*

I asked them to push harder, to get the core qualities. They reorganized and prioritized. They also decided to add something new to the list. This addition is revealing. The following excerpt from the transcript, slightly condensed for clarity, nicely captures the logic of their decision to expand the definition of a Good Family Man:

> I think if you could add one thing, it would be the word *flexibility.*
>
> What about if a woman was walking in, and she looked at that list? I'll say one of our wives looked in and she looked at it. What do you think she could add to that? And I'll tell you one she would say. It would be sharing household duties . . . going to the store, shopping, helping to put the dinner on on Sunday, washing the clothes, or whatever it is.
>
> Sharing the workload.
>
> You've got to be, yeah, a partner. There you go. You've got to be a spousal partner or something.
>
> Junior partner. (*Laughter.*)

Everybody seemed to concur. One father, seeking less to disagree than to clarify, insisted that

> I still think provider—whether it's traditional, or what you think about [our fathers] overdoing that when we were children, or whatever—the main role or the main emphasis is provider. And then secondary to that, or circled around that, would be the other qualities that you always hope would be provided [also].

The group consensus was clear: Flexibility, understood as sharing the domestic workload and establishing a more egalitarian marriage, constitutes an important characteristic of the Good Family Man in modern society. Indeed, this emphasis on flexibility, one father argued, was one key to rehabilitating the very idea of the good father in our time. As he put it:

> It carries somewhat of a sexist connotation to it now, if you could say a Good Family Man, because I think probably most everybody here, we

are sharing with the wife now. Whereas my Dad . . . provided for the family, but he wasn't around that much because he was working so much. And Mom took care of the house. He didn't.

For these men, the description was now complete. Here is their final collective definition of the Good Family Man:

1. Provider and protector
   knows the value of money
2. Shows love of spouse and children through actions
3. Biblical and moral values
   spiritual leader
   good role model
   good listener
   takes time for his family
   balances priorities
   problem solver, teacher, guidance counselor
4. Flexibility
   sharing workload as a partner.

We were out of time. One final question. What is happening to this type of father in our society? The answers from these men were anything but optimistic. One man summed it up for the group:

> You could put a double underline at the bottom of that list and put "rare breed." Because a good family man—whether you think he has more responsibilities in today's world or not—societywise . . . the people who are sitting in this room . . . are no longer the majority of what's out there in society.

The results from these Colorado interviews closely parallel the results from our interviews in other areas of the country. Indeed, the ideal of good-enough fatherhood, as enunciated by married fathers themselves, does not vary much from place to place, or between blue-collar and white-collar, or across racial, ethnic, or religious lines.

Of course, some variations did emerge. In Mississippi, for example, the fathers we interviewed tended to describe the good father in terms of abstinence. To them, the Good Family Man is frequently a man who refrains from doing certain things. He is "a good, clean, sober person." Recalling the phrase *good family man,* one Mississippi father said that "in the old days, you know, I used to hear it a lot. It means one that didn't drink or lie, didn't smoke, didn't chase a lot of women. . . . Clean-living father."

Fathers from New Jersey included the words *fidelity* and *compassion* in their list of core traits. (The mothers we interviewed also stressed the ideal of fidelity. As one mother from Ohio put it, the Good Family Man is "a one-woman man.") Moreover, our small number of interviews with unmarried fathers suggests that divorced and never-married men differ markedly from their married counterparts in their basic assumptions about fatherhood. Yet among the married fathers, the essential philosophical similarities, constituting what might be termed a shared understanding of the good father, are far more striking than any differences.

These men's shared understanding—their collective definition of the Good Family Man—stands in stark contrast to almost all contemporary elite discourse on fatherhood. Quite simply, these men are telling a different story, rooted in a different epistemology. The plot is different. The main character is different. The ending is different. Most of all, the moral of the story is different.

In the largest sense, these men are not simply listing a set of desirable attributes in a father. Their aim is much higher. They are proposing public norms of male behavior and defining fatherhood as an essential societal task for men. In many respects, they are describing nothing less than a model of male citizenship—standards of virtuous conduct for men in modern society.

Much of today's expert discourse insists upon both privatizing and disassembling fatherhood, removing it from the public square and breaking it down into abstract little pieces. The money piece. The biological piece. The psychological piece. The child-care piece. The housework piece. Any one piece, by itself, may be "not that important." Each piece, at least in theory, can be provided by someone or something other than a good father.

Conceptually, the fathers we interviewed do precisely the opposite. For them, all the pieces of the puzzle fit together, adding up to one man: the good father. In addition, their perspective is social as well as individual. Their ideals are public as well as private. For this reason, a good father is not simply a man who performs certain tasks for his children. He is a man who lives a certain kind of life. He is upright. He sets a good example. He has high moral character. He shows his love through his actions.

The contrast is crystal-clear: To accept the terms of today's elite discourse is to make the idea of fatherhood smaller. (Do child-support payments constitute good-enough fatherhood? Is no father any worse than a bad father? Can other men replace a father?) To listen to these men is to make the idea of fatherhood larger.

Moreover, in portraying the good father, these men rely upon a vocabulary that is unabashedly moral. A philosophy of right and wrong, good and bad, anchors their definition. At times, their ethical reasoning reveals the influence of the psychological and therapeutic ideas that dominate our expert conversation. But the heart of their moral philosophy derives from other sources. One main source is the classical language of civic virtue. The other is the language of the Judeo-Christian religious tradition.

To the Denver fathers, for example, the Good Family Man embodies "biblical and moral values." A father from Mississippi insisted: "In order to be a good family man you are going to have to be a religious man." A father from Ohio said that his main responsibility is to show his children "the value of family unity and be there to show them right from wrong and help them correct the wrongs they make." Another man from the same group said:

> I mean, keep to the basic morals, basic family idea, and try to just instill that in them. If you do that, and they don't go that route, all you can do is say that you did your best.

For this reason, many of these fathers are sharply critical of what they see as moral decline in the larger society. One said:

> I guess our parents were brought up in a culture that was very much different from the culture today. And they were brought up [to believe] that everyone around them is just as important as they are. . . . People today aren't brought up that way. Even with their own children, a lot of people put themselves ahead of them. . . . the children and the family is a secondary concern. I think you see a lot of that coming through today.

Another father made the same point:

> I think a very important one is spiritual. . . . In our family, in our home, in our lives, and in our community, we've gotten away from some of this, and it's the cause of a lot of trouble in the families today. That moral basic standard.

At the center of this moral vocabulary is the language of servanthood. The Good Family Man puts his family first. He is responsible for them. He sacrifices for them. These men stressed this point time and again. Seeking to sum up the essence of the Good Family Man, a father from New Jersey said:

> Well, basically you are there for them. You're not out carousing. You are putting them above yourself.

An Ohio man used almost the same words:

> Putting the family first, before anything. Putting the family's needs before his own.

A Colorado man said: "Put yourself last."

Equating masculinity with servanthood—I am a good man because I serve others—is a dominant idea in the Judeo-Christian religious tradition. Many of the most famous biblical stories and teachings, such as Jesus washing the feet of his disciples, convey precisely this message: The greatest leader is the greatest servant.[3] In social terms, such a message aims to domesticate masculinity, turning it away from warriorism and violence by linking codes of male conduct directly to the well-being of others, especially children.[4] In psychological terms, such a message helps the individual father to restrict his narcissistic impulses, ceding to his child and family his desire for omnipotentiality. Of course, most of our contemporary elite discourse, dominated by notions of individualism and self-expression, is either indifferent or overtly hostile to this message. Yet the fathers we interviewed place the ideal of male servanthood at the very center of their definition of the good father.

Again, the contrast is clear. These men speak a different language because they are telling a different story. Their essential purpose is different. Put simply, they reject the idea that fatherhood is superfluous. As a result, they resist the temptation to justify or explain away the decline of fatherhood in our society.

In today's dominant cultural conversation, probably the central prescription regarding fatherhood is to lower our standards. Expect and accept less. Instead of good fathers, settle for child-support payments, divorce reform, and other attempts to salvage something from the wreckage. Don't get too preachy. Focus more on rights than on responsibilities. Search for adequate substitutes for fathers.

These men say the opposite. They see the trend of fatherlessness in the society, but they do not embrace or condone it. They get preachy. Their morally robust description of the good father clearly implies that instead of lowering our standards for fatherhood, we should raise them. Instead of searching for good-enough substitutes for fatherhood, we should strive to become a society with more good-enough fathers.

Undergirding this entire way of thinking is one simple premise. Fathers are necessary. As a guarantor of child and societal well-being, the Good Family Man is unique and irreplaceable. These men do not debate this point as much as they assume it.

In part, of course, they are simply affirming their own worth. It is not surprising that these fathers would be reluctant to downplay the importance of fatherhood. But self-esteem is only part of their logic. More important, these men offer a remarkably rich account of the distinctive contributions that fathers make to their children and to the society. In a society that increasingly views fatherhood as nothing special, these men make the opposite case. Their reasoning on this matter deserves close inspection.

Provide, Protect, Nurture, Sponsor

First, largely ignoring the New Father imperative regarding breadwinning, these fathers reflexively assume that they are the primary breadwinners for their families. Not always or even typically the only breadwinner, but almost always the primary breadwinner. Numerous national surveys of parents confirm this finding: Compared to their wives, married fathers consistently display a larger commitment to the task of economic provision.[5]

Interestingly, the fathers we interviewed almost never bragged about their role as provider. In fact, they showed little interest in discussing it at all. For these men, the provider role is an assumption, a given. Nothing fascinating or controversial. When I asked these groups of fathers to list the most important things they do for their families, the word *provider* was almost always the first word spoken, but it was never the main focus of the discussion that followed. They preferred to talk about their children and their home life.

Perhaps for this reason, many of these men, when asked to sum up their basic responsibilities as fathers, chose to pair breadwinning with another component of their fatherhood, usually one more directly related to life at home. For example, one man summed up his fatherhood this way: "Provider and being there, spending as much time as possible." Another said:

> First thing would be, I work a lot. Second thing, when I'm at home, [I'm there to] actually participate in family things, not just sit on the couch or be a bump on the wall.

And another:

> Well, I think a father has to provide the necessities, the material stuff. I think example is probably real important. . . . I probably act different around the kids than I do with the guys because of that.

One of the mothers we interviewed offered a similar pairing of her husband's primary contributions: "income, that's probably number one, and love and support."

Of course, some discussion and even disagreements emerged. Many of the men pointed out that the demands of their work meant less time at home. Some fathers were sharply critical of runaway careerism, especially among "yuppies" and more affluent men:

> A lot of them consider their career far more important than their families. I can name several people. One guy, his son was in a car accident while he was in a Board of Directors meeting. And he said, "Well, he

is just going to have to wait until I'm finished. This is more important." Thank God his son didn't die.

Another father in the same group was troubled by this discussion:

I'm not a yuppie, but I work in an office as an accountant. And I take a lot of time out of my family time . . . to make my career better. For instance, right now I'm studying to become a CPA. That takes a lot of hours. I sacrifice family time for that, but I don't think I'm a bad father for that. Because I'm doing it so my family will have a better future.

A few moments later, he added:

My wife does a lot of stuff with the schools, and I'm not there because I work a lot. And you know, sitting here thinking of these things now, I wonder if other fathers who go there and volunteer their time for baseball and everything are saying about me, "Is he a good family man?" You know, we never see him here, you know? Does he care about his children and what they're doing? And you know, I do. But you know, society and taxes and everything else and the cost of living is keeping me away from there. Because in order to provide, I have to work longer.

Overall, however, these fathers displayed little anxiety or stress about the breadwinning task. Essentially, they seemed to view breadwinning in instrumental terms: I work hard because I need to support my family. In this sense, these men appear to understand economic provision as one aspect of the servanthood idea. I work to serve my family; my work is important to me because serving my family is important to me.

From this perspective, paternal provision becomes simultaneously celebrated and relativized. It is celebrated as a bedrock responsibility, and telltale sign, of the Good Family Man. But it is also relativized as part of, and therefore subordinate to, a larger purpose. In short, unlike the New Father model, in which breadwinning and fatherhood merely oppose each other, the servanthood model consecrates breadwinning in the service of fatherhood. In doing so, it creates an important imperative for men's work in the family—a primary pathway for men to become good fathers.

Second, these fathers believe that they protect their families. The word *protector* emerged frequently in our interviews. Some men used this word in its basic and literal sense of warding off physical danger:

If something happens, if somebody's trying to break in your house or something like that, you are the one who's going to stand up to that person and deal with whatever situation has to go down.

I consider my family the most precious thing I have and I will not let anybody do anything to harm them. That's the most important thing, protecting my family.

Several mothers we interviewed made the same point. Asked to describe any distinctive contributions that men bring to family life, one mother answered:

> Security. You know . . . if her husband's not home and the lights go out. The kids are going to go to Mom and they are going to feel that she is scared. Where they'll go to Dad—the kids aren't going to feel it, any more than she would if her husband was with her. She is going to feel a lot more secure, even if he is afraid.

Another mother agreed, offering a specific example:

> My daughter was about seven. We had just bought her a brand-new bike and we lived in suburbia. The bike was outside on the front lawn. My daughter . . . went outside and the bike was gone. Okay. Meanwhile a little boy down the street . . . [also] said his bike was taken. My husband gets in his van. . . . You know what he did? He took his van right to where the kids were and knocked them off the bikes. They dropped both of the bikes and they ran. Now, not only had he saved my daughter's bike, but the little kid down the street's. I mean everybody, the whole neighborhood, knew what my husband had done. My daughter was so proud of her daddy saving their bikes. Whereas if I had to . . . Well, let's see how much money we have. Maybe we can get you a new one later on. That's what I would have said.

The men also used the words *protect* and *protector* in a larger sense. Put simply, these men worry about their children and want to "protect" them from what they view as destructive forces in the larger society. Moreover, they recognize that a father's physical protection, while necessary, is insufficient. Fathers must also protect their children by teaching them a way of living.

In this sense, when these men say "protection," they typically mean more than immediate safety. Perhaps even more than mothers, who tend to define protection as defense, fathers define protection as preparation. One idea says: Protecting my children means safeguarding them. The other says: Protecting my children means preparing them for an uncertain and potentially dangerous future. Fathers lean decidedly toward this second notion. As a result, they frequently link the idea of protection to words such as *teaching* and *instilling*. Here is how one father put it:

> You have to be more protective now, especially with younger kids. Because the way the world is right now, children now are being exposed to a lot of things, and it's not coming out of the household. And parents don't have a chance to share that with their children before society already lets them know. So especially if you are a father of a young girl, you have to be very protective, and make sure that you instill inner quali-

ties and things that you know [are] the way it should be. . . . As far as music videos and things of this nature, what is going to happen when a five-year-old becomes a fourteen-year-old, you know? And you think about that because you always want to make sure your household is secure.

These comments display the same logic:

[In earlier times,] you could let your kids go outside and play with the other kids. You knew they were going to play ball or maybe climb. . . . Now you don't know where they are going to be. You don't know what is in the neighborhood. So you gotta *protect* them . . . you gotta *teach* a ten-year-old kid about something he shouldn't even learn about until he is eighteen or twenty.

My son just turned eleven, and I have got to talk to him already about sex, because he is getting all this garbage from the schoolyard and the TV and all that. So . . . I can't *protect* him because of all the media and everything. I try to *inform* him so that he gets the right view, rather than getting the street view of everything, whether it be sex or . . . the things that are prevalant in the society now.[6] [Emphasis mine.]

Third, these fathers help their wives to manage the household and assist their wives in providing the day-to-day affection and attention that children want and need from both of their parents. For example, echoing the Colorado fathers, many men stress the importance of flexibility regarding the sharing of household work. A father in Mississippi said:

You know, it's more, you've got to share. You've got to help wash the dishes, you've got to cook some meals . . . Sharing the responsibilities within the home, because there's not a lot of time that everybody is there at one time to get things done that need to be done. You know, the traditional American male . . . doesn't necessarily classify dishwashing as one of his favorite things to do. But it's something that really needs to be done. . . . My Dad never done that. Not very often, anyway.[7]

Most of the fathers we interviewed report that they spend more time with their children than their own fathers spent with them. Moreover, compared to their own fathers, these men frequently describe themselves as more physically affectionate and emotionally expressive:

I guess I was brought up in the old school . . . where you were just kind of stern . . . if you wanted to take your son out fishing or show him how to cut a tree down, that was good, but none of this "get in my lap" and that type of stuff. . . . I'm totally opposite from that, boy. I try to spend every day hugging my kids or touching them or telling them I love them, you know.

I'm taking more time with my children than my dad did with me. My dad was working a lot, he didn't have the time to show the affection and take the time with us that I'm taking with my children.

You know, me and my Daddy just shook hands. We've never hugged. . . . It's just something that we've never done, but we're close. But a firm handshake is about it.

These men are far more likely to hug their children, including their sons. Interestingly, however, almost none of these men blames or denigrates his father. He worked hard, they said. Times were tougher. Families were larger. Expectations were different. Indeed, several of these men attribute their affectionate style of fatherhood not to a desire to avoid the faults of their own fathers but rather to the fact that they grew up without fathers. As one man put it:

That's the kind of father I enjoy—burping, giving the bottle, changing diapers, whatever. My wife could leave the house and they're in good shape. And there's so much love. Because I come from a house that didn't have a father. And it stinked. I just want to give them more.

Yet even as these men describe the sharing of household duties, and even as they affirm the importance of close-in, emotionally bonded fatherhood, they clearly recognize that they are, at best, what the Colorado fathers wryly termed "junior partners" in the domain of child nurture and domestic management. Yes, they do more, sometimes much more, than their fathers did. But in this area, their wives are the leaders.

Both fathers and mothers frequently use humor to underscore this point. A New Jersey father joked: "I always said I was in charge until my wife gets home." Another man said: "Even though the man is the head of the family, the woman is the neck, and she turns the head any way she wants."

The mothers we interviewed were completely unambiguous regarding their authority in the domestic sphere. As one mother said: "I don't know if other people feel it, but you know that you have the final word." Another woman said: "My husband put it the best way. He says I run the train and I let him blow the whistle every now and then." (Laughter.)

This humor speaks truth. In a striking phrase, one Mississippi father praised the quality of "emotional strength." He said: "You know, regardless of how much a father cares to do . . . I think that the mother . . . most of the emotional strength is all her. And I think we as fathers see that."

One of the fathers in Colorado said that his wife frequently "has a keen sense to pick up on a mood, and I'm not even aware there is one." Another agreed:

I think she is a little more sensitive, too, than I am. When it comes to when they are developing an attitude about something . . . she seems to be a lot more receptive and sensitive. I hesitate to use the term that she is more interested in helping them get through that period or something, but I think maybe she is a little more sensitive to their needs and everything. So in that vein I am a little bit more like my father was, [except perhaps that] it is a conscious effort on my part to take part in what is going on in their little lives.

In the realms of household leadership and child nurturance, then, these men supplement and complement the strength of their wives, who are the conductors, the emotional quarterbacks, the primary day-to-day overseers of the children's well-being. These men defer to, and learn from, their wives' authority—in part because many of them consciously aim to deepen their fatherhood by striving, more than their fathers did, to participate actively with their wives in the care of their children.

Regarding domestic chores, these men display an essentially pragmatic, nonideological approach. There are jobs to be done. Fathers need to carry part of that load. Their wives expect no less. Especially in two-earner households, there is "not a lot of time . . . to get things done." So fathers must pitch in and "pick up the slack when you can."[8]

Regarding child nurturance, the issue is richer and more complex. Part of it is pitching in, participating, picking up the slack. But much more of it is about the intrinsic rewards of hands-on fatherhood. These men are involved, affectionate fathers not because they have to be but because they want to be. They believe that nurturant fatherhood is good for them, good for their families, and good for the society.

Regarding this entire domain of family life, these fathers display a relaxed familiarity with an ideal of gender roles that our elite discourse typically treats with great suspicion. That ideal is complementarity, or what might be termed the recognition of difference and dependency. One father put it this way:

> I think we both have a common goal, my wife and myself, but I think each one of us complements the kids differently. . . . You know, so the kids get more rounded than I might have gotten. You know, she can give them different things than I could. She can give them different insights that I couldn't.

What emerges repeatedly is the idea of mutual dependency, grounded in the realities of gender complementarity. I am not a whole, but part of a whole. By myself, I cannot "parent" my child. Only my wife and I together, in overlapping but distinctive ways, can "parent" our child. This way of thinking departs sharply from the philosophy of individual omnipotentiality that guides much of today's expert story of parenthood, especially the model of the New Father.

Fourth, and probably most important, these men invest in their children through paternal sponsorship. In examining what married fathers do, our elite discourse focuses almost exclusively on two tasks: breadwinning and nurturing. The typical conclusion of such examinations is that fathers must do less breadwinning and more nurturing, while mothers must do less nurturing and more breadwinning.

Cast in the familiar terms of gender conflict, this elite formula for discussing fatherhood is deeply flawed. First, it ignores and even opposes the ideal of gender complementarity as voiced by the parents we interviewed. In this sense, our expert conventional wisdom on this matter is simply an ideological construct, rooted in the ideal of androgynous fatherhood and bearing little resemblance to the actual beliefs and activities of good-enough fathers.

More important, this entire debate sidesteps the main point. Recall the key question: What does a good father do? From the perspective of child and societal well-being, our interviews with fathers suggest that the most essential task of modern fatherhood is sponsorship, or what could be called paternal cultural transmission.

Paternal sponsorship is different from economic provision. It is related to protection, but extends well beyond it. It is also distinct from the realm of household leadership and daily child nurturance. Because paternal sponsorship is not primarily about who earns money or who changes diapers, the topic rarely surfaces in today's expert story of fatherhood. But for children and for society, paternal sponsorhip is the heart of fatherhood.

A sponsor is someone who prepares a candidate for confirmation. For the men we interviewed, this idea nicely captures the essence of their identity as fathers. These men prepare their children for confirmation. Put simply, paternal sponsorship means fathers teaching children a way of life. More than providing for their material needs, or shielding them from danger, or even taking care of them and showing them affection, paternal sponsorship means cultural transmission—endowing children with competence and character by showing them how to live a certain kind of life.

For fathers, the language of sponsorship is typically a language of coaching or training. In describing the good father, the men we interviewed frequently chose words such as *instilling, advising, teaching, setting an example, preparing.* One man described his fatherhood activity as "counseling." Another defined his main objective as "learning a child to stay on his own two feet, especially in today's society." Another father sought especially to "help mold them, help teach them what they need to know to make a good life." And another said: "Well, try to teach them what are the right things, make the right decisions, not to go along with the crowd. So those are the main things. Think for yourself."

One described his essential fatherhood goal as "making sure that they're the best they can be as far as my limitations are." Another said: "Basically

just to have them know right from wrong and make good judgments."
Here are two other comments from Ohio fathers:

> At my house, I have only the girls. . . . I'm trying to set an example of
> the type of person that they'd want to marry.
>
> The moral and spiritual values, you instill that in them and hopefully
> when they get older . . . the values that are eroding is what I'm trying to
> instill in them the most.

Paternal sponsorship frequently differs from maternal sponsorship. There
is much overlap between the two, of course, and the differences are frequently subtle. But they are also crucial. Echoing a number of clinical and
social science investigations, our interviews suggest that paternal sponsorship tends to focus especially on preparation for the future and on children's
success in the larger society.[9]

If mothers are likely to devote special attention to their children's present physical and emotional needs, fathers are likely to devote special attention to character traits necessary for the future, especially qualities such as
independence, self-reliance, and the willingness to test limits and take
risks. If mothers frequently set the standards for children's conduct within
the home, fathers often take special interest and pride in their children's
conduct outside the home. When asked to describe the satisfactions of
parenthood, mothers are likely to describe the qualities of the mother-child
bond. But fathers, much more frequently than mothers, link parental satisfaction directly to successful outcomes for their children in the society.[10]

Accordingly, the language of paternal sponsorship is highly conditional,
filled with words such as *if* and *when*. When they take my advice. If they
turn out okay. If they pass the test. One father said: "My personal feeling
is, when somebody says to me, 'your kids are great, they are really good
kids,' that's the definition I feel."

Discussing his son, another man concluded: "I want him to have an
inner strength to make the right decision in a tough situation. That's, you
know if I can do that, then I have success as a parent. That's it."

This conditional nature of paternal sponsorship—I am a good father if
my children become good adults—often means that a father's love is quali-
tatively different from a mother's love. This difference takes us to the heart
of the matter. Compared to a mother's love, a father's love is frequently
more expectant, more instrumental, and significantly less unconditional.[11]

For the child, from the beginning, the mother's love is an unquestioned
source of comfort and the foundation of human attachment.[12] But the
father's love is almost always a bit farther away, more distant and contingent. Compared to the mother's love, the father's must frequently be
sought after, deserved, earned through achievement. My mother loves me
unconditionally because I am her child. My father loves me, but he tends

to make me work for it. Lucky is the child who receives both varieties of parental love.[13]

The special biases of fatherly love emerge frequently in the areas of discipline and protection. For example, for the same reason that fathers tend to equate protection with preparation for the future, fathers also tend to worry about the dangers of overprotection. One of the mothers we interviewed said that

> moms tend to be a little overprotective. And some of the things that he allows them to do, I wouldn't allow them. I would have inhibited them in a lot of ways. Whereas . . . I hear about it afterwards. "You know, Dad let me do this!" "What?!"

I asked the Ohio fathers what would happen first if they or their wives received a phone call from the local police saying that their son had been arrested. One answered:

> My wife would probably go down there and talk to him and say, "What happened? Let me know what happened." If I got a call like that, my first inclination would be to go down there and grab him in front of the police officer, by the collar, and say, "What the hell is going on?"

Interestingly, both of these comments are self-criticisms. The mother is clearly praising her husband's capacity to encourage independence and risk taking. The father clearly appreciates his wife's capacity to support, and assume the best about, their son. Both of these parents seem to recognize that neither fatherly love nor motherly love, by itself, is sufficient. Every child needs both.

Similarly, every child needs both maternal sponsorship and paternal sponsorship. Yet paternal sponsorship is declining rapidly in our society. It is declining in two respects. First, and most obviously, fatherlessness is spreading. As one mother put it, good fathers are becoming "a dying breed." Another woman added: "There's one-parent homes, and the good family man is gone." Second, for the men who still offer it, paternal sponsorship is becoming a harder and harder task. With each passing year, there is a lower probability of success for these men.

Recall the lodestars of the paternal mission. Teaching children right from wrong. Embodying and passing on a way of life. Preparing children for the future. Encouraging their competence and success in the larger society.

Yet even good fathers today believe that these paternal goals are increasingly hard to achieve. The men we interviewed are matter-of-fact about their breadwinning. They are proud and happy about their involved, affectionate style of nurturing their children. But about protection and sponsorship, especially sponsorship, they are pessimistic and alarmed.

They fear that the primary imperative of their fatherhood—to launch their children as competent adults—is increasingly endangered by a society that is spinning out of control.

When I asked the New Jersey fathers what it was like to be a father today, one man quickly answered, "Scary." He explained that "my oldest is twelve years old, and you just worry about the different things out there that he can get involved with. You try and teach him the best you can to know right and wrong, but there's a lot of people pulling him the wrong way."

Another man said that being a father today was

a little bit frightening, too, with all the crap that's going on outside. . . . It's pretty terrifying. I worry about them even before they leave the house in the morning. . . . AIDS, crime, crime in the schools, peer pressure. It's not what I remember when I was a kid.

One father predicted that while children today "are going to have incredible capacities," they "are also going to have incredible danger." Another man summed up the sense of the group: "Society's just falling apart out there and it's affecting your kids."

In Colorado, a father said that "the morals have degraded. Society basically accepts things that would not have been accepted in our day growing up as kids." I asked him to name three things. These fathers quickly listed seven. Sex. Movies. Music. Alcohol. Drugs. Respect for older people. Language.

These fathers worry that they are losing their ability to protect and guide their children. Inside the home, they and their wives are doing their best. But outside the home, the bad guys are winning. As one father put it: "You do your best and sometimes it doesn't seem to work out."

Fewer good fathers. Harder to be a good father. Fathers are necessary and irreplaceable. These are the bedrock assessments voiced by the fathers we interviewed. Not surprisingly, these assessments produce in many of these men a profound sense of loss and anxiety regarding the state of fatherhood today. What is happening to the good family man in our society? A New Jersey man said: "He has split from his role. Most fathers are gone." Another said: "They are disappearing. He is under siege right now."

CHAPTER 12

A Father for Every Child

The most urgent domestic challenge facing the United States at the close of the twentieth century is the re-creation of fatherhood as a vital social role for men. At stake is nothing less than the success of the American experiment. For unless we reverse the trend of fatherlessness, no other set of accomplishments—not economic growth or prison construction or welfare reform or better schools—will succeed in arresting the decline of child well-being and the spread of male violence. To tolerate the trend of fatherlessness is to accept the inevitability of continued societal recession.

Many voices today, including many expert voices, urge us to accept the decline of fatherhood with equanimity. Be realistic, they tell us. Divorce and out-of-wedlock childbearing are here to stay. Growing numbers of children will not have fathers. Nothing can be done to reverse the trend itself. The only solution is to remediate some of its consequences. More help for poor children. More sympathy for single mothers. Better divorce. More child-support payments. More prisons. More programs aimed at substituting for fathers.

Yet what Lincoln called the better angels of our nature have always guided us in the opposite direction. Passivity in the face of crisis is inconsistent with the American tradition. Managing decline has never been the hallmark of American expertise. In the inevitable and valuable tension between conditions and aspirations—between the social "is" and the moral "ought"—our birthright as Americans has always been our confidence that we can change for the better.

Does every child deserve a father? Our current answer hovers between "no" and "not necessarily." But we need not make permanent the lowering of our standards. We can change our minds. Moreover, we can change our minds without passing new laws, spending more tax dollars, or empaneling more expert commissions. Once we change our philosophy, we may well decide to pass laws, create programs, or commission research. But the first and most important thing to change is not our policies but our ideas.

Our essential goal must be the rediscovery in modern society of the fatherhood idea. Malinowski called it the "principle of legitimacy." For every child, a legally and morally responsible adult male. Others have described this idea as the imperative of paternal investment, achieved through a parental alliance with the mother. A more familiar name for such activity is married fatherhood.

The essence of the fatherhood idea is simple. A father for every child. But in our society, few ideas could be more radical. Embracing the fatherhood idea would require a fundamental shift in cultural values and in parental behavior. No other change in U.S. family life could produce such dramatic improvement in child and societal well-being.

To recover the fatherhood idea, we must fashion a new cultural story of fatherhood. The moral of today's story is that fatherhood is superfluous. The moral of the new story must be that fatherhood is essential. In today's script, the Unnecessary Father dominates the action. In addition, too many understudies are doing far too much. The star of the new script must be the Good Family Man. The understudies must leave the spotlight.

The new story will be simultaneously more positive and more negative, more celebratory and more reproachful, than today's anemic account of unimportant men. The good news, largely ignored in today's script, is that married fatherhood is a man's most important pathway to happiness. Being a loving husband and committed father is the best part of being a man. The bad news, similarly missing from today's watered-down narrative, is that high rates of divorce and out-of-wedlock childbearing, the twin generators of paternity without fatherhood, are incompatible with male happiness and societal success.

At the intellectual center of the new story, defining and sustaining the fatherhood idea, must be two propositions about men. The first is that marriage constitutes an irreplaceable life-support system for effective fatherhood. The second is that being a real man means being a good father. The first proposition aims to reconnect fathers and mothers. The second aims to reconnect fatherhood and masculinity. Both of these propositions carry profound societal implications. Each will powerfully shape the plot and characters of an invigorated cultural story.

In a large sense, the new story must help us change from a divorce culture to a marriage culture. In a divorce culture, divorce overshadows marriage as a defining metaphor for the male-female relationship. Divorce comes to be seen as modern, cutting-edge, a representative generational experience. The institution of marriage and the norm of marital permanence come to be seen as comparatively old-fashioned, beleaguered, even quaint—a way of life primarily suitable for older or boring people.

In a divorce culture, people are intensely interested in divorce and want to improve divorce. Family scholars study it. Children's books tell stories about it. Policy makers pursue the goal of better divorce. In contrast, marriage commands relatively little attention in a divorce culture. Even the primary custodians of the marital tradition—the clergy and marriage counselors—frequently lose their regard for that tradition and drift toward a preoccupation with divorce.[1]

For a basic contradiction defines our contemporary divorce culture. On the one hand, we are a marrying people. Indeed, American attitudes toward marriage remain distinctly romantic and even sentimental, especially regarding the potential in marriage for personal fulfillment and adult companionship. Yet at the same time, we are a society in the midst of a widespread collapse of confidence in marriage as an institution, in the ideal of marital permanence, and in the preeminence and necessity of marriage as a child-rearing environment.[2]

In short, while we believe in marrying, we are losing our belief in the institution of marriage. As a result, we are simultaneously institutionalizing divorce and deinstitutionalizing marriage. For divorce, our goals are to regularize it, destigmatize it, and improve its procedures. For marriage, our goals are the opposite. Deregulate and privatize it. Make it more flexible. Reduce its privileged legal status and cultural influence. Describe it in high school textbooks not as an ideal but as one of many options. In a divorce culture, marriage is increasingly viewed as a problem, divorce as a viable solution.

This view of marriage destroys fatherhood for millions of men. By normalizing the rupture of the parental alliance and the departure of men from their children's homes, the norms of a divorce culture decimate the foundations of good-enough fatherhood. To recover the fatherhood idea, we must recreate a marriage culture. The alternative is the continuing decline of fatherhood.

A stronger story of fatherhood must also reclaim and revise the connection between fatherhood and masculinity. Across cultures, as David D. Gilmore reminds us, manhood is regarded as a test, a challenge, a prize to be won. In general, societies assume that women possess traits of femininity. But men must typically "prove" their masculinity.[3] Of course, elite opinion today is frequently quite suspicious of this idea. Yet, for most men in our society, to "be a man" remains a matter of considerable importance.

Tragically, the weakening of fatherhood in our generation has produced a large and dangerous chasm between fatherhood and masculinity. Over here is the manhood test. Over there is fatherhood. Consequently, to "be a man" increasingly has very little to do with being a father.

In today's elite fatherhood script, the New Father constitutes an androgynous rejection of all traditional masculinity. As a cultural model, the New Father urges men simply to ignore or ridicule the manhood test. The New Father is expected to define his masculinity by either disavowing it or inverting it. As a result, the New Father model explicitly compels men to make a choice: Be a New Father or be a man. The pathway to the former is the rejection of the latter.

A similar split is occurring in popular culture and in the larger society. From Arnold Schwarzenegger–style fantasy movies of male omnipotence to the teenage gang culture in our central cities, the idea of "being a man" is increasingly identified with violence, materialism, and predatory sexual behavior. I am a man because I will hurt you if you disrespect me. I am a man because I have sex with lots of women and my girlfriends have my babies. I am a man because I have more money and more things than you do. Norms of good-enough fatherhood—I am a man because I cherish my wife and nurture my children—are simply not part of this manhood equation.

If our society forces men to choose between passing the New Father test and passing the manhood test, one result will be less fatherhood. Similarly, if we encourage men to pursue a manhood that is untempered by norms of responsible fatherhood, the primary results will be more violence and less fatherhood. The former urges fatherhood without masculinity. The latter stands for masculinity without fatherhood.

The challenge for a new story of fatherhood is to resocialize masculinity by reuniting it with fatherhood, recognizing that these two ideas for men stand best when they stand together. Fatherhood cannot destroy or oppose masculinity. But fatherhood must domesticate masculinity. In a good society, men prove their manhood by being good fathers. The alternative is the continuing decline of fatherhood and a deepening ambivalence and skepticism toward masculinity.

Twelve Proposals

Who will fashion this new story? What is the best strategy for igniting a culture shift? What will be the signs that our society is seeking to recover the fatherhood idea?

A culture shift in favor of the Good Family Man cannot draw its main strength from Washington politicians, Hollywood scriptwriters, Madison Avenue advertising firms, or the conferences of professional family scholars. Cultural elites can help or hinder social change, but their views, mercifully, are not all that matters. For fatherhood, the seedbeds of renewal must be local and immediate. The real shift must occur from the bottom up, around kitchen tables, less a reflection of elite fashion than a revolt against it. The most important leaders of the new movement will not be celebrities and experts on talk shows, but guys from Paducah and Dubuque who decide to strive for a certain kind of life. To encourage and give voice to such a movement, here are a dozen modest proposals.

First, every man in the United States should be requested to take the following pledge:

> *Many people today believe that fathers are unnecessary. I believe the opposite. I pledge to live my life according to the principle that every child deserves a father; that marriage is the pathway to effective fatherhood; that part of being a good man means being a good father; and that America needs more good men.*

In 1992, there were almost 94 million males in the United States over the age of fifteen. Of that total, about 28 percent, or 26.3 million, lived in family households with their own or adopted children under age eighteen.[4] A diverse coalition of civic and religious organizations, brought together for the purpose of strengthening fatherhood in the United States, could strive for 10 million fatherhood pledges in the first two years of the campaign.

Of course, talk is cheap. Making a promise is easier than keeping it. But promises can signal and shape our individual aspirations. They can also serve as public symbols of cultural change, or at least of the desire for cultural change. Moreover, taking such a pledge could also link men to more concrete ways of strengthening their fatherhood: literature to read, local initiatives to join, opportunities to get other men involved.

Second, the president of the United States, acting through the White House Domestic Policy Council, should issue a brief annual report to the nation on the state of fatherhood. These reports would document our society's progress, or lack of progress, regarding what might be called leading fatherhood indicators. The four most important indicators are presented in table 12.1.

For decades, administrations have routinely compiled and examined leading economic indicators. But here is a thought experiment. Ponder the state of the economy in your local community. Now ponder the state of fatherhood locally. Which number is higher: the proportion of adults who are unemployed or the proportion of children growing up without fathers? Which number concerns you more: the number of business failures or the number of divorces? Which number is going up faster: the rate of inflation or the rate of out-of-wedlock childbearing?

Which has the deepest impact on your community: the economic trend or the fatherhood trend? If you had to pick only one of these two trends to change for the better, which one would you choose?

During the 1992 presidential campaign, James Carville, the political

TABLE 12.1
Leading Fatherhood Indicators

	1960	1970	1980	1990
Percent of births outside of marriage	5.3	10.7	18.4	28.0
Divorced males per 1,000 married males	27.4	33.3	76.2	112.5
Male prisoners per 100,000 males	230	191	274	574
Percent of children living apart from their fathers	17.5	22.4	32.2	36.3

Sources: See note 5, p. 314.

strategist, famously summarized his view of public priorities: "It's the economy, stupid." But what if Carville is wrong? What if many Americans believe—or come to believe—that fatherhood standards are just as important as living standards? And that raising the former will also help to raise the latter? Annual reports on fatherhood, based on the leading indicators, might help to foster a serious national conversation about fatherhood in America.

Third, a few good men should start creating Fathers' Clubs in their local communities. If the idea caught on, Fathers' Clubs could spring up in communities across the country. In 1940, as the nation faced this century's first fatherhood crisis, the National Conference on Family Relations urged the "organization of community councils in every sizable American city for the express purpose of dealing with family problems arising from the war crisis."[6] In the 1990s, as we face the crisis of volitional fatherlessness, men in America should found Fathers' Clubs aimed at invigorating fatherhood at the grass roots through organized father-child activities and through community leadership, including reaching out to fatherless children.

The seeds for this idea have already been planted. In 1991 in Indianapolis, a group of fathers calling themselves the Security Dads began attending local ball games, dances, and other events that attract crowds of teenagers. Their goal, as one member of the group explains, is to help children in the community by making sure that "there won't be a lot of trouble." As another Security Dad put it: "What works is the father image, so we don't need to say very much. Just being there is what counts. With an officer, they think, 'Hey, I must be in trouble.' With us, they smile and say, 'Hey, what's up.' And we love it."[7]

In Omaha in 1989, in the basement of the Omaha Pilgrim Baptist

Church, eighteen African-American men formed a group called MAD DADS (an acronym for Men Against Destruction—Defending Against Drugs and Social disorder). The group called upon the city's "strong, drug-free Men and Fathers" to serve as "positive role models and concerned loving parents, as well as a visible presence in our city against the negative forces that are destroying our children, our homes, and our city." According to Eddie F. Staton, the group's president, these fathers

> report crime, drug sales and other destructive activities to the proper authorities. This strong group of Men paint over gang graffiti, and challenge drug dealers and gang members to get out of the area. These loving Fathers also provide positive community activities for youth, chaperone community events and provide street counseling for those in need.[8]

Over 800 fathers have come together across lines of race and class to form a "rainbow army" of MAD DADS in Omaha. The organization has opened local chapters in eight other states.[9] Much more than movie celebrities or sports stars who sell sneakers on TV, fathers who create organizations such as Security Dads and MAD DADS are the heroes of our time. Perhaps their example can help to inspire the emergence of a national Fathers' Club movement.

Fourth, the U.S. Congress could provide valuable assistance to community organizers, clergy, and other local leaders who are serious about creating higher standards of male responsibility. The Congress could permit localities across the nation to apply for designation as Safe Zones. Like a military Safe Zone in a war-torn society, a civilian-led Safe Zone in a U.S. city would be dedicated to the reduction of violence. To create a Safe Zone, local leaders would be required to fashion and implement a serious strategy for reducing male violence by increasing male responsibility. To increase the chances of success, Safe Zones would receive two types of special federal assistance: money and other in-kind resources, as well as regulatory relief aimed at establishing greater local control of community institutions, such as police, parks, and public housing.

Safe Zones would be Enterprise Zones for male responsibility. They would embody a new social contract, not only between the federal government and the locality but also between men and the surrounding community. The first Safe Zones would be frankly experimental—less prescriptions than laboratories. The basic idea is premised not on the necessity of social services and outside expertise but on the potential for social change through community empowerment.

Success would depend on local leaders. Each Safe Zone strategy would be designed according to what residents believe would work. Yet, despite the diversity of approaches, all Safe Zones would be evaluated by the same twin standards. Is this community reducing the violent crime victimization rate? And is this community reducing the proportion of children who live in father-absent homes?

New leaders would emerge. So would new approaches, or at least serious approaches. All-boys' residential schools with lots of male teachers, perhaps drawn from the ranks of decommissioned military officers. Jobs, including guaranteed after-school jobs for teenagers. Community policing. More YMCA's and Boys Clubs. Curfews for teenagers. Treating small offenses, such as shoplifting or loitering, with greater seriousness. Parents' patrols in parks and playgrounds. Permitting landlords to evict violent residents. Fathers' Clubs. Informing every boy and girl in the community that sexual promiscuity is wrong and that out-of-wedlock childbearing is unacceptable. Identifying the father of every child born. Finding men to serve as surrogate fathers to fatherless children. Encouraging unmarried girls to give up their babies for adoption by married couples.

Some residents might view the two Safe Zone standards as arbitrary or unrelated. But I suspect that most would recognize that the issues of violent crime and fatherless children are closely related. More good fathers, less violence. More weddings, fewer funerals for children. In an increasingly fatherless society, Safe Zones would become local experiments—radical pilot projects—for reducing male violence through restoring effective fatherhood.

Fifth, ask married fathers to transform public housing in the United States. With the possible exception of prisons, surely the most violent and fatherless places in our society are the 1.3 million units of public housing owned and operated by the federal government.[10] Routine violence, intimidation by gangs, destruction of property, teenage childbearing, an ethos of fear and fatalism—these are the defining characteristics of residential communities almost totally devoid of responsible male authority.

In large part due to regulations that effectively favor fatherless families and discourage marriage, very few married couples live in public housing. But why not change the rules? Put an end to the marriage disincentives.[11] Moreover, why not give priority in public housing to married couples?

Over a five-year period, the U.S. Department of Housing and Urban Development should pursue an explicit policy aimed at tilting the balance in public housing decisively toward married couples, especially married couples with children. At the same time, new regulations should also increase the opportunities for tenant management and tenant ownership—less power for bureaucrats and more for residents, including the power to evict unruly residents. Finally, during this transition period, in part to assist mother-headed families that otherwise might have been awarded a place in public housing, the Congress could also increase funding for housing vouchers available to all low-income families.

Let us see what would happen. If nothing much changed, we would have an empirical basis for doubting the thesis that fatherlessness generates violence and disorder. But what if almost everything changed? Less crime. Less teenage childbearing. Less violence against women. Better outcomes for children.

Public housing could provide a hardest-case test for a larger idea: the fatherhood idea. Perhaps married fathers can do what mothers, the police, social workers, and public housing officials are now manifestly unable to do: turn public housing developments into reasonably hospitable environments for raising children.

Sixth, a few good community organizers, veterans of the civil rights and poor people's movements and professional practitioners of Saul Alinsky's philosophy of "comforting the afflicted and afflicting the comfortable," could build the infrastructure for a broad new populist movement to empower families and strengthen community life. Unlike what is often called the "religious right," these new organizations would not affiliate with the Republican party and would not anchor themselves in the issues of homosexuality, abortion, and school prayer. Conversely, unlike what might be termed the secular left, these new efforts would strive unapologetically for family and civic renewal. In each local organizing site, the principal aims would be the reversal of family fragmentation, the recovery of the fatherhood idea, the protection of children, and the rehabilitation of community values and institutions.

The Industrial Areas Foundation, Alinsky's major institutional legacy, is already increasingly practicing what its organizers call "values-based organizing"—a strategy for igniting broad-based community action informed by ethical and spiritual reflection. They are pointing the way for others. Perhaps some good organizers could help unleash a serious demand for cultural renewal in the United States. Not simply more political jockeying between Republicans and Democrats, or another predictable ideological debate between liberals and conservatives, but some angry, responsible thunder from the grass roots that would help us all to shake off defeatism and face up to the challenge before us.[12]

Seventh, an interfaith council of religious leaders could speak up and act up on behalf of marriage. As odd as it may sound regarding a practice in which most adult Americans voluntarily participate, marriage has very few public defenders. For in a divorce culture, marriage is a subject surrounded by great uncertainty and ambivalence, as well as no small amount of overt hostility. To defend the marital institution in a divorce culture is to invite controversy.

So we need some leadership. Over the past three decades, many religious leaders—especially in the mainline Protestant denominations—have largely abandoned marriage as a vital area of religious attention, essentially handing the entire matter over to opinion leaders and divorce lawyers in the secular society. Some members of the clergy seem to have lost interest in defending and strengthening marriage. Others report that they worry about offending members of their congregations who are divorced or unmarried.

At the same time, about 75 percent of all couples who marry still choose to be married by a religious leader in a church or synagogue.[13] Religious leaders still counsel more young couples than any secular counseling program could ever hope to reach. In general, regularly attending religious services still correlates with a more durable marriage.[14] Most important, while our secular culture increasingly views an enduring marriage as simply an option, our religious tradition still teaches us that an enduring marriage is a commitment.

A new interfaith council on marriage could encourage local pastors and other religious leaders to recommit themselves to marital preparation and enrichment. When couples want to get married, for example, many church leaders do little more than rent them the space and preside at the ceremony. Yet several important efforts, such as the Catholic Church's "Engaged Encounters" and the Marriage Saver programs recently initiated by several religious organizations, clearly demonstrate that it is possible for local religious leaders to improve marriages and reduce divorce in their congregations.[15] In turn, based on such leadership by example, the interfaith council could also speak up for marriage in the public square, seeking to spark a national discussion about whether and how we might wish to change from a divorce culture to a marriage culture.

Eighth, the U.S. Congress should pass, and the president should support, a resolution stating that the first question of policy makers regarding all proposed domestic legislation is whether it will strengthen or weaken the institution of marriage. Not the sole question, of course, but always the first.

To take this question seriously would be to challenge a great many policies of the federal government. Much of the federal tax code, including the otherwise salutary 1993 expansion of the Earned Income Tax Credit, is indifferent or hostile to marriage. Almost the entire current welfare system, including Aid to Families with Dependent Children, constitutes a direct economic subsidy for out-of-wedlock childbearing. Taken together, far too many government activities end up taxing marriage to fund family fragmentation. Of course, one congressional resolution would not work magic in any of these policy areas. But it might create a valuable opportunity to discuss priorities.

Ninth, local and county officials from across the nation should follow the example of the Hennepin County Board of Commissioners in Minnesota. In 1994, these county commissioners drafted a "vision statement" to identify local priorities and to plan for the future. In the document, the commissioners called upon themselves and the citizenry to move toward a community "where healthy family structure is nurtured and fewer children are born out of wedlock."

This proposed goal for Hennepin County produced what the Minneapolis *Star Tribune* termed "a big ruckus." A reporter from the newspaper summed up what many local leaders were saying about the commissioners and their idea: "Exclusionary. Judgmental. Intolerant. Offensive. Stigmatizing. Degrading. Archaic."[16]

An assistant parks commissioner was outraged: "Why is this statement here? Why are you pointing fingers?" The county's community health director argued that "we have a lot of single parents who work here. A lot of them feel it was shaming to them as single parents and shaming to clients."

A lesbian leader chastised the commissioners for "discounting" gay and lesbian parents. A pastor said that the real issue was jobs, not marriage. A leader from the United Way said that the real issue was how to "nurture" children, not "how people choose to configure themselves." A state fiscal analyst told the commissioners that "there are a lot of good single-parent families and there are a lot of bad two-parent families, and you're not going to change that by hoping everybody's getting married."[17]

In the midst of this firestorm, the commissioners, or at least some of them, insisted that the county's escalating rate of unwed childbearing—about 27 percent in 1992—was causing or aggravating a plethora of local problems, from child poverty to infant mortality, thus lowering the quality of life for everyone in the county.[18] Their message was simple: We need to change our minds on this issue. Moreover, the commissioners hoped that the new goal would help them refocus policy priorities. The traditional goal had been to ameliorate some of the consequences of the trend. Now there was an additional and superordinate goal: to reverse the trend.

Two points stand out from this story. First, if you want to say something controversial, say that every child deserves a father and that unwed childbearing is wrong. Second, the vision statement of the Hennepin County Board of Commissioners ignited and gave shape to a serious local debate about the possibility of recovering a primary idea: the fatherhood idea. That possibility concerns not just the politics of Hennepin County but the future of the nation. It is time for all of us to consider this possibility.

Tenth, state legislatures across the nation should support fatherhood by regulating sperm banks. New laws should prohibit sperm banks and others from selling sperm to unmarried women and limit the use of artificial insemination to cases of married couples experiencing fertility problems. In a good society, people do not traffic commercially in the production of radically fatherless children.

Eleventh, a few well-known professional athletes should organize a public service campaign on the importance of fatherhood. Through public speaking in the schools and through a series of public service television advertisements, these sports stars could tell us what their fathers mean to them. They could also tell us what it means to them to be a father. It was great to score the winning basket in the playoffs, but I would never have been there without my father, my first coach and biggest fan. I am proud to be a professional athlete, but being a good father is the most important thing I will ever do.

During the 1994 National Basketball Association playoffs, Hubert Davis of the New York Knicks won a crucial victory for his team by calmly sinking two free throws with only seconds left on the clock. After the game, a reporter asked him what he was thinking about as he stepped up to the line. "I was thinking about my father," Davis said. To the sports stars of our time, much is given. Perhaps Hubert Davis and others like him can give something back by standing up for fatherhood.

Twelfth, a few prominent family scholars could write new textbooks for high school students about marriage and parenthood. Almost all of the current textbooks on this subject are remarkably weak—dumbed down, reluctant to say anything serious about the subject of marriage, and without a clue regarding the importance or even the meaning of the fatherhood idea. What do we wish to tell a fifteen-year-old boy about what a good society expects of fathers? Other than viewing masculinity as a problem to be overcome, most current textbooks have almost nothing to say on the subject.

But rather than cursing the darkness, a few scholars could light candles. Instead of more stories featuring the Unnecessary Father, perhaps a new guy could appear in some of these textbooks: the Good Family Man. Perhaps we are ready to attend to his story.

These dozen proposals suffer from several flaws. As responses to the trend of fatherlessness, they are limited, speculative, and fragmentary. Taken together, they do not constitute a blueprint. They are not intended as twelve new answers.

But they are intended as twelve attempts to ask one new question. The question is a fundamental one: Does our society wish to recover the fatherhood idea? If the answer is "no," then neither these proposals nor any like them will make much sense. They will seem jarring and arbitrary. But if the answer is "yes," or even "maybe," then these proposals might at least point us in a certain direction. That direction is away from a culture of fatherlessness, toward fatherhood.

Notes

INTRODUCTION

1. See Larry L. Bumpass, "Children and Marital Disruption: A Replication and Update," *Demography* 21, no. 1 (February 1984): 71–82; and Larry L. Bumpass and James A. Sweet, "Children's Experience in Single-Parent Families: Implications of Cohabitation and Marital Transitions," *Family Planning Perspectives* 21, no. 6 (November/December 1989): 256–60.

   Sweet and Bumpass's central finding is that "about half of all children born between 1970 and 1984 are likely to spend some time in a mother-only family" (p. 256). However, since nonmarital childbearing has increased dramatically since 1984—according to the National Center for Health Statistics, the number of births to unmarried mothers increased by 82 percent from 1980 to 1991—Sweet and Bumpass's estimation of "about half" is probably too low for children currently under age seventeen. Frank Furstenberg and Andrew Cherlin, revising Sweet and Bumpass's estimate, calculated in 1991 that "for children born in the 1990s, the figure could reach 60 percent if the divorce rate remains high and nonmarital childbearing continues its upward trend." See Frank F. Furstenberg, Jr., and Andrew J. Cherlin, *Divided Families: What Happens to Children When Parents Part* (Cambridge, Mass.: Harvard University Press, 1991), 11. For births to unmarried mothers, see National Center for Health Statistics, "Advance Report of Final Natality Statistics, 1991," vol. 42, no. 3, supplement, *Monthly Vital Statistics Report* (Hyattsville, Md.: U.S. Department of Health and Human Services, September 9, 1993), 9. See also Ronica N. Rooks, "Motherhood: Growing More Common Among Never-Married Women," *Population Today* (November 1993): 4.

2. My notion of a "fatherhood script" has been influenced by the discussion of "manhood codes" in David D. Gilmore, *Manhood in the Making: Cultural Concepts of Masculinity* (New Haven: Yale University Press, 1990). The idea of fatherhood as a "cultural invention" is taken from John Demos, *Past, Present, and Personal: The Family and the Life Course in American History* (Oxford, U.K.: Oxford University Press, 1986), 64. This same idea was presented earlier and at greater length by Margaret Mead, who concludes that "human fatherhood is a social invention." See Margaret Mead, *Male and Female: A Study of the Sexes in a Changing World* (New York: Dell, 1969), 190.

3. Mead insists that "the human family depends upon social inventions that will

make each generation of males want to nurture women and children" (ibid., 206). Moreover, "every known human society rests firmly on the learned nurturing behavior of men" (p. 195). In all societies, she concludes, "each new generation of young males learn the appropriate nurturing behavior and superimpose upon their biologically given maleness this learned parental role. When the family breaks down—as it does under slavery, under certain forms of indentured labor and serfdom, in periods of extreme social unrest during wars, revolutions, famines, and epidemics, or in periods of abrupt transition from one type of economy to another—this delicate line of transmission is broken. Men may flounder badly in these periods, during which the primary unit may again become the mother and child, the biologically given, and the special conditions under which man has held his social traditions in trust are violated and distorted. So far, in all known history, human societies have always re-established the forms they temporarily lost" (p. 198).

4. Gilmore, *Manhood in the Making,* 225.

5. David Gutmann, *Reclaimed Powers: Toward a New Psychology of Men and Women in Later Life* (New York: Basic Books, 1987), 235–53. See also Gutmann, "Culture and Mental Health in Later Life Revisited," in James E. Birren, R. Bruce Sloane, and Gene D. Cohen, eds., *Handbook of Mental Health and Aging,* 2d ed. (Orlando, Fla.: Academic Press, 1992), 75–97.

CHAPTER 1: THE DIMINISHMENT OF AMERICAN FATHERHOOD

1. Jordana Hart, "Michigan Girl Says Sundlun Is Her Father," *Boston Globe,* June 10, 1993, 29.

2. Jordana Hart, "R.I. Governor, Daughter Plan for Future as They Settle Suit," *Boston Globe,* June 18, 1993, 22.

3. Efrain Hernandez, Jr., "R.I. Governor Expects to Face Paternity Suit," *Boston Globe,* June 9, 1993, 25.

4. Hart, "R.I. Governor, Daughter Plan for Future."

5. "Speaking of Kids: A National Survey of Parents and Children" (Washington, D.C.: National Commission on Children, 1991), 23.

6. Current scholarly estimates suggest that paternity is legally established in only about 24 to 33 percent of all cases of births to unmarried mothers. See Office of Child Support Enforcement, "Seventeenth Annual Report to Congress" (Washington, D.C.: U.S. Department of Health and Human Services, 1994), 11; Freya Sonenstein, "Linking Children to Their Fathers," *Policy and Research Report* 23, no. 2 (Washington, D.C.: Urban Institute, Summer 1993), 24; and Daniel R. Meyer, "Paternity and Public Policy," *Focus* 14, no. 2 (Madison: University of Wisconsin Institute for Research on Poverty, summer 1992), 3–5.

7. Jeanne Warner Lindsay, *Do I Have a Daddy? A Story About a Single-Parent Child* (Buena Park, Calif.: Morning Glory Press, 1991).

8. Michele Lash, Sally Ives Loughridge, and David Fassler, *My Kind of Family: A Book for Kids in Single-Parent Homes* (Burlington, Vt.: Waterfront Books, 1990), 20–21, 93.

9. Ira Berkow, "The Call of a Lifetime," *New York Times,* June 27, 1993, sports section, 1.

10. Kay Lockridge, "Ronnell Williams Hasn't Answered All Questions," *New York Times,* letter to the editor, July 4, 1993, S-9.

11. See John Demos, *Past, Present, and Personal: The Family and the Life Course in American History* (Oxford, U.K.: Oxford University Press, 1986), 44–46; Carl N. Degler, *At Odds: Women and the Family in America from the Revolution to the Present* (Oxford, U.K.: Oxford University Press, 1981), 73; E. Anthony Rotundo, "American Fatherhood: A Historical Perspective," *American Behavioral Scientist* 29, no. 1 (September/October 1985): 7–25; and Stephen M. Frank, " 'Their Own Proper Task': The Construction of Meanings for Fatherhood in Nineteenth-Century America," paper presented at the conference "The History of Marriage and the Family in Western Society" (Ottawa: Carleton University, April 1992).

12. Alexander Mitscherlich, *Society Without the Father: A Contribution to Social Psychology* (New York: HarperCollins, 1993), 147. The effects of industrialization on family life, and especially on the father's role, are widely acknowledged by historians. Allan Carlson, for example, describes "the great divorce of labor from the home" as "one of the defining features of American domestic life since the 1840s." See Allan Carlson, *From Cottage to Work Station: The Family's Search for Social Harmony in the Industrial Age* (San Francisco: Ignatius Press, 1993), 4.

13. Degler, *At Odds,* 74, 77. Similarly, to the historian and literary scholar Ann Douglas, "it seems indisputable that paternal authority was a waning force in the middle-class American family" in the nineteenth century. For example, Douglas finds that during this period "mothers increasingly took over the formerly paternal task of conducting family prayers." See Ann Douglas, *The Feminization of American Culture* (New York: Anchor Press, 1988), 74–75.

    For a description of the spread of the ideal of the "companionate family" in the 1920s and 1930s, accompanied in part by the further "diminution of fatherhood," see Ralph LaRossa et al., "The Fluctuating Image of the 20th-Century Father," *Journal of Marriage and the Family* 53, no. 4 (November 1991): 988, 996; and Steven Mintz and Susan Kellogg, *Domestic Revolutions: A Social History of American Family Life* (New York: Free Press, 1988), 107–31.

14. Alexis de Tocqueville, *Democracy in America,* vol. 2 (New York: Schocken, 1961), 229.

15. Stephen M. Frank, " 'Rendering Aid and Comfort': Images of Fatherhood in the Letters of Civil War Soldiers from Massachusetts and Michigan," *Journal of Social History* 26, no. 1 (fall 1992): 5–6.

16. Susan M. Juster and Maris A. Vinovskis, "Changing Perspectives on the American Family in the Past," in W. Richard Scott and James F. Short, Jr., eds., *Annual Review of Sociology,* vol. 13 (Palo Alto, Calif.: Annual Reviews, 1987), 203.

17. Joseph H. Pleck, "American Fathering in Historical Perspective," in Michael Kimmel, ed., *Changing Men: New Directions in Research on Men and Masculinity* (New York: Russell Sage Foundation, 1987), 86.

18. Degler, *At Odds,* 77.

19. Frank, " 'Rendering Aid and Comfort,' " 23, 22.

20. Rev. John S. C. Abbott, "Paternal Neglect," *The Parent's Magazine and Young People's Friend* (March 1842): 147–48, cited in Frank, " 'Their Own Proper Task,' " 12. Abbott continues: "It is very rare that a family can be well regulated, unless there be cooperation of both parents in watching over and governing the children. Occasionally, there is a mother of such rare endowments of mind and heart, that, even without any aid from the father, she will impress her own noble image upon every child. Such cases, however, cannot be a frequent occurrence."

21. Demos, *Past, Present, and Personal,* 61.

22. Pleck, "American Fathering," 89.

23. Demos, *Past, Present, and Personal,* 60. As an example of this trend, popular cul-
    ture was increasingly valorizing male athleticism and competitive virility by the
    turn of the century—as seen in the rise of cowboy, adventure, and escapist litera-
    ture—while increasingly stigmatizing frailty and dependency. Masculine humor
    became more disparaging of marriage and family obligation during this period.
    Also, the equation of true masculinity with ideals of "toughness," while certainly
    evident throughout U.S. history, seemed to intensify during the late nineteenth
    and early twentieth centuries. See Rupert Wilkinson, *American Tough: The Tough-
    Guy Tradition and American Character* (Westport, Conn.: Greenwood Press,
    1984), 3–10.

24. Daniel Yankelovich, "How Changes in the Economy Are Reshaping American
    Values," in Henry J. Aaron, Thomas E. Mann, and Timothy Taylor, eds., *Values
    and Public Policy* (Washington, D.C.: Brookings Institution, 1994), 34.

    By 1993, about 63 percent of men said that "being a good provider" made
    them feel "most like a man," according to the Yankelovich Monitor, an annual
    survey of American values conducted by Yankelovich Partners. (Cited in Richard
    Morin, "Here's News for All You Men: You're Back," *Washington Post,* national
    weekly edition, August 30–September 5, 1993, 37.)

25. Peter N. Stearns, "Fatherhood in Historical Perspective: The Role of Social
    Change," in Frederick W. Bozett and Shirley M. H. Hanson, eds., *Fatherhood and
    Families in Cultural Context* (New York: Springer, 1991), 50.

26. Carol Lawson, "'Who Is My Daddy?' Can Be Answered in Different Ways," *New
    York Times,* August 5, 1993, C-1.

27. Elijah Anderson, *Streetwise: Race, Class, and Change in an Urban Community*
    (Chicago: University of Chicago Press, 1990), 112–37. See also Anderson, "The
    Code of the Streets," *Atlantic Monthly* (May 1994): 81–94. In many respects,
    Anderson's work is a successor to Elliot Liebow's classic anthropological study,
    Tally's Corner (Boston: Little, Brown, 1967).

28. Herbert Gold, *Fathers* (New York: Random House, 1966), 192. Similarly,
    Bertrand Russell once described fatherhood as "indirect, hypothetical and infer-
    ential." Fatherhood, much more than motherhood, is thus shaped by culture, or
    "bound up with beliefs." See Bertrand Russell, *Marriage and Morals* (New York:
    Bantam, 1968), 11.

29. See the introduction, note 1.

30. Opinion and dissenting opinion, Supreme Court of Texas, no. D-1742 (1993);
    and Marian M. Jones, "Wife's Lover Can Sue for Visitation," *Lawyers Weekly
    USA,* August 2, 1993, 1.

    For a discussion of the legal and family policy implications of permitting
    paternity tests to replace the traditional legal assumption that a married man is
    the father of his wife's child, see Wolfgang Hirczy, "A New Twist in Divorce:
    Paternity Tests as Solomon's Sword," *Journal of Divorce & Remarriage* 20, no. 1/2
    (1993): 85–104.

31. "Mother Files to Bar Adoption by Gay Couple," *New York Times,* September 20,
    1993, A-14.

32. A 1994 "fact-based" television movie, *Thicker Than Blood,* tells the story of Larry
    McKlinden, a California stockbroker who successfully sues his former girlfriend
    for custody of her son. At one point, Larry tries to explain things to the child: "I
    have a story to tell you. It's kind of complicated."

    Indeed it is complicated. Diane, the mother, has two children who are living
    with her former husband and his wife. Diane then gives birth to a little boy. She

names him Larry Jr., after Larry, her live-in boyfriend. When Diane and Larry break up, Larry takes the little boy to live with him in California. Meanwhile, Diane gets married. She and her new husband now want custody of her son. Larry does not like this idea. He hires a lawyer.

The plot thickens. Larry had assumed that he was the boy's father. But he is not. It turns out that a guy named Randy—who later shows up at the trial, also to seek custody—is in fact the child's biological father. On the witness stand, Diane asserts that her son does not have a "real father." Larry's lawyer replies: "One more father and we'd have a bridge club."

Of course, both claims are true. On the one hand, this child has a biological father, a boyfriend-father (described by the court as the "psychological father"), and a would-be stepfather. He also has a quasi-stepfather who has custody of his two half-siblings. At the same time, no one can agree on who the "real" father is.

In the end, Larry wins custody. The boy stays in California with his "psychological father." In the movie, as well as in most news reports of the case, the court's verdict was portrayed as a happy ending. After all, the case broke new ground, forcing paternity laws to recognize the rights of the growing number of "fathers" like Larry.

Well, that is one way to think about it. Another way, however, is to discern in this case, and in many others like it, the radical fragmentation and dispersal of fatherhood in our society.

33. Indira A. R. Lakshmanan and Bob Hohler, "Vt. Adoption May Become Custody Fight," *Boston Globe,* August 11, 1993, 1.

34. "A Familiar Custody Case, a Different Decision," *New York Times,* August 29, 1993, 28; and Susan Chira, "Adoption Is Getting Some Harder Looks," *New York Times,* April 25, 1993, E-1.

35. "For Once, the Baby Won," *New York Times,* September 1, 1993, A-18. For two other real-life tales of "fathers' rights" and the weakening of adoption, see David Quantz, "A Child Has a Right to a Parent," *Wall Street Journal,* April 14, 1994, A-14; and Janan Hanna, "U.S. Supreme Court Asked to Rule on the Rights of 'Baby Richard,'" *Chicago Tribune,* August 9, 1994, 1.

36. Peter Uhlenberg, "Changing Configurations of the Life Course," in Tamara K. Hareven, ed., *Transitions: The Family and the Life Course in Historical Perspective* (New York: Academic Press, 1978), 78–79.

37. Peter Uhlenberg, "Population Aging and Social Policy," in Judith Blake and John Hagan, eds., *Annual Review of Sociology,* vol. 18 (Palo Alto, Calif.: Annual Reviews, 1992), 459.

38. Uhlenberg, "Changing Configurations of the Life Course," 78–79.

39. Ibid., 87.

40. Linda Gordon and Sara S. McLanahan, "Single Parenthood in 1900," *Journal of Family History* 16, no. 2 (1991): 97, 100–101.

41. Uhlenberg, "Population Aging and Social Policy," 459.

42. The remaining 22 percent of these mother-headed homes in 1992 are classified by the U.S. Census Bureau as "married, spouse absent." See Steve W. Rawlings, "Household and Family Characteristics: March 1992," U.S. Bureau of the Census, Current Population Reports, series P-20, no. 467 (Washington, D.C.: U.S. Government Printing Office, April 1993), xvi.

43. Alvin L. Schorr and Phyllis Moen, "The Single Parent and Public Policy," in Arlene S. Skolnick and Jerome H. Skolnick, eds., *Family in Transition* (Boston: Little, Brown, 1983), 576.

44. Tamara K. Hareven, testimony before the Select Committee on Children, Youth, and Families, U.S. House of Representatives, February 25, 1986 (Washington, D.C.: U.S. Government Printing Office, 1986), 29, 26.

45. Stephanie Coontz, *The Way We Never Were: American Families and the Nostalgia Trap* (New York: Basic Books, 1992), 183–84.

46. Gordon and McLanahan, "Single Parenthood in 1900," 97; and Arlene F. Saluter, "Marital Status and Living Arrangements: March 1992," U.S. Bureau of the Census, Current Population Reports, series P-20, no. 468 (Washington, D.C.: U.S. Government Printing Office, December 1992), xii.

47. The differences for children between parental death and parental departure have been documented by clinical psychologists and other scholars. For example, as James M. Herzog concludes: "Children without fathers experience father hunger, an affective state of considerable tenacity and force . . . When the father is absent but revered (idealized or presented as an important and valued family member), as in times of war, or following death, the resulting state of father hunger seems less pronounced. The ambivalence, hurt, and hatred characteristic of divorce seem to maximize for the child the felt absence of a masculine parent and to exacerbate father hunger."

Paul L. Adams, Judith R. Milner, and Nancy A. Schrepf similarly conclude: "In summary, the child paternally deprived through death is often better off, emotionally and financially, than the child paternally deprived through divorce or desertion."

See James M. Herzog, "On Father Hunger: The Father's Role in the Modulation of Aggressive Drive and Fantasy," in Stanley H. Cath, Alan R. Gurwitt, and John Munder Ross, eds., *Father and Child: Developmental and Clinical Perspectives* (Boston: Little, Brown, 1982), 174; and Paul L. Adams, Judith R. Milner, and Nancy A. Schrepf, *Fatherless Children* (New York: Wiley, 1984), 105. See also Kathleen E. Kiernan, "The Impact of Family Disruption in Childhood on Transitions Made in Young Adult Life," *Population Studies,* no. 46 (London: Family Policy Studies Centre, 1992), 213–34.

CHAPTER 2: FATHERLESS SOCIETY

1. The most recent empirical confirmation of this thesis, drawing upon a four-decade study of fathers and their children, can be found in John Snarey, *How Fathers Care for the Next Generation* (Cambridge, Mass.: Harvard University Press, 1993), 84–119. Perhaps the most well-known statement of this theme comes from Erik H. Erikson's discussion of "generativity" in *Childhood and Society,* 2d ed. (New York: Norton, 1963), 266, passim.

2. Jane B. Lancaster and Chet S. Lancaster, "The Watershed: Change in Parental-Investment and Family Formation Strategies in the Course of Human Evolution," in Jane B. Lancaster et al., eds., *Parenting Across the Life Span: Biosocial Dimensions* (New York: Aldine de Gruyter, 1987), 189.

3. The leading cause of the decline of child well-being is the steady breakup of the mother-father child-raising unit. This proposition, for years the subject of heated scholarly and public debate, is now increasingly supported by the weight of scholarly evidence. This evidence has been summarized in recent years by numerous bipartisan national commissions. For example, see *Starting Points: Meeting the Needs of Our Youngest Children* (New York: Carnegie Corporation, 1994); *Fami-*

lies First: Report of the National Commission on America's Urban Families (Washington, D.C.: U.S. Government Printing Office, 1993); and National Commission on Children, *Beyond Rhetoric: A New American Agenda for Children and Families* (Washington, D.C.: U.S. Government Printing Office, 1991). See also Ronald J. Angel and Jacqueline L. Angel, *Painful Inheritance: Health and the New Generation of Fatherless Children* (Madison: University of Wisconsin Press, 1993).

4. Eleena de Lisser, "For Inner-City Youth, a Hard Life May Lead to a Hard Sentence," *Wall Street Journal,* November 30, 1993, 1. Across the nation, young males are committing more violent crimes, at younger ages, than ever before. From 1965 to 1991, the juvenile arrest rate for violent crime more than tripled, from 137 arrests per 100,000 juveniles in 1965 to 459 arrests per 100,000 juveniles in 1991. Between 1982 and 1991, the juvenile arrest rate for murder increased 93 percent; for aggravated assault, 72 percent; for forcible rape, 24 percent; and for motor vehicle theft, 97 percent.

Moreover, while for the past decade the number of young males has been declining as a proportion of the total population, the opposite will be the case for at least the next decade. As a result, some demographers predict that higher rates of violence among young males, combined with a growing proportion of young males in the population, will initiate a major new upsurge in violent crime during the second half of this decade.

See U.S. Department of Justice, Federal Bureau of Investigation, Uniform Crime Reports, *Crime in the United States, 1991* (Washington, D.C.: U.S. Government Printing Office, August 30, 1992), 279–80; U.S. Department of Justice, Bureau of Justice Statistics, *Sourcebook of Criminal Justice Statistics, 1992* (Washington, D.C.: U.S. Government Printing Office, 1993), 429; and Glenn L. Pierce and James Alan Fox, *Recent Trends in Violence: A Closer Look* (Boston: Northeastern University, National Crime Analysis Program, October 1992). The juvenile arrest rate for violent crime for 1991 was obtained in a telephone interview with FBI analysts in the Uniform Crime Reporting Program.

For an example of state-level recommendations embodying the current "get tougher" approach to youth violence, including the idea of eliminating or reducing distinctions between youthful offenders and adult criminals, see the Commission for the Study of Youth Crime and Violence and Reform of the Juvenile Justice System, *Preliminary Report to the Governor* (Albany, N.Y.: State of New York Executive Chamber, June 1994).

5. De Lisser, "For Inner-City Youth," 8.

6. "Saving Youth from Violence," *Carnegie Quarterly* 39, no. 1 (winter 1994): 1–15.

7. *Youth and Violence: Psychology's Response,* vol. 1 (Washington, D.C.: American Psychological Association Commission on Violence and Youth, 1993). See also Barbara Kantrowitz, "Wild in the Streets," *Newsweek,* August 2, 1993, 40.

For two additional scholarly examples of this basic understanding of the problem, see *Call for Violence Prevention and Intervention on Behalf of Very Young Children* (Arlington, Va.: Violence Study Group of the National Center for Clinical Infant Programs, 1993); and Deborah Prothrow-Stith, *Deadly Consequences: How Violence Is Destroying Our Teenage Population and a Plan to Begin Solving the Problem* (New York: HarperCollins, 1993).

Throughout this national discussion of youth violence, special emphasis has been placed on new ways for teachers and other professionals to help children both avoid and cope with violence. For example, in 1993, the Erikson Institute for Advanced Study in Child Development published *Let's Talk About Living in a*

World with Violence, an activity book for schoolchildren designed to "help children process their feelings and experiences about violence." See *Erikson* (fall/winter 1993): 25. See also Daniel Goleman, "Schools Try to Tame Violent Pupils, One Punch and One Taunt at a Time," *New York Times,* August 19, 1993, 12.

8. Testimony before the Select Committee on Children, Youth, and Families, U.S. House of Representatives, March 9, 1988 (Washington, D.C.: U.S. Government Printing Office, 1988), 67.

9. The following year, in 1989, the same congressional committee held a hearing on the subject of "Children and Guns." During the entire hearing, the role of fathers did not come up once, even indirectly, in part because committee members scrupulously spoke only of "parents," even when to do so was clearly obfuscatory. Consider one exchange between the committee chair, George Miller of California, and a teenage girl from Washington, D.C., in which the congressman recalls Shawn Grant's testimony from the previous hearing.

> CHAIRMAN MILLER: . . . When we asked a number of gang people "do your parents know you are a member of a gang," or "why would your parents let you become a member of a gang?" a couple of people . . . said that sometimes the child was bigger than the parent, that maybe parents didn't have as much control as some of us in Congress thought they might have, that some of these kids scare even their parents . . . So the pleas of the parents might simply go unheeded in this case, where kids aren't going to pay attention.
>
> MS. DETRA J.: Yes. It is not a family bond any more. The parents—okay, they might say stop or whatever, but that is not going to necessarily stop the child from doing what he or she wants to do, because while they are outside, the mother is inside, and she, you know, doesn't have any control of what her child does outside unless she really enforces her rules and regulations in her house.
>
> CHAIRMAN MILLER: . . . Do you find that to be the situation, I mean, where in many instances, parents are making the effort, but they have lost that element of control that we like to think we have as parents?

The congressman's determination to speak only of "parents" would border on comedy were it not such a revealing indicator of our reluctance to name or even discuss the nature of this problem.

   See the testimony before the Select Committee on Children, Youth, and Families, U.S. House of Representatives, June 15, 1989 (Washington, D.C.: U.S. Government Printing Office, 1988), 34.

10. Testimony of March 9, 1988, 11.

11. Alex Kotlowitz, *There Are No Children Here: The Story of Two Boys Growing Up in the Other America* (New York: Anchor Books, 1992).

12. Ibid., 14.

13. Myriam Miedzian, *Boys Will Be Boys: Breaking the Link Between Masculinity and Violence* (New York: Doubleday, 1991), 83.

14. Ibid.

15. See Frank S. Pittman, *Man Enough: Fathers, Sons, and the Search for Masculinity* (New York: Putnam's, 1993).

16. David D. Gilmore, *Manhood in the Making: Cultural Concepts of Masculinity* (New Haven: Yale University Press, 1990), 26–29; and David Gutmann, "The

Father and the Masculine Life Cycle," working paper no. 13 (New York: Institute for American Values, 1991), 2–6.

17. Kevin Merida, "Taking a Rap at the Images of Violence," *Washington Post,* national weekly edition, May 16–22, 1994, 33.

18. Michael R. Gottfredson and Travis Hirschi, *A General Theory of Crime* (Stanford, Calif.: Stanford University Press, 1990), 103. See also Douglas A. Smith and G. Roger Jarjoura, "Social Structure and Crime Victimization," *Journal of Research in Crime and Delinquency* 25, no. 1 (February 1988): 27–52.

19. See Deborah A. Dawson, "Family Structure and Children's Health and Well-Being: Data from the 1988 National Health Interview Survey on Child Health," *Journal of Marriage and the Family,* no. 53 (August 1991): 573–84; M. Anne Hill and June O'Neill, "Underclass Behaviors in the United States: Measurements and Analysis of Determinants" (New York: City University of New York, Baruch College, August 1993); and National Center for Educational Statistics, "Characteristics of At-Risk Students in NELS: 88" (Washington, D.C.: U.S. Department of Education, August 1992).

20. Elaine Ciulla Kamarck and William A. Galston, "Putting Children First: A Progressive Family Policy for the 1990s" (Washington, D.C.: Progressive Policy Institute, September 1990), 14.

21. James Q. Wilson, "Culture, Incentives, and the Underclass," in Henry J. Aaron, Thomas E. Mann, and Timothy Taylor, eds., *Values and Public Policy* (Washington, D.C.: Brookings Institution, 1994), 70–71. Wilson, one of the nation's leading authorities on crime, also concludes that, during the past two decades, "while the criminal justice system has become somewhat tougher, the family unit has become much weaker. This helps explain why the average young person is much more likely to commit a crime today than in the 1950s" (p. 57).

22. Susan Brownmiller's influential book, *Against Our Will,* was published in 1975. Between 1974 and 1980, according to Susan Schechter, a newly emergent battered women's movement founded more than three hundred shelters for abused women. The new movement also generated numerous state and national organizations dedicated to increasing awareness of the problem and developing strategies to combat it. Not coincidentally, congressional attention to the problem also blossomed during this period, leading to the creation or expansion of several federal initiatives and a significant increase in federal funding for programs aimed at reducing domestic violence. See Susan Brownmiller, *Against Our Will: Men, Women and Rape* (New York: Simon & Schuster, 1975); Susan Schechter, *Women and Male Violence: The Visions and Struggles of the Battered Women's Movement* (Boston: South End Press, 1982), 1, 11, 133–50, 192–95; and Jeffrey Fagan, "Contributions of Research to Criminal Justice Policy on Wife Assault," in Douglas J. Besharov, ed., *Family Violence: Research and Public Policy Issues* (Washington, D.C.: American Enterprise Institute Press, 1990), 53–81.

23. Nancy Gibbs, "'Til Death Do Us Part," *Time,* January 18, 1993, 41. Of course, Gibbs's suggestion that U.S. marriage law has historically sanctioned wife beating—or that it considered a wife to be the "legal property" of the husband—is deeply misleading. For a serious treatment of the legal history of marriage, see Mary Ann Glendon, *The New Family and the New Property* (Toronto: Butterworth, 1981).

24. Lenore E. Walker, *The Battered Woman* (New York: Harper & Row, 1979), 51. Similarly, R. Emerson Dobash and Russell Dobash argue that "for a woman to be

brutally or systematically assaulted she must usually enter our most sacred institution, the family. . . . Thus it is impossible to understand violence against women without also understanding the nature of the marital relationship in which it occurs and to which it is inextricably related." See R. Emerson Dobash and Russell Dobash, *Violence Against Wives: A Case Against the Patriarchy* (New York: Free Press, 1979), 75.

25. Schechter, *Women and Male Violence,* 218–19.

26. Naomi Wolf, "Radical Heterosexuality . . . or How to Love a Man and Save Your Feminist Soul," in Emilie Buchwald, Pamela R. Fletcher, and Martha Roth, eds., *Transforming a Rape Culture* (Minneapolis: Milkweed Editions, 1993), 361. In the same essay, in a further reflection on the meaning of marriage, Wolf tells us: "The phrase 'rule of thumb' descends from English common law that said a man could legally beat his wife with a switch 'no thicker than his thumb'" (p. 361). Wolf is certainly not the first author to shock readers with this statement. Indeed, as Christina Hoff Sommers has shown, the "rule of thumb" anecdote has become a commonplace in our media and public policy discussion of domestic violence.

Yet the assertion is a wild exaggeration. In America, state laws prohibiting wife-beating predate the nation's founding. Both legal and public opinion in the United States have consistently viewed wife-beating as a crime. The phrase "rule of thumb" has almost nothing to do with any aspect of Anglo-American legal history. Yet these facts do not deter Wolf, and many others, from regularly repeating the "rule of thumb" story in articles, books, and interviews. Obviously, their goal is to advance what they believe to be, regardless of the details, a deeper truth: that the marital institution permits, virtually encourages, men to beat their wives. See Christina Hoff Sommers, *Who Stole Feminism: How Women Have Betrayed Women* (New York: Simon & Schuster, 1994), 203–7.

27. In *Intimate Violence,* Richard J. Gelles and Murray A. Straus, two widely recognized scholars of family violence, repeatedly refer to "the marriage license as a hitting license." Similarly, Letty Cottin Pogrebin suggests that, for perhaps a majority of married men in the United States, "the wedding license is a 'hitting license'"—a permission slip for the married man who "views the marriage license as a license to abuse his wife in the sacrosanct privacy of his home." See Richard J. Gelles and Murray A. Straus, *Intimate Violence* (New York: Simon & Schuster, 1989), 26; and Letty Cottin Pogrebin, *Family Politics: Love and Power on an Intimate Frontier* (New York: McGraw-Hill, 1983), 98, 16. See also Diana E. H. Russell, *Rape in Marriage* (Bloomington: Indiana University Press, 1990); and Richard A. Stordeur and Richard Stille, *Ending Men's Violence Against Their Partners* (Newbury Park, Calif.: Sage Publications, 1989), 32–36.

28. "Frontlines," *News from the Homefront* (San Francisco: Family Violence Prevention Fund, spring/summer 1993), 2.

29. Shawn Sullivan, "Wife-Beating N the Hood," *Wall Street Journal,* July 6, 1993, 12. With more analytic clarity, Bob Herbert, the *New York Times* columnist, describes the "growing phenomenon" of teenage mothers being beaten by boyfriends. He interviewed Ronald Williams, a high school counselor in Brooklyn.: "Mr. Williams has no hard statistics, but he believes the problem of teen-age girls being beaten by their boyfriends is extensive, not only in New York but across the country. He sees four or five new cases each week. This is not a problem that gets much attention . . . there's limited sympathy for teen-age mothers in the ghetto, especially if they're hooked up with drug-abusing boyfriends. The girls are on their own and they know it. So, for the most part, they take their beat-

ings and keep their mouths shut." See Bob Herbert, "Battered Girls in School," *New York Times,* November 24, 1993, 25.

30. Susan Schechter is explicit about this terminology: "In this book, abused or battered women will be used interchangeably with battered wife." In the same way, Murray A. Straus and Richard J. Gelles, describing the results of their two national surveys of domestic violence, rely almost without exception on marriage-specific terms such as "wife-beating," "marital violence," and "abusive husbands," even though they specifically designed their surveys to include unmarried couples, a growing demographic category. See Schechter, *Women and Male Violence,* 11; and Murray A. Straus and Richard J. Gelles, "Societal Change and Change in Family Violence from 1975 to 1985 as Revealed by Two National Surveys," *Journal of Marriage and the Family* 48, no. 3 (August 1986): 465–79.

31. David Eggebeen and Peter Uhlenberg, "Changes in the Organization of Men's Lives: 1960–1980," *Family Relations* 34, no. 2 (April 1985): 256, 253. Since 1980, the trends described by Eggebeen and Uhlenberg have continued to accelerate.

32. Besharov, *Family Violence,* ix, passim.

33. Someone who disagrees with this analysis might well point out that, regardless of what happens outside of marriage, wife-battering remains a serious national problem. Each year, after all, hundreds of thousands of wives are physically abused by their husbands.

   Yes. Abuse by husbands is a large and deplorable phenomenon in our society. But this fact does nothing to disprove the thesis that married fatherhood serves as an institutional inhibitor of domestic violence against women. Consider two analogies. Each year, hundreds of thousands of people who attend religious services behave in an immoral way (that is, they sin). Each year, many people who attend Alcoholics Anonymous (AA) meetings hurt themselves and others by consuming alcohol. But regular church attendance does not cause or encourage sin, nor does attending AA meetings sanction or facilitate the consumption of alcohol. In both cases, the opposite is true. The fact that some (even many) participants in an institution violate its norms does not prove the institution itself responsible for, or complicit in, those violations.

34. Walter J. Ong, *Fighting for Life: Contest, Sexuality, and Consciousness* (Ithaca, N.Y.: Cornell University Press, 1981), 102, passim.

35. Martin Daly and Margo Wilson, *Homicide* (New York: Aldine de Gruyter, 1988), 147, 87, 80.

36. Centers for Disease Control and Prevention, *Morbidity and Mortality Weekly Report* 43, no. 8 (Washington, D.C.: U.S. Government Printing Office, March 4, 1994), 132–33.

37. Philip J. Hilts, "6% of Women Admit Beatings While Pregnant," *New York Times,* March 4, 1994, 23.

38. Centers for Disease Control and Prevention, *Morbidity and Mortality,* 135.

39. New Jersey State Police Uniform Crime Reporting Unit, *1991 Domestic Violence Report* (West Trenton, N.J.: Department of Law and Public Safety, 1991), 1. For the number of unmarried- versus married-couple households, see Arlene F. Saluter, "Marital Status and Living Arrangements: March 1992," U.S. Bureau of the Census, Current Population Reports, series P-20, no. 468 (Washington, D.C.: U.S. Government Printing Office, December 1992), xv.

40. Carolyn Wolf Harlow, *Female Victims of Violent Crime* (Washington, D.C.: U.S. Department of Justice, 1991), 1–2.

41. U.S. Bureau of Justice Statistics, *Highlights from 20 Years of Surveying Crime Vic-*

tims: The National Crime Victimization Survey, 1973–92 (Washington, D.C.: U.S. Department of Justice, 1993), 18.

42. Jules Crittenden and Andrea Estes, "Ex-boyfriend Held in Chelsea Slaying," *Boston Herald,* August 6, 1993, 6.

43. Jordana Hart, "Dorchester Woman Found Dead in Home," *Boston Globe,* August 2, 1993, 13.

44. Sarah Koch, "Slain Mom Posted Deadly Bail," *Boston Herald,* August 24, 1993, 1.

45. Dean K. Wong and Betsy Q. M. Tong, "Roxbury Rampage Kills 1, Injures 2; Husband Charged," *Boston Globe,* August 9, 1993, 1.

46. David Weber, "Child Support Seen Prompting Arlington Slaying," *Boston Herald,* August 6, 1993, 7.

47. Gerald F. Russell and Pamela Margarite, "N.H. Man Accused of Fatally Shooting Wife's Ex-Husband," *Boston Globe,* July 28, 1993, 17.

48. Sarah Koch, "Domestic Violence Expert Says Restraining Orders Don't Work," *Boston Herald,* August 10, 1993, 23.

49. Sara Koch, "Laws, $ Fail to Quell the Epidemic," *Boston Herald,* August 6, 1993, 6.

50. In the remarkable outpouring of commentary on the Simpson case, all the usual themes emerged. Men are terrible. Marriage is dangerous for women. Policy makers do not take domestic violence seriously. The "male mystique" of toughness and aggression, as exemplified by Simpson's association with football, is responsible for violence against women. Almost no one raised the issue of fatherlessness.

    Yet in two respects, Simpson's is a classic case of fatherlessness correlating with male violence. First, Simpson grew up without a father. Second, he became estranged, through his two divorces, from the status of married fatherhood. Both of these conditions are powerful predictors of male violence. In our intensive search for the larger meaning of the O. J. Simpson case, these issues were largely ignored. But if the Simpson case tells us anything about the roots of male violence, it tells us that boys need to have good fathers, and men need to be good fathers.

51. From 1976 to 1989, reported incidents of child abuse and neglect, a category that includes sexual abuse, rose an astonishing 259 percent. In recent years, about 35 percent of all reports each year have been confirmed; about 65 percent are classified as unconfirmed or unfounded. At the same time, analysts point out that many instances of child abuse are never reported. See National Commission on Children, *Beyond Rhetoric,* 284; Douglas J. Besharov, testimony before the Select Committee on Children, Youth, and Families, U.S. House of Representatives, March 3, 1987 (Washington, D.C.: U.S. Government Printing Office, 1987), 32–33; and Wade F. Horn, testimony before the Select Committee on Children, Youth, and Families, U.S. House of Representatives, September 15, 1991 (Washington, D.C.: U.S. Government Printing Office, 1992), 27.

52. Interview with Douglas J. Besharov, June 8, 1994.

53. Joshua Hammer, "The Sins of the Fathers," *Newsweek,* September 7, 1992, 69. *Something About Amelia* first aired in 1984; *Not in My Family* in 1993. *Ultimate Betrayal,* another television movie based on the same idea, aired in 1994.

54. Reanne S. Singer, *The Storm's Crossing: Maggie's Triumph over a Terrible Secret* (Minneapolis: Deaconess Press, 1993). The description of the book is taken from the press release from Deaconess Press.

55. Judith Lewis Herman with Lisa Hirschman, *Father-Daughter Incest* (Cambridge, Mass.: Harvard University Press, 1981), 110.

56. Don S. Browning, "Biology, Ethics, and Narrative in Christian Family Theory," working paper no. 41 (New York: Institute for American Values, 1993), 4–5.

57. Judith S. Wallerstein and Sandra Blakeslee, *Second Chances: Men, Women, and Children a Decade After Divorce* (New York: Ticknor & Fields, 1989), 249.

58. For example, see Martin Daly and Margo Wilson, "Child Abuse and Other Risks of Not Living with Both Parents," *Ethology and Sociobiology* 6, no. 4 (1985): 197–210.

59. The incest taboo is a distinguishing feature of the human species. Present in all human societies, it is a fundamental shaper of culture and determinant of sexual behavior. For an early and influential treatment of the subject in this century, see Sigmund Freud, *Totem and Taboo* (New York: Norton, 1950; first published, 1913), 1–17, 122–25.

60. According to an article in the *Chicago Tribune,* "play husband" is a frequently used street term for "boyfriend." In the same article, Dale Weigand, who prosecuted child abuse cases for eleven years in Cook County, Illinois, tells a reporter that "I'd say it's the boyfriend in about 95 percent of the child abuse cases." See Flynn McRoberts and John Gorman, "Child Abuse Often Points to Boyfriend," *Chicago Tribune,* March 11, 1993, 1.

61. Andrea J. Sedlak, *Supplementary Analyses of Data on the National Incidence of Child Abuse and Neglect* (Rockville, Md.: Westat, August 30, 1991), table 6-2, p. 6-5.

62. Leslie Margolin, "Child Abuse by Mothers' Boyfriends: Why the Overrepresentation?" *Child Abuse and Neglect* 16, no. 4 (July/August 1992): 545–46. See also Catherine M. Malkin and Michael E. Lamb, "Child Maltreatment: A Test of Sociobiological Theory," *Journal of Comparative Family Studies* 25, no. 1 (spring 1994): 121–33.

63. Sedlak, *Supplementary Analyses,* 6-5.

64. Michael Gordon and Susan J. Creighton, "Natal and Non-natal Fathers as Sexual Abusers in the United Kingdom: A Comparative Analysis," *Journal of Marriage and the Family* 50, no. 1 (March 1988): 99.

65. Judith S. Musick, *Young, Poor and Pregnant: The Psychology of Teenage Motherhood* (New Haven: Yale University Press, 1993), 83. Musick concludes: "It is not only the absence of a father that harms a child, but the presence of a stream of men who move in and out of the life of her mother, behaving toward her with disdain or cruelty and mistreating her or her children" (p. 83).

66. Sedlak, *Supplementary Analyses,* 6-5.

67. Elijah Anderson, *Streetwise: Race, Class, and Change in an Urban Community* (Chicago: University of Chicago Press, 1990), 123.

68. *Sex and America's Teenagers* (New York: Alan Guttmacher Institute, 1994), 22, 28.

69. Musick, *Young, Poor and Pregnant,* 89.

70. Michelle C. Quinn, "Sympathy for a Mother Accused of Slaying Molester in Revenge," *New York Times,* April 12, 1993, 14.

In the Hampstead Heath nurseries established to care for British children during World War II, Anna Freud observed that "many children will adopt every father who enters the nursery as if he were their own. They will demand to sit on his lap or wish to be carried around by him. A visiting mother will never be claimed in this manner by strange children." Freud's observation may help explain the special susceptibility of fatherless children to the overtures of male strangers. See Anna Freud and Dorothy T. Burlingham, *War and Children* (Westport, Conn.: Greenwood Press, 1973), 60.

71. Much contemporary writing on fatherhood dwells almost exclusively on what might be termed the affective potential of paternity: the need for fathers to become more sensitive, more communicative, more nurturing, more egalitarian, and more emotionally accessible. This concern is important; but we misunderstand the issue if we isolate it from the larger context of male behavior in families and society.

Yes, paternal behavior includes an important affective dimension. Yet in all human societies, for better or worse, paternal behavior (and maternal behavior, too, for that matter) ranges well beyond the affective dimension, with great social consequences for children and society. The evidence is fairly clear: There is more to the male animal than its potential for nurturing.

Consider two of the harder truths about male behavior. Men compete with one another, often violently, over money, status, and sex. The overwhelming majority of violent acts in our increasingly disordered society are committed by men. Although the gap is lessening, men still earn and control most of the money in our society.

These are basic things that men do. They are not small matters. They can change, but they will not disappear anytime soon. Such enduring male problems are related to issues of emotional sensitivity and nurturant behavior, but they also extend well beyond them, pointing us toward the problematic essence of what it means to be a man. Moreover, these core dilemmas of masculinity—including the ultimate question of whether male behavior can be guided toward prosocial ends—are inextricably linked to the status of fatherhood. Consequently, a serious analysis of fatherhood must directly confront these primary questions concerning violence and money.

72. U.S. Bureau of the Census, "Poverty in the United States: 1992," Current Population Reports, series P-60, no. 185 (Washington, D.C.: U.S. Government Printing Office, September 1993), x.

73. U.S. Bureau of the Census, "Money Income of Households, Families, and Persons in the United States: 1992," Current Population Reports, series P-60, no. 184 (Washington, D.C.: U.S. Government Printing Office, September 1993), 68–69.

74. U.S. Bureau of the Census, "Poverty in the United States: 1992," xv.

75. Ibid., table 4, p. 8.

76. Irwin Garfinkel and Sara S. McLanahan, *Single Mothers and Their Children: A New American Dilemma* (Washington, D.C.: Urban Institute, 1986), 11.

77. David T. Ellwood, *Poor Support: Poverty in the American Family* (New York: Basic Books, 1988), 46.

78. William Julius Wilson and Kathryn M. Neckerman, "Poverty and Family Structure: The Widening Gap Between Evidence and Public Policy Issues," in Sheldon H. Danziger and Daniel H. Weinberg, eds., *Fighting Poverty: What Works and What Doesn't* (Cambridge, Mass.: Harvard University Press, 1986), 240.

79. Leif Jensen, David J. Eggebeen, and Daniel T. Lichter, "Child Poverty and the Ameliorative Effects of Public Assistance," *Social Science Quarterly* 74, no. 3 (September 1993): 542, 544.

The increase in child poverty during the past two decades reverses the progress made in the years between 1949 and 1973, when child poverty dropped dramatically. From close to 50 percent in 1949, the child poverty rate was halved by 1959, and almost halved again by 1973. But then it began to rise. By 1991, the child poverty rate had climbed back nearly to the level of 1965, the year that President Lyndon Johnson announced the War on Poverty.

Moreover, in looking at the historical trends, what stands out most clearly is the growing income gap between two-parent and single-parent homes, regardless of race. For example, two-parent black families today are economically better off than white single-parent families. Indeed, the poverty rate for two-parent black families has fallen substantially since 1969. As a predictor of poverty, the influence of race is declining; the influence of family structure is rising. See Sandra K. Danziger and Sheldon Danziger, "Child Poverty and Public Policy: Toward a Comprehensive Antipoverty Agenda," *Daedalus* 122, no. 1 (winter 1993): 59–61.

80. William A. Galston, "Causes of Declining Well-Being Among U.S. Children," *Aspen Institute Quarterly* 5, no. 1 (winter 1993): 68.

81. U.S. Bureau of the Census, "Poverty in the United States: 1992," xvi.

82. The contrast of rising public spending on children and declining child well-being is examined in Victor R. Fuchs and Diane M. Reklis, "America's Children: Economic Perspectives and Policy Options," *Science* 255, no. 3 (January 1992): 41–46; Peter Uhlenberg and David Eggebeen, "The Declining Well-Being of American Adolescents," *The Public Interest,* no. 82 (winter 1986): 25–38; Uhlenberg and Eggebeen, "Hard Times for American Youth: A Look at the Reasons," *National Association of Secondary School Principals Bulletin* 72, no. 508 (May 1988): 47–51; and Jensen, Eggebeen, and Lichter, "Child Poverty."

83. U.S. Bureau of the Census, "Poverty in the United States: 1992," x.

84. Saul D. Hoffman and Greg J. Duncan, "What Are the Economic Consequences of Divorce?" *Demography* 25, no. 4 (November 1988): 641.

85. Jay D. Teachman, "Contributions to Children by Divorced Fathers," *Social Problems* 38, no. 3 (August 1991): 368.

86. Judith S. Wallerstein and Shauna B. Corbin, "Father-Child Relationships After Divorce: Child Support and Educational Opportunity," *Family Law Quarterly* 20, no. 2 (summer 1986): 110.

87. See Timothy J. Biblarz and Adrian E. Raftery, "The Effects of Family Disruption on Social Mobility," *American Sociological Review* 58, no. 1 (February 1993): 97–109. They conclude: "Family disruption affects occupational mobility in contemporary American society in two ways. First is the direct effect of family disruption: Men from nonintact family backgrounds have greater odds of entering low status occupations as opposed to high status occupations. Second is the conditional effect of family disruption: Family disruption weakens intergenerational inheritance and resemblance, even after the disruption's direct effects are taken into account. Hence, including family structure in studies of social mobility adds to our understanding of the present distribution of occupations" (p. 107). See also Jiang Hong Li and Roger A. Wojtkiewicz, "A New Look at the Effects of Family Structure on Status Attainment," *Social Science Quarterly* 73, no. 3 (September 1992): 581–95.

88. Urie Bronfenbrenner of Cornell University, one of the nation's leading family scholars, powerfully underscores this point: "Controlling for associated factors such as low income, children growing up in such [female-headed] households are at greater risk for experiencing a variety of behavioral and educational problems, including extremes of hyperactivity or withdrawal, lack of attentiveness in the classroom, difficulty in deferring gratification, impaired academic achievement, school misbehavior, absenteeism, dropping out, involvement in socially alienated peer groups, and especially, the so-called 'teenage syndrome' of behaviors that

tend to hang together—smoking, drinking, early and frequent sexual experience, and, in the more extreme cases, drugs, suicide, vandalism, violence, and criminal acts." See Urie Bronfenbrenner, "Discovering What Families Do," in David Blankenhorn, Steven Bayme, and Jean Bethke Elshtain, eds., *Rebuilding the Nest: A New Commitment to the American Family* (Milwaukee: Family Service America, 1990), 34.

89. National Center for Health Statistics, "Advance Report of Final Natality Statistics, 1991," vol. 42, no. 3, supplement, *Monthly Vital Statistics Report* (Hyattsville, Md.: U.S. Department of Health and Human Services, September 9, 1993), 3, 30.

90. Blankenhorn, Bayme, and Elshtain, *Rebuilding the Nest,* 15.

91. Annie E. Casey Foundation, *1994 Kids Count Data Book: State Profiles of Child Well-Being* (Greenwich, Conn.: Annie E. Casey Foundation, 1994), 12.

92. Interestingly, the research on sexual satisfaction challenges the belief that, for daughters, fathers simply reinforce sexual inhibition. In this common view, a father's influence on his daughter's sexuality is essentially restrictive rather than empowering. The father's goal for his daughter is sexual modesty, not pleasurable sexual experiences. Yet research on female sexual satisfaction suggests that, in addition to lowering the risk for precocious sexual behavior and adolescent childbearing, effective fatherhood contributes significantly to the later sexual happiness of daughters. For example, Seymour Fisher, in his research on the psychological aspects of orgasmic difficulties in women, concludes that "the greater the difficulty women had in becoming orgiastically excited the more anxiously preoccupied they were about loss." What kind of loss? In Fisher's study, preoccupation with loss among low-orgasmic women—anxiety about losing something that is love giving but undependable—stems in large measure from nonexistent or highly tenuous father-daughter relationships. Other studies confirm the importance of father loss as a foundation of female sexual anxiety about "loss of love." Moreover, "in contrast to the confluence of findings affirming the role of fear of loss in inhibiting orgasm, largely negative results have emerged from the study of many other variables. Orgasm consistency has proven to be unrelated to such diverse factors as early dating history, reaction to first menstrual period, anxiety about sexual stimuli, mode of expressing hostility, masochism, anxiety level, achievement drive, sense of humor, amount of use of alcohol and cigarettes, various personality traits, and political conservatism-liberalism. The positive findings pinpointing the significance of concern about loss stand out in an otherwise largely negative array." See Seymour Fisher, *Sexual Images of the Self* (Hillsdale, N.J.: Lawrence Erlbaum, 1989), 43–44, 46.

93. Garfinkel and McLanahan, *Single Mothers and Their Children,* 30–31.

94. Ibid., 33. See also Sara S. McLanahan and Gary D. Sandefur, *Growing Up with a Single Parent: What Hurts and What Helps* (Cambridge, Mass.: Harvard University Press, 1994), 6; Joan R. Kahn and Kay E. Anderson, "Intergenerational Patterns of Teenage Fertility," *Demography* 29, no. 1 (February 1992): 39–57; and Lawrence L. Wu and Brian C. Martinson, "Family Structure and the Risk of a Premarital Birth," *American Sociological Review* 58 (April 1993): 210–32.

95. Judith S. Wallerstein, "The Long-Term Effects of Divorce on Children: A Review," *Journal of the American Academy of Child Adolescent Psychiatry* 30, no. 3 (May 1991): 353.

96. E. Mavis Hetherington, "Effects of Father Absence on Personality Development in Adolescent Daughters," *Developmental Psychology* 7, no. 3 (1972): 313–26.

97. Musick, *Young, Poor and Pregnant,* 60.

98. Erikson, *Childhood and Society,* 258–61.
99. Musick, *Young, Poor and Pregnant,* 60.

CHAPTER 3: THE LOST IDEA

1.   Bronislaw Malinowski, *Sex, Culture, and Myth* (New York: Harcourt, Brace & World, 1962), 63. The anthropological evidence suggests that the legitimacy principle—a responsible father for every child—is primarily a legal manifestation of the desire for paternal certainty: the sure knowledge that this child is my child, not another man's child. The reason is that paternal certainty is the most important precondition for paternal investment. Paternal investment, in turn, is an essential determinant of child and societal well-being. Of course, all three of these concepts—legitimacy, paternal certainty, and paternal investment—underlie and largely define a universal human institution with a much more familiar name: marriage. See also Steven J. C. Gaulin and Alice Schlegel, "Paternal Confidence and Paternal Investment: A Cross-Cultural Test of a Sociobiological Hypothesis," *Ethology and Sociobiology* 1 (1980): 301–9.

2.   See Harold Rosenberg, *The Tradition of the New* (New York: Horizon Press, 1959).

3.   Andrew Billingsley, building on a theme developed by Eugene D. Genovese and other historians, cautions against our acceptance of the idea that slavery destroyed the black family. Analyzing slave narratives collected in the 1930s by the Federal Writers Project, Billingsley shows that ex-slaves retained strong memories of family life. Among ex-slaves from South Carolina, for example, 85 percent had vivid recollections of their mothers; 76 percent vividly remembered their fathers. See Andrew Billingsley, *Climbing Jacob's Ladder: The Enduring Legacy of African-American Families* (New York: Simon & Schuster, 1992), 104–5. See also Eugene D. Genovese, *Roll, Jordan, Roll: The World the Slaves Made* (New York: Pantheon, 1974).

4.   New York City, Nursery and Child's Hospital, *Eleventh Annual Report, 1865* (New York, 1865), cited in Robert H. Bremner, ed., *Children and Youth in America,* vol. 1 (Cambridge, Mass.: Harvard University Press, 1970), 800.

5.   Amy Holmes and Maris A. Vinovskis, "The Impact of the Civil War on American Widowhood," in Scott J. South and Stewart E. Tolnay, eds., *The Changing American Family: Sociological and Demographic Perspectives* (Boulder, Colo.: Westview Press, 1992), 67–68.

6.   Stephen M. Frank, "'Rendering Aid and Comfort': Images of Fatherhood in the Letters of Civil War Soldiers from Massachusetts and Michigan," *Journal of Social History* 26, no. 1 (fall 1992): 22.

7.   Bell Irvin Wiley, *The Life of Johnny Reb: The Common Soldier of the Confederacy* (Lewisberry, Penn.: Charter Press, 1943), 208.

8.   Ibid.

9.   More than a century later, Dr. Benjamin Spock encouraged similar paternal involvement in his advice to the wives of World War II servicemen: "If a father is far away when his baby is born and growing up, it doesn't mean he can't take part in the baby's care . . . The father needs lots of news and pictures . . . Take as many snapshots as you can, and send along any that don't look like midnight." See Benjamin Spock, *Baby and Child Care* (New York: Pocket Books, 1946), 465.

10. Testimony before the Committee on Military Affairs, U.S. Senate, September

15–17, 1943 (Washington, D.C.: U.S. Government Printing Office, 1943), 32.

11. Ibid., 31.

12. C. P. Trussell, "M'Nutt, Hershey Demand Fathers Be Drafted in '43," *New York Times,* September 17, 1943, 1.

13. George Gallup, "Draft of Fathers Opposed by Public," *New York Times,* September 15, 1943, 17.

14. Trussell, "M'Nutt, Hershey Demand Fathers Be Drafted in '43."

15. Davis R. B. Ross, *Preparing for Ulysses: Politics and Veterans During World War II* (New York: Columbia University Press, 1969), 169.

16. Ibid., 176–77.

17. Ibid., 176.

18. Francis E. Merrill, *Social Problems on the Home Front: A Study of War-time Influences* (New York: Harper & Brothers, 1948), 26.

19. Ibid., 72.

20. Ray E. Barber, "Marriage and the Family After the War," in Roy H. Abrams, ed., *The American Family in World War II,* vol. 229, *The Annals of the American Academy of Political and Social Science* (Philadelphia: American Academy of Political and Social Science, 1943), 171.

21. Merrill, *Social Problems,* 72.

22. Anna Freud and Dorothy T. Burlingham, *War and Children* (Westport, Conn.: Greenwood Press, 1973), 16.

23. Ibid., 37.

24. Anna Freud and Dorothy Burlingham, *Infants Without Families and Reports on the Hampstead Heath Nurseries 1939–1945* (London: Hogarth Press, 1974), 635.

25. Ibid., 637. It is worth noting that the children did call out for their father in the one instance where they felt in need of physical protection.

26. Ibid., 636.

27. Ibid., 641–42.

28. Ibid., 645–47.

29. As Anna Freud noted in 1944: "It is a matter of common knowledge that one cause of the delinquency of adolescents and pre-adolescents in war and post-war periods is the incompleteness of the family-setting owing to the father's absence in the Forces." See Anna Freud and Dorothy Burlingham, *Infants Without Families: The Case For and Against Residential Nurseries* (New York: International University Press, 1944), 102–3.

30. Richard Polenberg, *War and Society: The United States, 1941–1945* (Philadelphia: Lippincott, 1972), 150–51.

31. Cited in Robert L. Griswold, *Fatherhood in America: A History* (New York: Basic Books, 1993), 169.

32. Barber, "Marriage and the Family After the War," 170.

33. Polenberg, *War and Society,* 148.

34. Ernest R. Mowrer, "War and Family Solidarity and Stability," in Abrams, *The American Family in World War II,* 105.

35. Lois Meek Stolz, *Father Relations of War-Born Children: The Effect of Postwar Adjustment of Fathers on the Behavior and Personality of First Children Born While the Fathers Were at War* (New York: Greenwood Press, 1968), 323–24.

36. William M. Tuttle, Jr., *"Daddy's Gone to War": The Second World War in the Lives of America's Children* (New York: Oxford University Press, 1993), 218.

37. Ibid.

38. Ibid., 221.

39. Stolz, *Father Relations,* 222.

40. Cited in ibid., 62–63.

41. Merrill, *Social Problems,* 34.

42. Cited in Tuttle, *"Daddy's Gone to War,"* 223.

43. Ibid., 28.

44. Eleanor S. Boll, "The Child," in Abrams, *The American Family in World War II,* 77.

45. Ibid., 78.

46. Barber, "Marriage and the Family After the War," 169.

47. Tuttle, *"Daddy's Gone to War,"* 219–20.

48. Barber, "Marriage and the Family After the War," 167.

49. Jeanette Hanford, "Some Case-Work Notes on the Impact of the War on Family Relationships," *Social Service Review* 17, no. 3 (September 1943): 359.

50. Tuttle, *"Daddy's Gone to War,"* 44.

51. These estimates are very crude. Using U.S. Census Bureau data, I estimate that there were approximately 16 million families with children under age eighteen during the war years, and that about 3.5 million of these families, or about 22 percent, experienced war-related father absence during any one year. Data for 1992, which are much more precise, are from the U.S. Census Bureau. For data on both periods, see U.S. Bureau of the Census, "Household and Family Characteristics: March 1992," *Current Population Reports,* series P-20, no. 467 (Washington, D.C.: U.S. Government Printing Office, April 1993), A-2, A-6.

52. Jonathan Bach, *Above the Clouds: A Reunion of Father and Son* (New York: William Morrow, 1993), 11.

CHAPTER 4: THE UNNECESSARY FATHER

1. George Gerbner, "Society's Storyteller: How Television Creates the Myths by Which We Live," *Media & Values,* no. 59/60 (Los Angeles: Center for Media and Values, fall 1992), 9. In part, of course, the concept of a cultural "story" is less an academic construct than a literary device for deciphering a set of important cultural symbols. Yet in a larger sense, a cultural story cannot be dismissed as merely a metaphor. For to detect a cultural story is simply to recognize that the messages of certain cultural products—such as textbooks, magazine articles, scholarly monographs, or testimony before legislative committees—are bound together by shared norms conveying a common moral.

   Elite cultural stories are powerful precisely because they draw upon, and build upon, a core component of human psychology that might be termed the narrative impulse. Beginning in childhood, as Bruno Bettelheim and others have found, stories become the individual's primary form for ordering and interpreting daily experiences. Children not only love stories, they require them. Indeed, as all parents know, children strive for stories, often with great intensity, precisely because narratives, more than other ways of knowing, permit the child to envisage life as coherent.

   For the adult, as well, stories remain the most common and natural mode of discourse. As Wayne Booth reminds us, "fictions are the most powerful of all the architects of our souls and societies." He insists that "even those few tough-minded ones among us who claim to reject all 'unreality'; even those who read no novels, watch no soap operas, and share no jokes; even those (if there are any) who echo Mr. Gadgrind and have truck only with 'the facts'; even the statisticians and accountants must in fact conduct their daily business largely in stories." Or as William Kilpatrick argues: "This desire to be a hero, so common to children and adults, is part of a larger wish: the hope that one's life can be like a story. It is such a basic wish that we hardly reflect on it. For the most part we simply assume that our lives will make sense. And the kind of 'making sense' that we intuitively have in mind is not the sense of a mathematical equation or of a scientific theorem but the kind of sense a story makes." George Gerbner argues that we "live our lives in terms of the stories we tell" and he describes storytelling as "the great process that makes us recognizably human."

This deeply rooted human propensity to comprehend life as a narrative constitutes the foundation, and explains the unusual normative power, of our cultural stories. These stories are not simply external influences, like the weather. They both derive from and construct the vital social dimension of the disposition in all of us to understand our lives as a story.

See Bruno Bettelheim, *The Uses of Enchantment: The Meaning and Importance of Fairy Tales* (New York: Knopf, 1976); Wayne Booth, *The Company We Keep: An Ethics of Fiction* (Berkeley: University of California Press, 1988), 19, 15; William Kilpatrick, *Why Johnny Can't Tell Right from Wrong: Moral Illiteracy and the Case for Character Education* (New York: Simon & Schuster, 1992), 191; and Gerbner, "Society's Storyteller," 8.

2. Carl E. Schneider, "The Law and the Stability of Marriage: The Family as a Social Institution," working paper no. 18 (New York: Institute for American Values, 1992), 4–7.

3. Peter L. Berger, *Facing Up to Modernity: Excursions in Society, Politics, and Religion* (New York: Basic Books, 1977), 77.

4. Alfred North Whitehead, *An Introduction to Mathematics* (New York: Oxford University Press, 1958), 41–42. To acknowledge the importance in human societies of habit, custom, and what I am calling cultural stories—and therefore to qualify the social importance of rational individual choice—is, of course, to qualify a central premise of modernist thought, which holds few values in higher regard than those of reason and self-creation. "The Western ideal," writes Daniel Bell in *The Cultural Contradictions of Capitalism,* "was the autonomous man who, in becoming self-determining, would achieve freedom" in order to "make of oneself what one can, and even, in discarding old roots, to remake oneself altogether." The limitations of this powerfully attractive ideal, especially insofar as it comes to govern cultural expression and family life, have been examined with great insight by Bell and also by Michael Oakeshott in *Rationalism in Politics.* However, cultural analysts are not required to choose sides in the larger epistemological contest between modernism and tradition in order simply to acknowledge the power of cultural stories to influence human relationships, especially those rooted in paternity. See Daniel Bell, *The Cultural Contradictions of Capitalism* (New York: Basic Books, 1976), 16; and Michael Oakeshott, *Rationalism in Politics* (New York: Basic Books, 1962), 59–79.

5. "Riding 'Murphy Brown's' Coattails," *New York Times,* September 21, 1992, C-1.

6. "Place Where 'Reality Ends, Fiction Begins,'" *USA Today,* September 22, 1992, 1.

7. Ibid., and "Over 'Murphy Brown,' Art Is Bigger Than Life," *New York Times,* September 23, 1992, A-17.

8. This success, in turn, generated a significant cultural ripple effect, especially on Madison Avenue. Within months, for example, *Good Housekeeping* magazine had significantly revamped its five-year-old "New Traditionalist" advertising cam-

paign to emphasize the "new" and downplay the "traditional." The inaugural ad of the magazine's new "New Traditionalist" campaign featured a single mother as "living proof that family values are as strong as ever, even though the family 'structure' is changing." Just so everyone would get the point, the *Good Housekeeping* press release stressed: "There's plenty of room for 'Murphy Brown' in the American values system." Indeed, there is.

See "Riding 'Murphy Brown's' Coattails"; "After Months of Political Attack, the 'Cultural Elite' Fires Back," *New York Times,* September 1, 1992, C-11; Barbara Dafoe Whitehead, "Dan Quayle Was Right," *Atlantic Monthly* (April 1993): 55; "Good Housekeeping Modifies Its Campaign Celebrating Families to Embrace the Nontraditional," *New York Times,* March 29, 1993, D-10; and "Generation Gap Is Narrowing; 'Family Values' Running Strong," *Good Housekeeping* press release, March 30, 1993, 2.

9. Malcolm Gladwell, "Conventional Family's Value Is Being Reevaluated," *Washington Post,* September 21, 1992, 1. Two weeks later, an article on the front page of the *New York Times* reached the same conclusion, declaring that "sociologists say there are little data showing that single parenthood in itself causes dire problems for children." See Tamar Lewin, "Rise in Single Parenthood Is Reshaping U.S.," *New York Times,* October 5, 1992, 1.

10. "Conventional Family's Value Is Being Reevaluated."

11. "Fathers in the Home: Important, But Not That Important," press release (Columbus: Ohio State University Communications, August 18, 1992), 1.

12. Frank L. Mott, "The Impact of Fathers' Absence from the Home on Subsequent Cognitive Development of Younger Children: Linkages Between Socio-Emotional and Cognitive Well-Being," paper presented at the annual meeting of the American Sociological Association, August 1992.

13. In its January/February 1993 issue, *Psychology Today* published an article on Mott's research called "Disposable Dads?" In the next issue, in a letter to the editor, one reader complained that the "most consistent finding in Dr. Mott's study is that white boys do more poorly when not living with their biological father. This result persists after he includes all the covariates about the boys' mothers. Perhaps you should have titled your article 'Disposable Black Dads?'" After further analysis, the reader concludes that Mott's study is "virtually worthless." See *Psychology Today* (March/April 1993): 5; and ibid. (January/February 1993): 20.

14. In a subsequent paper focusing on the same group of children, Mott goes even further in postulating research conclusions that contradict, rather than support, his public statements. For example, in 1993, he finds "significant . . . male figure presence-absence effects for both black and white children" and, remarkably, concludes that "family structure effects are perhaps more significant predictors of behavior problems than are income effects." See Frank L. Mott and Elizabeth G. Menaghan, "Linkages Between Early Childhood Family Structure, Socio-Economic Well-Being and Middle-Childhood Socio-Emotional Development," paper presented at the annual meeting of the Population Association of America, March 1993, ii.

15. Ronald J. Angel and Jacqueline L. Angel recently completed a careful review of current social science research findings regarding the impact of father absence on children's health. They conclude that "the preponderance of evidence suggests that father absence results in fairly serious emotional and behavioral problems in children. Children in single-parent families suffer more psychiatric illness and are at a developmental disadvantage in comparison to children in two-parent fami-

lies. These children have more problems at school, have less self-control, and engage in more delinquent acts than children who live with both parents. Children in father-absent families are more vulnerable to peer pressure and are more easily led to commit delinquent acts than children with a father present. A mother with no husband may often be a poor disciplinarian, and her children may seek moral authority from others. Often that source is their peers, and children who grow up in the streets are unlikely to be exposed to the best role models. The evidence also indicates that fathers are important for a girl's sexual development and her ability to form relationships with men. Taken as a whole, then, the research we reviewed indicates that father absence places both girls and boys at elevated risk of emotional, educational, and developmental problems." See Ronald J. Angel and Jacqueline L. Angel, *Painful Inheritance: Health and the New Generation of Fatherless Children* (Madison: University of Wisconsin Press, 1993), 118.

16. Mott's confusion surrounding both the age of the children in his sample and the role of black fathers—as well as the lapse of journalistic standards at the *Washington Post* on September 21, 1992—is further illustrated by his subsequent work. In his 1993 study, which examines the same children three years later, Mott finds a significantly stronger relationship between fatherlessness and poor child outcomes. Fathers, it seems after all, are not "not that important"—especially as children get older, and particularly for black children. Remember that in the 1992 study, for which the oldest children in the sample were eight years old, Mott finds almost no evidence that fatherlessness harms black children. But in the 1993 study, for which the oldest children were now eleven years old, Mott suddenly reverses course, finding that fatherlessness does indeed harm these black children as they get older. "For black children," he concludes, "we do find that children that had no father figure present during the period . . . have some deterioration in their behavior during the period." This finding was not reported in the *Washington Post*. See Mott and Menaghan, "Linkages," 12.

17. Writing in the *Journal of Family Issues* in 1994, Mott further elaborates this theme. Fatherless girls, it turns out, derive measurable benefits from the absence of male sexism in their home environment. Mott reports "fairly systematic evidence that in several domains a father's absence is associated with greater gender equality in child rearing" and that white girls, in particular, "are relatively more likely than their male counterparts to have a preferable home cognitive environment when the father is absent." Here Mott has uncovered yet another reason not to worry about fatherlessness. See Frank L. Mott, "Sons, Daughters and Fathers' Absence: Differentials in Father-Leaving Probabilities and in Home Environments," *Journal of Family Issues* 15, no. 1 (March 1994): 121–22.

18. See Katherine Trent and Scott J. South, "Sociodemographic Status, Parental Background, Childhood Family Structure, and Attitudes Toward Family Formation," *Journal of Marriage and the Family* 54, no. 2 (May 1992): 427–39; J. Roland Fleck et al., "Father Psychological Absence and Heterosexual Behavior, Personal Adjustment and Sex-Typing in Adolescent Girls," *Adolescence* 15, no. 60 (winter 1980): 847–60; E. Mavis Hetherington, "Effects of Father Absence on Personality Development in Adolescent Daughters," *Developmental Psychology* 7, no. 3 (1972): 313–26; and Patrick C. Fowler and Herbert C. Richards, "Father Absence, Educational Preparedness, and Academic Achievement: A Test of the Confluence Model," *Journal of Educational Psychology* 70, no. 4 (1978): 595–601.

19. Similarly, is never knowing your father preferable to losing him? Mott believes it is. He finds that "'never' presence may from a socio-emotional perspective

involve fewer traumas for a child than those associated with a parental absenting process." As Mott later explained in an interview for *American Health* magazine: "From a child's perspective, never having had a father in the home may be better, at least in a psychological sense, than having had one who left."

In her 1994 novel, *Delusions of Grandma*, Carrie Fisher stresses the same point. Cora, who is pregnant, is sorry that things do not work out with her boyfriend, Ray, the father-to-be. But, she tells him, "better we know now, before she (I've decided she's a she) is old enough to wish it was back to how it was before it got so bad." In short, an empty glass of fatherhood is better for a child than a half-empty glass. All things considered, better that the little girl never know what she is missing.

Here we see Mott, the social scientist, and Fisher, the novelist, each doing what Daniel Patrick Moynihan calls "defining deviancy down" by proposing what I will term a "Could Be Worse" philosophy of fatherhood. For what interests them is not whether fatherhood may be better than father absence, but instead—here is the lowering of standards—whether one type of father absence may be less bad than another type of father absence. Relying on similar standards of social science research, both Mott and Fisher advise us that partial fatherhood could be worse than zero fatherhood.

Yet consider this utterly unsubstantiated thesis in light of several real-life examples of women who have never known their fathers. The novelist and playwright Laura Cunningham, for example, never knew her father and never knew why. She begins the story of her childhood with this sentence: "I began my life waiting for him." Growing up, she was regularly possessed by the belief that "my father was alive somewhere. I could find him. . . . I wrote to the Hall of Records. My letter was returned, stamped 'INSUFFICIENT INFORMATION.' I wrote again: How many Larry Moores could have been stationed in Miami in 1946? Too many, I was told . . . My father's name was too common. I would have to give up."

She did not give up. Even today, as a middle-aged woman, the possibility of finding him "lurks never too distant at the back of my mind. Hope is sneaky; it hides behind reason. As recently as three years ago I might pause at a communications center to flip under the M's, in the book marked 'Alabama.'"

Elyce Wakerman, in her book *Father Loss,* describes her sister, Caren, who never knew her father: "'The older I get, the more I think about him,' Caren says, 'because I wasn't encouraged to do so as a child. People used to say, "Lucky for Caren, she never knew him; she doesn't know what she missed." Naturally, I created a father who was all out of proportion to reality. I don't even remember seeing a picture of him when we were kids.'"

Wakerman quotes Barbra Streisand, who never knew her father: "My mother never mentioned him, never talked about him. I guess she thought if the subject wasn't brought up, I wouldn't notice that something was missing."

See Mott, "The Impact of Fathers' Absence," 14; Susan Chollar, "Happy Families," *American Health* 12, no. 6 (July/August 1993): 56–57; Carrie Fisher, *Delusions of Grandma* (New York: Simon & Schuster, 1994), 248; Laura Cunningham, *Sleeping Arrangements* (New York: Plume, 1991), 3, 192–93; and Elyce Wakerman, *Father Loss: Daughters Discuss the Man That Got Away* (Garden City, N.Y.: Doubleday, 1984), 58–59. See also Suzanne Fields, *Like Father, Like Daughter: How Father Shapes the Woman His Daughter Becomes* (Boston: Little, Brown, 1983); and Ursula Owen, ed., *Fathers: Reflections by Daughters* (New York: Pantheon, 1983).

20. Frank L. Mott, "When Is a Father Really Gone? Paternal-Child Contact in Father-Absent Homes," *Demography* 27, no. 4 (November 1990): 513, 511, 499, 510.

21. Travis Hirschi and Hannan C. Selvin, "False Criteria of Causality in Delinquency Research," *Social Problems* 13, no. 3 (winter 1966): 254, 268.

22. Mott is mistaken to suppose that, using his data, he can even attempt any valid conclusion about the relative importance of fatherlessness as a cause of childhood problems. Norval Glenn, a distinguished social scientist from the University of Texas and a former editor of the *Journal of Family Issues,* explains the scale and consequence of Mott's technical confusion: "Mott is quoted as saying that there are much greater issues to worry about than father absence, but the data reported are not an adequate basis for that conclusion. The data reported are regression coefficients, and a regression coefficient is the amount of change in the dependent variable (or outcome variable) associated with a unit of change in the independent variable (or the variable assumed to have had an effect on the dependent variable). Since the different independent variables are measured in different metrics, the regression coefficients are not comparable from one independent variable to another, and therefore they provide no basis for conclusions about which variable is more important than any other . . . With the unstandardized regression coefficients reported for this study, there is no clear-cut and generally recognized criterion for judging what is a weak or strong effect."

Let Travis Hirschi and Hannan Selvin have the last word on this matter: "It is sometimes better to say nothing about the effects of a variable whose range is restricted than to attempt to reach some idea of its importance with inadequate data."

See the memorandum from Norval Glenn to David Blankenhorn, March 17, 1993; and Hirschi and Selvin, "False Criteria," 262.

23. Why would the *Washington Post* build a front-page article around such deeply flawed research? This question becomes even more intriguing upon consideration of the other scholars cited in the article.

The *Post* quotes Paul Amato, a sociologist from the University of Nebraska, as saying that "different family structures can work very well. They are different. But different doesn't mean bad." Much of Amato's work focuses on family trends in Australia. His most recent book, *Children in Australian Families,* is based on in-depth interviews with 402 school-age children in Victoria. Yet this book's findings decisively contradict Mott's thesis and the thesis of the *Post* article. Amato concludes, for example, that "lack of attention from fathers was related to low self-esteem, low self-control, low life skills, and low social competence among sons and daughters of primary school age." See Paul Amato, *Children in Australian Families: The Growth of Competence* (New York: Prentice Hall, 1987), 99.

Amato's work on divorce in the United States reaches similar conclusions. Writing in *Social Forces* in 1991, he and Alan Booth conclude that "parental divorce appears to have negative consequences [for children] that, under some circumstances, persist well into adulthood; parental divorce increases the risk of psychological, social, and marital difficulties in later life." Writing in the *Journal of Marriage and the Family* in 1993, Amato summarizes his meta-analyses of 125 recent studies of the effects of divorce on children and adult children. His conclusion: "Parental divorce (or some factor connected with it) is associated with lowered well-being among both children and adult children of divorce." See Paul R. Amato and Alan Booth, "Consequences of Parental Divorce and Marital Unhappiness for Adult Well-Being," *Social Forces* 69, no. 3 (March 1991):

912; and Amato, "Children's Adjustment to Divorce: Theories, Hypotheses, and Empirical Support," *Journal of Marriage and the Family* 55 (February 1993): 23.

But what about his contrary-sounding comments to the *Post?* Amato now insists that he was quoted selectively and out of context. He describes the *Post* article as "much too slanted" and "pretty much one-sided" and agrees that the article's core thesis "cannot be supported" by either his own research findings or the overall weight of social scientific evidence. (From an interview with David Blankenhorn, April 13, 1993.)

The *Post* also cites a study by David H. Demo, a sociologist from the University of Missouri. Demo, interpreting his research for the *Post,* finds it "absurd" to suppose that childhood problems are strongly linked to fatherlessness. With eerie precision, Demo replicates the conceptual and technical mistakes of Frank Mott. For example, like Mott, Demo concludes that fatherless children do worse than other children in areas such as academic achievement and personal behavior. But also like Mott, he deploys false criteria of causality in an effort to deny the importance of fatherlessness in causing childhood problems.

For example, as the *Post* puts it, Demo discovered that a child who lives with her father usually "had a greater family income" than the typical fatherless child, thus "raising the question of whether it was the presence of the father or the greater resources" that made the difference. Like Mott, then, Demo methodologically disassembles fatherhood, in this case twisting the harmful consequences of the absence of a paternal breadwinner into evidence that the importance of fathers to their children has been, in Demo's words, "greatly exaggerated." Similarly, Demo proposes that "family process," rather than father presence per se, is what matters most for children. This argument is a staple among scholars who seek to minimize the importance of fathers. In general, "family process" refers to the internal dynamics of family relationships, such as how well family members communicate and get along with one another, or which parenting styles produce the best outcomes for children. Again, Demo's conceptual confusion is to anchor his findings in the premise that family process and father presence have nothing to do with one another. Accordingly, to the degree that Demo can prove that family process matters, he has proven that fathers do not matter.

Indeed, Demo provides a classic iteration of this false criterion of causation: "Children, although certainly affected by divorce and single-parent family structure, are more profoundly influenced by socioeconomic resources and by the degree of involvement, support and discipline provided by their parents." Travis Hirschi could not have said it better. See David H. Demo, "Parent-Child Relations: Assessing Recent Changes," *Journal of Marriage and the Family,* no. 54 (February 1992): 111.

The *Post* story briefly mentions three other scholars. Nicholas Zill observes that assessing the depth of problems in fatherless homes can be like assessing "whether the glass is half empty or half full." True enough. But ironically, Zill's own scholarly work, even more than Amato's, has focused national attention on the harmful consequences of fatherlessness. For Zill, half-empty glasses are cause for alarm. In a 1993 study of the long-term consequences of divorce for children, Zill and his colleagues conclude: "Even after controlling for variations across groups in parent education, race, and other child and family factors, 18- to 22-year-olds from disrupted families were twice as likely as other youths to have poor relationships with their fathers and mothers, to show high levels of emotional distress or problem behavior, to have received psychological help, and to have dropped out of high school at some point." See Nicholas Zill, Donna Ruane Morrison, and Mary Jo Coiro, "Long-Term Effects of Parental Divorce on Parent-Child Relationships, Adjustment, and Achievement in Young Adulthood," *Journal of Family Psychology* 7, no. 1 (1993): 96.

The *Post* cites a study by John Guidubaldi of Kent State University showing the harmful effects of fatherlessness: "Children of divorce are more likely than children in traditional, intact families to engage in drug abuse, violent behavior, suicide and out-of-wedlock childbearing."

The article concludes with a quotation from E. Mavis Hetherington, a psychologist from the University of Virginia, who says that children basically need to learn "responsibility" and "reasonable social values," which "can be taught in a lot of different family forms."

These six sources—Mott's highly questionable study, surrounded by ambiguous (and, in several cases, misleading) references to five other scholars—constitute the entire basis for the *Post*'s dramatic announcement of a "searching reevaluation by social scientists" showing that fathers are "far less critical to the healthy development of children than previously believed."

24. James Q. Wilson, "The Family-Values Debate," *Commentary* 95, no. 4 (April 1993): 26; Irwin Garfinkel and Sara S. McLanahan, *Single Mothers and Their Children: A New American Dilemma* (Washington, D.C.: Urban Institute, 1986); Norval D. Glenn, "Continuity Versus Change, Sanguineness Versus Concern: Views of the American Family in the Late 1980s," *Journal of Family Issues* 8, no. 4 (December 1987): 348–54; and Sar A. Levitan and Richard Belous, *What's Happening to the American Family?* (Baltimore: Johns Hopkins University Press, 1988).

25. Mott's study won him widespread media attention. For example, in *USA Today,* which devoted an article to his study, Mott recommends: "We need to get mothers better educated and boost income, because it's this rather than having a father in the home that affects kids most." The article summarizes Mott's research this way: "Murphy Brown's baby is likely to be as well-behaved and academically successful in elementary school as traditionally-reared kids." Playing along with this patently silly story line, Mott observes: "A very strong case could be made that in many respects the Brown kid is perfectly well off." See Marilyn Elias, "Impact of the Absent Father," *USA Today,* August 24, 1992, 1-D.

Surely the most remarkable aspect of this interview is the radical disjunction between what Mott actually studied and what Mott is commenting on. Mott studied several problems affecting the young children of lower-income, extremely young (primarily teenage) mothers. Quite specific. The study itself is filled with technical qualifications and reminders of its limited scope. But for his press releases and newspaper interviews, Mott offers this same study as a scholarly justification for the most sweeping commentary on national education policy, national economic policy, and the very nature of fatherhood—including, of all things, his beliefs regarding the unimportance of fathers for the (fictional) children of upper-income, middle-aged single mothers by choice. Clearly, Mott wants it both ways. On some days, he is a scientist in a lab coat, presenting carefully circumscribed "data" to other specialists. But on other days, still wearing his lab coat to impress us, he is a public policy expert and a philosopher of American family life. Mott is obviously not the only academic ever to succumb to this temptation, but he may be the most unself-conscious.

26. Among whites, the proportion of children born outside of marriage doubled dur-

ing the 1980s, increasing from 11 percent in 1980 to 22 percent in 1991. Among
blacks, the proportion increased from 55 percent to 68 percent. Among Hispan-
ics, the increase was from 24 percent to 39 percent. See National Center for
Health Statistics, "Advance Report of Final Natality Statistics, 1991," vol. 42, no.
3, supplement, *Monthly Vital Statistics Report* (Hyattsville, Md.: U.S. Department
of Health and Human Services, September 9, 1993), 9, 31–32.

27. Daniel Yankelovich, *New Rules: Searching for Self-Fulfillment in a World Turned
Upside Down* (New York: Random House, 1981), 88, 99.

28. Personal correspondence from Alice S. Rossi, May 20, 1994, regarding a 1994 pilot
survey on health, work, and family, with a random probability sample of 1,276
adults age nineteen or older, for a forthcoming study of midlife development sponsored by the John D. and Catherine T. MacArthur Foundation of Chicago.

29. William A. Galston, "Beyond the Murphy Brown Debate: Ideas for Family Policy" (New York: Institute for American Values, 1993), 8. The opinion poll cited
by Galston was conducted by Voter/Consumer Research of Washington, D.C., in
September 1993 for the Family Research Council, also based in Washington, D.C.

30. Lena Williams, "Pregnant Teen-Agers Are Outcasts No Longer," *New York
Times,* December 2, 1993, C-1. April Schuldt's father, Richard Schuldt, reveals, at
least in this interview, a curiously passive and ambivalent attitude about his
daughter's behavior. On the one hand, he's "glad the old days of wearing the scar-
let 'P' are gone." On the other hand, he seems a bit shocked that his daughter
"goes on the 'Montel Williams Show'" as a spokesperson for unwed-teen motherhood and that "today, teen pregnancy is being treated like it's no big thing, it's the
norm." In short, Mr. Schuldt seems to be unsure of what he thinks about the
issue. He also describes his daughter's behavior as if he were an outside observer.
April, by contrast, certainly knows what she believes. To her, unwed-teen childbearing is about the right to make one's own decisions and to be treated with
respect. Of course, teenagers frequently voice such sentiments, on matters ranging from whether homework is really necessary to whether they should be
allowed to take the car and stay out all night. Yet one is tempted to ask: Don't
these children need parents to guide them?

31. Katha Pollitt, "Bothered and Bewildered," *New York Times,* July 22, 1993, 23. In
August 1994, *USA Today* announced the imminent arrival of a new magazine
called *Single-Parent Family.* See "Short Takes," *USA Today,* August 9, 1994, 3-D.

32. Leslie Bennetts, "Belle Michelle," *Vanity Fair,* September 1993, 164. Indeed, adoption seems to be an increasingly popular "option" for affluent Hollywood stars who
want to enjoy motherhood without the complications of a husband and father.

33. Caryn James, "A Baby Boom on TV as Biological Clocks Cruelly Tick Away,"
New York Times, October 16, 1991, C-15.

34. Stanley R. Graham, "What Does a Man Want?" *American Psychologist* 47, no. 7
(July 1992): 837.

35. Gretchen Super, *What Kind of Family Do You Have?* (Troll Associates, 1991), 30.
While a growing number of children's storybooks address this issue directly, by
making fatherlessness an explicit component of the narrative, many other contemporary children's books seek to solve the problem indirectly, by simply omitting any mention of fathers in the text. In *Fred's First Day,* for example, we learn
all about Fred and his family on Fred's first day at school. Yet none of the illustra-
tions in the book portrays an adult male, and the word *father* does not appear in
the text. See Cathy Warren, *Fred's First Day* (New York: Lothrop, Lee & Shep-
ard, 1984).

36. Anne Lamott, *Operating Instructions: A Journal of My Son's First Year* (New York: Pantheon, 1993), 111.

37. Ibid., 86, 88.

38. Jerry Carroll and Ruthe Stein, "Anne Lamott on Raising a Boy by Herself," *San Francisco Chronicle,* July 20, 1993, C-4.

39. Anne Lamott, "When Going It Alone Turns Out to Be Not So Alone at All," *New York Times,* August 5, 1993, C-5.

40. Stephanie Coontz, letter to the editors, *The New Republic,* September 20 and 27, 1993, 4. Articulating another version of this new "Could Be Worse" philosophy, David H. Demo offers a highly original interpretation of a 1992 study in which he and Alan C. Acock compare outcomes for children living in four family types: first-marriage, divorced, stepfamily, and never-married homes. Data from the study suggest that, after controlling for income, race, and other socioeconomic variables, children of never-married mothers do better in some areas, such as school performance and reported conflict with parents, than do children from either divorced or stepfamily homes.

   On the surface, of course, these data are unremarkable. Numerous studies have revealed the unstable and conflictual aspects of divorced and especially step-family homes. Specifically, is it any surprise that children of never-married mothers, most of whom never see their fathers, much less experience "conflict" with them, would report less "conflict" with parents than do children in divorced homes and children who live with stepfathers?

   But consider Demo's quite remarkable interpretation of this finding. In an interview for *The Washingtonian* magazine, Demo concludes that fathers are unnecessary. Here is how he puts it: "People have this mentality that children are going to be disadvantaged if they grow up in a single-parent home, and this study disproves that notion. It may be that adolescents with never-married mothers benefit from their intact, non-disrupted family history."

   Leave aside Demo's remark that growing up without a father can constitute an "intact, non-disrupted family history." In addition, leave aside the inconvenient fact that Demo's study specifically contradicts Demo's public summary of the study. (The study's core finding: "Adolescents whose mothers and fathers are both in their first marriage have the fewest problems with personal adjustment, emotional adjustment, completion of homework, and grades.") Consider instead the "Could Be Worse" logic that informs these otherwise inexplicable comments to *The Washingtonian.* Demo's study examines four groups of children, three of which do not live with their fathers. He finds that one of the three groups of fatherless children experiences somewhat fewer problems than do the other two groups of fatherless children. On this basis, he tells *The Washingtonian* that "this study disproves" the "notion" that children without fathers "are going to be disadvantaged."

   Here is a perfect, almost comical, example of defining deviancy down. Demo the scholar shows us that fathers matter. On every measurement he uses, children who live with their fathers report better outcomes than those who do not. Yet Demo the public advocate insists to *The Washingtonian* that fathers do not matter. Indeed, his study "disproves that notion."

   The explanation for this non sequitur is that Demo is seeking to lower the traditional standard for what is normative. To Demo the opinion leader, father-hood is not what counts. (Let's just forget about that part of the study.) What matters is that some forms of fatherlessness may be less bad, in some ways, than other forms of fatherlessness. Apparently, this view of what matters is also the view of *The Washingtonian,* whose reporter Tamar Abrams seems more than willing to play this little game. See David H. Demo and Alan C. Acock, "Family Structure and Adolescent Behavior," paper presented at the 1992 annual meeting of the American Sociological Association, 17; and Tamar Abrams, "My Test-Tube Daddy," *The Washingtonian,* March 1994, 116.

41. Daniel Patrick Moynihan, "Defining Deviancy Down," *American Scholar* 62, no. 1 (winter 1993): 17–30.

42. Gloria Norris and Jo Ann Miller, *The Working Mother's Complete Handbook* (New York: New American Library, 1984), 299.

43. Ibid., 261, 283.

44. Alvin L. Schorr and Phyllis Moen, "The Single Parent and Public Policy," in Arlene S. Skolnick and Jerome H. Skolnick, eds., *Family in Transition: Rethinking Marriage, Sexuality, Child Rearing, and Family Organization* (Boston: Little, Brown, 1983), 579.

45. Genevieve Clapp, *Divorce and New Beginnings* (New York: Wiley, 1992), 198–99.

46. Quoted in Chollar, "Happy Families," 57. In the same article, Chollar concludes that "the quality of a home is more important than its cast of characters" (p. 55) and that fathers, in particular, are nonessential, since "other nurturing adults can also provide the support and stability all children need" (p. 54).

47. Martin Wolins, "The Gender Dilemma in Social Welfare: Who Cares for Children?" in Michael E. Lamb and Abraham Sagi, eds., *Fatherhood and Family Policy* (Hillsdale, N.J.: Erlbaum Associates, 1983), 113, 121.

48. See testimony of Stephanie Coontz before the Select Committee on Children, Youth, and Families, U.S. House of Representatives, July 23, 1992 (Washington, D.C.: U.S. Government Printing Office, 1992), 72; Marietta Morrissey, "Female-Headed Families: Poor Women and Choice," and Frances Fox Piven, "Women and the State: Ideology, Power, and the Welfare State," in Naomi Gerstel and Harriet Engel Gross, eds., *Families and Work* (Philadelphia: Temple University Press, 1987), 302, 512–19; Nan D. Hunter, "Women and Child Support," in Irene Diamond, ed., *Families, Politics and Public Policy: A Feminist Dialogue on Women and the State* (New York: Longman, 1983), 212–15; and Barbara Ehrenreich and Frances Fox Piven, "Women and the Welfare State," in Irving Howe, ed., *Alternatives: Proposals for America from the Democratic Left* (New York: Pantheon, 1984), 41–60.

49. Cited in Bryan Appleyard, "Only Nuclear Families Can Defuse This Social A-Bomb," *London Sunday Times,* September 22, 1991, 2-2.

50. John N. Edwards, "Changing Family Structure and Youthful Well-Being," *Journal of Family Issues* 8, no. 4 (December 1987): 369.

51. Joseph Pleck, response dated November 14, 1991, to the Fatherhood Questionnaire of the Institute for American Values (New York: Institute for American Values, 1991).

52. Susan E. Krantz, "Divorce and Children," in Sanford M. Dornbusch and Myra H. Strober, eds., *Feminism, Children, and the New Families* (New York: Guilford Press, 1988), 250.

53. Lula Beatty and Lawrence E. Gary, testimony before the Select Committee on Children, Youth, and Families, U.S. House of Representatives, February 25, 1986 (Washington, D.C.: U.S. Government Printing Office, 1986), 53.

54. Steven Mintz and Susan Kellogg, *Domestic Revolutions: A Social History of Family Life* (New York: Free Press, 1988), 226.

55. Alan J. Hawkins and David J. Eggebeen, "Are Fathers Fungible? Patterns of Coresident Adult Men in Maritally Disrupted Families and Young Children's Well-being," *Journal of Marriage and the Family* 53, no. 4 (November 1991): 959–60. Like Frank Mott's study, this one examines only a narrow range of outcome variables in very young children (ages four to six) born to very young (mostly teenage) mothers. Thus, many of the inherent problems of the Mott study, all of which serve to undermeasure paternal influence, also limit the validity of this study.

56. Barbara G. Cashion, "Female-Headed Families: Effects on Children and Clinical Implications," *Journal of Marital and Family Therapy* 8, no. 2 (April 1982): 80, 82. This same point is made by Norris and Miller in *The Working Mother's Complete Handbook:* "One of the happiest results of being single can be a deepened companionship with your children . . . Without another adult to share their problems, many single mothers discuss their thoughts more freely with their children. 'My eight-year-old daughter loves to know just where I stand with my latest boyfriend,' says Annie [a single mother interviewed by the authors]. 'And you know, she has better instincts about them than my adult friends'" (p. 281).

    Of course, this view is not so much empirically incorrect as it is almost comically one-dimensional, rigorously excluding any positive consideration of what fathers do. Yes, a home without a father is a home in which the mother-child relationship can become closer and more intimate; a home in which adult decision making is, almost by definition, a smoother process; and a home in which children can and usually do exercise greater measures of both authority and responsibility. This same home, however, precisely because it lacks a father, is a home in which children can suffer from being treated more as friends and confidants than as children ("My eight-year-old daughter loves to know just where I stand with my latest boyfriend"); a home in which children can grow up too fast, for the wrong reasons; and a home in which children can ultimately pay a heavy price for the decline of adult authority.

    For a balanced, nuanced discussion of father-absent parenting as "a different kind of parenting," see Robert S. Weiss, *Going It Alone: The Family Life and Social Situation of the Single Parent* (New York: Basic Books, 1979), 66–96, 259–80.

57. Interviews with single mothers conducted on August 2, 1992, in Chicago, Illinois. The interviews were carried out under the auspices of the National Commission on America's Urban Families.

58. Consider two hypotheses. If, as of 1991, one of every three out-of-wedlock childbirths is "by choice," then approximately 400,000 children per year are now born to "single mothers by choice," representing about 9 percent of all births per year. Alternatively, if only 15 percent of nonmarital births are "by choice," then about 175,000 children per year are born "by choice," representing about 4 percent of all births per year. Accordingly, we can estimate that, at a minimum, somewhere from 175,000 to 400,000 children per year, representing from 4 to 9 percent of all newborns today, are born to "single mothers by choice."

    Compare this estimate to the phenomenon of unwed teenage childbearing. In 1990, about 368,000 births—or about 9 percent of all births—occurred to unmarried teenage mothers. Accordingly, if my higher-end estimate is correct, the number of "single mothers by choice"—adult unmarried women who make a conscious decision to bear children—is now approaching a rough parity with the number of unwed teenage mothers.

This estimate is derived from the following data. In 1991, about 1.2 million children were born to unmarried mothers, representing 29.5 percent of all births, up from 19.4 percent in 1982. Moreover, unmarried mothers age thirty or over in 1990 accounted for some 182,000 births, or about 15 percent of all nonmarital births and about 4 percent of all births. See National Center for Health Statistics, "Advance Report of Final Natality Statistics, 1991," vol. 42, no. 3, supplement, *Monthly Vital Statistics Report* (Hyattsville, Md.: U.S. Department of Health and Human Services, September 9, 1993), 9, 30.

Similarly, according to the U.S. Census Bureau, among all never-married women who have attended at least one year of college, the proportion who have become mothers has approximately doubled over the course of one decade, from 5.5 percent in 1982 to 11.3 percent in 1992. This doubling of the rate is consistent across subcategories. For example, among never-married women with bachelor's degrees, the rate rose from 3 percent to 6.4 percent. Among never-married women with professional and managerial jobs, the rate increased from 3.1 percent to 8.3 percent. See Amara Bachu, "Fertility of American Women: June 1992," U.S. Bureau of the Census, Current Population Reports, series P-20, no. 470 (Washington, D.C.: U.S. Government Printing Office, June 1993), xix.

Of course, it is inherently difficult to quantify a trend involving a subjective dimension such as "choice." But most analysts agree that the astonishing recent surge in unwed childbearing, especially among older (and therefore more educated and affluent) women, does represent, to a large degree, as the National Center for Health Statistics puts it, "deliberate choices to accept single parenthood." See Linda B. Williams and William F. Pratt, "Wanted and Unwanted Childbearing in the United States, 1973–1988," *Advance Data from Vital and Health Statistics,* National Center for Health Statistics (Hyattsville, Md.: U.S. Department of Health and Human Services, 1990), 5.

Indeed, my estimate is a cautious one; other analysts might reasonably argue that the actual number is much higher. The importance of "choice" in explaining current trends in natality is strongly confirmed by the testimony of unmarried mothers themselves, who consistently cite recent changes in the cultural climate as the catalyst for their decision to bear and raise children apart from fathers. A 1993 *San Francisco Chronicle* story calls this cultural shift "the mainstreaming of single motherhood." Beginning in the late 1970s, as a lesbian mother puts it in *The Lesbian and Gay Parenting Handbook,* "unmarried, middle-class heterosexual women who wanted children were becoming single parents by choice. Though it wasn't common, it wasn't a rarity either. The ancient specter of illegitimacy became a dowdy old notion. There were possibilities. If it hadn't been for these changes, Susan and I probably never would have considered having children. . . . The social climate had given us an opening." See Jerry Carroll and Ruthe Stein, "The Mainstreaming of Single Motherhood," *San Francisco Chronicle,* July 29, 1993, C-3; and April Martin, *The Lesbian and Gay Parenting Handbook: Creating and Raising Our Families* (New York: HarperCollins, 1993), 3–4.

Several organizations now exist to support single mothers by choice, including Single Mothers by Choice (with a reported two thousand members in twenty chapters in 1993), Parents Without Partners, and New York's Single Parent Resource Center.

59. Naomi Miller, *Single Parents by Choice: A Growing Trend in Family Life* (New York: Plenum Press, 1992).

60. Ibid., 25–26, 28–29, 32, 37, 46–47. Rachel's viewpoint is frequently endorsed by

the editors of leading newspapers. For example, commenting on the rising rate of unwed childbearing among professional women, the *Boston Globe* opines: "It doesn't take a rocket scientist to figure out why a growing number of women have chosen to bear children without the 'benefit' of marriage: They want to be mothers." (Placing "benefit" in quotation marks, thus mocking the idea that marriage is beneficial, is a nice touch.) These mothers, the *Globe* explains, "facing the prospect of not finding a mate during their fertile years, choose not to forgo the joys of parenthood." To the *Globe,* this trend is perfectly fine—it represents "new families, old values"—so long as women achieve pay equity and policy makers "wake up to the fact that all kinds of families need support." See "New Families, Old Values," *Boston Globe,* July 19, 1993, 10.

CHAPTER 5: THE OLD FATHER

1. Frank S. Pittman, "The Masculine Mystique," *Networker* (May/June 1990): 40–41, 48. See also Pittman, "The Secret Passions of Men," *Journal of Marital and Family Therapy* 17, no. 1 (January 1991): 17–23.

2. Scott Heller, "Scholars Debunk the Marlboro Man: Examining Stereotypes of Masculinity," *Chronicle of Higher Education,* February 3, 1993, A-6.

3. Michael S. Kimmel, "Reading Men: Men, Masculinity, and Publishing," *Contemporary Sociology* 21, no. 2 (March 1992): 162. Similarly, a 1993 review of five new books on masculinity and fatherhood for *In These Times* reports that: "By and large, the authors assert that men are constrained by rigid social expectations that dictate emotional distance, heterosexuality, breadwinning responsibility and a competitive edge." All bad things, it seems, such that "the image of the manly man is, at bottom, vacuous and even dangerous." See Leora Tanenbaum, "Man Watchers," *In These Times,* August 23, 1993, 34.

4. Phil Donahue, *The Human Animal* (New York: Simon & Schuster, 1985), 186, 231.

5. Kyle D. Pruett, *The Nurturing Father: Journey Toward the Complete Man* (New York: Warner, 1987), 40.

6. Ruth Egel Khowais, "Today's Dads Face Stress of Balancing Kids and Success," *Boston Herald,* June 21, 1992, 11.

7. Ralph Keyes, "If Only I Could Say, 'I Love You, Dad,'" *Parade,* February 7, 1993, 4.

8. Andrew Ferguson, "America's New Man," *American Spectator* (January 1992): 26, 30. For a literature review of the contemporary men's movement, including both its mytho-poetic and fathers' rights branches, see the Changing Men Collection in the Special Collections Division of the Michigan State University Libraries in Lansing, Michigan.

9. David Halberstam, *The Fifties* (New York: Villard, 1993), 520.

10. Stephanie Coontz, *The Way We Never Were: American Families and the Nostalgia Trap* (New York: Basic Books, 1992), 34–35. Interestingly, Coontz's only source for this historical claim is a 1991 issue of *People* magazine. It was in 1991, it seems, when Van Derbur first announced that her father, by then deceased, had abused her decades earlier. For years, Van Derbur said, she had repressed all memory of the abuse. (The actress Roseanne Barr also appeared on the cover of *People* in 1991 when she announced her recovery of previously repressed memories of childhood abuse.)

Yet Coontz declines to consider the possible meanings of any of these facts. She does not even report them. For her, the issue is uncomplicated. The father abused the daughter; the father is a symbol of his era. Why pursue the details?

Coontz notwithstanding, no serious historian would ever rely uncritically on *People* magazine as a sole source for determining the facticity of an uncorroborated historical allegation of child abuse, much less rely on such a problematic case as a retroactive metaphor for an entire generation of men. To locate the Van Derbur case within the larger and exceedingly complex phenomenon of contemporary claims of "recovered" memories of abuse, see Elizabeth F. Loftus, "The Reality of Repressed Memories," *American Psychologist* 48, no. 5 (May 1993): 519, passim; and Lawrence Wright, "Remembering Satan," *The New Yorker,* May 24, 1993, 69, passim.

11. Barbara J. Berg, *The Crisis of the Working Mother: Resolving the Conflict Between Family and Work* (New York: Summit, 1986), 32.

12. William H. Chafe, *The Unfinished Journey: America Since World War II* (New York: Oxford University Press, 1991), 123–24.

13. Steven Mintz and Susan Kellogg, *Domestic Revolutions: A Social History of Family Life* (New York: Free Press, 1988), 186, 196.

14. Wini Breines, *Young, White, and Miserable: Growing Up Female in the Fifties* (Boston: Beacon, 1992), 43–44.

15. Ibid., 40. A *New York Times* editorial describes the larger culture of the 1950s as "gray and repressive." See "Deconstructing 'Tommy,'" *New York Times,* July 6, 1993, A-16.

16. Coontz, *The Way We Never Were,* 32.

17. Chafe, *The Unfinished Journey,* 125.

18. Elaine Tyler May, *Homeward Bound: American Families in the Cold War Era* (New York: Basic Books, 1987), 14.

19. James Garbarino, "Reinventing Fatherhood," *Families in Society: The Journal of Contemporary Human Services* 74, no. 1 (January 1993): 52.

20. Linda Thompson and Alexis J. Walker, "Gender in Families: Women and Men in Marriage, Work, and Parenthood," *Journal of Marriage and the Family* 51, no. 4 (November 1989): 860.

21. James Dittes, "Yale Weekly Bulletin and Calendar" (New Haven: Yale University, November 19, 1984), 2, cited in Pruett, *The Nurturing Father,* 17.

22. Adrienne Rich, *Of Woman Born* (New York: Bantam, 1977), 39, 290.

23. Catharine R. Stimpson, "Foreword," in Harry Brod, ed., *The Making of the Masculinities: The New Men's Studies* (Boston: Allen & Unwin, 1987), xii.

24. Ursula Owen, ed., *Fathers: Reflections by Daughters* (New York: Pantheon, 1983), x.

25. Sara Maitland, "Two for the Price of One," in ibid., 20, 28.

26. Walt Whitman, "There Was a Child Went Forth," in *Leaves of Grass* (New York: New American Library, 1958), 291.

27. Dylan Thomas, "Do Not Go Gentle into That Good Night," in Helen Gardner, ed., *The New Oxford Book of English Verse, 1250–1950* (New York: Oxford University Press, 1972), 942.

28. In the bitter struggle between the captain and his wife, Laura, regarding the rearing of Bertha, their young daughter, the captain finally loses his mind and dies, literally tormented to death by the idea, suggested to him by his wife, that he may not be Bertha's biological father. Concerning fatherhood, two themes stand out in this play. First, the core meaning of a man's life, Strindberg suggests, is inextricably linked to fatherhood. The captain tells Laura: "For me, since I don't believe in a life to come, my child was my afterlife. She was my idea of immortality—perhaps the only one that has any foundation in reality. Take that away and you wipe me out." When the captain loses understanding of his fatherhood, he dies.

Second, social fatherhood presupposes—is rooted in—the notion of paternal certainty. Frequently called the legitimacy principle, paternal certainty denotes a man's sure belief, confirmed by the surrounding society, that he is the biological father of a particular child. Without paternal certainty, Strindberg suggests, fatherhood is impossible. From the opening moments, this issue—of much salience in today's increasingly fatherless society—dominates the play.

The captain, now going mad, exclaims: "Here it is in the Odyssey—Book I, line 215; in the Uppsala translation. Telemachus is speaking to Athene. 'My mother indeed declares that he—meaning Odysseus—is my father; but I myself cannot be sure; since no man ever yet knew his own begettor.' And it was Penelope, the most virtuous of women, whom Telemachus was suspecting. That's a fine thing, eh? And then we have the prophet Ezekiel: 'The fool saith: Lo, here is my father, but who can tell whose loins have engendered him?' That's clear enough, isn't it?" As he approaches death, Laura asks if he wants to see his child. He replies: "My child? A man doesn't have children, it's only women who get children. That's why the future is theirs, and we die childless." (August Strindberg, *Three Plays* [New York: Penguin, 1958], 65–66, 73.)

29.   The Old Father also appears in Robert Anderson's 1968 play *I Never Sang for My Father*, as well as in Lanford Wilson's 1985 play, *Talley & Son*.

30.   Donald Barthelme, *The Dead Father* (New York: Farrar, Straus and Giroux, 1975), 129–31.

31.   Peter Taylor, *A Summons to Memphis* (New York: Ballantine, 1987), 11, 61.

32.   Ibid., 153.

33.   Mary Sinclair, *The Three Sisters* (London: Virago, 1982; first published, 1914), 12.

34.   Cited in Alexander Towle, ed., *Fathers* (New York: Simon & Schuster, 1986), 183.

35.   Jessica Benjamin, *The Bonds of Love: Psychoanalysis, Feminism, and the Problem of Domination* (New York: Pantheon, 1988), 171.

36.   Ibid., 86.

37.   Ibid., 133.

38.   Ibid., 109.

39.   Ibid., 102.

40.   Ibid., 105, 133.

41.   Ibid., 107, 221–22.

42.   Ibid., 113.

43.   Ibid., 217–18.

44.   In *Reinventing Womanhood,* for example, Carolyn G. Heilbrun concisely presages *The Bonds of Love.* Like Benjamin, she locates the root of female exploitation in "the absence of any role model for a woman of purpose other than her father." She warns: "If you bring children up with a mother in constant attendance, as the only object of early infant bonding, and if the father is largely absent and comes to represent to the growing infant the only alternative to the mother's encompassing love, you will precisely reproduce the family condition that will impel girls toward mothering and boys to seek their destiny in the world apart from parenting." To remedy this evil, she explicitly urges, like Benjamin, the ungendering of fatherhood and the invention of androgynous parenthood: "a new order of individuals" living in "the symmetrical family." In the symmetrical family, "both parents care for the children in equal turns ... Neither boys nor girls will then identify separation as separation from the mother, nor conceive of the only alternative to her and her all-encompassing love as inevitably male." Thus "the parent-child bond is profound until such time as the child undergoes

initiation rites into selfhood, but is not inevitably established with one parent or the other simply because of gender." As a result, daughters can "appropriate the male model without giving up the female person." Moreover, we can "then begin to mystify fatherhood not, as in the past, as some distant, godlike, authority figure, but as a parent, like the mother, partaking in daily adventures in intimacy and affection." More recently, Sandra Lipsitz Bem of Cornell University has reiterated these themes in *The Lens of Gender.* Like Benjamin, Bem views "eradicating gender polarization" as the primary social imperative. Achieving this goal would mean that "the distinction between male and female no longer organizes either the culture or the psyche." In *Toward a Recognition of Androgyny,* Heilbrun makes this same point, insisting that "our future salvation lies in a movement away from sexual polarization and the prison of gender toward a world in which individual roles and modes of personal behavior can be freely chosen."

See Carolyn G. Heilbrun, *Reinventing Womanhood* (New York: Norton, 1979), 156–58, 192–96, 212; Heilbrun, *Toward a Recognition of Androgyny* (New York: Norton, 1993), ix–x; and Sandra Lipsitz Bem, *The Lens of Gender: Transforming the Debate on Sexual Inequality* (New Haven: Yale University Press, 1993), 192. Benjamin's basic themes are also iterated in Dorothy Dinnerstein, *The Mermaid and the Minotaur: Sexual Arrangements and Human Malaise* (New York: Harper & Row, 1977); and Nancy J. Chodorow, *Feminism and Psychoanalytic Theory* (New Haven: Yale University Press, 1989), 45–65.

45. Olga Silverstein and Beth Rashbaum, *The Courage to Raise Good Men* (New York: Viking, 1994), 76, 237.

46. Susan Moller Okin, *Justice, Gender, and the Family* (New York: Basic Books, 1989), 181, 171.

47. Judith Lorber, "Dismantling Noah's Ark," in Judith Lorber and Susan A. Farrell, eds., *The Social Construction of Gender* (Newbury Park, Calif.: Sage Publications, 1991), 355, 359–60.

48. Ibid., 361–63. See also Lorber, *Paradoxes of Gender* (New Haven: Yale University Press, 1994). Sara Ruddick agrees with Lorber. In urging the abolition of fatherhood as a male role and as a cultural idea, Ruddick looks forward "to the day when men are willing and able to share equally and actively in transformed maternal practices . . . On that day there will be no more 'fathers,' no more people of either sex who have power over their children's lives and moral authority in their children's world, though they do not do the work of attentive love. There will [instead] be mothers of both sexes." See Sara Ruddick, "Maternal Thinking," in Barrie Thorne and Marilyn Yalom, eds., *Rethinking the Family: Some Feminist Questions* (New York: Longman, 1982), 91.

49. In *The Hearts of Men,* Barbara Ehrenreich seeks to unite these two modes of analysis, provocatively synthesizing feminist cultural criticism with socialist theory. The focal point of her argument is the cultural demise of married fatherhood in the United States, or what she terms "the collapse of the breadwinner ethic." In a sense, then, her subject is the demise of the Old Father.

To Ehrenreich, the major underlying cause of this demise has not been the women's movement, but rather an inchoate men's movement, or what she describes as "the male revolt." Over the last four decades, men have simply changed their minds about masculinity, sexuality, and marriage. By the 1980s, Ehrenreich concludes, "manhood was no longer burdened with the automatic expectation of marriage and breadwinning." More freedom. Fewer "burdens." More divorce. More children growing up without fathers.

What is the proper response to this shift? Ehrenreich's thesis is that we must "accept the male revolt as a historical fait accompli, and begin to act on its economic consequences for women." Specifically: "The collapse of the family wage system demands nothing less than the creation of a welfare state; that is, a state committed to the welfare of its citizens and prepared to meet their needs—for financial assistance, medical care, education, child care, etc.—when they are unable to meet these needs themselves."

Since increasing numbers of women and children can no longer rely on men for support, they must rely on society as a whole. The Old Father is gone. His logical replacement is the state. Ehrenreich presses the point: "Those who believe that it is somehow more honorable to rely on an individual man than on agencies created by public wealth are, I think, simply clinging to an idealized memory of male paternalism . . . If men [today] cannot be held responsible as individuals—and there is no way consistent with democracy to do so—then we must all become more responsible collectively." In sum: "In a 'world without a father,' that is, without the private system of paternalism built into the family wage system, we will have to learn to be brothers and sisters."

Well, here at least is a plan. A world without fathers necessitates the creation of socialism. Clear enough. Yet several problems escape Ehrenreich's attention. For example, what leads Ehrenreich to suppose that men ("brothers") who are unwilling or unable to support their own children would be willing or able to support other people's children, or children in general?

Moreover, consider the single most obvious lacuna in her logic. Throughout her book, Ehrenreich bases her recommendations on the assumption that fatherhood is reducible to economics. But she is wrong. Fatherhood is not reducible to economics. Fatherhood is not a synonym for "breadwinning," or income. Fatherhood is a social role: a pattern of expectations for male behavior that socializes men by encouraging them to protect and nurture their offspring. Ehrenreich is unable to recognize this basic fact.

Instead, Ehrenreich is interested in "the hearts of men" for one reason only: She wants mothers without husbands to have enough money. As a result, in a book purportedly about the male role in the family, Ehrenreich hardly deigns to mention the subject of the father-child relationship. To her, the topic is irrelevant. She thus sustains her basic proposal—replace fathers with socialism—only by assuming that fathers, understood as anything other than an income source, do not and need not exist. In this sense, *The Hearts of Men* is a culturally diagnostic book: Its entire argument is rooted in the assumption that fathers, as fathers, are superfluous. See Barbara Ehrenreich, *The Hearts of Men: American Dreams and the Flight from Commitment* (New York: Anchor Books, 1983), 12–13, 177–78, 181–82.

50. Weston La Barre, *The Ghost Dance: Origins of Religion* (Garden City, N.Y.: Doubleday, 1970), 592. Accordingly, La Barre views the father-son relationship as "the most critical and dangerous animal relationship on this earth" precisely because the son's relationship to the father forms the paradigm of the son's understanding of how to "accept and how to embody male authority, how to express and when to modulate aggressiveness against other men" (pp. 591–92).

51. Weston La Barre, *The Human Animal* (Chicago: University of Chicago Press, 1954), 29.

52. Walter J. Ong, *Fighting for Life: Contest, Sexuality, and Consciousness* (Ithaca, N.Y.: Cornell University Press, 1981), 102. As a prosaic and more positive exam-

ple of this idea, consider the story of Hubert Davis, a professional basketball player with the New York Knicks. Davis credits his father—"My Dad's my best friend"—with teaching him how to play basketball and how to succeed in life. What did Hubert Davis, Sr., teach his son? When the two played basketball together, "Hubert Davis Sr. gave no quarter. He would knock his son down. Talk trash to him. Foul him. Whatever it took to win. Davis's mother would look out the window in anguish, and inevitably she would run outside and stop the game, sparing her son any more lumps. 'I wanted Hubert to know that it takes toughness to succeed,' said the elder Davis . . . 'He learned. I knew it would help him compete later . . . the only tough part was dealing with his mother when she thought he'd had enough.'" See Clifton Brown, "Knicks' Davis: The Choir Boy with the Killer Shot," *New York Times,* November 26, 1993, D-1.

53. Sigmund Freud, *Totem and Taboo* (New York: Norton, 1950), 51, 141. The process in the child by which fear of external authority becomes internalized as the superego—that is, the external conflict with the parent (especially the father) becomes an internal conflict between the ego and conscience—is described in Sigmund Freud, *Civilization and Its Discontents* (New York: Norton, 1961), 70–80.

54. Even as strong an advocate of the New Father model as Samuel Osheron can report that "distance indeed may be the curse of fatherhood." Interestingly, although Osheron clearly disapproves of the Old Father, "it is not yet at all clear" to him that "some of the distance of the father . . . is all bad." See Samuel Osheron, *Finding Our Fathers: The Unfinished Business of Manhood* (New York: Free Press, 1986), 175.

55. One consequence of this phenomenon is that the issue of paternal authority—what it is and what it does—has virtually disappeared from contemporary sociological analyses of family life. It is almost as if the subject itself has vanished. Of course, a few scholars have declined to abandon the topic. Moira Eastman, an Australian family scholar, worries about the "widespread lack of appreciation of the value, the essential nature of authority in families," especially among "social welfare professionals." This scholarly and professional neglect is significant, since Eastman finds a clear correlation between family dysfunction and weak or passive fathers. Christopher Lasch has also analyzed the consequences of the long-term decline in paternal and familial authority. See Moira Eastman, *Family: The Vital Factor* (Victoria, Australia: CollinsDove, 1989), 79; and Christopher Lasch, *Haven in a Heartless World: The Family Besieged* (New York: Basic Books, 1977), and *The Culture of Narcissism: American Life in an Age of Diminished Expectations* (New York: Norton, 1978).

56. Robert Bly, "Foreword: Mitscherlich and His Uncomfortable Thoughts," in Alexander Mitscherlich, *Society Without the Father: A Contribution to Social Psychology* (New York: HarperCollins, 1993), xvi.

CHAPTER 6: THE NEW FATHER

1. Julie Wheelock, "The 'New' Father: Are Old Sexist Stereotypes About Childrearing Breaking Down?" *Television & Families* (summer 1991): 14.

2. Anthony Astracham, *How Men Feel* (Garden City, N.Y.: Anchor Press/Doubleday, 1986), 401–2.

3. David Giveans and Michael Robinson, "Old and New Images of Fatherhood," in Charles Scull, ed., *Fathers, Sons, and Daughters: Exploring Fatherhood, Renewing*

the Bond (Los Angeles: Jeremy P. Tarcher, 1992), 11. Virtually the same definition is offered by Graeme Russell, who recommends fundamental social changes—including "changes in beliefs and attitudes, social policy, education, and the economic and employment and political structures"—to support "fathers who have rejected traditional notions of fatherhood and who either share or have the major responsibility for child care." See Graeme Russell, *The Changing Role of Fathers?* (New York: University of Queensland Press, 1983), 221, 2. See also Russell, "Primary Caretaking and Role-Sharing Fathers," in Michael E. Lamb, ed., *The Father's Role: Applied Perspectives* (New York: Wiley, 1986), 29–57.

4. Letty Cottin Pogrebin, *Family Politics: Love and Power on an Intimate Frontier* (New York: McGraw-Hill, 1983), 206.

5. Ibid., 197, 209.

6. Robert A. Lewis and Joseph H. Pleck, eds., "Men's Roles in the Family," *The Family Coordinator* 28, no. 4 (October 1979), 430–31.

7. Peter Coolsen, ed., "Half Full or Half Empty?" *Families in Society: The Journal of Contemporary Human Services* 74, no. 1 (January 1993): 3.

8. Nijole V. Benokraitis, *Marriage and Families: Changes, Choices, and Constraints* (Englewood Cliffs, N.J.: Prentice-Hall, 1993), 98–99.

9. Ronald G. Stover and Christen A. Hope, *Marriage, Family, and Intimate Relations* (Orlando, Fla.: Harcourt Brace Jovanovich, 1993), 73.

10. Janet G. Hunt and Larry L. Hunt, "Male Resistance to Role Symmetry in Dual-Earner Households: Three Alternative Explanations," in Naomi Gerstel and Harriet Engel Gross, eds., *Families and Work* (Philadelphia: Temple University Press, 1987), 192–94. This theme is also developed by Beth Willinger, "Resistance and Change: College Men's Attitudes Toward Family and Work in the 1980s," in Jane C. Hood, ed., *Men, Work, and Family* (Newbury Park, Calif.: Sage Publications, 1993), 108–30. For a longer reflection on this theme, see Arlie R. Hochschild, *The Second Shift: Working Parents and the Revolution at Home* (New York: Viking, 1989).

11. Augustus Napier, "Heroism, Men and Marriage," *Journal of Marital and Family Therapy* 17, no. 1 (January 1991): 9–10, 13–14.

12. Clayton Barbeau, "The Man-Woman Crisis," in James M. Henslin, ed., *Marriage and Family in a Changing Society* (New York: Free Press, 1985), 169, 173–75.

13. James Garbarino, "Reinventing Fatherhood," *Families in Society: The Journal of Contemporary Human Services* 74, no. 1 (January 1993): 53.

14. Ronald F. Levant, "Education for Fatherhood," in Phyllis Bronstein and Carolyn Pape Cowan, eds., *Fatherhood Today: Men's Changing Roles in the Family* (New York: Wiley, 1988), 256, 269–70. In the same vein, Kerry Daly argues that a primary obstacle to the socially vital goal of "reshaping fatherhood" is the lingering presence of "deficient" paternal role models from earlier generations. In particular, for the men Daly studied, their own fathers "served only as a negative role model" and thus as "the antithesis of who they wanted to be as fathers."

    Daly's conclusion is unsupported by the results of my own interviews with married fathers. The men I interviewed typically want to be, and believe that they are, different from their fathers—more nurturant, more emotionally accessible, more flexible, less strict. But they also offer a much richer, more nuanced, and more generous assessment of their fathers than Daly's blanket assertions suggest. Daly casually dismisses an entire earlier generation of fathers as "deficient" and the "antithesis" of good fatherhood. The men I interviewed do not. In a larger sense, of course, the tendency among elites to denigrate their own fathers—to assert, even as they witness the collapse of fatherhood in our time, that they are good fathers while their own fathers were bad—reflects a remarkable but ubiquitous feature of contemporary public discourse. See Kerry Daly, "Reshaping Fatherhood: Finding the Models," *Journal of Family Issues* 14, no. 4 (December 1993): 517–18, 526.

15. Beth M. Erickson, *Helping Men Change: The Role of the Female Therapist* (Thousand Oaks, Calif.: Sage Publications, 1993).

16. Shirley M. H. Hanson and Frederick W. Bozett, "Fatherhood: A Review and Resources," *Family Relations* 36, no. 3 (July 1987): 336.

17. Beverly Beckham, "Here's a Dad Who Sets the Standard for Sharing, Caring," *Boston Herald,* June 21, 1992, 11.

18. Arthur D. Colman and Libby Lee Colman, *The Father* (New York: Avon, 1988), xvi–xvii.

19. "The 90s Father: Who Is He?"; James A. Levine, "Is Your Husband a Good Enough Father?"; and Curtis Austin, "Dads and Kids," *Child* (March 1993): 95, 97, 101, 138.

20. Jerry Adler, "The Good Father," *Redbook* (June 1993): 79–83, 131.

21. "The Parenting Poll: Does Dad Really Do Diapers?" *Parenting* (August 1993): 17.

22. "What's It Like to Be a Dad," *Parents* (June 1993): 39–44.

23. David Gutmann, *Reclaimed Powers: Toward a New Psychology of Men and Women in Later Life* (New York: Basic Books, 1987), 197–98.

24. Ibid., 202–4. See also Gutmann, "Good Outcomes and Pathological Consequences of Post-Parental Androgyny," unpublished paper (Evanston, Ill.: Northwestern University, 1991), 1–2.

25. Alice S. Rossi, "Gender and Parenthood," *American Sociological Review* 49 (February 1984): 1. See also Rossi, "Sex and Gender in an Aging Society," *Daedalus* 115, no. 1 (winter 1986): 141–69; and Rossi, "Eros and Caritas: A Biopsychosocial Approach to Human Sexuality and Reproduction," in Alice S. Rossi, ed., *Sexuality Across the Life Course* (Chicago: University of Chicago Press, 1994), 3–36.

26. Jean-Jacques Rousseau, *The First and Second Discourses* (New York: St. Martin's Press, 1964), 146–47.

27. Alexis de Tocqueville, *Democracy in America,* vol. 2 (New York: Schocken, 1961), 233.

28. Stephen M. Frank, "'Their Own Proper Task': The Construction of Meanings for Fatherhood in Nineteenth-Century America,' paper presented at the conference "The History of Marriage and the Family in Western Society" (Ottawa: Carleton University, April 1992), 13, 30.

29. Ibid., 10, 33.

30. Rev. Artemus B. Muzzey, *The Fireside: An Aid to Parents* (Boston, 1854), 153–54, cited in ibid., 34.

31. Sloan Wilson, *The Man in the Gray Flannel Suit* (New York: Simon & Schuster, 1955), 251–52.

32. David Riesman, "The College Student in an Age of Organization," in Hendrik M. Ruitenbeek, ed., *The Dilemma of Organizational Society* (New York: Dutton, 1963), 103. In this valuable essay, Riesman appears to contest, or at least qualify, William Whyte's critique of 1950s familism as merely symptomatic of a larger value shift toward what Whyte terms the Social Ethic, or adherence to the newly regnant values of the large-scale organization. To Riesman, by contrast, "the very emphasis on family life which is one of the striking and in so many ways attractive

qualities of young people today is an implicit rejection of large organization. The suburban family with its garden, its barbeque, its lack of privacy in the open-plan house, is itself a manifesto of decentralization . . . The wish to build a nest, even if a somewhat transient one, is a striking feature of the interviews, in contrast to the wish to build a fortune or a career which might have dominated some comparable interviews a generation earlier" (p. 102).

33. William H. Whyte, Jr., *The Organization Man* (New York: Simon & Schuster, 1956), 342, 355. For similar, and largely unsympathetic, assessments of the child-centeredness of the era, see A. C. Spectorsky, *The Exurbanites* (Philadelphia: Lippincott, 1955), 248–52; and Martha Weinman Lear, *The Child Worshippers* (New York: Crown, 1963), 120–35. For example, Lear makes considerable fun of a group of fathers from suburban New York who organized a communitywide network of "Dads' Clubs." Trained by a "Coaching for Dads" course and directed by a "Central Dads' Committee," the fathers in these local clubs seemed curiously dedicated to the idea, as Lear teasingly puts it, that "no Pop who's a real Pop lets his offspring play alone." These clubs, Lear tells us, constituted a "cornerstone of local culture" (p. 131).

34. Ibid., 131–32.

35. David Riesman with Nathan Glazer and Ruel Denney, *The Lonely Crowd: A Study of the Changing American Character* (New Haven: Yale University Press, 1973), see especially 280–83. See also Wini Breines, *Young, White, and Miserable: Growing Up Female in the Fifties* (Boston: Beacon, 1992), 30–37. This assessment was widely shared by contemporary scholars. As William G. Dyer and Dick Urban put it in 1958: "A basic postulate held by many sociologists in the area of the family is that the American family is in a stage of transition from the older patriarchal family to a system of a democratic, equalitarian arrangement." See William G. Dyer and Dick Urban, "The Institutionalization of Equalitarian Family Norms," in John N. Edwards, ed., *The Family and Change* (New York: Knopf, 1969), 201.

36. In 1950, the prominent marriage counselor Paul Popenoe listed ten traits of the "perfect father." Three of them capture the essence of his thinking and also typify the fatherhood advice of the era. Number one: "He modestly recognizes that there is no such thing as a perfect father." Number seven: "He is convinced that bringing up children is not 'women's work.'" Number ten: "He recognizes that fatherhood is an experience which greatly helps a man to grow up emotionally, and he is determined to give frequent evidence of his growth." See Paul Popenoe, *Marriage Is What You Make It* (New York: Macmillan, 1950), 135–36.

37. Margaret Mead, "Job of the Children's Mother's Husband," *New York Times Magazine,* May 10, 1959, 66. Mead presses the point even further: "There seems to be a real danger that the care of young children will prove both so time-consuming and so fascinating that many men will skimp their careers in order to get more time with their families." She worries that the new postwar society is "turning being a father into a full-time job, too, with all a man's best energies going into the home, and too little left over for work outside." Of course, this is precisely the worry of William Whyte in *The Organization Man,* and precisely the dilemma confronting Tom Rath in *The Man in the Gray Flannel Suit*—a dilemma that he resolves in favor of "skimping" his career so that he can spend more time with his family.

38. J. M. Mogey, "A Century of Declining Paternal Authority," in Edwards, *The Family and Change,* 256–58. Of course, the obvious inaccuracy of Mogey's key pre-

diction—that "the redefinition of the father role" would lead to greater "family stability" in the future—raises a disturbing question. Is it possible that what he praises in 1955 as the decline of the father's "rigorous insistence on responsibility with a concomitant of social distance" actually began to contribute, especially as the trend intensified in later years, not to family stability but to family fragmentation? Obviously something was about to happen that he did not foresee in 1955. Perhaps part of that something was the continuing decline of paternal authority and responsibility.

39. Interviews with married fathers confirm this point. On the one hand, many of them are proud to be "newer," more involved fathers than their own fathers were. On the other hand, they do not demean or caricature their fathers. They recognize their fathers' strengths and accomplishments; they try to see their fathers in context. In Ohio, for example, one father said: "My father was working 15 hours a day just to make a few dollars and it was rough for him . . . whereas today . . . we have a lot of time with the children. We have, like, family day set aside." Another said: "Well, I have a good job, my wife has a good job—money is no problem, okay? We don't live high on the hog or nothing, but we have enough to live like we want, so there's no pressures like the money standpoint. Where my dad, we struggled for a while. He didn't have the opportunity that I had, you know." Similarly, in Colorado, one man said: "I'm much better educated than my father was, so I work with the kids education-wise, music-wise." Another father perfectly captured this combination of respect, rivalry, and affection when he concluded about his father: "He did his best, and by God, I'm going to do a little bit more than what Dad did." (Cleveland, Ohio, interviews of November 9, 1992; Denver, Colorado, interviews of August 24, 1992.)

40. In their three-year study of 1,100 California families during the late 1980s, Eleanor E. Maccoby and Robert H. Mnookin confirm this finding: "When fathers are asked what it means to be a father, they are likely to mention first their role as breadwinner." See Eleanor E. Maccoby and Robert H. Mnookin, *Dividing the Child: Social and Legal Dilemmas of Custody* (Cambridge, Mass.: Harvard University Press, 1992), 25.

41. Steve Fainary, "McDaniel Gives Celtics Some Punch," *Boston Globe,* March 26, 1993, 49.

42. For a protean analysis of "the disposition to contest in the human male"—including the biological and cultural roots of "the felt need by males . . . to fight each other"—see Walter J. Ong, *Fighting for Life: Contest, Sexuality, and Consciousness* (Ithaca, N.Y.: Cornell University Press, 1981), 64, 77 passim (especially chapter 2).

43. Robert Zussman, "Work and Family in the New Middle Class," in Gerstel and Gross, *Families and Work,* 344–45.

44. For example, Barbara J. Berg concludes that, for men, "being both father and breadwinner are positively synonymous with being men . . . this double role merely comprises two components of a well-integrated whole. There is no sense of incompatibility, no discontinuity and certainly no guilt." To Berg, this fact is deplorable. It signals gender inequality and proves that most men are "ossified in time and tradition." Similarly, Maureen Perry-Jenkins and Ann C. Crouter confirm "husbands' deep-seated attitudes about provider-role duties," but call for "men's relinquishment of the provider role," since male commitment to this role explains "why some husbands continue to do less in the home." Laura Lein agrees. She concludes: "Men do not see their wage-earning activities apart from

family life. As they see it, working in the paid labor force is their primary contribution to the well-being of their families." But to Lein, this attitude is harmful, since these men "are reluctant to acknowledge either that they need help in performing this [breadwinning] function or have a responsibility to participate in the homemaking function." To Janet Shibley Hyde, Marilyn J. Essex, and Francine Horton, the key conflict is equally simple: Male commitment to "the good-provider role" erodes male commitment to "the family role," thus decreasing the likelihood that men will participate in paternity-leave programs. Similarly, Jane C. Hood dislikes male attitudes toward breadwinning because they stand in the way of the "reallocation of household work."

Not only are scholars typically suspicious of male attitudes toward breadwinning, but many also mix their disapproval with confusion, often producing a strange brew. Theodore F. Cohen, for example, writing in the *Journal of Family Issues,* seems baffled by his findings. On the one hand, he concludes from his interviews that fathers love their children, wish they could spend more time with them, and rank family at the top of their life's priorities. On the other hand, they work long and hard at their jobs. To Cohen, these facts are unreconcilable. To make sense of them, he speculates that "jobs can demand a level of investment in work that ignores the family needs of workers" and that our culture is "still less than wholehearted in embracing the idea of family-oriented men." Thus he concludes that the important social goal of "remaking men"—of "reconceptualizing men's lives" away from preoccupation with "success at work"—will require "looking beyond what men do to what they say and feel."

This logic is tortured but typical. To Cohen, breadwinning conflicts with fatherhood. The two activities are separate, even opposite. His whole argument flows from this premise. Yet his view is not shared by most fathers, who view their work as a component of their paternal responsibility, not as an evasion of it or a barrier to it. Thus Cohen's core question—How can these fathers love their kids yet devote themselves to breadwinning?—is literally meaningless to men who work hard not despite their paternal love but in large part because of it. Indeed, these fathers need not "look beyond" what they do in order to affirm "what they say and feel." For them, the two fit together fairly well, thank you.

See Barbara J. Berg, *The Crisis of the Working Mother: Resolving the Conflict Between Family and Work* (New York: Summit, 1986), 25; Maureen Perry-Jenkins and Ann C. Crouter, "Men's Provider-Role Attitudes: Implications for Household Work and Marital Satisfaction," *Journal of Family Issues* 11, no. 2 (June 1990): 153, 157; Laura Lein, "Male Participation in Home Life: Impact of Social Supports and Breadwinner Responsibility on the Allocation of Tasks," *The Family Coordinator* (October 1979): 489, 493–94; Janet Shibley Hyde, Marilyn J. Essex, and Francine Horton, "Fathers and Parental Leave: Attitudes and Experiences," *Journal of Family Issues* 14, no. 4 (December 1993): 620–21; Jane C. Hood, "The Provider Role: Its Meaning and Measurement," *Journal of Marriage and the Family,* no. 48 (May 1986): 351; and Theodore F. Cohen, "Remaking Men: Men's Experiences Becoming and Being Husbands and Fathers and Their Implications for Reconceptualizing Men's Lives," *Journal of Family Issues* 8, no. 1 (March 1987): 72, 74. See also Maureen Perry-Jenkins, Brenda Seery, and Ann C. Crouter, "Linkages Between Women's Provider-Role Attitudes, Psychological Well-Being, and Family Relationships," *Psychology of Women Quarterly* 16, no. 3 (September 1992): 311–29.

45.   Robert S. Weiss, "Men and Their Wives' Work," in Faye J. Crosby, ed., *Spouse,*

Parent, Worker: On Gender and Multiple Roles (New Haven: Yale University Press, 1987), 110.

46. Ibid., 114, 120.

47. Some authorities, of course, insist on denying these facts. Caryl Rivers and Rosalind Barnett, for example, are disappointed that "family leave" and "juggling work and family" should be seen by corporate managers as issues primarily affecting mothers, since, according to Rivers and Barnett, "there is no gender difference in this area." Such a conclusion clearly reflects the triumph of belief over evidence. See Caryl Rivers and Rosalind Barnett, "Fathers Do Best," *Washington Post,* June 20, 1993, C-5.

48. Teresa M. Cooney and Peter Uhlenberg, "Changes in Work-Family Connections Among Highly Educated Men and Women: 1970 to 1980," *Journal of Family Issues* 12, no. 1 (March 1991): 69.

49. Jean L. Potuchek, "Who's Responsible for Supporting the Family? Employed Wives and the Breadwinner Role," working paper no. 186 (Wellesley, Mass.: Wellesley College Center for Research on Women, 1988), 9. Potuchek argues that "a husband and wife could be said to share the breadwinner role if both participated to the same degree in the labor force . . . and if both felt equally responsible for the financial support of the family." However, she concludes, research findings demonstrate that "such role sharing is rare," even among two-earner married couples (p. 13).

50. Linda Duxbury, Christopher Higgins, and Catherine Lee, "Work-Family Conflict," *Transition* 23, no. 2 (June 1993): 11, 12.

51. Harriet B. Presser, "Can We Make Time for Children? The Economy, Work Schedules, and Child Care," *Demography* 26, no. 3 (August 1989): 523–43.

52. Erik Larson, "The New Father," *Parents* (June 1991): 91. Interestingly, much of the writing on the New Father makes it quite clear that he is a man who does not like, or at least does not wish to be like, his own father. Larson recounts his interview with Kyle Pruett, whose study of real-life New Fathers confirms that these men typically view their own fathers negatively, or as anti–role models: "Pruett found that when the home front got rough, the fathers in his study tried to imagine how their wives would manage things. 'If that didn't work, they often conjured up their mothers,' Pruett explains" (p. 91).

53. Levine, "Is Your Husband a Good Enough Father?" 99, 146.

54. Gayle Kimball, *50-50 Parenting: Sharing Family Rewards and Responsibilities* (Lexington, Mass.: Lexington Books, 1988), 135, 132.

55. Herb Goldberg, *The Hazards of Being Male: Surviving the Myth of Masculine Privilege* (New York: Signet, 1977), 1, 91. Goldberg has emerged as an influential advocate of what he terms "the new male." See also Goldberg, *The New Male: From Self-Destruction to Self-Care* (New York: Signet, 1980); and Goldberg, *What Men Really Want* (New York: Signet, 1991). The central premise of *The New Male* is that "the gender orientation known as masculinity has serious and troubling limitations" (p. 1). Thus the "blueprint for masculinity is a blueprint for self-destruction" (p. 5).

56. Christopher P. Anderson, *Father: The Figure and the Force* (New York: Warner, 1983), 44.

57. Jessie Bernard, "The Good-Provider Role," *American Psychologist* 36, no. 1 (January 1981): 2–3, 8–11.

58. Robert L. Griswold, *Fatherhood in America: A History* (New York: Basic Books, 1993), 3.

59. Kathleen Gerson, *No Man's Land: Men's Changing Commitments to Family and Work* (New York: Basic Books, 1993), 17, 19, 229. Gerson's argument nicely encapsulates conventional scholarly wisdom on this subject. She concludes that inherited male norms of masculinity, including family breadwinning, are "myths" that harm everyone by reinforcing "rigid definitions of manhood." She divides fathers today into three basic groups. The first group holds a "primary bread-winning outlook." Very bad. The second group consists of "estranged dads" who abandon their families. Also very bad. The third group, tiny but growing, consists of "equal fathers" who are "willing and able to defy social expectations, to over-come social constraints, and to reject the pathways of the past" in pursuit of "equal parenting" and thus of "more work flexibility and fewer work demands." Very good. What is needed, therefore, is nothing less than "a profound transfor-mation in men's lives," including "fundamental changes in the organization of the workplace." (See pp. 259–61, 285–86, 254.)

60. Bryan Strong and Christine DeVault, *The Marriage and Family Experience* (St. Paul, Minn.: West Publishing, 1992), 102.

61. Elaine Tyler May, *Homeward Bound: American Families in the Cold War Era* (New York: Basic Books, 1987), 177.

62. Henry B. Biller, *Fathers and Families: Paternal Factors in Child Development* (Westport, Conn.: Auburn House, 1993), 27.

63. Ralph LaRossa, "Fatherhood and Social Change," *Family Relations* 37, no. 4 (October 1988): 457.

64. Anna Coote, Harriet Harman, and Patricia Hewitt, *The Family Way: A New Approach to Policy-Making*, social policy paper no. 1 (London: Institute for Pub-lic Policy Research, 1990), 36. They conclude that "it is essential for men to change their role in the household, and do more of the unpaid work" and that society must "create the conditions for men and women to be equally capable of supporting themselves and contributing at least half to the support of their chil-dren" (p. 37). Unless I misread this last recommendation, it would seem that no father, for example, should earn more than half of the family income, lest such an imbalance suggest at least the possibility of less-than-equal maternal capability.

65. Mark Gerzon, *A Choice of Heroes: The Changing Faces of American Manhood* (Boston: Houghton Mifflin, 1984), 122.

66. Gordon Rothman, testimony before the Select Committee on Children, Youth, and Families, U.S. House of Representatives, June 11, 1991 (Washington, D.C.: U.S. Government Printing Office, 1991), 10.

67. James Warren, "A Real 'Mr. Mom,'" *Chicago Tribune*, April 4, 1993, sec. 5, 2. Indeed, a number of fathers in recent years have won favorable public attention by staying home to care for their newborn children—and to write books about the experience. For example, see Mike Clary, *Daddy's Home: The Personal Story of a Modern Father Who Opted to Raise the Baby and Master the Craft of Mother-hood* (New York: Seaview, 1982).

68. Shari Rudavsky, "New Fathers Reluctant to Take Time Out," *Washington Post*, July 7, 1992, A-3.

69. "Discouraging Words Hit Home for Men," *Wall Street Journal*, December 1, 1992, B-1.

70. In the United States in 1991, there were 11.9 million married couples with at least one child under age six. Of those families, 9.2 million (77 percent) had a father who worked full-time throughout the year; 3.4 million (28 percent) had a mother who worked full-time throughout the year; and 2.7 million (22 percent) had two

parents who worked full-time throughout the year. These data should—but probably will not—give at least some pause to journalists and other analysts who endlessly assert, as if it were an obvious truth, that the two-career couple is now the norm among today's young parents. The numbers presented here are unpublished data from the U.S. Bureau of Labor Statistics, "Current Population Survey," March 1992.

71. Joseph H. Pleck, *The Myth of Masculinity* (Cambridge, Mass.: MIT Press, 1981), 151.

72. Leigh A. Leslie, Elaine A. Anderson, and Meredith P. Branson, "Responsibility for Children: The Role of Gender and Employment," *Journal of Family Issues* 12, no. 2 (June 1991): 209. See also James A. Levine, "Daddy Stress," *Child* (June/July 1994): 86–91.

73. If the commitment of married fathers to the breadwinning ideal served to thwart the goals of wives, or was resented by wives, surely this phenomenon would be revealed by national surveys of women's attitudes toward work and family. But existing survey and interview data offer little contemporary evidence of such a phenomenon.

See *The 1990 Virginia Slims Opinion Poll* (New York: Roper Organization, 1990); Mary Komarnicki, "Public Attitudes Toward the American Family: An Overview of Survey Responses Covering 1963–1991," working paper no. 9 (New York: Institute for American Values, June 1991); and Barbara Dafoe Whitehead, "Maryland Focus Group Report on Family Time," working paper no. 2 (New York: Institute for American Values, November 1990).

74. Interview with Heidi Brennen on May 17, 1993. Mothers at Home, headquartered in Vienna, Virginia, has 14,000 subscribers to its monthly publication, *Welcome Home.*

75. Why do men and women work? Of course, at the most basic level, both men and women work to earn money and support their families. But there are also important gender differences in the motivation to work and in styles of work. Compared to men, for example, women frequently value achievement more than money at work. Opinion poll data suggest that employed women are also substantially more likely than men to place a high priority on having lots of contact with coworkers, doing work that can help others, having flexible and limited work hours, and having jobs with limited amounts of stress. See "Relations Between the Sexes," *The American Enterprise* 4, no. 5 (September/October 1993): 89–90, 94.

Moreover, and more central to an exploration of paternal breadwinning, men at work, more than women, are typically motivated in large part by the need to compete with other men and to establish hierarchical relationships of power. Of course, since this gender-related goal is increasingly criticized and denied in our culture, many men now refrain from talking about it, but it remains at the center of male motivation in the workplace. Turning this motivation toward the support of children and child rearing is the cultural basis of the breadwinner role for men.

76. Michael E. Lamb, "The Changing Role of Fathers," in Lamb, *The Father's Role,* 14. Kyle D. Pruett stresses virtually the same point: "Nurturing fathers do not treat their sons much differently from their daughters. In fact, these particular fathers resemble traditional mothers, in that they seem less occupied with shaping gender-appropriate behavior and beliefs in their children than are traditional fathers." See Kyle D. Pruett, *The Nurturing Father: Journey Toward the Complete Man* (New York: Warner, 1987), 37.

77. Andrew M. Greeley, "Necessity of Feminism," *Society* 30, no. 6 (September 1993): 13–14.

78. Biller, *Fathers and Families,* 28, 35, 48, 60.
79. Diane Ehrensaft, *Parenting Together: Men and Women Sharing the Care of Their Children* (Urbana: University of Illinois Press, 1990), x, 13, 35.
80. Ibid., 78–79, 85, 139.
81. Pogrebin, *Family Politics,* 211.
82. Gayle Kimball similarly believes that fathers must "move in an androgynous direction." To help them, she recommends certain children's books "that show boys and men in nurturing roles [that] provide useful role models. Examples of such books are *The Daddy Book, George the Babysitter,* and *My Daddy Is a Nurse.*" See Kimball, *50-50 Parenting,* 142–43.
83. In endorsing this idea, Adrienne Rich does admit that such rewired little boys—those who "grow up unmutilated by gender roles"—are apt to be lonely: "We also have to face the fact that in the present stage of history our sons may feel profoundly alone in the masculine world, with few if any close relationships with other men." Arguably a small price to pay for such progress. And presumably we may take comfort in the fact that this suffering will not occur in future stages of history. See Adrienne Rich, *Of Women Born* (New York: Bantam, 1977), 206.
84. Cited in Phil Donahue, *The Human Animal* (New York: Simon & Schuster, 1985), 308–9.
85. This idea—that moral import lies not primarily in what I do, or even in what I choose, but instead in the act of choosing freely—has become a defining norm of contemporary elite discourse, not only regarding fatherhood, but also regarding our culture as a whole. This regnant idea carries particularly important social consequences for fatherhood. As Joseph Veroff, Elizabeth Douvan, and Richard A. Kulka put it in their important 1981 book, *The Inner American:* "While earlier generations took marriage and parenthood for granted as necessary parts of adulthood, such unconsidered assumptions now gave way to processes of choice, deliberation, and decision. Once parenthood is cast as a choice, the experience is compared to the outcomes of other possible choices and some metric (personal satisfaction, cost-benefit, etc.) must be found on which alternative outcomes can be scaled."

 Yet fatherhood, much more than motherhood, depends for its very existence on shared cultural norms. Social paternity is largely the fragile result of applying effective cultural pressures on males. The current transformation of fatherhood from cultural expectation to personal option must powerfully contribute to the decline of fatherhood in our society—especially since the transformation is occurring in the context of widespread cultural ambivalence, and even hostility, toward most forms of authority, including paternal authority. Despite these facts, the valorization of personal choice and the denigration of social roles remain almost universally celebrated ideals in our elite discourse on fatherhood. Pepper Schwartz, for example, warns us against allowing "nostalgia for the institution of the past" to obscure the new reality (for which she offers at least two cheers), namely, that "the contemporary family is composed of voluntary associations" in which "all family actors are essentially using individual rather than group welfare as their basis for everyday action." More poetically, Charles Scull offers this appreciation: "Fathers come in varied guises. We live in a time of many options as to the form fathering can take—divorced single fathers, stepfathers, gay fathers.... There are as many ways of fathering as there are fathers." See Joseph Veroff, Elizabeth Douvan, and Richard A. Kulka, *The Inner American: A Self-Portrait from 1957 to*

1976 (New York: Basic Books, 1981), 239; Pepper Schwartz, "The Family as a Changed Institution," *Journal of Family Issues* 8, no. 4 (December 1987): 455; and Charles S. Scull, ed., *Fathers, Sons, and Daughters: Exploring Fatherhood, Renewing the Bond* (Los Angeles: Jeremy P. Tarcher, 1992), xvii, 1.

86. Benjamin Spock and Michael B. Rothenberg, *Baby and Child Care* (New York: Pocket Books, 1985), 38.

87. Gerzon, *A Choice of Heroes,* 237.

88. Walt Whitman, "Song of the Open Road," in *Leaves of Grass* (New York: New American Library, 1958), 138.

89. Clearly, proposals for androgynous parenthood spring not primarily from the timeless needs of children but rather from the modern desires of adults. At the same time, ironically, considerable evidence now suggests that the pursuit of androgyny actually undermines, rather than fosters, the modern adult pursuit of intimacy, particularly sexual intimacy, and therefore reduces the likelihood of adult marital satisfaction.

Most scholars agree that the current drift toward parental androgyny is occurring during a period of declining levels of marital satisfaction. More important, however, some recent research concludes that the growing espousal of androgynous parental norms directly contributes to this increase in marital unhappiness. For example, Jay Belsky, Mary Lang, and Ted L. Huston find that, particularly among couples espousing androgynous norms, marital happiness drops with the arrival of children, since the transition to parenthood is typically, almost regardless of parental attitudes, accompanied by greater gender-role divergence. Similarly, Judith Wallerstein finds that first-time fathers who are committed to "co-parenting" frequently cause marital strain by misunderstanding what their wives need from them. The hardest challenge for these fathers, Wallerstein observes, is less to nurture the infant than to love and support the new mother, including supporting her decision to focus primarily on the needs of the newborn child rather than on his needs, including his desire for sex. Yet nothing in the androgynous ideal is likely to prepare the male co-parent for these challenges, or even alert him to their likely existence.

Recent research from Sweden and Norway—two cultures deeply influenced by androgynous parental norms—confirms these trends. Marriage counselors from Sweden, for example, report that increasing numbers of divorcing wives attribute their decision to divorce to sheer boredom with their husbands, including loss of sexual interest. Why? One reason, surely, is that sexual attraction between men and women is based not on sameness but on differences. As Marianne Gullestad, an anthropologist from Norway, has summarized the problem: "There is a contradiction between romantic love and the desired equality in the division of tasks, because romantic love implies imagination and mystery, and, therefore, some cultivation of otherness. Romantic love implies imagination, adventure, excitement, that the two genders are able to be a little secretive to each other, and that is doubtless difficult if they strive to define their relationship in terms of being more and more similar, more and more the same."

Closer to home, Suzanne Fields puts it less delicately. Recalling a woman who complained that her "husband suffers from premature emasculation," Fields reasons: "When men pursue a feminine sensibility, women are inevitably shortchanged in their own fundamental psychic and sensual needs. 'In my practice,' says F. Joseph Whelan . . . 'I have noted that today's women want to have a placid, pliable man to deal with most of the time. However, they also want a virile, aggressive male when it comes to bedroom activities . . . a tiger in bed and a lamb in the living room. Such a creature is hard to find.'"

See Norval D. Glenn, "The Recent Trend in Marital Success in the United States," *Journal of Marriage and the Family* 53, no. 2 (May 1991): 261–70; Diane N. Lye and Timothy J. Biblarz, "The Effects of Attitudes Toward Family Life and Gender Roles on Marital Satisfaction," *Journal of Family Issues* 14, no. 2 (June 1993): 157–88; Jay Belsky, Mary Lang, and Ted L. Huston, "Sex Typing and Division of Labor as Determinants of Marital Change Across the Transition to Parenthood," *Journal of Personality and Social Psychology* 50, no. 3 (March 1986): 517–22; David Popenoe, "Parental Androgyny," *Society* 30, no. 6 (September/October 1993): 5–11; Suzanne Fields, *Like Father, Like Daughter: How Father Shapes the Woman His Daughter Becomes* (Boston: Little, Brown, 1983), 273. Comments from Judith Wallerstein are from an interview on June 4, 1993. Relevant to the consideration of androgyny and the pursuit of intimacy is Milton C. Regan, Jr., *Family Law and the Pursuit of Intimacy* (New York: New York University Press, 1993). For a criticism of measuring fathers according to a "deficit model" of parenthood—that is, a model that posits maternity as the standard—see Ronald D. Day and Wade C. Mackey, "An Alternative Standard for Evaluating American Fathers," *Journal of Family Issues* 10, no. 3 (September 1989): 401–8; and Wade C. Mackey, *Fathering Behaviors: The Dynamics of the Man-Child Bond* (New York: Plenum, 1985), especially 149–66.

90. The archetypal male hero in American literature is frequently identified with freedom from civilization, especially as represented by women and children. From Natty Bumpo to Sam Spade to Travis McGee, this hero is the man who got away—the man who lives in what R. W. B. Lewis calls "the area of total possibility." Yet this understanding of masculinity as juvenility and the escape from adulthood—so ubiquitous in American culture—directly challenges the ideal of responsible fatherhood. See R. W. B. Lewis, *The American Adam: Innocence, Tragedy and Tradition in the Nineteenth Century* (Chicago: University of Chicago Press, 1955), 91 passim. See also Leslie Fielder, "Adolescence and Maturity in the American Novel," in Fielder, *An End to Innocence* (Boston: Beacon Press, 1955), 191–210; and Ann Swidler, "Love and Adulthood in American Culture," in Neil J. Smelzer and Erik H. Erikson, eds., *Themes of Work and Love in Adulthood* (Cambridge, Mass.: Harvard University Press, 1980), 120–47.

91. See Francis Fukuyama, "The End of History?" *The National Interest* 16 (summer 1989): 3–18.

92. Gutmann, *Reclaimed Powers,* 198.

93. Lawrence Kubie, "The Desire to Become Both Sexes," *Psychoanalytic Quarterly* 43, no. 3 (July 1974): 370. See also Robert May, *Sex and Fantasy: Patterns of Male and Female Development* (New York: Norton, 1980), 163–77.

CHAPTER 7: THE DEADBEAT DAD

1. Steven Waldman, "Deadbeat Dads," *Newsweek,* May 4, 1992, 46–52.

2. "Imaginary Letters to Absent Parents Reveal Anguish," *Kansas City Star,* May 2, 1993, G-5.

3. Quoted in Joe Klein, "'Make the Daddies Pay,'" *Newsweek,* June 21, 1993, 33.

4. Andrew J. Cherlin, testimony before the Select Committee on Children, Youth, and Families, U.S. House of Representatives, February 25, 1986 (Washington, D.C.: U.S. Government Printing Office, 1986), 69. Frank J. Furstenburg, a family scholar from the University of Pennsylvania, agrees with Cherlin: "The economic differences between children from one-parent families and children from two-parent families are much greater than the psychological differences." Remembering James Carville's famous quip about the importance of economics, we might describe the contemporary cultural significance of Deadbeat Dads as: "It's the paycheck, stupid." See Tamar Lewin, "Rise in Single Parenthood Is Reshaping U.S.," *New York Times,* October 5, 1992, B-6.

5. "Speed the Search for Deadbeat Dads," *New York Times,* July 17, 1993, 18. This editorial is a minor classic in the psychology of denial and the politics of gesture. It describes as "surprising news" a U.S. Census Bureau report that merely confirmed the widely known fact that the rate of unwed childbearing continues to increase. It opines, a year after the same editors had excoriated Dan Quayle for criticizing Murphy Brown, that Quayle had made a valid point, although he somehow did so "unintentionally." As our main societal response to the spread of unwed childbearing, it recommends tracking down Deadbeat Dads. To achieve that goal, it applauds a new "Federal task force" that is "working on improvements in the enforcement system." The *Times* bids the task force to "quicken its pace." Finally, a bold new solution to the problem of fatherlessness.

6. For example, see Richard L. Rashke, *Runaway Father: The True Story of Pat Bennett, Her Daughters, and Their Seventeen-Year Search* (San Diego: Harcourt Brace Jovanovich, 1988). *Runaway Father,* a television movie based on the book, was first broadcast in 1991.

   Predictably, societal targeting of the Deadbeat Dad has also generated an organized counter-response from irate absent fathers, including an emerging popular literature on how to beat, or at least avoid being overwhelmed by, the child support–enforcement system. For example, see Jon Conine, *Fathers' Rights: The Sourcebook for Dealing with the Child Support System* (New York: Walker, 1989). For exactly the opposite point of view, see Lois Brenner and Robert Stein, *Getting Your Share: A Woman's Guide to Successful Divorce Strategies* (New York: Signet, 1991); and Carole A. Chambers, *Child Support: How to Get What Your Child Needs and Deserves* (New York: Summit, 1991).

7. Steve Plamann, "ENQUIRER Honored for Deadbeat Dad Series," *National Enquirer,* April 13, 1993, 18; and Plamann, "Help Find the Cruel Louse Who Deserted His Four Children," *National Enquirer,* June 15, 1993, 23.

8. Irwin Garfinkel, *Assuring Child Support: An Extension of Social Security* (New York: Russell Sage Foundation, 1992), 7, 18–22. Indeed, as late as 1978, an authority in the field could write that "the topic of child support . . . has not been a topic of general concern until rather recently." See Judith Cassetty, *Child Support and Public Policy: Securing Support from Absent Fathers* (Lexington, Mass.: Lexington Books, 1978), 3.

9. Ibid., 8–10.

10. By 1981, for example, less than 2 percent of all children of single parents receiving AFDC were the children of widows, while 49 percent were children whose parents had never married and 47 percent were children whose parents were divorced or separated. Ten years later, in 1991, about 60 percent of all children of single parents receiving AFDC were the children of never-married parents, up

from approximately 26 percent in 1961. (From data collected by the Office of Family Assistance, U.S. Department of Health and Human Services, Washington, D.C., transmitted via facsimile on September 8, 1993.)

11. William Julius Wilson and Kathryn M. Neckerman, "Poverty and Family Structure: The Widening Gap Between Evidence and Public Policy Issues," in Sheldon H. Danziger and Daniel H. Weinberg, eds., *Fighting Poverty: What Works and What Doesn't* (Cambridge, Mass.: Harvard University Press, 1986), 239.

12. This idea—that making fathers pay could reduce AFDC caseloads—clearly drives much of the popular and public policy concern about Deadbeat Dads. For example, the *Boston Globe,* citing a 1993 report by the Massachusetts Revenue Department, concludes that about 3,200 AFDC families in Boston alone "could get off welfare if their 'deadbeat dads' paid child support." See Peter J. Howe, "State Could Save $155 Million If 'Deadbeat Dads' Paid Up, Study Says," *Boston Globe,* November 4, 1993, 33.

13. Garfinkel, *Assuring Child Support,* 22.

14. Office of Child Support Enforcement, "The Changing Face of Child Support Enforcement: Incentives to Work with Young Parents" (Washington, D.C.: U.S. Department of Health and Human Services, 1990); and Garfinkel, *Assuring Child Support,* 31.

15. To my knowledge, the earliest use of the phrase "deadbeat dad" in the national press occurred in 1983 in *U.S. News & World Report.* Remarkably, however, this article defines deadbeat dads as fathers who "do not honor agreements to support children of broken marriages." A mere decade later, of course, that definition sounds old-fashioned, almost quaint. Indeed, the new demographics of father absence—particularly the rapid rise of nonmarital childbearing—has prompted a dramatic expansion and redefinition of the term. As a result, deadbeat dads no longer emerge simply from broken marriages—or, for that matter, from "agreements" of any kind. Andrew Cherlin has succinctly iterated the new definition. A "deadbeat," Cherlin writes in 1993, is a father who does not pay child support "after the breakup of a marital, live-in or even casual relationship." This is the new idea. Accordingly, the *New York Times* could report in 1993 that "as the number of unwed mothers grows, so does the number of deadbeat dads." Today, then, the regnant definition of a deadbeat dad is simply an absent father who does not pay child support. See Patricia A. Avery, "On the Trail of Those Deadbeat Dads," *U.S. News & World Report,* March 21, 1983, 70; Andrew Cherlin, "Making Deadbeats Pay Up at Work," *New York Times,* December 30, 1993, A-19; and "Speed the Search for Deadbeat Dads," 18.

16. E. Clay Shaw, Nancy L. Johnson, and Fred Grandy, "Moving Ahead: How America Can Reduce Poverty and Welfare Dependency Through Work" (Washington, D.C.: Human Resources Subcommittee of the Committee on Ways and Means, U.S. House of Representatives, June 1992), 31.

17. These tables, as well as much of the rest of this chapter, rely extensively on data collected by the U.S. Census Bureau. Yet Census Bureau analyses of child support contain an important methodological weakness: Their data are derived almost solely from the self-reports of custodial mothers. Other possible methods of determining the level and frequency of payments—such as examining court data or seeking information from noncustodial fathers—are not employed. Not surprisingly, a 1991 study found that, when asked, noncustodial divorced fathers report higher rates of payment compliance—as well as more socially acceptable reasons for nonpayment, such as unemployment—than are reported by custodial

mothers. In sum, it would seem logical to assume that some custodial mothers underreport what they receive, just as some noncustodial fathers overreport what they pay. As the authors of the 1991 study reasonably conclude: "It is certainly not being argued that the noncustodial parents' report should be uncritically accepted as truth. Present practice, however, of accepting the mothers' report as truth without qualification, has been equally erroneous ... Clearly, no judge would decide a case after listening to only one of the two sides to a disagreement, but this is just what the Census Bureau researchers and policymakers did, when they believed the results from custodial parents without qualification." See Sanford L. Braver, Pamela J. Fitzpatrick, and R. Curtis Bay, "Noncustodial Parents' Report of Child Support Payments," *Family Relations* 40, no. 2 (April 1991): 184.

Despite this shortcoming, however, the U.S. Census Bureau remains, to my knowledge, the most important and reliable source of national data on trends in child-support payments and enforcement.

18. Of the approximately 9 million single mothers living with children under age eighteen in 1992, about 3 million were divorced and 3 million were never married. Similarly, of the approximately 15 million children living in mother-headed households in 1992, about 5.5 million were children whose parents had divorced and about 5.4 million were children whose parents had never married.

See Steve W. Rawlings, "Household and Family Characteristics: March 1992," U.S. Bureau of the Census, Current Populations Reports, series P-20, no. 467 (Washington, D.C.: U.S. Government Printing Office, April 1993), xvi; Arlene F. Saluter, "Marital Status and Living Arrangements: March 1992," U.S. Bureau of the Census, Current Population Reports, series P-20, no. 468 (Washington, D.C.: U.S. Government Printing Office, December 1992), 29; and Ronica N. Rooks, "Motherhood: Growing More Common Among Never-Married Women," *Population Today* (November 1993): 4.

19. However, this statement must be qualified by the fact that divorced mothers may be more likely than unmarried mothers to form mother-stepfather families. If so, children of divorce are more likely than children of nonmarriage to spend some portion of their childhood with stepfathers. However, although these children of divorce and remarriage no longer live in mother-headed homes, they certainly do not live with their biological fathers and thus still fundamentally experience fatherlessness.

20. Among all mother-headed households with children under age eighteen in 1970, only about 7 percent were headed by never-married women. About 40 percent were headed by married women who were separated or whose spouses were absent; about 32 percent were headed by divorced women; and about 20 percent were headed by widows. See Rawlings, "Household and Family Characteristics," xvi.

21. Anne Lamott, *Operating Instructions: A Journal of My Son's First Year* (New York: Pantheon, 1993), 111.

22. Anne Lamott, "When Going It Alone Turns Out to Be Not So Alone at All," *New York Times*, August 5, 1993, C-5.

23. David T. Ellwood of Harvard University, currently serving as a senior official in the U.S. Department of Health and Human Services for the Clinton administration, spells out this argument quite explicitly. Under Ellwood's proposal for getting tough with Deadbeat Dads, a "man would know that when he fathered a child, he would be fiscally responsible for providing some support for the next eighteen years, regardless of whether he married or lived with the child's mother."

Like many who study this issue, Ellwood seems to believe that our ability to achieve this goal is solely a function of our desire to achieve it. Indeed, other than pointing to remediable bureaucratic shortcomings, combined with what he views as our inexplicably weak public determination to make these men pay, Ellwood does not even consider why rapidly growing numbers of new-style absent fathers in our society would no more consider themselves "fiscally responsible" for their children "for the next eighteen years" than they would consider themselves—or would be considered by the children's mothers—to be emotionally or ethically responsible. See David T. Ellwood, *Poor Support: Poverty in the American Family* (New York: Basic Books, 1988), 166.

24. As Sar A. Levitan points out, all fifty states today "recognize supporting children as a legal responsibility, whether the offspring is born out of wedlock or in a legally established family." See Sar A. Levitan, *Programs in Aid of the Poor* (Baltimore: Johns Hopkins University Press, 1990), 124.

25. Gordon H. Lester, "Child Support and Alimony: 1989," U.S. Bureau of the Census, Current Population Reports, series P-60, no. 173 (Washington, D.C.: U.S. Government Printing Office, September 1991), 5.

26. Jay D. Teachman and Kathleen Paasch, "The Economics of Parenting Apart," in Charlene E. Depner and James H. Bray, eds., *Nonresidential Parenting: New Vistas in Family Living* (Newbury Park, Calif.: Sage Publications, 1993), 76.

27. Many analysts, of course, insist that the new-style, nonmarrying absent fathers typically fail to pay child support because they are unable to pay it, due to low wages or joblessness. In this view, the problem is not the decline of fatherhood but rather the decline of the economy. Interestingly, however, the U.S. Census Bureau finds little difference between divorced and never-married mothers on this issue. For 1989, only 14 percent of never-married mothers who did not receive a child-support award cited "father unable to pay" as the reason for non-support—virtually the same proportion as the 13 percent of divorced mothers without awards who cited this reason (ibid., 17). Certainly, for a father to pay child support, a good-paying job is important. But a willingness to pay, sustained by the surrounding community's firm expectation of paternal responsibility, is at least as important—and apparently, in most of these cases, at least as problematic.

28. Ibid., 8.

29. Unpublished data from the U.S. Census Bureau, 1990 Current Population Survey, provided by the Housing and Household Economic Statistics Division, U.S. Census Bureau.

30. By contrast, about 44 percent of all divorced fathers with visitation privileges did not visit their children at all during 1989. See Nicholas Zill, Christine Winquist Nord, and William Prosser, "How Often Do Absent Fathers See Their Children? Evidence from a Recent National Survey," presentation to the annual meeting of the National Council for Children's Rights, April 30, 1993.

31. Judith A. Seltzer, "Relationships Between Fathers and Children Who Live Apart: The Father's Role After Separation," *Journal of Marriage and the Family* 53 (February 1991): 87, 96.

32. Lester, "Child Support and Alimony: 1989," 17.

33. Robert P. Hey, "Making Fathers Accountable for Children Born to Unwed Teens," *Christian Science Monitor,* December 2, 1987, 3.

34. Nancy Herndon, "Garnish: Dad," *Christian Science Monitor,* November 28, 1988, 25.

35. Ann Schreiber, "Enforcing Child-Support Obligations," letter to the editor, *Wall Street Journal,* February 19, 1988, 19.

36. Julie Rovner, "Child Support Enforcement Pays Off," *Governing* (February 1988): 53.

37. Spencer Rich, "Child-Support Collections Jump in '88," *Washington Post,* December 8, 1989, 13.

38. Office of Child Support Enforcement, "Seventeenth Annual Report to Congress" (Washington, D.C.: U.S. Department of Health and Human Services, 1994), 19.

39. Shaw, Johnson, and Grandy, "Moving Ahead," 32.

40. Lester, "Child Support and Alimony: 1989," 9.

41. Teachman and Paasch, "The Economics of Parenting Apart," 74.

42. Family Economics Research Group, "Expenditures on a Child by Husband-Wife Families: 1990" (Hyattsville, Md.: U.S. Department of Agriculture, January 1991), 7.

43. Ibid., 9.

44. Robert S. Weiss is one of the few scholars to describe this difference carefully. In *Going It Alone: The Family Life and Social Situation of the Single Parent* (New York: Basic Books, 1979), he concludes: "The money the husband sends his former wife for her support and the support of their children is not only much less than he contributed when he was a member of the household, but it is also a contribution of a different kind. No longer does the husband share responsibility for the household's financial security. Now he functions only as an income source and, like any other income source, is responsible for a certain amount and no more" (p. 18).

45. Consider three recent cases from New York and California:

> A state parole officer shot and killed his estranged wife in a waiting room at Brooklyn Family Court yesterday just before the start of a custody hearing . . . [The chief probation officer for the federal courts in Brooklyn said:] "People fall in and out of love, and when there are children involved it becomes more and more tragic." . . . At the courthouse, [the suspect gave his wife] two notes as they waited . . . The notes discussed "how the hearing and divorce would have an effect on their child." After each note, Mr. Almonor walked away and watched his estranged wife's response. Mrs. Almonor read the second note and tore it up. "He saw her rip that note up and that was it," Detective Singleton said, "and he walked back over to her, put the gun to her head and fired." (Josh Barbanel, "Divorce Case Has Deadly Ending at Courthouse," *New York Times,* February 13, 1993, 23.)
>
> John T. Miller nursed his anger over child-support payments from the moment his pregnant, 19-year-old girlfriend demanded them in 1966 through two six-month jail terms and 26 years as an intermittent fugitive from welfare authorities. Yet few who knew the heavy-set, 50-year-old trucker believed him capable of the fury that left him and four female welfare workers dead in this lake town Thursday. Interviews . . . produced the picture of a man who believed he was not the father of the child he had been ordered to support, a man who battled for years to evade paying that support and who had been tracked down after Congress changed the system to make it harder for parents to evade financial responsibility . . . Mr. Miller owed $6,780 in back payments, the authorities said, and they had recently begun to garnish his wages . . . Thursday morning, Mr. Miller . . . walked the two blocks from his hotel to the county-government building. He shot the four women on duty in the child-support unit . . . and then turned the pistol on himself. (Sam Dillon, "Shooting Followed Tougher Efforts to Collect Child Support," *New York Times,* October 17, 1992, 27.)
>
> Joel Souza, a self-described "Mr. Mom," showed so much outward affection for his two children that his estranged wife did not challenge his visitation rights

... Most family members and friends ... could not imagine him inflicting any harm on the children, let alone shoot them—and then himself—as he did at their Antioch home Sunday. Although Jennifer Souza obtained a restraining order to keep her husband away from her, she apparently did not sense that her children were in serious danger ... But investigators said the husband's rage about the divorce became murderous when he saw Jennifer with another man ... [The victim's attorney] said that Jennifer Souza had done everything right by getting a restraining order ... but sometimes that is not enough. "You can't stop a bullet with a piece of paper," Johnson said ... The seeds [of the tragedy] were sown earlier this year ... when Jennifer told Souza she wanted to separate and he refused to move out ... [Souza later sent Jennifer a threatening letter which said:] "You have chosen your path, and you will be sorry for this ... My children and I will go to our resting place since our lives here will just be shattered." (Erin Hallisay, "Behind Killer Dad's Deadly Rampage," *San Francisco Chronicle,* July 13, 1993, 17.)

46. Martin Daly and Margo Wilson cut to the heart of this issue when they report that "familocide—often but not always followed by suicide—is a peculiarly male crime." Moreover: "In every society for which we have been able to find a sample of spousal homicides, the story is basically the same: Most cases arise out of the husband's jealous, proprietary, violent response to his wife's (real or imagined) infidelity or desertion." They conclude with an insight directly relevant to both *Falling Down* and, more importantly, the dramatic increase in violence in our society perpetrated by Killer Ex-Dads: "That a desperate man should formulate the bitter intent to kill and then to die—and should act upon that intent—must somehow be a byproduct of his more adaptive concerns with social competence, material success, fidelity, paternity, deterrent power, reputation, self-esteem, and his authority as a husband and father." See Martin Daly and Margo Wilson, *Homicide* (New York: Aldine de Gruyter, 1988), 82, 202, 219.

47. A 1992 movie, *Hero,* similarly examines the importance of fatherhood in the life of a troubled man, but offers a less harsh ending. The divorced father, played by Dustin Hoffman, is clearly a loser—a small-time grifter, a failure as a husband, always whining about child-support payments. But in the end, his concern for how his son will see him—his desire, after all, to be a father to his son—provides him with a small measure of redemption. Even he can be a hero, of sorts, as a father. Someone tells him that he is a loser, a nothing. His response captures the movie's main idea: "I got a kid. I'm a person, for Chrissakes."

48. "Massachusetts Governor Seeks Stiffest Law to Collect Child Support," *New York Times,* November 11, 1992, A-14.

49. Charles Stile, "'Deadbeat Dads' Get Deserved Attention," *Trenton Times,* July 30, 1993, 3.

50. This strategy originated in the state of Washington in 1989. An Associated Press news story waxes enthusiastic about its potential in Virginia: "To the people responsible for tracking down what President Clinton, among others, calls 'deadbeat dads,' the 3-year-old paternity program in Virginia is exciting news. 'It's a really hot, trendy issue in child support,' observed Mike Henry, Virginia's director of child support enforcement. It is trendy enough that states around the country have begun [passing legislation] to allow men to declare their paternity in the hospital." See Mitchell Landsberg, "Fathers Held Responsible from the Start," *Kalamazoo Gazette,* September 2, 1993, B-1.

51. Edward Walsh, "Going After Fathers Who Turn Their Backs," *Washington Post,* national weekly edition, January 11–17, 1993, 32; "Child Support Enforcement

News," *Child Support Bulletin* (Washington, D.C.: Children's Foundation, March 1993), 1–2; idem. (September 1993), 2; "High Tech and Child Support," *Boston Globe,* November 2, 1993, 14; Kenneth Cole, "State Wants to Go After 'Deadbeat Dads' Who Fail to Make Child Support Payments," *Detroit News,* June 25, 1992, 5-F; "County Will Televise Names of Worst Deadbeat Parents," *New York Times,* October 1, 1993, A-18; and Wayne King, "A Crackdown Is Proposed on Overdue Child Support," *New York Times,* April 29, 1993, B-6.

52. Writing in the *Journal of Marriage and the Family,* Jay D. Teachman is persuaded that "receipt of child support is linked to the motivation of absent fathers to provide cash transfers to the mother." Such "motivation," in turn, derives much more from the status of the man's fatherhood—his proximity to his children, how often he visits them, whether he has married someone else, and whether and how long he was married to the mother—than from the current needs of the mother and children. This fact leads Teachman to pessimistic predictions. For example, he suggests that the current focus on increasing the number of mothers who receive awards is "likely to face rapidly diminishing returns under the current collection system." He is similarly skeptical of efforts to increase the size of awards: "Increased intervention on the part of the state in arranging the size of awards may actually reduce the motivation of fathers to pay support." See Jay D. Teachman, "Who Pays? Receipt of Child Support in the United States," *Journal of Marriage and the Family* 53, no. 3 (August 1991): 769–70.

Frank F. Furstenberg, Jr., offers a similar but even more disturbing warning. Among the low-income, never-married young parents in Baltimore whom he interviewed, the child-support system "is coming to be viewed in the same light as the welfare and criminal justice bureaucracies." Indeed, Furstenberg was "impressed by how much informal resistance to child support was evident among the very people whom it was designed to help." These ground-level observations have the ring of authenticity. If they point to a trend, that trend does not bode well for our current approach.

As Furstenberg puts it: "Without taking full account of the complexity of the process by which paternal responsibility is secured, child support enforcement programs may do little to increase paternal assistance and may even undermine the goal of getting fathers to do their fair share." In speaking of the "complexity of the process by which paternal responsibility is secured," I take Furstenberg to be saying that the young men he interviewed will not pay child support simply because government agencies order them to pay. They will pay child support only if they think of themselves as fathers and believe that they should act like fathers—an eventuality that state child-support bureaucracies can do little to foster and may even discourage.

This level of scholarly pessimism should give serious pause to those who express the hope, based on little more than wishful thinking, that stricter demands for child-support payments will lead to more frequent visitation and overall improvements in father-child relationships. As Teachman suggests, the exact opposite may be more likely to occur. We can only speculate, however, since very little is known about this issue. As Teachman and Kathleen Paasch reported in 1993: "To date, there has been no research of which we are aware that examines the impact of actual or simulated child support regimes on subsequent life-course behavior" of absent fathers. Similarly, Judith A. Seltzer ponders: "To what extent can findings about nonresidential fathers who participate voluntarily in childrearing after separation predict the effects of laws that require greater paternal involvement?" She is not sure. Although her study "shows that paying support and spending time with children are positively related, it does not address the problem of how fathers respond to policies that constrain their strategies of postdivorce parenting." Indeed, Seltzer speculates, as Teachman does, that our current strategy of "getting tougher" about child support may, in many cases, actually decrease the frequency and quality of father-child visitations.

In sum, we simply do not know—and if the serious attention devoted to the subject is any guide, we do not care very much—whether our current approach to child-support enforcement is likely to strengthen or weaken the mother-father bond or the father-child bond. Again, today's societal concern with the Deadbeat Dad is almost exclusively a matter of money, not fatherhood.

See Frank F. Furstenberg, Jr., "Daddies and Fathers: Men Who Do for Their Children and Men Who Don't," in Furstenberg, Kay E. Sherwood, and Mercer L. Sullivan, *Caring and Paying: What Fathers and Mothers Say About Child Support* (New York: Manpower Demonstration Research Corporation, 1992), 56, 37; Teachman and Paasch, "The Economics of Parenting Apart," 83; and Seltzer, "Relationships Between Fathers and Children Who Live Apart," 97.

53. Children's Defense Fund, "The State of America's Children: 1992" (Washington, D.C.: Children's Defense Fund, 1992), 120. See also, Office of Child Support Enforcement, "Sixteenth Annual Report to Congress," table 39, 85.

54. Klein, "'Make the Daddies Pay,'" 33.

55. "Families First: Report of the National Commission on America's Urban Families" (Washington, D.C.: U.S. Government Printing Office, January 1993), 52; Daniel R. Meyer, "Paternity and Public Policy," *Focus* 14, no. 2 (Madison: University of Wisconsin Institute for Research on Poverty, summer 1992), 3–5; and Freya Lund Sonenstein, "Linking Children to Their Fathers" (Washington, D.C.: Urban Institute, summer 1993), 24.

56. David L. Chambers, *Making Fathers Pay: The Enforcement of Child Support* (Chicago: University of Chicago Press, 1979), 278–81.

57. U.S. Representatives Thomas J. Downey and Henry Hyde, "The Downey/Hyde Child Support Enforcement and Assurance Proposal" (Washington, D.C.: U.S. House of Representatives, Committee on Ways and Means, May 1992). See also Paul Taylor, "A New 'Blueprint' for Child Support," *Washington Post*, May 13, 1992, 21; and "Who Pays for Children?" *Washington Post*, July 27, 1992, 16. Garfinkel's idea is also endorsed by Ellwood, *Poor Support*, 165–74; and by the editors of the *Washington Post* in ". . . And the Dads Issue," *Washington Post*, national weekly edition, December 13–19, 1993, 27.

58. Garfinkel, *Assuring Child Support*, 147–53 passim. This basic idea is also endorsed by Theda Skocpol and William Julius Wilson, "Welfare As We Need It," *New York Times*, February 9, 1994, A-21.

59. To date, however, this idea does not enjoy widespread public support. In a May 1992 survey by Yankelovich Clancy Shulman, for example, 93 percent of Americans favored "taking money out of paychecks and tax refunds of fathers who refuse to make child support payments that a court has ordered," but only 44 percent favored "paying child support directly out of public funds to mothers on welfare if the government cannot make the father pay." See "Public Opinion and Demographic Report," *The Public Perspective* (Storrs, Conn.: The Roper Center, September/October 1993), 87.

60. This curious two-sidedness, in which the second part of an idea so clearly

undermines the first, is not unique to Garfinkel's proposal. Indeed, it is a recurring paradigm in today's policy discourse, especially regarding sex and procreation. For example, a deep internal ambivalence—a wish to both do and not do something—characterizes proposals that seek to discourage adolescent sexual intercourse while simultaneously dispensing contraceptive devices to students. Do not do it. But here is how to do it.

CHAPTER 8: THE VISITING FATHER

1. Gordon H. Lester, "Child Support and Alimony: 1989," Bureau of the Census, Current Population Reports, series P-60, no. 173 (Washington, D.C.: Government Printing Office, September 1991), 8.

2. Ibid., 7.

3. In 1990, just under 4 million people over age fifteen received AFDC benefits. In 1990, the number of unemployed men was about 3.8 million, constituting about 5.6 percent of the civilian male labor force. Also in 1990, the number of unemployed married fathers with at least one child living in the home was 854,000, or about 3.7 percent of all married fathers living with children.

    For AFDC data, see U.S. Bureau of the Census, "Money Income of Households, Families and Persons in the United States: 1990," Current Population Reports, series P-60, no. 174 (Washington, D.C.: U.S. Government Printing Office, 1991), 186. For unemployment data, see "Employment and Earnings," U.S. Department of Labor, Bureau of Labor Statistics, vol. 40, no. 1 (Washington, D.C.: U.S. Government Printing Office, January 1993), 173; and unpublished data from the March 1990 Current Population Survey, U.S. Department of Labor, Bureau of Labor Statistics.

4. Bronislaw Malinowski, *Sex, Culture, and Myth* (New York: Harcourt, Brace & World, 1962), 69.

5. Jill Krementz, *How It Feels When Parents Divorce* (New York: Knopf, 1992), 19–20.

6. Ibid., 95–97.

7. Eda LeShan, *What's Going to Happen to Me?* (New York: Alladin, 1986), 37, 81.

8. Peter Mayle, *Why Are We Getting a Divorce?* (New York: Harmony, 1988), 16, 21.

9. In her clinical studies, Judith Wallerstein documents the pervasive sadness experienced by these children of visiting fathers who "taught us very early that to be separated from their father was intolerable. The poignancy of their reactions is astounding, especially among the six-, seven-, and eight-year-olds. They cry for their daddies—be they good, bad, or indifferent daddies. I have been deeply struck by the distress children of every age suffer at losing their fathers." Indeed, one of Wallerstein's most arresting findings is that the intense sadness and father hunger typically experienced by children after divorce are unrelated to either the quality of the father-child relationship prior to divorce or the frequency of visits after divorce.

    Consider the implications of this startling fact. If you believe that fatherhood is basically superfluous, your case is greatly strengthened by the proposition—described elsewhere in this book as a "could be worse" thesis—that not having any father is better than having a bad or indifferent father. But perhaps this idea reflects the needs of adults more than children. Perhaps, on some fundamental level, what a child needs and yearns for is less a good father than simply a father. See Judith S.

Wallerstein and Sandra Blakeslee, *Second Chances: Men, Women, and Children a Decade After Divorce* (New York: Ticknor & Fields, 1989), 234, 238.

10. Linda Walvoord Girard, *At Daddy's on Saturdays* (Morton Grove, Ill.: Albert Whitman, 1987). In Danielle Steel's *Martha's New Daddy,* five-year-old Martha worries about her mother's decision to remarry. She discusses her fears with her daddy, who sees her every Wednesday and every other weekend. On a Wednesday night, when she and Daddy are out eating pizza, Martha asks, "And what if they have a baby?"

   "Her Daddy nodded thoughtfully. 'They might. And I might get married and have more children too. But that wouldn't make us love you less. You're our special, special little girl, and you always will be.'"

   In the last sentence of the book, Martha—like Katie in *At Daddy's on Saturdays*—learns the most important lesson: "And even though her Mommy was married again, she knew she would always have her very, very special Daddy." See Danielle Steel, *Martha's New Daddy* (New York: Delacorte, 1989). Other children's books about Visiting Fathers include Louis Baum, *One More Time* (New York: William Morrow, 1986); and C. B. Christiansen, *My Mother's House, My Father's House* (New York: Puffin, 1989). See also Marge Heegaard, *When Mom and Dad Separate: Children Can Learn to Cope with Grief from Divorce* (Minneapolis: Woodland, 1991).

11. Girard, *At Daddy's on Saturdays.*

12. Richard H. Gatley and David Koulack, *Single Father's Handbook: A Guide for Separated and Divorced Fathers* (Garden City, N.Y.: Anchor Books, 1979), 41–42.

13. Anna Keller, "Parenting Post-Divorce: Problems, Concerns," in David L. Levy, ed., *The Best Parent Is Both Parents: A Guide to Shared Parenting in the 21st Century* (Norfolk, Va.: Hampton Roads, 1993), 59.

14. The frequency and duration of these visits vary from case to case, of course, depending upon both formal determinations by courts as well as informal procedures negotiated by the ex-spouses. Moreover, visitation patterns frequently change over time, usually toward less visitation. But "reasonable visitation," as defined by the courts, frequently means that a father has permission to see his child the equivalent of every other weekend, or about forty-eight days each year, plus portions of some holidays. See Alexander Hillery II, "The Case for Joint Custody," in Levy, *The Best Parent Is Both Parents,* 31.

15. Joseph Epstein, *Divorced in America: Marriage in an Age of Possibility* (New York: Dutton, 1974), 289.

16. Hillery, "The Case for Joint Custody," 31.

17. Frank F. Furstenberg, Jr., and Andrew J. Cherlin, *Divided Families: What Happens to Children When Parents Part* (Cambridge, Mass.: Harvard University Press, 1991), 38.

18. In psychological terms, it is hard to understand why so many divorced fathers eventually choose to sever all ties with their children. But it is necessary to try to understand, for while the behavior of these men is certainly blameworthy, simply blaming them—viewing them only as hard, cold men—does not capture the complexity and pathos of this phenomenon.

   For example, as John Munder Ross points out, many divorced fathers are "overwhelmed by feelings of failure and self-hatred." For these men, visiting their children only reminds them of their failure. The response to this terrible feeling is withdrawal, "the tendency of divorced men to invest their energies elsewhere, disengaging from a family that is no longer really theirs."

Moreover, it is a cruelly ironic fact that some divorced fathers abandon their children more out of love than lack of love. As Judith Wallerstein observes, postdivorce visits with children "can lead to depression and sorrow in men who love their children." Why? Because it is precisely the loving father who most acutely "realizes, with each visit, that he is not part of the children's lives." In such cases, seemingly intolerable sorrow and self-blame, deriving partly from paternal love, cause these men to turn away from their children.

Finally, many of these men also come to believe that they are helping their children by leaving them. As Richard Gatley and David Koulack put it: "Consistent with our sense of diminished importance and responsibility, we may see the children's mother as the main person in their lives. Honestly wanting to do what we think is best for our children, we may feel that doing well by them means letting their mother raise them." In short, as in the biblical story of the good mother who proved herself to King Solomon by begging to give her child away rather than having Solomon literally cut the child in half, these men ultimately decide to prove their paternity by forswearing it; they decide that it is better for a loving parent to give a child away than to harm or split a child.

Robert S. Weiss nicely sums up this bundle of issues. For many fathers who leave their children, "it is not that they are without commitment to their children; it is that they feel helpless to realize that commitment fully, no matter what they do; that they can justify their withdrawal from the children on grounds of the children's well-being and their own; and that withdrawal becomes increasingly tolerable emotionally as time goes on. Furthermore, there may be other demands on them to which they believe they must respond, in addition to those of their first families."

See John Munder Ross, *The Male Paradox* (New York: Simon & Schuster, 1992), 154, 157; Wallerstein and Blakeslee, *Second Chances,* 235; Gatley and Koulack, *Single Father's Handbook,* 24; and Robert S. Weiss, "Parenting Together and Parenting Apart," working paper no. 35 (New York: Institute for American Values, May 1993), 33. See also Judith A. Seltzer, "Relationships Between Fathers and Children Who Live Apart: The Father's Role After Separation," *Journal of Marriage and the Family* 53 (February 1991): 80.

19. Richard A. Warshak, "The Custody Revolution: Beyond Fathers' Rights and Mothers' Rights" (Dallas: Clinical Psychology Associates, 1993), 18.

20. Furstenberg and Cherlin, *Divided Families,* 39.

21. One recent study of 1,100 divorcing couples from California, conducted by Eleanor E. Maccoby and Robert H. Mnookin during the late 1980s, found a somewhat higher incidence of co-parenting after divorce than is estimated by Furstenberg and Cherlin. Specifically, Maccoby and Mnookin found that, within a year and a half after separating, nearly 17 percent of the divorced fathers in their sample had established a pattern of cooperative co-parenting with the mother. On the other hand, 83 percent had not. For example, within three and a half years after separation, among all the fathers who were seeing their children at least once every two weeks, more than 70 percent had established relationships with the mother that Maccoby and Mnookin described as either "conflicted" (high levels of conflict and disagreement) or "disengaged" (little or no direct communication) or a combination of the two. By far the biggest category (41 percent) was "disengaged."

Maccoby and Mnookin's core findings, then, are largely consistent with Furstenberg and Cherlin's estimates. Indeed, Maccoby and Mnookin conclude that "spousal disengagement became the norm as time passed." Similarly, Furstenberg and Cherlin report that "the pattern of modest initial contact and a sharp drop-off over time is strikingly similar across studies." This finding leads Furstenberg and Kathleen Mullan Harris (in a separate essay) to warn that, in the area of divorce reform, "policies that assume a high level of collaboration between parents are doomed to produce disappointing results."

See Eleanor E. Maccoby and Robert H. Mnookin, *Dividing the Child: Social and Legal Dilemmas of Custody* (Cambridge, Mass.: Harvard University Press, 1992), 236, 285; Furstenberg and Cherlin, *Divided Families,* 36, 42–43; and Furstenberg and Kathleen Mullan Harris, "The Disappearing American Father? Divorce and the Waning Significance of Biological Parenthood," in Scott J. South and Stewart E. Tolnay, eds., *The Changing American Family: Sociological and Demographic Perspectives* (Boulder, Colo.: Westview Press, 1992), 217.

22. Ibid., 40–41.

23. The rhetoric both of the fathers' rights movement and of gender egalitarianism notwithstanding, most married fathers depend heavily on the mediating influence of the mother to sustain good father-child relationships. As a rule, the competent father is, among other things, a man who has been extensively and patiently tutored by the mother. For example, the mother is usually the father's single most valuable source of advice and information about his child. Because mothers typically have a greater and more intimate knowledge of their children's moods, quirks, habits, preferences, and vulnerabilities, most fathers necessarily rely on the mother to interpret the child's behavior and provide direction for their fatherhood.

This fact does not mean that mothers know how to be, or can be, fathers. Learning from and depending on mothers are a necessary, but not sufficient, definition of effective fatherhood. Nor does this fact of paternal dependency diminish the father's competence or importance, any more than recognizing aspects of maternal dependency would diminish the mother's competence or importance. It simply tells us the circumstances under which fathers are most likely to be good fathers.

24. Robert S. Weiss, *Going It Alone: The Family Life and Social Situation of the Single Parent* (New York: Basic Books, 1979), 142, 146.

25. Ibid., 134, 141.

26. Epstein, *Divorce in America,* 290, 292.

27. For many visiting fathers, the predictable, almost inevitable, failure to meet these expectations of postdivorce fatherhood can exact a heavy psychological toll. The sense of guilt and defeat in these men can be overpowering: First I failed at my marriage, now I am failing as a visiting father. For these reasons, Debra Umberson and Christine L. Williams, in their investigation of the psychological wellbeing of divorced fathers, report that these men "exhibit substantially higher rates of psychological distress and alcohol consumption than do married men," in large part because of the intensified "parental role strain" associated with visiting fatherhood. See Debra Umberson and Christine L. Williams, "Divorced Fathers: Parental Role Strain and Psychological Distress," *Journal of Family Issues* 14, no. 3 (September 1993): 385, 378.

28. Furstenberg and Cherlin, *Divided Families,* 38.

29. Melinda Blau, *Families Apart: Ten Keys to Successful Co-Parenting* (New York: Putnam's, 1993).

30. Ibid., 19, 24, 18.

31. Ibid., 21, 18–19.
32. Ibid., 130, passim.
33. Ibid., 233, 235–36.
34. Ibid., 155, 24.
35. Ibid., 29–30. This statement is astonishing. Leave aside the fact that Blau seeks to prettify her divorce by denigrating, at some length, her own parents. (For example, on page 29: "Bitterness resounded up and down the generations, and family occasions were tainted by melodrama: Would Dad arrive with Shirley, his new wife, who was once my mother's best friend? Where would we seat them? No room seemed big enough to contain their collective animosity.") What is truly remarkable is Blau's insistence that her divorce constitutes evidence not of failure but success. Blau repeatedly deploys her "better divorce" as a cultural credential—as a monument to her wisdom regarding family life and how to be a good parent. Her book makes it plain: "She and her ex-husband are successful co-parents." In this statement—reported as an empirical fact rather than her opinion of herself—she is clearly asserting a claim to authority based on how she handled her divorce. Put simply, she is bragging. Listen to me, she says, I am good at divorce.

    Curiously, this kind of bragging is almost never heard today from married people. Perhaps if Blau were married her book would have reminded us: "Her marriage is successful and she and her husband are good parents." But it seems unlikely. Similarly, at conferences and symposia on family topics today, it is quite common to hear someone preface a comment by saying, "Speaking as a single parent. . . " Sometimes, perhaps, such a remark reflects defensiveness or insecurity. But increasingly this self-identification is intended to serve, and does serve, as evidence of authenticity and even cachet—a reason to give special credence to the ideas being expressed and to the person expressing them. By contrast, one seldom hears anyone introduce an idea by saying, "Speaking as a married parent. . . " or "Speaking as someone who has succeeded in my marriage. . . " Rarely today does a married person assert his or her own marriage as a badge of honor, or even as an explanation.

    What explains this discrepancy? The answer seems clear enough. In an era of family disintegration, people claim credibility based on the fact that their own life reflects the larger trend. They can affirm as paradigmatic their own experience of family decline. More importantly, they present as therapeutic—as the remedy to the problem—their own "success" in handling decline. For in a divorce-oriented culture—where divorce in many ways outranks marriage as an authentic, interesting, and culturally authoritative experience—the idea of better divorce commands our attention far more readily than the idea of better marriage. For this reason, people who are personally and professionally concerned with divorce, as opposed to marriage, tend to become the dominant voices in our cultural conversation on these matters. This phenomenon contributes significantly to the growing cultural acceptance of fatherlessness.
36. Susan Steinman, "Joint Custody: What We Know, What We Have Yet to Learn, and the Judicial and Legislative Implications," in Jay Folberg, ed., *Joint Custody and Shared Parenting* (Washington, D.C.: Bureau of National Affairs, 1984), 127.
37. James H. Bray and Charlene E. Depner, "Perspectives on Nonresidential Parenting," in Depner and Bray, eds., *Nonresidential Parenting: New Vistas in Family Living* (Newbury Park, Calif.: Sage Publications, 1993), 184–85, 3. See also Lawrie Moloney, "Beyond Custody and Access: Post-separation Parenting in the

Nineties," *Family Matters,* no. 34 (Melbourne: Australian Institute of Family Studies, May 1993), 11–15.

38. William J. Goode, *World Changes in Divorce Patterns* (New Haven: Yale University Press, 1993), 345.

39. Barbara Vobejda, "Making Divorce as Painless as Possible," *Washington Post,* national weekly edition, July 19–25, 1993, 33.

40. Florence Bienenfeld, *Helping Your Child Succeed After Divorce* (Claremount, Calif.: Hunter House, 1987), xi. For similar themes, see Robert B. Shapiro, *Separate Houses: A Practical Guide for Divorced Parents* (New York: Simon & Schuster, 1989); Linda Bird Francke, *Growing Up Divorced* (New York: Simon & Schuster, 1983); and Glynnis Walker, *Solomon's Children: Exploding the Myths of Divorce* (New York: Arbor House, 1986).

    Like Blau, Lansky, and many others, Walker repeatedly stresses that "for the child, divorce per se is not necessarily the big, bad event we usually make it out to be" (p. 9). What matters is not "divorce per se," but instead "the way individual parents handle divorce." For it turns out that children "don't care so much about the fact that their parents got divorced as they do about 'the way' they got divorced" (p. 12).

41. Vicki Lansky, *Divorce Book for Parents: Helping Your Children Cope with Divorce and Its Aftermath* (New York: Signet, 1991), 97; and a 1993 press release from the publisher, G. P. Putnam's Sons, entitled "Advance Praise for *Families Apart.*" See also Lansky, "How Can We Do It Better—Divorce American-style," in Levy, *The Best Parent Is Both Parents,* 13–14. What Blau terms "families apart," Lansky terms "restructured families." Her main point in *Divorce Book for Parents* is that "children are affected more by the way a family restructures itself and the way the feelings are handled afterward than by the divorce itself." Indeed, done properly, "reorganization has the potential for growth and happiness for all family members. We know that children can prosper in single-parent homes as well as in two-parent homes. Some children even become stronger by acquiring new coping skills" (pp. 2–3). Translation: Some children even become stronger by learning to live without a father.

42. Melvin G. Goldzband, *Quality Time: Easing the Children Through Divorce* (New York: McGraw-Hill, 1985), 1.

43. "Children of Divorce," *Mothering* (spring 1994): 25. Of course, much of the popular writing on this subject owes a great deal to Mel Krantzler's influential bestseller, *Creative Divorce: A New Opportunity for Personal Growth* (New York: M. Evans, 1973).

44. Gatley and Koulack, *Single Father's Handbook,* 116.

45. E. Mavis Hetherington and Margaret Stanley Hagan, "Divorced Fathers: Stress, Coping, and Adjustment," in Micheal E. Lamb, ed., *The Father's Role: Applied Perspectives* (New York: Wiley, 1986), 128.

46. At the 1993 annual convention of the National Congress for Men and Children, entitled "Fathers Fighting Back," three sessions were devoted to the subject of child-abuse allegations, including a lecture on "Defense Against False Allegations of Child Abuse." I have no firsthand knowledge of any of the specific charges leveled against any of these fathers, and thus can offer no opinion regarding the veracity of the allegations.

47. Jeffery M. Leving, a Chicago attorney who represents divorced fathers, makes the case for his clients this way: "The courts place a greater emphasis on child sup-

port than on visitation rights. There is a stronger likelihood that a man would go to jail for not paying child support than a woman for denying visitation rights."

For example, the right of a custodial mother to relocate to another state frequently outweighs, and can in effect nullify, a father's right to visitation. Leving describes "the helpless feelings many fathers experience in attempting simply to visit their children" or "in not even knowing where their children live or what schools they are attending." For these reasons, fathers' rights groups such as the Fathers' Resource Center in Minneapolis urge the courts to enforce visitation rights as strictly as they enforce child-support orders.

At a minimum, these facts should add complexity—and even pathos—to our current cultural portrait of the Deadbeat Dad as a one-dimensional villain, a moral leper. Not surprisingly, these men view their situation quite differently. As one father put it: "To a father denied the sight of his daughter's piano recital or his son's jump shot at the buzzer, child support is the modern equivalent of taxation without representation" (quoted in Randy Salzman, "Deadbeat Dad Divorces Fact from Fiction," *Wall Street Journal,* February 3, 1993, A-14).

What is the ultimate validity of this argument? Let me hazard an answer. After parents divorce, there is typically a mother's side of the story. (He broke his promise, he is a deadbeat.) For many reasons, this side of the story tends to get a respectful hearing in our society. But there is also a father's side. (She broke her promise, she took my children.) Our society today is much less receptive to this side of the argument.

In individual cases, of course, the facts vary. But as a societal proposition, it seems clear that neither the mother's nor the father's side of the story, by itself, can adequately explain the dimensions and consequences of parental divorce. Each allegation of failure, each assignment of blame, is only one thread of a larger tragedy. That tragedy is the failure of marriage: the largely inevitable consequences of the inability of fathers and mothers to sustain a common life together.

See "Chicago-area Attorney Jeff Leving Champions Men's Rights," *North Shore Journal* (April 1993): 15; Jeffery M. Leving, "Divorced Dads Don't Deserve Humiliation," *Chicago Sun-Times,* March 11, 1988, 42; Marilyn Gardner, "Finding Fairness in Family Court," and "Fathers' Group Proposes Ways to Equalize Child Care," *Christian Science Monitor,* October 12, 1993, 12; and Salzman, "Deadbeat Dad." For an analysis of what we might term the father's story versus the mother's story of divorce, see Scott Coltrane and Neal Hickman, "The Rhetoric of Rights and Needs: Moral Discourse in the Reform of Child Custody and Child Support Laws," *Social Problems* 39, no. 4 (November 1992): 400–20.

48. A local fathers' rights group from Missouri, Parents Demanding Equal Justice, adopted a similar slogan: "Dedicated to Assuring Equal Parenthood After Divorce." See the 1993 brochure of the National Congress for Men and Children in Washington, D.C., and literature from Parents Demanding Equal Justice in Florissant, Missouri.

49. Levy, *The Best Parent Is Both Parents,* 12. Indeed, a growing advice literature is now available to help "long distance dads" keep in touch with their children. Writing in *Full-Time Dads,* for example, George Larson teaches absent fathers to become good "telephone dads." In Larson's own case, "it was the telephone that enabled me to be the equal of any live-in father."

Similarly, the singer-songwriter Dwight Twilley, separated from his daughter since her birth, has written a book, *Questions from Dad,* in which he explains how his "quizzes," in which he regularly mails questions to his daughter and she mails back the answers, have helped him and his daughter, as his publisher puts it, "build a very close personal relationship that is, in many ways, as rich as those experienced by parents and children living together."

See George Larson, "A 'Telephone Dad' Can Make All the Difference," *Full-Time Dads* 1, no. 2 (March 1993): 4; and Dwight Twilley, *Questions from Dad: A Very Cool Way to Communicate with Kids* (Boston: Charles E. Tuttle, 1994). Similarly, see George Newman, *101 Ways to Be a Long Distance Super-Dad* (Saratoga, Calif.: R & E, 1989); and Miriam Galper Cohen, *Long-Distance Parenting: A Guide for Divorced Parents* (New York: Signet, 1991).

50. Don Chavez, "Let the Fathers Return," Minority Report of the Report to Congress of the U.S. Commission on Interstate Child Support (Washington, D.C.: U.S. Government Printing Office, 1992), 357.

51. For an example of the curriculum used in such a mandatory program, see Beverly Willis and Mickey James, *Sensible Approach to Divorce* (Kansas City, Kans.: Wyandotte County District Court, 1986). This idea is spreading. In 1993 alone, according to a report in *RE: Rights & Responsibilities,* parenting classes for divorcing couples ("divorce education") became mandatory in various counties in Kentucky, Illinois, Georgia, Indiana, Missouri, New York, and Ohio. See "Divorce School," *RE: Rights & Responsibilities* (Washington, D.C.: American Alliance for Rights & Responsibilities, January 1994), 5.

52. Memorandum of November 20, 1993, from George R. McCasland. *Parent* magazine of San Francisco predicted that this movie concerning "the timely topic of family life in the 90s" would "turn out to be the biggest family entertainment hit since *Home Alone!*" See Joanne Bracco, "Cinemascoop," *Parent* (December 1993): 24.

53. Art imitates life. The movie stars Robin Williams, who plays Daniel Hillard/Mrs. Doubtfire. One of the movie's producers is Marsha Garces Williams, who is Robin Williams's wife. Prior to marrying Mr. Williams and becoming a movie producer, Marsha Garces worked as a nanny for Robin Williams and his previous wife.

54. Paul Freeman interviewed Robin Williams about his role in the movie for San Francisco's *Parent* magazine: "The first script that Williams read had an artificially happy ending. [Said Williams:] 'It has the parents getting back together again.'"

In the movies today, then, portraying the ultimate success of a troubled marriage would constitute "an artificially happy ending." Yet portraying a good divorce—in which, for example, the divorced mother hires her wonderful ex-husband to clean house and babysit the children—presumably constitutes a realistically happy ending. See Paul Freeman, "Parenting No Laughing Matter for Talented Robin Williams," *Parent* (January 1994): 45.

55. Some current films, of course, decline to conform to the prevailing sensibility. The little-noticed 1992 *Gas Food Lodging,* for example, looks unflinchingly at the impact of fatherlessness—or more broadly, of families without any men in them—on the emerging sexual identity of a teenage girl. A 1993 movie, *Josh and S.A.M.,* examines how a couple's divorce frightens their two young sons. Both *Boyz N the Hood* (1991) and *South Central* (1992) explore the societal and personal meanings of fatherlessness for African-American young people in Los Angeles. Similarly, a 1992 documentary film, *In Search of Our Fathers,* tells the story of a young African-American man's search for the father he never knew.

Yet these films lean against the trend. Moreover, as depictions of a divorce culture, they are primarily descriptions of the problem. Sympathetic depictions of marriage as the solution—portrayals of the good-enough marriage as a worthy life goal for interesting adults—have been relatively rare in American movies for quite some time.

A good example of a cinematic turning point on this theme—signifying a transition in the movies from a marriage culture to a divorce culture—is *Two for the Road,* released in 1966. The movie offers a relentless criticism of marriage. ("What kind of people sit together in a restaurant and don't even try to talk to each other?" "Married people.") Yet in the end, Audrey Hepburn and Albert Finney decide against divorce. They stay together, certainly not out of romanticism or naivete, or even out of cynicism, defeat, or social conformity, but rather out of the desire for a shared life. This movie, despite its modernist critique of marriage, affirms marriage rather than divorce. Since then, however, divorce has increasingly displaced marriage as a prevailing ethos in the movies.

56. Greer Litton Fox and Priscilla White Blanton, "Noncustodial Fathers Following Divorce," *Marriage and Family Review* (forthcoming).

57. Ibid.

58. Paul R. Amato, "Contact with Non-custodial Fathers and Children's Well-Being," *Family Matters,* no. 36 (Melbourne: Australian Institute of Family Studies, December 1993), 33. In his examination of 725 children of divorce, drawing upon data from the 1987–88 National Survey of Families and Households in the U.S., Amato found that continuing father-child contact after divorce "was positively related to interparental conflict, which suggests that contact provides opportunities for conflict to occur" (p. 33). Accordingly, he concludes that "when the relationship between ex-spouses is marked by hostility, frequent visits may do more harm than good" (p. 34).

Some observers, particularly clinical analysts such as Judith Wallerstein, do conclude that children of divorce are better off when they see their fathers regularly. Mary Lund, for example, in her examination of thirty divorced families in England, concludes that keeping "this new kind of father" involved with the children "is probably important for children's well-being. Non-custodial fathers do matter to children."

Yet as Amato suggests, current survey research findings regarding this thesis are inconclusive at best. Greer Litton Fox and Priscilla White Blanton, in their review of larger-scale sociological surveys, conclude that "the empirical evidence to support this assumption is surprisingly thin." Valerie King, examining data from the National Longitudinal Survey of Youth, finds "no evidence for the hypothesis that father visitation has beneficial effects for child well-being." Furstenberg and Cherlin, in their study drawing upon data from the National Survey of Children, find that "the amount of contact that children had with their fathers seemed to make little difference for their well-being."

What explains these inconsistent findings? More unsettling, what explains the paucity of survey evidence to support the seemingly self-evident proposition that children benefit from contact with their fathers? Amato points carefully to the "moderating factor" of "interparental conflict" following divorce. Furstenberg and Cherlin hint that it "may be that evidence is difficult to obtain because so few fathers living outside the home are intimately involved in childrearing." Moreover, many visiting fathers "have difficulty establishing a collaborative style of childrearing" after divorce.

What all these "factors" add up to seems plain enough, despite the recondite language of much contemporary scholarship. Visitation confers almost none of the predictable benefits of fatherhood because visitation is not fatherhood. Consequently, while children benefit dramatically from fathers, they often benefit little, if at all, from periodic visits with ex-fathers. Visitation is a shadow, a painful reminder, of fatherhood—observable and even measurable in clinical settings, but not nearly substantial enough to register as fatherhood, or even almost-fatherhood, on most large-scale surveys of quantifiable outcomes for children of divorce.

See Wallerstein and Blakeslee, *Second Chances,* 229–40 passim; Mary Lund, "The Non-Custodial Father: Common Challenges in Parenting After Divorce," in Charlie Lewis and Margaret O'Brien, eds., *Reassessing Fatherhood: New Observations on Fathers and the Modern Family* (Newbury Park, Calif.: Sage Publications, 1987), 223; Fox and Blanton, "Noncustodial Fathers Following Divorce," 19; Valerie King, "Nonresidential Father Involvement and Child Well-Being: Can Dads Make a Difference?" *Journal of Family Issues* 15, no. 1 (March 1994): 87; and Furstenberg and Cherlin, *Divided Families,* 72–73.

59. As previously cited, Furstenberg and Cherlin estimate that fewer than 10 percent of all divorced fathers approach the norm of cooperative co-parenting after divorce. Maccoby and Mnookin offer an estimate of 17 percent. Summarizing data from a number of studies, Fox and Blanton conclude that "for most fathers contact with children tapers off sharply following marital separation . . . [Studies show] decreasing levels of father involvement over time, such that most children reported rare or no contact with their fathers in the preceding year."

A recent Australian study of parenting after divorce similarly concludes that "children remained central to mothers' sense of wellbeing, but became peripheral in their fathers' post-separation adaptation, mirroring the attenuation of contact between fathers and their children."

See Fox and Blanton, "Noncustodial Fathers Following Divorce," 10; and Kathleen Funder, Margaret Harrison, and Ruth Weston, *Settling Down: Pathways of Parents After Divorce* (Melbourne: Australian Institute of Family Studies, 1993), 238.

60. Keller, "Parenting Post-Divorce," 62.

61. Some analysts have explored this discrepancy between the public and private dimensions of the fathers' rights movement. Their critiques have focused largely on these men's purportedly hypocritical endorsement of gender equality. For example, Joanne Schulmann and Valerie Pitt describe legislation favoring joint custody, a key goal of the fathers' rights movement, as "in effect, an attack on women," since these laws, though ostensibly affirming gender equality, seek essentially "to expand the rights of the parent who is not responsible for the day-to-day job of raising children. The non-caretaking parent is given 'equal' rights or control when he/she does not contribute equally to the day-to-day care and support of the child, either pre-divorce or post-divorce." Or as Carl Bertoia and Janice Drakich put it in the *Journal of Family Issues:* "Although fathers rightists portray themselves as caring, loving fathers who have been denied their rights to equal custody and access to their children, they are more concerned about the equality of their legal status than their equality in everyday parenting." Through "appeals to the popular gender-neutral ideals of contemporary society," these men have "coopted the language of equality but not the spirit of equality." For the real intention of these divorced fathers "is one that contradicts the fathers rightists' public depiction of fathers as participatory dads and co-parents to their children. Indeed, fathers want to play a role in their children's lives; but for the

most part, that role is merely a continuation of their predivorce role of the traditional father who exercises his power and control."

In short, despite the egalitarian rhetoric, these men are still the same old guys. They pretend to want to be New Fathers. But in fact they are divorced Old Fathers, enraged by the loss of their traditional privileges.

There is truth in this charge. Fathers' rights leaders do frequently, and self-consciously, use the fashionable language of gender neutrality to advance a distinctly gender-related agenda, just as they frequently invoke "children's rights" to describe what are clearly the interests and goals of divorced fathers.

At the same time, this criticism of the fathers' rights movement—that it fails, despite its rhetoric, to transcend masculinity—suffers from its own myopia. It is a criticism that insists on casting every issue as a zero-sum contest of women versus men, another battle in the gender wars, in which the only important issue is whether we are making progress toward eliminating gender roles.

But surely this is not the only, or even the main, significance of the fathers' rights phenomenon. Surely the core issue is effective fatherhood: not whether divorced men can or should overcome gender roles but whether children will grow up with fathers and whether men and women will have the desire and capacity to find a common life in marriage.

See Joanne Schulmann and Valerie Pitt, "Second Thoughts on Joint Child Custody: Analysis of Legislation and Its Implications for Women and Children," in Folberg, *Joint Custody and Shared Parenting,* 222; and Carl Bertoia and Janice Drakich, "The Fathers' Rights Movement: Contradictions in Rhetoric and Practice," *Journal of Family Issues* 14, no. 4 (December 1993): 611–13.

CHAPTER 9: THE SPERM FATHER

1. In 1991, unmarried parents accounted for about 1.2 million childbirths, or about 30 percent of all childbirths that year, up from 18 percent in 1980.

Children Born to Unmarried Parents

	1980	1991
Percent of all births occurring to unwed mothers	18.4	29.5
White	11.0	21.8
Black	55.2	67.9
Hispanic	23.6	38.5

Sources: National Center for Health Statistics, "Advance Report of Final Natality Statistics, 1991," vol. 42, no. 3, supplement, November 30, 1982; and "Advance Report of Final Nativity Statistics, 1991," vol. 42, no. 3, supplement, *Monthly Vital Statistics Report* (Hyattsville, Md.: U.S. Department of Health and Human Services, September 9, 1993).

Note: 1980 data reflect race of mother; 1991 data reflect race of child.

Moreover, in 1990, among all mothers living with children under age twenty-one whose fathers were absent, about 3 million of these mothers, or 30 percent, were never married. Accordingly, if nonmarriage is the single most reliable indicator of the Sperm Father model, then the key figure is approximately 30 percent: 30 percent of all births per year and 30 percent of all nonresidential fathers in the nation with children under age twenty-one. Some of these never-married nonresidential fathers, of course, do know their children and maintain some type of relationship with them, even if the relationship is sporadic and difficult to measure. About 24 percent of never-married mothers in 1989, for example, were awarded child-support payments, which roughly corresponds to the sociologist Sara S. McLanahan's estimation of the proportion of never-married fathers in 1987 who saw their children on a regular basis.

Conversely, however, a sizable number of married fathers each year get divorced and abandon their very young children almost entirely. No child support, no visits, no fathering. Indeed, in 1992, 4 percent of all children under age three—and 6 percent of all children under age six—had already experienced parental divorce, proportions that have doubled since 1970. Certainly many of these fathers, even though they were married when their children were born, closely resemble the Sperm Father model.

It seems reasonable to estimate, therefore, that these two qualifications cancel out one another. Specifically, we can estimate that the number of never-married nonresidential fathers who are not Sperm Fathers is roughly equal to the number of quickly divorced fathers who are. This reasoning, then, brings us back to the figure of 30 percent. In short, we can assume that the Sperm Father model of paternity now accounts for about 30 percent of all childbirths and about 30 percent of all families with absent fathers. If current trends continue, of course, this proportion will increase dramatically in coming years.

Regarding the proportion of single mothers who are never married, see Gordon H. Lester, "Child Support and Alimony: 1989," U.S. Bureau of the Census, Current Population Reports, series P-60, no. 173 (Washington, D.C.: U.S. Government Printing Office, September 1991), 3. Regarding never-married mothers receiving child support, see the Lester report, page 1. McLanahan estimates come from an interview with her on July 29, 1993, and from Roni Rabin, "When Baby Makes Two," *New York Newsday,* July 29, 1993, 65. Regarding young children experiencing parental divorce, see Arlene F. Saluter, "Marital Status and Living Arrangements: March 1992," U.S. Bureau of the Census, Current Population Reports, series P-20, no. 468 (Washington, D.C.: U.S. Government Printing Office, December 1992), tables 4 and 5; and unpublished tabulations from the revised 1970 Current Population Survey of the U.S. Bureau of the Census.

2. Don S. Browning, "Biology, Ethics, and Narrative in Christian Family Theory," working paper no. 41 (New York: Institute for American Values, 1993), 46.

3. Jeanne Warren Lindsay, *Do I Have a Daddy? A Story About a Single-Parent Child* (Buena Park, Calif.: Morning Glory Press, 1991).

4. In the highly popular 1991 action-fantasy movie *Terminator 2,* Arnold Schwarzenegger plays a high-tech robot who becomes a father figure to a boy named John Conner. "I wish I could've met my real Dad," the boy says. "Mom and him were only together for one night." Sara, John's mother, watching her son bond with the robot named Terminator, finally finds her answer to the father problem. To Sara, "it was suddenly so clear. The Terminator would never stop, it would never leave him, and it would never hurt him, never shout at him, or get drunk and hit him, or say it was too busy to spend time with him. It would always be there, and it would die to protect

him. Of all the would-be fathers who came and went over the years, this thing, this machine, was the only one who measured up."

In Sergio M. Castilla's 1994 film, *The Girl in the Watermelon,* a seventeen-year-old girl, Samantha, learns by reading her mother's diary that the deceased man she had always believed was her father probably was not. Instead, Samantha learns, one of two other of her mother's former boyfriends from 1976—neither of whom Samantha has ever seen but who turn out to be very nice guys—is probably her biological father. The movie centers on Samantha's search for her "real" father.

The same question—who fathered this child?—also drives the narrative of another provocative 1994 film, *The Snapper,* a comedy-drama in which an Irish father learns to accept and ultimately support his daughter's unwed pregnancy, including her obviously improbable claim that "a Spanish sailor" is the father of her child. Indeed, the daughter's petulant naming of "a Spanish sailor" as the father emerges as a central means of conveying the film's core message. Insisting that the father is "a Spanish sailor" conveys not only the idea of "none of your business" but also, at least symbolically, advances the idea that there truly is no father for this child, other than (perhaps) the grandfather, who in the end proves his decency by his willingness to accept things as they are rather than judge or blame his daughter.

Angie and Henry Jaglom's *Babyfever* are yet two more 1994 movies that focus on the growing societal phenomenon of childbearing via Sperm Fathers. In *Babyfever,* Gena, a fashionable young professional, finds herself happily pregnant by a current boyfriend, whom she does not like very much, at the same time that she is dealing with the reappearance in her life of an old boyfriend, whom she also does not like very much. Similarly, *Angie,* starring Geena Davis, is the story of a woman whose pregnancy, by a boyfriend she does not like very much, causes her to reassess her life, searching for independence and ultimately embracing the adventure of single motherhood.

5. Mary Morris, *A Mother's Love* (New York: Doubleday, 1993), 31. Carrie Fisher's 1994 novel about motherhood, *Delusions of Grandma,* tells a similar story. Cora, finding herself pregnant, writes a letter to Ray, her sort of current, sort of ex-, boyfriend: "I'm proud—and a little inexperienced—to announce the inadvertent impending arrival of the child we appear to have made during our recent stressful albeit heroic circumstances . . . I'm not telling you this so that you'll feel obliged to marry me or support me for the next eighteen years . . . I'm sorry we weren't and aren't about to configure ourselves into a more convenient constellation."

   Yet Cora, facing parenthood alone, concludes on this optimistic note: "Although we couldn't make a relationship that worked, we managed to fashion a human being." See Carrie Fisher, *Delusions of Grandma* (New York: Simon & Schuster, 1994), 248.

6. Ibid., 96.

7. Barbara Kingsolver, *Pigs in Heaven* (New York: HarperCollins, 1993), 10.

8. This fantasy of asexual female generativity—women becoming mothers without having sex with a man—now appears with some regularity in contemporary fiction. For example, in addition to Morris and Kingsolver, Tama Janowitz's *The Male Cross-Dresser Support Group* tells the story of a single woman in New York who simply meets a little boy on the street. She becomes his family, his mother. See Tama Janowitz, *The Male Cross-Dresser Support Group* (New York: Washington Square Press, 1992).

9.   Kingsolver, *Pigs in Heaven,* 3, 24, 27.

10. Ibid., 11.

11. Ibid., 337, 339.

12. One tentative qualification of this theme does emerge at the end of the story, when Taylor tells her mother that she misses Jax and now wants to "start thinking of me and Jax as kind of more permanent . . . I don't know if married is really the point, but you know what I mean" (p. 327).

13. "Parent & Child," *Single Mother,* no. 9 (November/December 1992): 3. Similarly, in Bryan Miller's profile of the Chicago chapter of Single Mothers by Choice, we learn that each chapter meeting "features a topic for discussion; 'What do I tell my child about Daddy?' is a perennial." See Bryan Miller, "Life Without Father," *Chicago Reader,* October 9, 1992, 20.

14. Jane Mattes, "What to Say About Dad," *Single Mother,* no. 9 (November/December 1992): 3.

15. Marge Kennedy and Janet Spencer King, *The Single-Parent Family: Living Happily in a Changing World* (New York: Crown, 1994), 28.

16. "Forum: Where's Daddy?" *Single Mother,* no. 3 (November/December 1991): 7. In a 1994 "Mother to Mother" column in *Working Mother* magazine, a mother writes in to ask Engber for advice: "My preschooler came home the other day complaining of feeling left out because all the kids at his child care center had been making Father's Day cards. Because we have no contact with Joey's father, I don't know how to deal with this holiday. How can I help my son to feel more included?"

     Engber advises Joey's mother to encourage Joey to make a Father's Day card for "any male family member or friend who has shown significant fathering qualities." Father's Day can also be an occasion for teaching important lessons. Engber urges Joey's mother to "use the holiday to initiate a talk about why Joey's father isn't part of your family. Let your son know that it's okay not to have a dad in the house. Point out that families come in all shapes and sizes: the kind gentleman down the street who is raising his granddaughter or the happy little boy next door who was adopted by a loving couple." See "How Single Moms Can Handle Father's Day," *Working Mother* (June 1994): 10.

17. John K. Rosemond, *Parent Power! A Common-Sense Approach to Parenting in the '90s and Beyond* (Kansas City, Mo.: Andrews and McMeel, 1990), 7–8.

18. "Ask the Experts," *Single Mother,* no. 10 (January/February 1993): 11.

19. April Martin, *The Lesbian and Gay Parenting Handbook: Creating and Raising Our Families* (New York: HarperCollins, 1993), 188. Martin is advising lesbians and gays, but the same idea is increasingly prevalent in the wider society. Rebecca Rawson, a successful forty-six-year-old lawyer from New York, is a single mother by choice. She did not want to marry the father, who now lives in another city and has expressed "not the slightest interest" in the child, Jenny. Now age six, Jenny tells people who ask that "my father doesn't want me." Rawson tries to reassure her: "I told her a father was a biological thing; it doesn't have to do with someone who is around the house."

     This is the core assumption of the new advice literature. The idea of "father" is broken into pieces. One piece is "a biological thing." But the biological thing has nothing to do with the parenthood thing. Making Jenny is one thing; raising her is another. The two need not go together. This analysis is both a perfect apologia for the Sperm Father and the most radical assault possible on the idea of fatherhood as a coherent social role for men. See Stephanie Gutmann, "Rebecca's Law: Work—or Else," *New York Post,* April 20, 1994, 27.

20. Ibid., 83.

21. Other recent movies focusing on sperm mix-ups include *Leon the Pig Farmer,* a 1993 comedy, and *Babymaker,* a 1994 television movie based on the real-life exploits of Dr. Cecil Jacobson, whose habit of using his own sperm to inseminate his patients earned him the nickname "The Sperminator."

22. "Artificial Insemination: Practice in the United States" (Washington, D.C.: U.S. Congress, Office of Technology Assessment, 1988), 3, 23. According to this survey conducted in 1987, fully half of all physicians who perform artificial inseminations do not screen prospective patients according to marital status. Since then, this trend seems to have accelerated. In 1991, for example, doctors at the University of Michigan, instituting what they described as a "major policy change," began offering donor insemination to unmarried women. See Richard Louv, *Fatherlove* (New York: Pocket Books, 1993), 39.

23. David Wasserman and Robert Wachbroit, "Defining Families: The Impact of Reproductive Technology," *Philosophy and Public Policy* 13, no. 3 (summer 1993): 4–6.

24. John A. Robertson, testimony before the Select Committee on Children, Youth, and Families, U.S. House of Representatives, May 21, 1987 (Washington, D.C.: U.S. Government Printing Office, 1987), 84, 89.

25. Daniel Callahan, "Bioethics and Fatherhood," *Utah Law Review,* no. 3 (1992): 735, 739. In this provocative essay, Callahan ponders with regret our society's "acceptance of the systematic downgrading of fatherhood brought about by the introduction of anonymous sperm donors. Or perhaps it was the case that fatherhood had already sunk to such a low state, and male irresponsibility was already so accepted, that no one saw a problem. It is as if everyone argued: Look, males have always been fathering children anonymously and irresponsibly; why not put this otherwise noxious trait to good use?" (p. 741). For a similarly against-the-grain argument, see James Lindemann Nelson, "Parental Obligations and the Ethics of Surrogacy: A Causal Perspective," *Public Affairs Quarterly* 5, no. 1 (January 1991): 49–61.

26. Wasserman and Wachbroit, "Defining Families," 8.

27. Anne Donchin, "Procreation, Power and Subjectivity: Feminist Approaches to the New Reproductive Technologies," working paper no. 260 (Wellesley, Mass.: Wellesley College Center for Research on Women, 1993), 13.

28. Thomas Hobbes, *Leviathan* (New York: Penguin, 1985; first published, 1651), 186.

29. Ibid., 254.

30. Philip Abbott, *The Family on Trial: Special Relationships in Modern Political Thought* (University Park: Pennsylvania State University Press, 1981), 23.

31. Interview with Jean Bethke Elshtain, June 23, 1993. See also Gordon J. Schochet, *Patriarchalism in Political Thought: The Authoritarian Family and Political Speculation and Attitudes Especially in Seventeenth-Century England* (New York: Basic Books, 1975), 233.

32. See Jean Bethke Elshtain, *Public Man, Private Woman: Women in Social and Political Thought* (Princeton: Princeton University Press, 1993), 108–31 passim. See also John W. Yolton, *John Locke: Problems and Perspectives* (Cambridge, U.K.: Cambridge University Press, 1969).

33. Abbott, *The Family on Trial,* 28. Indeed, much of Locke's argument, including almost all of the *First Treatise,* is presented in the form of a sustained polemic against a book entitled *Patriarcha,* written by Sir Robert Filmer, a seventeenth-century English royalist. In *Patriarcha,* Filmer defended monarchial absolutism by linking it to familial patriarchy. To him, the political ordering of society derived from the private ordering of the family. Consequently, as the father exercised a divine right to rule the family—a lesson that Filmer drew from the biblical story of Adam and Eve—so the king exercised a divine right to rule the people.

    Locke vigorously disputed both aspects of this patriarchal thesis. (Moreover, in both intellectual and historical terms, Locke clearly won the argument. Indeed, it seems safe to assume that, were it not for Locke's famous attack against him, Filmer's name today would have long since been forgotten.) As a result, *Two Treatises* is almost as much about the nature of the family and fatherhood as it is about the nature of government.

34. John Locke, *Two Treatises on Government* (Cambridge, U.K.: Cambridge University Press, 1965; first published, 1698), 179.

35. Ibid., 206. Of course, Locke's observation about whether man should "be alone" directly echoes the biblical story of creation (Genesis 2:18): "And the Lord God said, It is not good that the man should be alone."

36. Ibid., 319.

37. Ibid., 214, 337.

38. Ibid., 214, 306.

39. Ibid., 310.

40. Sam Howe Verhovek, "Michigan's High Court Says Adopted Girl Must Be Sent to Biological Parents," *New York Times,* July 3, 1993, 5; Charlotte Allen, "Our Archaic Adoption Laws," *Wall Street Journal,* August 11, 1993, 19; "Standing Up for Fathers," *Newsweek,* May 3, 1993, 52; and "Whose Daughter Is Jessica?" *Washington Post,* national weekly edition, August 9–15, 1993, 27.

CHAPTER 10: THE STEPFATHER AND THE NEARBY GUY

1. David Popenoe, "The Evolution of Marriage and the Problem of Stepfamilies," paper presented at the National Symposium on Stepfamilies (University Park: Pennsylvania State University, October 14–15, 1993), 19. Popenoe defines this principle of "biological favoritism," or what is often called "inclusive fitness" or "kin altruism," as the universal human "predisposition to advance the interests of genetic relatives before those of unrelated individuals.... With respect to children, this means that both men and women have likely evolved to invest more in children who are related to them than in those who are not. The world over, such biological favoritism tends to be the rule" (p. 7). See also W. D. Hamilton, "The Genetic Evolution of Social Behaviour," *Journal of Theoretical Biology* 7, no. 1 (July 1964): 1–52; and Martin S. Smith, "Research in Developmental Sociobiology: Parenting and Family Behavior," in Kevin B. MacDonald, ed., *Sociobiological Perspectives on Human Development* (New York: Springer-Verlag, 1988), 271–92.

2. William R. Beer, *Strangers in the House: The World of Stepsiblings and Half-Stepsiblings* (New Brunswick, N.J.: Transaction, 1989), 9.

3. In adumbrating the Stepfather and the Nearby Guy as ideal types, I am not seek-

ing to account for the relatively small proportion of actual cases in which the biological father has died. Instead, in describing these two cultural models, I am referring only to situations in which the biological father is alive but is not married to the mother and does not reside with his children.

Today, the prevalence of the Stepfather and the Nearby Guy in our society is overwhelmingly due to divorce and nonmarriage, not death. For example, in 1990, among all women age fifteen to sixty-five who had been married more than once, only about 10 percent of remarriages involved remarriage after widowhood. See unpublished data from the U.S. Bureau of the Census, Current Population Survey, June 1990, Marital History Supplement.

4. Contemporary Hollywood screenwriters increasingly seeking to produce simplified or "high concept" movie plots must frequently follow this maxim: Exclude nonessential characters. In this sense, the seemingly conscious decision to erase the children's biological father from this story—he does not merit even one indirect reference—reveals two underlying and related ideas. First, in a story for children about the importance of faithfulness and family commitment, there is no need to refer at all to the biological father. Quite literally, he is an unnecessary character in this story, easily and logically excludable. Second, a stepfather can easily become "Dad" to his stepchildren, thus producing a happy ending for the entire family.

5. Consider this equation. Over the past fifteen years, the fastest-growing family-structure trend in the nation has been out-of-wedlock childbearing. The second fastest-growing trend has been the formation of stepfamilies. The third fastest-growing trend has been divorce. Of these three, considered as harmful environments for child rearing, the least bad seems to be divorce. The second worst appears to be stepfamilies. The worst, almost certainly, is out-of-wedlock childbearing. In sum, a perfectly inverse relationship between family-structure trends and child well-being.

6. For numbers of stepfathers, see Arthur J. Norton and Louisa F. Miller, "Marriage, Divorce, and Remarriage in the 1990's," U.S. Bureau of the Census, Current Population Reports, series P-23, no. 180 (Washington, D.C.: U.S. Government Printing Office, October 1992), 10. For married-couple households with children, see Steve W. Rawlings, "Household and Family Characteristics: March 1992," U.S. Bureau of the Census, Current Population Reports, series P-20, no. 467 (Washington, D.C.: U.S. Government Printing Office, April 1993), vii.

7. Lenore J. Weitzman, *The Divorce Revolution* (New York: Free Press, 1985), 256–57; and Ross A. Thompson, "The Role of the Father After Divorce," *The Future of Children* 4, no. 1 (Los Altos, Calif.: Center for the Future of Children, spring 1994), 215.

8. Norton and Miller, "Marriage, Divorce, and Remarriage," 10.

9. Harold H. Bloomfield, *Making Peace in Your Stepfamily* (New York: Hyperion, 1993), 5, 63.

10. Tamara K. Hareven, testimony before the Select Committee on Children, Youth, and Families, U.S. House of Representatives, February 25, 1986 (Washington, D.C.: U.S. Government Printing Office, 1986), 31, 27.

11. Claire Berman, *Making It as a Stepparent: New Roles/New Rules* (New York: Harper & Row, 1986), 10. A leading college textbook, written by Bryan Strong and Christine DeVault, calls stepfamilies "as American as Beaver Cleaver's family and apple pie." Although some people still believe in negative "cultural stereo-

types" about stepfamilies, the "actual picture of these families" is quite reassuring. Accordingly: "Stepfamilies, indeed, may not be especially different from traditional nuclear families."

Echoing Berman and others, Strong and DeVault find that stepfamilies may "offer children a number of benefits that can compensate for the negative consequences of divorce." These new benefits might be described as the six "mores." First, more parental "role models" for children to choose from. Second, more "flexibility" for children, gained through exposure to diverse living arrangements. Third, more "sounding boards" for children, especially in "areas in which the biological parents feel unknowledgeable or uncomfortable." Fourth, more siblings, acquired either as stepsiblings or half-siblings. Fifth, a more "extended kin network," which for children "may become as important and loving (or more) as their original kin network." And sixth, parents who are more happily married, since children are "better adjusted" in "happily remarried families" than in "conflict-ridden traditional nuclear families." See Bryan Strong and Christine DeVault, *The Marriage and Family Experience* (St. Paul, Minn.: West Publishing, 1992), 556, 539.

12. Ross A. Thompson, "Fathers and the Child's 'Best Interests': Judicial Decision Making in Custody Disputes," in Micheal E. Lamb, ed., *The Father's Role: Applied Perspectives* (New York: Wiley, 1986), 86.

13. Kyle D. Pruett, "The Paternal Presence," *Families in Society* 74, no. 1 (January 1993): 49.

14. Lawrence Balter, *The Wedding* (New York: Barron's, 1989). In Claire Berman's advice book for children, *What Am I Doing in a Stepfamily?* (New York: Carol Publishing, 1992), children learn "how two families can be better than one." Near the end of the book, Berman writes: "Now you are finding out that children can love more than one set of parents."

15. James H. Bray et al., "Longitudinal Changes in Stepfamilies: Impact on Children's Adjustment" (Washington, D.C.: American Psychological Association, August 15, 1992), 7–8.

16. Laurence Steinberg, "Single Parents, Stepparents, and the Susceptibility of Adolescents to Antisocial Peer Pressure," *Child Development* 58 (1987): 275.

17. Nicholas Zill, Donna Ruane Morrison, and Mary Jo Coiro, "Long-Term Effects of Parental Divorce on Parent-Child Relationships, Adjustment, and Achievement in Young Adulthood," *Journal of Family Psychology* 7, no. 1 (1993): 101.

18. Frank F. Furstenberg, Jr., "History and Current Status of Divorce in the United States," *The Future of Children* 4, no. 1 (Los Altos, Calif.: Center for the Future of Children, spring 1994), 37.

19. Kathleen E. Keirnan, "The Impact of Family Disruption in Childhood on Transitions Made in Young Adult Life," *Population Studies* 46, no. 2 (July 1992): 213–34. Seeking to explain the worse outcomes for children from stepfamilies as compared to children from mother-only homes, Keirnan offers this hypothesis: "The answer probably lies in the emotional-psychological domain rather than in the socio-economic one, and is likely to be the result of qualitative differences in family processes between the two sets of families" (p. 233).

To distinguish the effects of family structure from the effects of economic and other influences, this study incorporates two major control variables: social class at birth and nonverbal ability scores at age eleven. Consequently, the outcomes for children in various family structures are compared to one another only after "controlling" for these (at least arguably) extraneous factors.

20. Maggie Drummond, "Step This Way for the Growing Cause of Family Breakdown" (London) *Daily Telegraph,* December 2, 1991, 18.

21. Paul Amato, *Children in Australian Families: The Growth of Competence* (New York: Prentice Hall, 1987), 115, 118.

22. Ibid., 147–48.

23. For example, second marriages are significantly more likely to end in divorce than are first marriages. Among younger couples today, a redivorce may be as much as 25 percent more likely than a first divorce. One national survey finds that more than one-third of all children living in stepfamilies have already experienced a second parental divorce by the time they reach their early teens. As a result, about 15 percent of all the children in the nation today are likely to experience at least two parental divorces by the time they reach late adolescence.

    Describing this aspect of stepfamily life from the child's perspective, William R. Beer observes: "Over all hangs the possibility that everything will fall apart again; for children of divorce are no longer innocent in this regard. They know that adults can stop loving one another, that a marriage can be shattered and a household torn apart. They have seen it happen before their very eyes. They have a feeling for the transience and delicacy of human emotions that few other people acquire before adulthood." See Norton and Miller, "Marriage, Divorce, and Remarriage," 6–7; Frank F. Furstenberg, Jr., "Divorce and the American Family," in W. Richard Scott, ed., *Annual Review of Sociology,* vol. 16 (Palo Alto, Calif.: Annual Reviews, 1990), 382, 384; and Beer, *Strangers in the House,* xii.

24. Frank F. Furstenberg, Jr., and Andrew J. Cherlin, *Divided Families: What Happens to Children When Parents Part* (Cambridge, Mass.: Harvard University Press, 1991), 59.

25. Furstenberg, "Divorce and the American Family," 388.

26. John W. Santrock, Karen A. Sitterle, and Richard A. Warshak, "Parent-Child Relationships in Stepfather Families," in Phyllis Bronstein and Carolyn Pape Cowan, eds., *Fatherhood Today: Men's Changing Role in the Family* (New York: Wiley, 1988), 159.

27. E. Mavis Hetherington, Margaret Stanley-Hagan, and Edward R. Anderson, "Marital Transitions: A Child's Perspective," *American Psychologist* 44, no. 2 (February 1989): 308. See also Lawrence A. Kurdek and Mark A. Fine, "The Relationship Between Family Structure and Young Adolescents' Appraisals of Family Climate and Parenting Behavior," *Journal of Family Issues* 14, no. 2 (June 1993): 279–90; Elizabeth Thomson, Sara S. McLanahan, and Roberta Braun Curtin, "Family Structure, Gender, and Parental Socialization," *Journal of Marriage and the Family* 54 (May 1992): 368–78; and Stephen Claxton-Oldfield, "Perceptions of Stepfathers," *Journal of Family Issues* 13, no. 3 (September 1992): 378–89.

28. Harold H. Bloomfield, "Stepparents: Getting to the Heart of Problems," *Parenting* (April 1993): 161–62.

29. Sandi Kahn Shelton, "Happily Remarried," *Working Mother* (April 1993): 62–64.

30. Even the word *stepchild* is so fraught with negative meaning that it is frequently used to suggest a state of deprivation. For example, one current dictionary defines *stepchild* as either "a child of one's wife or husband by a former marriage" or "one that fails to receive proper care or attention." See *Merriam Webster's Collegiate Dictionary* (Springfield, Mass.: Merriam-Webster, 1993).

31. Bloomfield, *Making Peace in Your Stepfamily,* 75. Linda Bird Francke, finding "no rational solution to the name problem" in stepfamilies, recommends a major

societal change. She urges couples to switch over to a matrilineal system of naming children. In a divorce-oriented society, such a system would be simpler and more equitable: "In stepfamilies, the children then would at least have the same last name as one of the adults."

I disagree with Francke's proposal, but her underlying thesis is logical and highly suggestive. As fatherhood decomposes in our society, the idea of children taking their father's name—a practice historically rooted in the desire to increase paternal certainty and to connect the father unambiguously to his child and the mother of his child—becomes impractical and increasingly hard to justify. Indeed, for growing numbers of families in our society, the practice may no longer be worth the trouble. See Linda Bird Francke, *Growing Up Divorced* (New York: Simon & Schuster, 1983), 199–200.

32. See Emily and John Visher, *How to Win as a Stepfamily* (New York: Dembner Books, 1982), 67–69; and Berman, *Making It as a Stepparent,* 37–41.

33. Berman, *What Am I Doing in a Stepfamily?*

34. Amy Stevens, "A Los Angeles Lawyer Specializes in Helping Nonbiological Fathers," *Wall Street Journal,* June 17, 1993, 1.

35. Anne Burke, "Nonbiological Father, Mother at Odds," *San Fernando Valley Daily News,* July 24, 1994, 1.

36. Anne Burke, "Van Nuys Man Ruled 'Better Caretaker,'" *San Fernando Valley Daily News,* June 30, 1993, 1.

37. Stevens, "A Los Angeles Lawyer"; and Burke, "Nonbiological Father."

38. Benjamin Spock, "A Father's Companionship," *Redbook* (October 1974): 24.

39. David Ray, "The Endless Search," *New York Times Magazine,* August 28, 1994, 32.

40. David Giveans and Michael Robinson, "Old and New Images of Fatherhood," in Charles S. Scull, ed., *Fathers, Sons, and Daughters: Exploring Fatherhood, Renewing the Bond* (Los Angeles: Jeremy P. Tarcher, 1992), 11.

41. Harold P. Gershenson, "Redefining Fatherhood in Families with White Adolescent Mothers," *Journal of Marriage and the Family* 45, no. 3 (August 1983): 591, 598.

42. Ibid., 591–92, 597–98.

43. Margaret Crosbie-Burnett, Ada Skyles, and Jane Becker-Haven, "Exploring Stepfamilies from a Feminist Perspective," in Sanford M. Dornbusch and Myra H. Strober, eds., *Feminism, Children, and the New Families* (New York: Guilford Press, 1988), 321.

44. James A. Levine, "Involving Fathers in Head Start: A Framework for Public Policy and Program Development," *Families in Society* 74, no. 1 (January 1993): 15.

45. Frank L. Mott, "When Is a Father Really Gone? Paternal-Child Contact in Father-Absent Homes," *Demography* 27, no. 4 (November 1990): 514.

46. Numerous scholars have offered analogous arguments regarding young, never-married biological fathers. According to this view, to describe these men as essentially "absent" is incorrect. Some of these young men visit their children. Some of them give money to the mother or buy gifts for the child. Yet they do these things "informally," thus constituting a kind of underground fatherhood—often difficult for outsiders to recognize but effective and important for the children.

Like the thesis of the Nearby Guy as a father, however, the "underground father" thesis is based largely on speculation and wishful thinking. There is very little solid evidence that these young, unmarried men who do not live with their children are providing them with even a semblance of good-enough fatherhood.

For an example of the opposite argument, see Sandra K. Danziger and Norma Radin, "Absent Does Not Equal Uninvolved: Predictors of Fathering in

Teen Mother Families," *Journal of Marriage and the Family* 52, no. 3 (August 1990): 636–42.

47. Iris Marion Young, "Making Single Motherhood Normal," *Dissent* (winter 1994): 90.
48. Michele Willens, "Breaking a Stereotype, More Men Are Being Hired as Nannies," *New York Times,* May 13, 1993, p. C-6.

CHAPTER 11: THE GOOD FAMILY MAN

1. Most of the interviews quoted in this chapter were conducted in Denver, Colorado, on August 24, 1992; in Cleveland, Ohio, on November 9, 1992; in Teaneck, New Jersey, on April 16, 1992; and in Jackson, Mississippi, on July 7, 1992.
2. This theme emerged frequently in our interviews. First, the definition of a good father today is more complex. His list of basic traits is longer. He is expected to do more, especially in the areas of daily child care and the sharing of household responsibilities. As one father from New Jersey put it: "[Back in my father's generation] there were more good family men, probably because only three things [were expected] . . . One, a good provider. A disciplinarian, two. And three is probably takes his kids to church. [Today] there is a lot more that has to be added to that . . . to qualify as a good family man."

    Second, effective fatherhood today derives less from social expectations than from individual choice. Combined with the longer list of traits, the result is that fatherhood today has both a lower floor and a higher ceiling. On the one hand, with each passing year, there is more fatherlessness. On the other hand, a significant group of men are choosing to be very good fathers. A father from Colorado said: "The ones who have made a decision—this is what they want to do—they are now going to put all their efforts and all their knowledge . . . to try to meet this goal. Rather than before, you might have just blundered through it because it's the proper thing to do."

3. In the Gospel according to St. Mark (King James Bible, Book of Mark, 10: 42–44), Jesus tells his disciples: "Ye know that they which are accounted to rule over the Gentiles exercise lordship over them; and their great ones exercise authority upon them. But so shall it not be among you: but whosoever will be great among you, shall be your minister: And whosoever of you will be the chiefest, shall be servant of all."

    On February 4, 1968, at the Ebenezer Baptist Church in Atlanta, Dr. Martin Luther King, Jr., examined this same theme in "The Drum Major Instinct," one of his most famous sermons. King defines the drum major instinct as "a desire to be out front, a desire to lead the parade, a desire to be first." Frequently, King warns, this instinct reflects selfishness and egotism. Indeed, from a societal perspective, the drum major instinct often constitutes the psychological underpinnings of authoritarianism and bigotry.

    Yet the Scriptures do not tell us to eliminate or destroy this basic human desire. Instead, the Scriptures teach us to harness this instinct to prosocial purposes by understanding leadership as servanthood. According to King, Jesus offers his disciples "a new definition of greatness" by teaching them that "he who is greatest among you can be your servant." King concludes the sermon by describing the redemptive power and social worth of this "new norm of greatness": "Everybody can be great, because everybody can serve."

    What might be termed the contemporary Christian fatherhood movement frequently incorporates this same idea: Every man can be a great father, because every man can serve his family. For example, the ideal of service to family and God constitutes the philosophical essence of "Promise Keepers"—one of the largest and fastest-growing Christian ministries in the nation devoted to helping men become better husbands and fathers. The theme of service also permeates many religiously informed contemporary advice books for fathers.

See E. Glenn Wagner, *Strategies for a Successful Marriage: A Study Guide for Men* (Colorado Springs: NavPress, 1994); Stephen A. Bly, *How to Be a Good Dad* (Chicago: Moody Press, 1986); and Frank Minirth, Brian Newman, and Paul Warren, *The Father Book* (Nashville, Tenn.: Thomas Nelson Publishers, 1992). For a description of a contemporary men's and fatherhood ministry in an African-American congregation, see Don S. Browing, *A Fundamental Practical Theology: Descriptive and Strategic Proposals* (Minneapolis: Fortress Press, 1991), 243–77.

4. In his investigation of cultural concepts of masculinity, David D. Gilmore ultimately rejects the popular view that "masculinity is self-serving, egotistical, and uncaring." Instead, across cultures, Gilmore finds that "manhood ideologies always include a criterion of selfless generosity, even to the point of sacrifice. Again and again we find that 'real' men are those who give more than they take; they serve others . . . Manhood therefore is also a nurturing concept, if we define that term as giving, subventing, or other-directed." See David D. Gilmore, *Manhood in the Making: Cultural Concepts of Masculinity* (New Haven: Yale University Press, 1990), 229.

5. For example, see Linda Thompson and Alexis J. Walker, "Gender in Families: Women and Men in Marriage, Work, and Parenthood," *Journal of Marriage and the Family* 51, no. 4 (November 1989): 845–71; Eleanor E. Maccoby and Robert H. Mnookin, *Dividing the Child: Social and Legal Dilemmas of Custody* (Cambridge, Mass.: Harvard University Press, 1992), 25–26; and Rosalind C. Barnett and Grace K. Baruch, "Social Roles, Gender, and Psychological Stress," in Rosalind C. Barnett, Lois Beiner, and Grace K. Baruch, eds., *Gender and Stress* (New York: Free Press, 1987), 122–43.

6. Many of the fathers we interviewed were deeply disturbed about what might be termed the dangerous state of the culture. Speaking of teaching his children right from wrong, a father from New Jersey said: "The bottom line is that it has to be done at home first, because if the world gets hold of them, it's over." The following conversation excerpt from Austin, Texas, makes the same point:

> FATHER 1: Within the home, within the family structure, you can communicate, you can talk, you can do these things. But the minute they are outside of that home, what I call my defensive perimeter . . .
> FATHER 2: You have no control.
> FATHER 1: That's it.
> FATHER 3: The only control you have is what you have taught them . . .
> FATHER 1: That's right. You hope to God that that seed you have put in them carries them away from the temptations and all the peer pressure that these kids are under.

7. Nationally, Joseph H. Pleck finds that married fathers today spend significantly more time in child care and domestic work than did married fathers in the early 1960s. Interestingly, Pleck also finds that, among two-earner couples, nearly one mother in five reports that her husband is the primary caregiver while she is

working. This trend—largely a consequence of the increasing number of "tag team" couples in which parents have nonoverlapping work schedules—means that more children of employed mothers are being cared for by their fathers than are in day-care centers. See Joseph H. Pleck, "Are Family-Supportive Employer Policies Relevant to Men?" in Jane C. Hood, ed., *Men, Work, and Family* (Newbury Park, Calif.: Sage Publications, 1993), 219–22.

Pleck also asserts that "two-shift" couples select these schedules "as a conscious strategy to reduce child care costs" (p. 222). Yet our interview findings disconfirm this conclusion. The "tag team" parents we interviewed repeatedly stressed the quality of child care, not the cost. Specifically, as Barbara Dafoe Whitehead has put it, most working parents "believe that the safest and best care is provided by a parent or close relative. Their actual child-care arrangements follow this principle. They frequently arrange their working lives to maximize the time their child spends in the care of a parent or relative and to minimize the time spent with nonrelatives." See Barbara Dafoe Whitehead, "The Family in an Unfriendly Culture," *Family Affairs* 3, no. 1/2 (spring/summer 1990): 2; and Whitehead, "Maryland Focus Group Report on Family Time," working paper no. 2 (New York: Institute for American Values, 1990).

8. One Denver father explained that he and his wife divide household work according to "convenience." When she was an at-home mother, she cooked dinner, but when she went back to work, on some nights she got home later than he did: "To come home and sit down and wait for her to get in and then start cooking—when I had been there for an hour and a half to two hours—didn't make any sense. (laughter) So I was hungry. And you know, kids are coming in and we are sitting around waiting for Mom to, you know (laughter) . . . And I am saying, well, we are hungry, you know? So that . . . no problem with less of a man because I brought out the skillet."

9. An unusually insightful exploration of this issue can be found in Robert S. Weiss, *Staying the Course: The Emotional and Social Lives of Men Who Do Well at Work* (New York: Free Press, 1990).

10. As Joseph Veroff, Elizabeth Douvan, and Richard A. Kulka put it: "When they think of the nicest things about having children, mothers allude more often to the love and warmth, aspects of affiliative pleasure with their children, while men more often focus on the influence or power implicit in the parental role. Men are more likely to say that having an influence, forming the character of the child, is a major pleasure of parenthood." See Joseph Veroff, Elizabeth Douvan, and Richard A. Kulka, *The Inner American: A Self-Portrait from 1957 to 1976* (New York: Basic Books, 1981), 216.

11. See Kyle P. Pruett, "The Paternal Presence," *Families in Society* 74, no. 1 (January 1993): 49.

12. The theory of human attachment, rooted in the mother-infant relationship, is a centrally important topic of modern psychology. See Robert Karen, *Becoming Attached: Unfolding the Mystery of the Infant-Mother Bond and Its Impact on Later Life* (New York: Warner, 1994); and John Bowlby, *The Making and Breaking of Affectional Bonds* (New York: Routledge, 1979).

13. Of course, to describe differences between maternal love and paternal love is to describe tendencies and matters of degree, not absolutes or stark polarities. For this reason, differences between what Erich Fromm called "motherly love" and "fatherly love" are often explicated theoretically through what Max Weber called

"ideal types" or what C. G. Jung called "archetypes." See Erich Fromm, *The Art of Loving* (New York: Harper & Row, 1989), 35–41; and Guy Corneau, *Absent Fathers, Lost Sons: The Search for Masculine Identity* (Boston: Shambhala, 1991).

CHAPTER 12: A FATHER FOR EVERY CHILD

1. Consider the case of the American Association for Marriage and Family Therapy (AAMFT). Founded in 1942, AAMFT, with over 16,000 members, is the nation's premier professional association of marriage and family counselors. Yet at its annual conferences, the topic of marriage is literally nowhere to be found. For example, at AAMFT's fifty-first annual conference, held in 1993, the conference's "Subject Guide" listed forty-three major topics to be explored. These topics included: Abuse, AIDS, Couples, Custody, Divorce, Gender, Models, Sexual Issues, Stepfamilies/Single Parents, and Teaching Family Therapy. These major topics were further divided into 234 subtopics. Under the topic of Couples, for example, there were sixteen subtopics, including Communications, Gender Construction, Psychoeducation, and Substance Abuse. Yet in this total of 277 subject listings, the word *marriage* did not appear once. The closest we get is the subtopic called Remarriage Ceremony, listed under Stepfamilies/Single Parents. As odd as it may seem, the American Association for Marriage and Family Therapy has excised the word *marriage* from its basic vocabulary. If these professionals were naming their organization today, instead of living with a name chosen by others in 1942, it seems highly unlikely that *marriage* would appear in its name.

    The same revealing trend is evident in high school and college textbooks on family life. In 1942, or even in 1982, most of these books had straightforward titles such as *Marriage and Family Life*. Today, far fewer of these book titles contain the "m" word. In 1994, at a Wisconsin conference on the International Year of the Family, a sales representative from Macmillan/McGraw-Hill, a major publisher of these textbooks, told me that her company increasingly declines to publish books featuring the word *marriage* in the title, since educators complain that the word sounds too "old-fashioned" and "preachy." Better simply to leave it out.

    These curious phenomena—marriage counselors who avoid discussing marriage, and family-life textbooks that shy away from the "m" word—are almost comical. But they represent increasingly typical examples of how a divorce culture seeks to avoid the topic of marriage.

2. For empirically based adumbrations of this idea, see Norval D. Glenn, "The Family Values of Americans," working paper no. 7 (New York: Institute for American Values, 1991); and Barbara Dafoe Whitehead, "The Experts' Story of Marriage," working paper no. 14 (New York: Institute for American Values, 1992).

3. David D. Gilmore, *Manhood in the Making: Cultural Concepts of Masculinity* (New Haven: Yale University Press, 1990).

4. Arlene F. Saluter, "Marital Status and Living Arrangements: March 1992," U.S. Bureau of the Census, Current Population Reports, series P-20, no. 468 (Washington, D.C.: U.S. Government Printing Office, December 1992), 1; Steve W. Rawlings, "Household and Family Characteristics: March 1992," U.S. Bureau of the Census, Current Population Reports, series P-20, no. 467 (Washington, D.C.: U.S. Government Printing Office, April 1993), xiv.

5. The following are the sources for table 12.1. For percent of births outside marriage: Stephanie J. Ventura, "Trends and Differentials in Births to Unmarried

Women: United States, 1970–76," U.S. Department of Health and Human Services, series 21, no. 38 (Washington, D.C.: U.S. Government Printing Office, May 1980), 47; National Center for Health Statistics, *Vital Statistics of the United States, 1980*, vol. 1, *Natality* (Washington, D.C.: U.S. Government Printing Office, 1984), 1-59; National Center for Health Statistics, "Advance Report of Final Natality Statistics, 1990," *Monthly Vital Statistics Report*, vol. 41, no. 9, supplement (Hyattsville, Md.: U.S. Department of Health and Human Services, February 25, 1993), 33.

For divorced males per 1,000 married males: Helena Znaniecki Lopata, ed., *Family Factbook* (Chicago: Marquis Academic Media, 1978), 199; "Marital Status and Living Arrangements: March 1980," U.S. Bureau of the Census, Current Population Reports, series P-20, no. 365 (Washington, D.C.: U.S. Government Printing Office, October 1981), 7; Arlene F. Saluter, "Marital Status and Living Arrangements: March 1990," U.S. Bureau of the Census, Current Population Reports, series P-20, no. 450 (Washington, D.C.: U.S. Government Printing Office, May 1991), 17.

For male prisoners per 1,000 males: Timothy J. Flanagan and Kathleen Maguire, eds., *Sourcebook of Criminal Justice Statistics, 1991,* U.S. Department of Justice (Washington, D.C.: U.S. Government Printing Office, 1992), 636; Frederick W. Hollmann, "U.S. Population Estimates, by Age, Sex, Race, and Hispanic Origin: 1980 to 1991," U.S. Bureau of the Census, Current Population Reports, series P-25, no. 1095 (Washington, D.C.: U.S. Government Printing Office, February 1993), 4.

For percent of children living apart from their fathers: see sources for table 1.2.

6. Ruth H. Jewson and James Walter, *The National Council on Family Relations: A Fifty-Year History, 1938–1987* (St. Paul, Minn.: National Council on Family Relations, 1988), 7. For a description of "Dads' Clubs" in suburban New York in the 1950s, see Martha Weinman Lear, *The Child Worshippers* (New York: Crown, 1963), 131.

7. Hank Whittemore, "Dads Who Shaped Up a School," *Parade,* September 27, 1992, 20.

8. Private correspondence of Eddie F. Staton to David Blankenhorn, August 5, 1993.

9. Ibid.

10. Unpublished data obtained from a telephone interview with the Occupancy Division, U.S. Department of Housing and Urban Development, Washington, D.C., July 25, 1994.

11. For example, establishing rent ceilings in public housing, as opposed to fixing rent as a percentage of income, would almost certainly reduce the disincentive for marriage facing many current residents. See *Families First: Report of the National Commission on America's Urban Families* (Washington, D.C.: U.S. Government Printing Office, 1993), 43–44.

12. For a discussion of Saul Alinsky and the work of the Industrial Areas Foundation, see P. David Finks, *The Radical Vision of Saul Alinsky* (New York: Paulist Press, 1984); Sanford D. Horwitt, *Let Them Call Me Rebel* (New York: Knopf, 1989); and Mary Beth Rogers, *Cold Anger: Faith and Power Politics* (Denton: University of North Texas Press, 1990). See also Saul D. Alinsky, *Rules for Radicals: A Practical Primer for Realistic Radicals* (New York: Random House, 1971).

13. Public Health Service, "Vital Statistics of the United States, 1988," vol. 3 (Washington, D.C.: U.S. Government Printing Office, forthcoming), table 1-18.

14. *Families First,* 46. See also W. Shrum, "Religion and Marital Instability: Changes in the 1970's," *Review of Religious Research* 21, no. 2 (1980): 135–47; and M. G. Dudley and F. A. Konsinski, "Religiosity and Marital Satisfaction: A Research Note," *Review of Religious Research* 32, no. 1 (1990): 78–86.

15. See Michael McManus, *Marriage Savers: Helping Your Friends and Family Stay Married* (Grand Rapids, Mich.: Zondervan, 1993). See also Ray Waddle, "Ministers Hope Program Can Dam Flood of Divorce," *Tennessean,* December 19, 1993, 1.

16. Steve Brandt, "Out of Wedlock, into Controversy," *Star Tribune,* May 13, 1994, 1-B.

17. Ibid.

18. Ibid.

Index

Note: Page numbers followed by *n* indicate material in endnotes.

Abandonment, by fathers, 1, 18–19, 22–24
Abbott, John S. C., 237*n*20
Abbott, Philip, 181
Abrams, Tamar, 262–63*n*40
Acock, Alan C., 262–63*n*40
Adams, Paul L., 240*n*47
Adolescent childbearing, 45–48, 76, 191–92, 264–65*n*58
Adoption, and fragmentation of fatherhood, 20–21, 183, 238*n*32
African-Americans: child poverty among, 43; fatherlessness among, 129; and slavery, 50, 251*n*3
Aid to Families with Dependent Children (AFDC), 128, 231, 283–84*n*10, 284*n*12, 291*n*3
Alan Guttmacher Institute, 42
Alinsky, Saul, 230
Amato, Paul R., 168, 258–60*n*23, 299–300*n*58, 309–10*n*21
American Association for Marriage and Family Therapy (AAMFT), 314*n*1
American Psychological Association, Commission on Violence and Youth, 27
Anderson, Christopher P., 111
Anderson, Elaine A., 113–14
Anderson, Elijah, 17, 41
Anderson, Kay E., 250*n*94
Androgyny, 281–82*n*89; of New Fathers, 98, 101–3, 117–23, 224–25; of noncustodial fathers, 168

Angel, Jacqueline L., 240–41*n*3, 255–56*n*15
Angel, Ronald J., 240–41*n*3, 255–56*n*15
Angie (movie), 302–3*n*4
Artificial insemination, 178–80, 233, 305*n*22
Assuring Child Support (Garfinkel), 146
Astrachan, Anthony, 96
At Daddy's on Saturdays (Girard), 153–54, 292*n*10
Athletes, and fatherhood, 108–9, 233, 270–71*n*52
Australia, stepfamilies in, 192
Authority: abuse of, by fathers, 87–93, 104–5; decline of paternal, 237*n*13, 271*n*55; and father-child relationship, 93–95; of Good Family Man, 202

Baby and Child Care (Spock), 120, 251*n*9
Babyfever (movie), 302–3*n*4
Babymaker (movie), 305*n*21
Bachu, Amara, 264–65*n*58
Barbanel, Josh, 287–88*n*45
Barbeau, Clayton, 99
Barnett, Rosalind, 277*n*47, 312*n*5
Barthelme, Donald, 88–89
Baruch, Grace K., 312*n*5
Battered Woman, The (Walker), 32
Baum, Lois, 292*n*10
Bay, R. Curtis, 284–85*n*17
Bayme, Steven, 249–50*n*88
Beatty, Lula, 80
Becker-Haven, Jane, 197
Beckham, Beverly, 99–100
Beer, William R., 186, 309*n*23

Bell, Daniel, 254n4
Belous, Richard, 260n24
Belsky, Jay, 281–82n89
Bem, Sandra Lipsitz, 268–69n44
Benjamin, Jessica, 90, 91, 92
Berg, Barbara J., 86, 275–76n44
Bergen, Candice, 69–70
Berger, Peter L., 66
Berkow, Ira, 11
Berman, Claire, 189, 307–8n11
Bernard, Jessie, 111
Bertoia, Carl, 300–301n61
Besharov, Douglas J., 39, 246n51
Bettelheim, Bruno, 253–54n1
Biblarz, Timothy J., 249n87
Bienenfeld, Florence, 161
Big Chill, The (movie), 173
Biller, Henry B., 112, 117
Billingsley, Andrew, 251n3
Biological fathers, 10, 19, 183, 238–39n32
Birth certificates, 10, 174
Births, out-of-wedlock, 10, 56, 69, 145, 222, 223, 264–65n58, 301n1
Blakeslee, Sandra, 291n9
Blankenhorn, David, 249–50n88, 250n90
Blanton, Priscilla White, 168, 299–300n58
Blau, Melinda, 159–60, 168–70, 201, 295n35, 296n41
Blended families, 189. *See also* Stepfathers
Bloomfield, Harold H., 189, 193, 194
Bly, Robert, 95
Bly, Stephen A., 311–12n3
Bonds of Love, The (Benjamin), 90
Booth, Alan, 258–60n23
Booth, Wayne, 253–54n1
Boston Globe, 246n43, 246n45, 246n47, 265–66n60, 284n12, 288–89n51
Boston Herald, 85, 99–100
Bowlby, John, 313n12
Boyfriends: and child sexual abuse, 40–42. *See also* Nearby Guys
Boys Will Be Boys (Miedzian), 29–30
Boyz N the Hood (movie), 298–99n55
Bozett, Frederick W., 99
Branson, Meredith P., 113–14
Braver, Sanford L., 284–85n17
Bray, James H., 160, 190
Breadwinners: Deadbeat Dads as, 124–25, 128–41, 143–47; fathers as, 107–17, 278–79n70, 279n73, 279n75;

Good Family Men as, 212–13, 221; mothers as, 110–17, 278–79n70, 279n75
Breines, Wini, 86–87, 274n35
Brennen, Heidi, 115–16
Brenner, Lois, 283n6
Bronfenbrenner, Urie, 249–50n88
Brown, Wayland, 11
Browning, Don S., 172, 247n56, 311–12n3
Brownmiller, Susan, 243n22
Bumpass, Larry L., 235n1
Burlingham, Dorothy T., 247–48n70, 252n29
Burning Bed, The (movie), 33
Bush, George, 126

California Children of Divorce Study, 47
Callahan, Daniel, 179, 305n25
Carlson, Allan, 237n12
Carnegie Corporation, 27
Carroll, Jerry, 264–65n58
Carville, James, 226–27, 283n4
Cashion, Barbara G., 80–81, 264n56
Cassetty, Judith, 283n8
Castilla, Sergio M., 302–3n4
Census Bureau, 132, 134, 135, 253n52, 284–85n17, 286n27
Centers for Disease Control and Prevention, 35
Chafe, William H., 86
Chambers, Carole A., 283n6
Chambers, David L., 145–47
Chaney, Joseph, Jr., 26–28, 29, 32
Chaney, Joseph, Sr., 26–28
Chavez, Don, 163
Cherlin, Andrew J., 124, 127, 130, 155–58, 235n1, 283n4, 284n15, 293–94n21, 299–300n58, 300n59
Chicago Tribune, 112–13, 239n35, 247n60
Child magazine, 100, 111, 159
Child-rearing manuals, 13, 14, 120, 251n9
Children in Families study (Australia), 192
Children's Defense Fund, 144
Children's Rights Council, 161, 163
Child sexual abuse, 39–42, 246n51
Child support, 44; and Deadbeat Dads, 124–25, 128–41, 143–47, 286n27. *See also* Visiting Fathers
Child Support Enforcement Program, 129, 135–36

Chodorow, Nancy J., 268–69*n*44
Choice of Heroes, A (Gerzon), 112
Chollar, Susan, 256–57*n*19, 263*n*46
Christian fatherhood movement, 104,
    310*n*3
Christian Science Monitor, 135,
    296–97*n*47
Christiansen, C. D., 292*n*10
Civil War, and fatherlessness, 14, 50
Clapp, Genevieve, 79
Clary, Mike, 278*n*67
Clausen, Clara, 183
Claxton-Oldfield, Stephen, 309*n*27
Clinton, Bill, 126, 288*n*50
Coats, Dan, 28–29
Cohen, Miriam Galper, 297–98*n*49
Cohen, Theodore F., 275–76*n*44
Coiro, Mary Jo, 258–60*n*23
Colman, Arthur D., 100
Colman, Libby Lee, 100
Colonial America, 13
Coltrane, Scott, 296–97*n*47
Companionate marriage, 13–14, 60,
    237*n*13
Conine, Jon, 283*n*6
Connecticut, and artificial insemination,
    179
Cooney, Teresa M., 110
Coontz, Stephanie, 23, 78, 86–87,
    262–63*n*40, 266–67*n*10
Coote, Anna, 80, 112, 278*n*64
Co-parenting arrangements, 151, 156,
    159, 160, 163, 168, 293–94*n*21
Corneau, Guy, 313*n*13
Cosby Show, The (TV show), 77
Crafts, Steve, 85
Creighton, Susan J., 41
Crime: domestic violence against women,
    32–39; and single-parent families,
    31–32; youth violence, 26–32, 241*n*4,
    241–42*n*7
Crime and Human Nature (Wilson), 75
Crosbie-Burnett, Margaret, 197
Crouter, Ann C., 275–76*n*44
Cruz, Hernando, 36–37
Cunningham, Laura, 256–57*n*19
Curtin, Roberta Braun, 309*n*27

Daddy trackers, 112
Daly, Kerry, 272–73*n*14
Daly, Martin, 34, 288*n*46
Danson, Ted, 178

Danziger, Sandra K., 248–49*n*79,
    310–11*n*46
Danziger, Sheldon, 248–49*n*79
Davis, Hubert, 233, 270–71*n*52
Dawson, Deborah A., 243*n*19
Day, Clarence, 88
Deadbeat Dads, 68, 114, 124–47, 150,
    185; as breadwinners, 124–25, 128–41,
    143–47; and child-support payments,
    124–25, 128–41, 143–47, 286*n*27;
    media images of, 11, 124–27, 129,
    141–42, 284*n*15; New Fathers versus,
    125–26; Old Fathers versus, 125–26;
    Sperm Fathers versus, 172; strategy of
    tracking down, 127–28, 130–41,
    143–47; as term, 284*n*15; tragedy of,
    141–47
"Deculturation" of paternity, 4, 16–18
"Defining deviancy down" (Moynihan),
    78, 177, 256–57*n*19, 262*n*40
Degler, Carl, 13
Delusions of Grandma (Fisher),
    256–57*n*19, 303*n*5
Demo, David H., 258–60*n*23, 262–63*n*40
Demos, John, 235*n*2, 238*n*23
Depner, Charlene E., 160
DeVault, Christine, 307–8*n*11
Dillon, Sam, 287–88*n*45
Dinnerstein, Dorothy, 119, 268–69*n*44
Dittes, James, 87
Divorce, 222, 223; and child poverty, 44;
    child support following, 145–46; co-
    parenting arrangements in, 151, 156,
    159, 160, 163, 168, 293–94*n*21; and
    gender roles, 159–61, 165; impact on
    children, 44, 47, 191; during and after
    World War II, 60. *See also* Deadbeat
    Dads; Divorce culture; Stepfathers;
    Visiting Fathers
Divorce and New Beginnings (Clapp), 79
Divorce Book for Parents (Lansky), 161
Divorce culture, 166–67, 223–24, 230,
    295*n*35, 296–97*n*47, 298*n*54,
    298–99*n*55, 314*n*1
Divorce reform, 158–70
Dobash, R. Emerson, 243–44*n*23
Dobash, Russell, 243–44*n*23
Do I Have A Daddy? (Lindsay), 10, 173
Domestic Revolutions (Mintz and Kel-
    logg), 80, 86, 237*n*13
Domestic violence, 32–39, 141–43,
    287*n*45

Donahue, Phil, 85
Donchin, Anne, 180
Douglas, Ann, 237n13
Douglas, Michael, 141
Douvan, Elizabeth, 280–81n85, 313n10
Downey, Thomas J., 136
Downward social mobility, 44–45
Drakich, Janice, 300–301n61
Driver, Daniel Mark, 42
Dudley, M. G., 315–16n14
Duxbury, Linda, 110
Dyer, William G., 274n35

Earned Income Tax Credit, 231
Eastman, Moira, 271n55
Edwards, John N., 80
Eggebeen, David J., 43, 80, 248–49n79, 264n55
Ehrenreich, Barbara, 263n48, 269–70n49
Ehrensaft, Diane, 117–18
Elias, Marilyn, 260n25
Ellwood, David T., 43, 285–86n23
Elshtain, Jean Bethke, 181, 249–50n88, 305n32
Engber, Andrea L., 175, 304n16
English, Diane, 69–70
Epstein, Joseph, 157
Erickson, Beth M., 99
Erikson, Erik H., 47, 240n1, 282n90
Essex, Marilyn J., 275–76n44

Falling Down (movie), 141–42, 163, 288n46
Families Apart (Blau), 159–60
Familocide, 288n46
Family law, 186, 243n23, 244n26
Family Politics (Pogrebin), 97, 101, 118
Family Relations (LaRossa), 112
Family Support Act (1988), 129, 135, 136
Family Way (Coote, Harman, and Hewitt), 278n64
Father, The (Colman and Colman), 100
Father, The (Strindberg), 142, 267–68n28
Father-child relationship, 90–91, 93–95, 134, 154–70, 294n23. See also Father–daughter relationship; Father–son relationship
"Father-complex" (Freud), 94
Father-daughter relationship, 90–91; and child sexual abuse, 39–42; importance of, 72, 250n92
Fatherhood: androgynous, 98, 101–3, 117–23, 224–25; biological, 10, 183,

238–39n32; breadwinner role in, 107–17, 278–79n70, 279n73, 279n75; capacity for, 3; "Could Be Worse" philosophy of, 78–83, 176, 262–63n40; cultural story of, 65–69, 253–54n1; dimensions of, 3, 10–11; diminishment of, 12–17, 19; effective, conditions for, 18, 125–26, 150; explaining away, 173–77; fragmentation of, 10–11, 19–20, 38, 304–5n19, 309–10n31; good-enough, collapse of, 18–22; masculinity as key to, 224–25; Mott's study of, 70–73, 74, 75; as "not that important," 69–75; purpose of, 65; rise of, 25–26; social, 10, 13–17, 183; socialization for, 3–4, 65, 107–17, 180–81; as unnecessary, 68–83, 119
Fatherlessness: and adolescent childbearing, 45–48; and child poverty, 42–45, 248–49n79; and child sexual abuse, 39–42, 246n51; culture of, 2–3, 60–62, 198; and domestic violence against women, 32–39; as harmful trend, 1–2; increase in, 22–24, 130; stepfather as embodiment of, 192–93; war-induced, 50–60; and youth violence, 26–32, 241n4, 241–42n7
Father Loss (Wakerman), 256–57n19
Fathers and Families (Biller), 112, 117
Fathers' Clubs, 227–28
Father-son relationship, 90–91, 93, 270n50
Fathers' Resource Center, 296–97n47
Fathers' rights movement, 149, 161–63, 294n23, 300–301n61
Feminization of domestic sphere, 13
Feminization of poverty, 115
Ferguson, Andrew, 85–86, 266n8
Fielder, Leslie, 282n90
Fields, Suzanne, 256–57n19, 281–82n89
Fifties, The (Halberstam), 86
50-50 Parenting (Kimball), 111
Fighting for Life (Ong), 34, 93
Filmer, Sir Robert, 306n33
Fine, Mark A., 309n27
Fisher, Carrie, 256–57n19, 303n5
Fisher, Seymour, 250n92
Fitzpatrick, Pamela J., 284–85n17
Fleck, Roland, 256n18
Florio, Jim, 143
Fowler, Patrick C., 256n18
Fox, Greer Litton, 168, 299–300n58

Fox, James Alan, 241*n4*
Francke, Linda Bird, 296*n40*, 309*n31*
Frank, Stephen M., 14, 50, 104
Fred's First Day (Warren), 261*n35*
Freud, Anna, 54–56, 247–48*n70*, 252*n29*
Freud, Sigmund, 94, 247*n59*, 271*n53*
Fromm, Erich, 313*n13*
Fukuyama, Francis, 282*n90*
Full-Time Dads (Larson), 297–98*n49*
Funder, Kathleen, 300*n59*
Furstenberg, Frank F., Jr., 155–58, 191, 192, 235*n1*, 283*n4*, 289–90*n52*, 293–94*n21*, 299–300*n58*, 300*n59*, 309*n23*

Gallup, George, 52
Galston, William A., 43, 243*n20*, 261*n29*
Garbarino, James, 87, 99
Garfinkel, Irwin, 43, 46, 129, 146–47, 260*n24*
Gary, Lawrence E., 80
Gas Food Lodging (movie), 298–99*n55*
Gatley, Richard H., 155, 161, 292–93*n18*
Gaulin, Steven J. C., 251*n1*
Gay parents, 20, 177, 232, 304–5*n19*
Gazmararian, Julie, 35
Gelles, Richard J., 244*n27*, 245*n30*
Gender conflict, 90–93; and breadwinner role, 111–17; and Good Family Man, 218
Gender roles: androgyny versus, 98, 101–3, 117–23, 168, 224–25, 281–82*n89*; breadwinner role and, 107–17; and divorce, 159–61, 165; and Good Family Men, 217–18; and "separate spheres," 172
Genovese, Eugene D., 251*n3*
Gerbner, George, 66, 253–54*n1*
Gershenson, Harold P., 196–97
Gerson, Kathleen, 111, 278*n59*
Gerzon, Mark, 112, 120
Gibbs, Nancy, 243*n23*
Gilmore, David D., 224, 235*n2*, 312*n4*
Girard, Linda Walvoord, 153, 292*n10*
Girl in the Watermelon, The (movie), 302–3*n4*
Giveans, David, 96–97, 196, 271–72*n3*
Glendon, Mary Ann, 20, 243*n23*
Glenn, Norval, 75, 258*n22*, 260*n24*, 281–82*n89*, 314*n2*
Going It Alone: The Family Life and Social Situation of the Single Parent (Weiss), 287*n44*

Gold, Herbert, 17, 238*n28*
Goldberg, Herb, 111
Goldberg, Whoopi, 178
Goldzband, Melvin G., 161
Goleman, Daniel, 241–42*n7*
Goode, William J., 160
Good-enough fatherhood: collapse of, 18–22; components of, 18, 126, 202–11; Visiting Fathers and, 150, 156–57, 167
Good Family Man, 5, 201–21, 223; as breadwinner, 212–13, 221; culture shift toward, encouraging, 225–33; decline of, 201, 204–8, 221; described, 201–2; and good-enough fatherhood, 202–11; meaning of, 203–10; as nurturer, 215–17, 221; as protector, 213–15, 221; as sponsor of children, 217–21
Good Housekeeping magazine, 254–55*n8*
Gordon, Michael, 41
Gottfredson, Michael R., 31
Graham, Stanley R., 77
Grant, Shawn, 28–29, 242*n9*
Great Britain, stepfamilies in, 191–92
Greeley, Andrew M., 117
Griswold, Robert L., 111
Guidubaldi, John, 258–60*n23*
Gullestad, Marianne, 281–82*n89*
Guthrie, Francisca, 37
Gutmann, David, 4, 101–2, 121–22, 242–43*n16*
Gutmann, Stephanie, 304–5*n19*

Hagan, Margaret Stanley, 161
Halberstam, David, 86
Hanson, Shirley M. H., 99
Hareven, Tamara K., 23, 189
Harman, Harriet, 112, 278*n64*
Harriman, Angela, 21
Harriman, Daniel, 21
Harris, Kathleen Mullan, 293–94*n21*
Harrison, Margaret, 300*n59*
Hawkins, Alan J., 80, 264*n55*
Hearts of Men, The (Ehrenreich), 269–70*n49*
Heegaard, Marge, 292*n10*
Heilbrun, Carolyn G., 268–69*n44*
Helping Men Change (Erickson), 99
Helping Your Child Succeed After Divorce (Bienenfeld), 160
Henry, Mike, 288*n50*
Herbert, Bob, 244–45*n29*

Herman, Judith Lewis, 39
Hernandez, Donald J., 19
Hero (movie), 288*n*47
Hershey, Lewis B., 52
Herzog, James M., 240*n*47
Hetherington, E. Mavis, 47, 161, 256*n*18, 258–60*n*23, 309*n*27
Hewes, Kara, 9–10
Hewitt, Patricia, 112, 278*n*64
Hickman, Neal, 296–97*n*47
Higgins, Christopher, 110
Hillery, Alexander, 155, 292*n*14
Hirczy, Wolfgang, 238*n*30
Hirschi, Travis, 31, 73, 258*n*22
Hobbes, Thomas, 181
Hochschild, Arlie R., 272*n*10
Hoffman, Dustin, 288*n*47
Homeward Bound: The Incredible Journey (movie), 187–88, 189, 194
Homicide: Life on the Run (TV show), 77
Hood, Jane C., 272*n*10, 275–76*n*44
Horn, Wade F., 246*n*51
Horton, Francine, 275–76*n*44
Housing, upgrading public, 229–30
Howe, Peter J., 284*n*12
How Men Feel (Astracham), 96
Hunt, Janet G., 98
Hunt, Larry, 98
Huston, Ted L., 281–82*n*89
Hyde, Janet Shibley, 275–76*n*44
Hypermasculinity, 31

Incredible Journey, The (movie), 187–88
Indiana, Fathers' Clubs in, 227
Industrial Areas Foundation, 230
Industrialization, 13–14, 237*n*12
Inner American, The (Veroff, Douvan, and Kulka), 280–81*n*85, 313*n*10
In Search of Our Fathers (movie), 298–99*n*55
In These Times magazine, 266*n*3
Intimate Violence (Gelles and Straus), 244*n*27

Jackson, Yvonne, 26
James, Caryn, 77
Jensen, Leif, 43, 248–49*n*79
Joint Custody and Shared Parenting (Steinman), 160
Jones, Marian M., 238*n*30
Josh and S.A.M. (movie), 298–99*n*55
Jung, C. G., 313*n*13

Juster, Susan, 14
Juvenile delinquency: absence of father and, 75; during wartime, 56, 252*n*29

Kahn, Joan R., 250*n*94
Kamark, Elaine Ciulla, 243*n*20
Kantrowitz, Barbara, 241–42*n*7
Karan, Robert, 313*n*12
Kasdan, Lawrence, 173
Kaufman, Gus, Jr., 32
Keirnan, Kathleen E., 240*n*47, 308*n*19
Keller, Anna, 155, 169
Kellogg, Susan, 80, 86, 237*n*13
Kennedy, Marge, 175
Keyes, Ralph, 85–86
Kilpatrick, William, 253–54*n*1
Kimball, Gayle, 111, 280*n*82
Kimmel, Michael S., 266*n*3
King, Janet Spencer, 175
King, Martin Luther, Jr., 311–12*n*3
King, Valerie, 299–300*n*58
Kingsolver, Barbara, 174–75
Klein, Joe, 145, 282*n*3
Klungness, Leah, 176
Komarnicki, Mary, 279*n*73
Konsinski, F. A., 315–16*n*4
Kotlowitz, Alex, 29
Koulack, David, 155, 161, 292–93*n*18
Krantz, Susan E., 80
Krantzler, Mel, 296*n*43
Krementz, Jill, 151
Kubie, Lawrence, 122
Kulka, Richard A., 280–81*n*85, 313*n*10
Kurdek, Lawrence A., 309*n*27

La Barre, Weston, 93, 270*n*50
Lamb, Michael E., 117, 247*n*62, 279*n*76
Lamott, Anne, 77–78, 132
Lancaster, Chet, 25
Lancaster, Jane, 25
Lang, Mary, 281–82*n*89
Lansky, Vicki, 160–61, 296*n*41
LaRossa, Ralph, 112, 237*n*13
Larson, Erik, 277*n*52
Larson, George, 297–98*n*49
Lasch, Christopher, 271*n*55
Lear, Martha Weinman, 274*n*33, 315*n*6
Lee, Catherine, 110
Legitimacy principle (Malinowski), 49, 61, 223, 251*n*1, 267–68*n*28
Lein, Laura, 275–76*n*44
Lenroot, Katherine, 56

Lens of Gender, The (Bem), 268–69*n*44
Leon the Pig Farmer (movie), 305*n*21
Lesbian and Gay Parenting Handbook (Martin), 264–65*n*58, 304–5*n*19
Lesbian parents, 177, 232, 264–65*n*58, 304–5*n*19
LeShan, Eda, 152
Leslie, Leigh A., 113–14
Lester, Gordon H., 131
Levant, Ronald F., 99, 272–73*n*14
Leviathan (Hobbes), 181
Levine, James A., 113, 197, 279*n*72
Leving, Jeffery M., 296–97*n*47
Levitan, Sar, 75, 286*n*24
Levy, David L., 163, 297–98*n*49
Lewis, R. W. B., 282*n*90
Li, Jiang Hon, 249*n*87
Lichter, Daniel T., 43, 248–49*n*79
Lindsay, Jeanne Warren, 173
Lisser, Eleena de, 241*n*4
Locke, John, 181–83, 306*n*33
Loftus, Elizabeth F., 266–67*n*10
Lorber, Judith, 91–92, 269*n*48
Louv, Richard, 305*n*22
Lucas, Megan, 20
Lund, Mary, 299–300*n*58

Maccoby, Eleanor E., 275*n*40, 293–94*n*21, 300*n*59
Mackey, Wade C., 281–82*n*89
MAD DADS (Men Against Destruction–Defending Against Drugs and Social disorder), 228
Made in America (movie), 178
Maitland, Sara, 88
Making Fathers Pay (Chambers), 145
Making It As a Stepparent (Berman), 189
Making Peace in Your Stepfamily (Bloomfield), 189, 193
Male Cross-Dresser Support Group, The (Janowitz), 303*n*8
"Male mystique" (Miedzian), 29–30
Male nannies, 198
Malinowski, Bronislaw, 49, 50, 61, 150–51, 223, 251*n*1
Man in the Gray Flannel Suit, The (Wilson), 105, 274*n*37
Marriage, 223; companionate, 13–14, 60, 237*n*13; domestic legislation and, 231; and domestic violence against women, 32–39, 243–46*n*22–50; and father absence during war, 57, 59–60; religious community support for, 230–31
Marriage and Family Experience, The (Strong and DeVault), 307–8*n*11
Martha's New Daddy (Steele), 292*n*10
Martin, April, 177, 304–5*n*19
Martinson, Brian C., 250*n*94
Marx, Karl, 92
Masculinity, 2; androgyny of New Fathers versus, 98, 101–3, 117–23, 224–25; changing concepts of, 13–15, 96–100, 238*n*23; as key to fatherhood, 224–25
"Mascupathology," of Old Father, 84–85
Mattes, Jane, 175
May, Elaine Tyler, 87, 112
McCasland, George R., 164, 298*n*52
McCormick, Katie, 166
McDaniel, James, 108–9, 112
McDaniel, Xavier, 108–9
McKlinden, Larry, 238–39*n*32
McLanahan, Sara S., 43, 46, 75, 250*n*94, 260*n*24, 301–2*n*1, 309*n*27
McManus, Michael, 316*n*15
Mead, Margaret, 3–4, 106, 235*n*2, 235–36*n*3, 274*n*37
Menaghan, Elizabeth G., 255*n*14
Merrill, Francis, 53
Meyer, Daniel R., 236*n*6
Michaelson, Julius, 9
Midnight Run (movie), 154
Miedzian, Myriam, 29–30, 31
Miller, George, 242*n*9
Miller, John T., 287–88*n*45
Miller, Naomi, 81–83
Milner, Judith R., 240*n*47
Minirth, Frank, 311–12*n*3
Minnesota, Hennepin County "vision statement," 232
Mintz, Steven, 80, 86, 237*n*13
Misogyny, 30
Mitscherlich, Alexander, 13, 237*n*12
Mnookin, Robert H., 275*n*40, 293–94*n*21, 300*n*59
Moen, Phyllis, 23, 79
Mogey, J. M., 106–7, 274–75*n*38
Moloney, Lawrie, 295–96*n*37
Morin, Richard, 238*n*24
Morris, Mary, 173–74
Morrison, Donna Ruane, 258–60*n*23
Mother-child bond, weakening of, during wartime, 56–57
Motherhood, increasing importance of, 14–17

Mothers: as breadwinners, 110–17, 278–79*n*70, 279*n*75; as nurturers, 215–17; separation of boys from, 30, 54; sponsorship of children by, 219–20
Mother's Love, A (Morris), 173–74
Mott, Frank L., 70–73, 74, 75, 80, 133, 197, 255*n*13, 255*n*14, 256*n*16, 256*n*17, 256–57*n*19, 258*n*22, 260*n*25
Moynihan, Daniel Patrick, 78, 124, 256–57*n*19
Mrs. Doubtfire (movie), 163–68
Murphy Brown (TV show), 69–70, 75, 283*n*5
Musick, Judith S., 41, 47, 247*n*65
Myth of Masculinity, The (Pleck), 113

Napier, Augustus, 98–99
Narcissism, 4, 101–2, 121, 123
National Center for Health Statistics, 132, 235*n*1
National Commission on Children, 10
National Conference on Family Relations, 227
National Congress for Men and Children, 161, 163, 164, 296*n*46, 297*n*48
National Council on Family Relations, 97–98, 227
National Crime Victimization Survey, 35–36, 37
Nearby Guys, 68–69, 126, 195–98; and child sexual abuse, 40–41; described, 195–96; as fathers, 195–98; Stepfathers versus, 185–87; types of, 185–86
Nebraska, Fathers' Clubs in, 227–28
Neckerman, Kathryn, 43, 129
Nelson, James Lindemann, 305*n*25
Nelson, Ozzie, 86
Nelson, Ricky, 86
New Fathers, 68, 96–123, 202; affection toward children, 103–7; androgyny of, 98, 101–3, 117–23, 224–25, 281–82*n*89; and breadwinner role, 107–17; Deadbeat Dads versus, 125–26; described, 96–100; historical meaning of fatherhood versus, 101–3; media images of, 100, 105–6, 111, 112–13; Old Fathers versus, 118; as Unnecessary Fathers of the future, 102–3, 119
New Jersey, and Deadbeat Dads, 143
Newman, Brian, 311–12*n*3
Newman, George, 297–98*n*49

Newsweek, 27, 145
New York Times, 11, 16, 21, 69, 76, 77, 78, 124–25, 143, 198, 267*n*15, 284*n*15, 287*n*45, 288–89*n*51
No Man's Land: Men's Changing Commitments to Family and Work (Gerson), 278*n*59
Nonresidential Parenting (Depner and Bray), 160
Norway, androgyny in, 281–82*n*89
Novak, Michael, 115
Nurturers: Good Family Men as, 215–17, 221; men as, 3–4, 235–36*n*3
Nurturing Father, The (Pruett), 85

Oakeshott, Michael, 254*n*4
Office of Child Support Enforcement, 129, 136
Okin, Susan Moller, 91
Oklahoma, and artificial insemination, 178–79
Old Fathers, 68, 84–95, 202; abuse of power by, 87–93, 104–5; Deadbeat Dads versus, 125–26; described, 84–87; and father-child relationship, 93–95; "mascupathology" of, 84–85; media images of, 86; New Fathers versus, 118; Unnecessary Fathers versus, 84
Ong, Walter J., 34, 93, 270–71*n*52, 275*n*42
Organization Man, The (Whyte), 105–6, 274*n*37
Osheron, Samuel, 271*n*54
Owen, Ursula, 88, 256–57*n*19
Ozzie and Harriet (TV show), 86

Paasch, Kathleen, 134, 289–90*n*52
Parallel parenting, 156
Parenting magazine, 193
Parenting Together (Ehrensaft), 117–18
Parent Power! (Rosemond), 176
Parents magazine, 100, 111
Past, Present, and Personal (Demos), 235*n*2, 237*n*11, 238*n*23
Paternal sponsorship, 217–21
Paternity: "deculturation" of, 4, 16–18; and unmarried mothers, 236*n*6
Paternity leave, 112–13
Paternity suits, 9, 10
Paternity tests, 238*n*30
Patterson, Charlotte, 79

Perry-Jenkins, Maureen, 275–76n44
Pfeiffer, Michelle, 76
Pierce, Glenn L., 241n4
Pigs in Heaven (Kingsolver), 174–75
Pitt, Valerie, 300–301n61
Pittman, Frank, 84, 242n15
Pleck, Joseph H., 14–15, 80, 113, 312–13n7
Pogrebin, Letty Cottin, 97, 101, 118, 244n27
Pollack, William, 113
Pollitt, Katha, 76
Poor Support (Ellwood), 43
Popenoe, David, 186, 281–82n89, 306n1
Popenoe, Paul, 274n36
"Post-parental androgyny" (Gutmann), 101–2
Potuchek, Jean L., 110, 277n49
Poverty: child, and fatherlessness, 42–45, 248–49n79; feminization of, 115
Power, abuse of, by fathers, 87–93, 104–5
Pratt, William F., 264–65n58
Pregnancy, domestic violence and, 35
Presser, Harriet, 110
Prisons, 32
Progressive Policy Institute, 31
Promise Keepers, 311–12n3
Protectors, Good Family Men as, 213–15, 221
Protest masculinity, 31
Pruett, Kyle D., 85, 190, 277n52, 279n76, 313n11
Psychological fathers, 196, 238–39n32
Public housing, upgrading, 229–30
Public Perspective, The magazine, 290n59

Quality Time (Goldzband), 161
Quayle, Dan, 69, 70, 283n5
Quinn, Michelle C., 247–48n70

Radin, Norma, 310–11n46
Raftery, Adrian E., 249n87
"Rape culture" (Wolf), 33, 244n26
Rashke, Richard L., 283n6
Rawlings, Steve W., 239n42
Ray, David, 196
Reclaimed Powers (Gutmann), 101–2
Redbook magazine, 100
Regan, Milton C., Jr., 281–82n89
Reinventing Womanhood (Heilbrun), 268–69n44
Religious community, support for marriage, 230–31

Replacement fathers, stepfathers as, 188, 190–95
Rich, Adrienne, 87, 95, 280n83
Richards, Herbert C., 256n18
Riesman, David, 105–6, 273–74n32
Rivers, Caryl, 277n47
Robertson, John A., 179
Robinson, Michael, 96–97, 196, 271–72n3
Role strain, 113–14, 294n27
Roseanne (TV show), 77
Rosemond, John, 176
Rosenberg, Harold, 49
Ross, Davis R. B., 252n15
Ross, John Munder, 292–93n18
Rossi, Alice, 102, 121–22, 261n28
Rousseau, Jean-Jacques, 103
Ruddick, Sara, 269n48
Ruitenbeek, Hendrik M., 273–74n32
Russell, Bertrand, 238n28
Russell, Graeme, 271–72n3

Safe Zones, 228–29
St. Elmo's Fire (movie), 76
Salzman, Randy, 296–97n47
San Francisco Chronicle, 78, 287–88n45
Schechter, Susan, 32, 243n22, 245n30
Schlegel, Alice, 251n1
Schmidt, Daniel, 183
Schneider, Carl E., 66
Schochet, Gordon J., 305n31
Schorr, Alvin L., 23, 79
Schreiber, Ann, 136
Schrepf, Nancy A., 240n47
Schuldt, April, 76, 261n30
Schulmann, Joanne, 300–301n61
Schwartz, Glen H., 195
Schwartz, Pepper, 280–81n85
Schwarzenegger, Arnold, 225, 302–3n4
Scull, Charles, 280–81n85
Seltzer, Judith A., 134, 289–90n52, 292–93n18
Selvin, Hannan, 73, 258n22
Sex, Culture, and Myth (Malinowski), 150, 251n1
Sexual abuse, child, 39–42, 246n51
Sexual history, end of, 121
Sex without responsibility, 17
Shapiro, Robert B., 296n40
Shelton, Sandi Kahn, 194
Sherwood, Kay E., 289–90n52
Shrum, W., 315–16n14
Silverstein, Olga, 91

Simpson, O. J., 38, 246n50

Sinclair, Mary, 89

Single Father's Handbook (Gatley and Koulack), 155, 161

Single Mother (newsletter), 175, 176

Single Mothers and Their Children (Garfinkel and McLanahan), 43

Single Mothers by Choice, 175, 304n13

Single-parent families, 240n47, 285n18; adolescent, 45–48, 76, 191–92, 264–65n58; crime and, 31–32; *Murphy Brown* episode, 69–70, 75; paternal death versus abandonment in, 22–24, 240n47; prevalence of, 18–19, 75–76, 130, 301n1; problems of children in, 255–56n15

Single-Parent Family (Kennedy and King), 175

Single Parents by Choice (Miller), 81–83

Skocpol, Theda, 290n58

Skyles, Ada, 197

Slavery, 50, 251n3

Smelzer, Neil J., 282n90

Snapper, The (movie), 302–3n4

Snarey, John, 240n1

Social fathers, 10, 13–17, 183

Social Problems on the Home Front (Merrill), 53

Sommers, Christina Hoff, 244n26

Sonenstein, Freya, 236n6, 290n55

South, Scott J., 256n18

South Central (movie), 298–99n55

Souza, Joel, 287–88n45

Spectorsky, A. C., 274n33

Sperm banks, 178–80, 233

Sperm Fathers, 68, 126, 171–84, 185; in artificial insemination, 178–80, 233, 305n22; children's fantasies of, 175–77; Deadbeat Dads versus, 172; described, 171–73; explaining away, 173–77; media images of, 173–76, 183, 302–3n4; as postmodern and primeval, 180–84

Spock, Benjamin, 120, 196, 251n9

Sponsors of children, Good Family Men as, 217–21

Stanford University, 57, 58

Staton, Eddie F., 228

Stay-at-home Dads, 112

Stearns, Peter N., 16

Steele, Danielle, 292n10

Stein, Robert, 283n6

Stein, Ruthe, 264–65n58

Steinberg, Laurence, 191

Steinman, Susan, 160

Stepfathers, 68–69, 187–95; and child sexual abuse, 40; child's perspective on, 190–95; as embodiment of father-lessness, 192–93; media images of, 187–88, 190, 193–95; Nearby Guys versus, 185–87; prevalence of, 188–89; as replacement fathers, 188, 190–95

Stimpson, Catharine R., 87–88

Stoddard, Marcus, 21

Stone, Oliver, 87

Straus, Murray A., 244n27, 245n30

"Street culture," 17

Streisand, Barbra, 256–57n19

Strindberg, August, 88, 142, 267–68n28

Strong, Bryan, 307–8n11

Sullivan, Mercer L., 289–90n52

Sullivan, Shawn, 33

Summons to Memphis, A (Taylor), 89

Sundlun, Bruce, 9–10, 12

Super, Gretchen, 261n35

Sweden, androgyny in, 281–82n89

Sweet, James A., 235n1

Swidler, Ann, 282n90

Taxes, and marriage, 231

Taylor, Peter, 89

Teachman, Jay D., 134, 289–90n52

Television: Old Father and, 86; Unnecessary Father in, 69–70, 75, 76–77

Terminator 2 (movie), 302–3n4

There Are No Children Here (Kotlowitz), 29

Thicker Than Blood (movie), 238–39n32

Thomas, Dylan, 88

Thomas, Kevin, 195–96

Thompson, Linda, 87, 312n5

Thompson, Ross A., 189–90

Thompson, Tommy, 144

Thomson, Elizabeth, 309n27

Three Sisters, The (Sinclair), 89

Tocqueville, Alexis de, 14, 103

Toward a Recognition of Androgyny (Hielbrun), 268–69n44

Trent, Katherine, 256n18

Tuttle, Nathaniel, 38

Tuttle, William M., 57–58

Twilley, Dwight, 297–98n49

Two for the Road (movie), 298–99n55

Two Treatises of Government (Locke), 181–83

Uhlenberg, Peter, 22, 110
Umberson, Debra, 294*n*27
U.S. Department of Housing and Urban
    Development, 229
University of Iowa, 41
Unnecessary Fathers, 68, 76, 81, 223;
    Deadbeat Dads as, 125; media
    images of, 69–70, 75–77; Mott's
    study of, 70–73, 74, 75, 133,
    255*n*12–14, 256*n*16–17, 256–57*n*19,
    260*n*25; New Fathers as, 102–3, 119;
    Old Fathers versus, 84; Visiting
    Fathers as, 149–50
Unwed parenthood, 10, 20, 132, 232,
    301–2*n*1; adolescent, 45–48, 76,
    191–92, 264–65*n*58; and child-support
    payments, 133–35; during wartime,
    56, 59. *See also* Deadbeat Dads
Urban, Dick, 274*n*35
USA Today, 260*n*25, 261*n*31

"Values-based organizing," 230
Van Derbur, Marilyn, 86, 266–67*n*10
Veroff, Joseph, 280–81*n*85, 313*n*10
Vinovskis, Maris, 14, 251*n*5
Violence: child sexual abuse, 39–42; of
    Deadbeat Dads, 141–43; domestic,
    against women, 32–39, 243–46*n*22–50;
    and Safe Zones, 228–29; youth, 26–32,
    241*n*4, 241–42*n*7
Visher, Emily, 310*n*32
Visher, John, 310*n*32
Visiting Fathers, 68, 126, 148–70, 185;
    and co-parenting arrangements, 151,
    156, 159, 160, 163, 168, 293–94*n*21;
    described, 148–49; and divorce
    reform, 158–70; and fathers' rights
    movement, 149, 161–63, 294*n*23,
    300–301*n*61; media images of, 152–54,
    163–68, 298–99*n*55; number of, 149;
    as real fathers, 150–58; as term, 149,
    155; tragedy of, 154–58, 169, 291*n*9,
    299–300*n*58; as version of Unneces-
    sary Fathers, 149–50

Wachbroit, Robert, 179–80
Wagner, E. Glenn, 311–12*n*3
Wakerman, Elyce, 256–57*n*19
Walker, Alexis J., 87, 312*n*5
Walker, Glynnis, 296*n*40
Walker, Lenore E., 32, 243–44*n*23
Wallerstein, Judith, 40, 44, 47, 187,

    281–82*n*89, 291*n*9, 292–93*n*18,
    299–300*n*58
Wall Street Journal, 26, 296–97*n*47,
    310–11*n*34
War, and fatherlessness, 50–60
Warren, Cathy, 261*n*35
Warren, James, 278*n*67
Warren, Paul, 311–12*n*3
Warshak, Richard A., 155
Washington Post, 70, 71, 74, 75, 113, 136,
    160, 258–60*n*23
Wasserman, David, 179–80
Way We Never Were, The (Coontz), 23, 86
Weber, Max, 4–5, 313*n*13
Wedding, The (Bulter), 190
Weiss, Robert S., 109, 156, 264*n*56,
    287*n*44, 292–93*n*18, 313*n*9
Welcome Home magazine, 279*n*74
Weld, William F., 38, 143
Weston, Ruth, 300*n*59
What Am I Doing in a Stepfamily?
    (Berman), 195, 308*n*14
What's Going to Happen to Me?
    (LeShan), 152
Wheeler, Burton, 51–52
Whelan, F. Joseph, 281–82*n*89
Whitehead, Alfred North, 66, 254*n*4
Whitehead, Barbara Dafoe, 254–55*n*8,
    279*n*73, 312–13*n*7, 314*n*2
Whitman, Walt, 120
Why Are We Getting a Divorce? (Mayle),
    152–53
Whyte, William, 105–6, 273–74*n*32
Wickell, Barbara, 161
Wiley, Bell Irvin, 251*n*7
Wilkinson, Rupert, 238*n*23
Williams, Christine L., 294*n*27
Williams, Lena, 261*n*30
Williams, Linda B., 264–65*n*58
Williams, Robin, 165, 298*n*53, 298*n*54
Williams, Ronald, 244–45*n*29
Williams, Ronnell, 11, 12
Williams, Tennessee, 88
Willinger, Beth, 272*n*10
Wilson, James Q., 31, 75, 243*n*21
Wilson, Margo, 34, 288*n*46
Wilson, Sloan, 105
Wilson, William Julius, 43, 129, 290*n*58
Wisconsin, and Deadbeat Dads, 144–45
Wojtkiewicz, Roger A., 249*n*87
Wolf, Naomi, 33, 244*n*26
Wolins, Martin, 79

Women: domestic violence against,
    32–39; hatred of, 30; violent crimes
    against, 35–36. *See also* Motherhood;
    Mothers
Women of Brewster Place, The (TV show),
    76–77
Working Mother magazine, 175, 194,
    304*n*16
World War II, 51–60, 247–48*n*70;
    absence of fathers during, 51–57;
    return of fathers after, 57–60
Wright, Lawrence, 266–69*n*10

Wu, Lawrence L., 250*n*94

Yankelovich, Daniel, 15–16, 76, 238*n*24
Yolton, John W., 305*n*32
Young, Iris Marion, 198
Young, Poor, and Pregnant (Musick), 41,
    47
Youth violence, 26–32, 241*n*4, 241–42*n*7

Zill, Nicholas, 191, 258–60*n*23, 286*n*30
Zussman, Robert, 109